LATIN
AMERICAN
CINEMAS

LATIN AMERICAN AND CARIBBEAN SERIES

Christon I. Archer, General Editor

ISSN 1498 –2366

This series sheds light on historical and cultural topics in Latin America and the Caribbean by publishing works that challenge the canon in history, literature, and postcolonial studies. It seeks to print cutting-edge studies and research that redefine our understanding of historical and current issues in Latin America and the Caribbean.

No. 1 · **Waking the Dictator: Veracruz, the Struggle for Federalism and the Mexican Revolution** Karl B. Koth

No. 2 · **The Spirit of Hidalgo: The Mexican Revolution in Coahuila** Suzanne B. Pasztor · Copublished with Michigan State University Press

No. 3 · **Clerical Ideology in a Revolutionary Age: The Guadalajara Church and the Idea of the Mexican Nation, 1788–1853** Brian F. Connaughton, translated by Mark Allan Healey · Copublished with University Press of Colorado

No. 4 · **Monuments of Progress: Modernization and Public Health in Mexico City, 1876–1910** Claudia Agostoni · Copublished with University Press of Colorado

No. 5 · **Madness in Buenos Aires: Patients, Psychiatrists and the Argentine State, 1880–1983** Jonathan Ablard · Copublished with Ohio University Press

No. 6 · **Patrons, Partisans, and Palace Intrigues: The Court Society of Colonial Mexico, 1702–1710** Christoph Rosenmüller

No. 7 · **From Many, One: Indians, Peasants, Borders, and Education in Callista Mexico, 1924–1935** Andrae Marak

No. 8 · **Violence in Argentine Literature and Film (1989–2005)** Edited by Carolina Rocha and Elizabeth Montes Garcés

No. 9 · **Latin American Cinemas: Local Views and Transnational Connections** Edited by Nayibe Bermúdez Barrios

LATIN AMERICAN CINEMAS

Local Views and Transnational Connections

Edited by
NAYIBE BERMÚDEZ BARRIOS

UNIVERSITY OF
CALGARY
LATIN AMERICAN
RESEARCH CENTRE

UNIVERSITY OF
CALGARY
PRESS

Copublished with the Latin American Research Centre at the University of Calgary

University of Calgary Press
2500 University Drive NW
Calgary, Alberta
Canada T2N 1N4
www.uofcpress.com

LIBRARY AND ARCHIVES CANADA CATALOGUING IN PUBLICATION

Latin American cinemas : local views and transnational connections / edited by
Nayibe Bermúdez Barrios.

(Latin American and Caribbean series ; 9)
Includes bibliographical references and index.
Issued also in electronic format.
ISBN 978-1-55238-514-2

1. Motion pictures—Latin America—Reviews. 2. Motion pictures—Social aspects—
Latin America. I. Bermúdez Barrios, Nayibe II. Series: Latin American and Caribbean
series ; 9

PN1993.5.L3L282 2011   791.43098   C2010-907485-8

The University of Calgary Press acknowledges the support of the Alberta Foundation
for the Arts for our publications. We acknowledge the financial support of the
Government of Canada through the Canada Book Fund for our publishing activities.
We acknowledge the financial support of the Canada Council for the Arts for our
publishing program.

Printed and bound in Canada by Marquis Book Printing Inc.
∞ This book is printed on FSC Silva Edition

Cover design by Melina Cusano
Page design and typesetting by Melina Cusano

For Charlène,
who is my past, my present, and my future.

TABLE OF CONTENTS

Part III: Visions of the Transnational

ACKNOWLEDGMENTS

I would like to thank the University International Grants Committee of the University of Calgary for a Research Grant that allowed me to organize the "Jornada de cine latinoamericano" conference (March 30–31, 2007) and to make this book possible. Two of the essays in this anthology are revised versions of papers presented during the conference. The others are contributions that arose from a call for papers.

Thanks also to the anonymous reviewers for their invaluable time and perceptive comments and to Christon Archer for his enthusiasm and willingness to include this book in the Latin American Studies Series. Special thanks go to Elissa J. Rashkin for her generosity, for the warm conversations that helped me keep focused, and for meticulously copyediting many of the articles of this book.

I have to thank my spouse Charlène for her firm optimism and belief in my work and in this project.

INTRODUCTION

Latin American cinemas have had a considerable upsurge during the past twenty years, prompting many film critics and scholars to hail a new era in the development of at least some of the film industries in this region.[1] This, however, does not mean that these national cinemas have at last found solutions for their endemic financial troubles. Some, such as the cinemas of Colombia and Peru, in fact, lack an industrial infrastructure.[2] What this upsurge signals, more than thriving industries or healthy contexts for production and distribution, are renovated cinematic visions and a notable alertness towards the everyday experiences of citizens that help connect the contemporary cinemas of Latin America even more closely to social and cultural concerns. The films analyzed in this anthology reflect and examine contemporary lives in their diversity and singularity, through their focus on identity politics, sexuality, the body, the family, and/or community.

This emphasis on the local implies a questioning of modernity, in the vein proposed by philosopher Enrique Dussel, as a homogenizing force underlying, among others, conventional ethnic and patriarchal discourses about the nation.[3] It also challenges inclusionary/exclusionary as well as assimilatory dynamics and makes explicit a desire for community, which, following Jean-Luc Nancy, far from expressing nostalgia for an idealized cohesive myth, opens the way to new forms of imagining communal interrelations which thrive on singularity. These challenges to the hierarchical reasoning of modernity and to widespread ideas about community also give prominence to transnational contexts of exchange, as depicted by Philip Crang, Claire Dwyer and Peter Jackson. These are common threads linking the major cinematic traditions of the region, including Argentina, Brazil, and Mexico, but also the lesser-known cinemas from Colombia and Peru.

Postcolonial Studies, in spite of Jorge Klor de Alba's initial critique of its application in Latin America, has been a prominent discipline for the study of the region.[4] Rolena Adorno, Enrique Dussel, Walter Mignolo, and Aníbal Quijano are but some of the names linked to theorizations of modernity, coloniality, and postcolonialism in Latin America. Although the essays that comprise this anthology work with a variety of themes and theories, I find that Dussel's critique of modernity, coupled with Quijano's emphasis on corporality, offer a useful contextualization for the local views and transnational connections that join the contributions making up this book. In Dussel's interpretation, modernity has functioned as a universal, univocal project that has conflated Occidental culture with the human in general and has sought violently to impose European rationality, unilateral machismo, and white racism upon its Others (1995, 138). The project of modernity, which in Latin America has often been linked with national projects, is thus ridden with colonial cultural undertones, even if most of those countries gained political independence from their colonizers almost two centuries ago. Hegemonic discourses of national and pan-national identity have typically posited *mestizaje* as the prevailing cohesive force for Latin American countries, often in detriment of the cultures and rights of indigenous, Afro-Latin American, Jewish, and other populations. Simultaneous with this, patriarchal and heterosexual national projects that have placed women as biological reproducers of citizens have violently ignored or diminished the rights not only of women but also of sexually diverse citizens. These homogenizing strategies for imagining and building the nation prove that coloniality still has a strong cultural hold.

In the 1980s and 1990s, national projects were challenged by social and political crises which, if not necessarily triggered by the introduction of neoliberal economic models, did have a relationship to them. As a result of these crises, networks and groups emerged to bring their particular interests and demands to the fore in a dialogue that showed that traditional nationalisms had fallen far short of responding to the concerns of all. For example, in Mexico after the 1985 earthquake, as Lynn Stephen notes, several loosely allied networks such as the Network against Violence toward Women, the Feminist Peasant Network, and the Network of Popular Educators developed a discourse characterized as *feminismo popular*, or grassroots feminism, that linked class and women's issues (251). The 1990s also saw the formation of the Continental Network of Indigenous Women, an initiative of First Nations women of Canada, which has allowed the development of shared strategies for indigenous women across the Americas (Blackwell, 144). In that same decade, social movements for indigenous rights and autonomy became even stronger in Mexico with the advent of the influential Zapatista movement (Stephen, 241). In Ecuador too, indigenous movements reacted to the crisis of the nation-state by calling for the creation of a plurinational state (Walsh, 510). As this widespread organizing and voicing of citizens' concerns in resistance to established political systems implies, nation-states' capacity to control and discipline populations through views and practices imposed from above has been challenged. Although Latin American social movements were not spontaneously born in the 1980s and 1990s, and indeed have a long history, it was not until this period that their discourses explicitly highlighted ethnicity, sexuality, and the need for civil society, among others, as experiential components of corporality, cultural identity, and community life.[5]

It is in this context that Quijano's call for a linkage between capitalism and corporality offers a way to tie the crisis of the nation-state with citizens' commitments to finding solutions from below. As Quijano states: "En la explotación, es el 'cuerpo' el que es usado y consumido en el trabajo y, en la mayor parte del mundo, en la pobreza, en el hambre, en la malnutrición, en la enfermedad" (380) [Under relationships of exploitation, it is the "body" that is used and consumed by work, and almost everywhere in the world, by poverty, hunger, malnutrition and disease]. Relations of power inscribe themselves on the body to try to mould it according to a capitalist logic. Besides those forces mentioned by Quijano, social categories such as gender, race, ethnicity, heterosexuality, and nationalism, among other imperatives, seek to claim and appropriate the body much in the manner in which *requerimientos* laid claim to the land in colonial times in order to control its subsequent status and use. Such writing implies the possibility of a rewriting, especially as modernization projects continue to be mostly one-sided in spite of governments' rhetoric regarding multicultural citizenship (Hooker; Speed et al.). Under these conditions, nation-states' time-honoured discourses lose more and more credibility in the face of their inability to provide for citizen's minimal needs and demands.

To counter modernity's negative impact, Dussel has called upon liberation theology, an ideology which opens up a space for the voicing of perspectives from the point of view of dominated races, women in patriarchal systems, and disadvantaged children living in misery (Dussel 2008, 342). Thus, Dussel pinpoints the central role of alterity in a transformative project that would go against inclusionary/exclusionary politics of identity in which the white man has functioned as universal subject and would instead engage in a process of mutual, creative fecundation among groups (1995, 138). As a consequence, *mestizaje* or heterosexuality, for example, would not be understood as the norm, but only as ways of being in the world alongside other, equally possible ethno-sexual identity configurations. Furthermore, besides traditional subjects, such as those marked by race and social class, this grounding on the body opens the door for other forms of corporality. Quijano's identification of the body as the site of struggle against all forms of power (380) furthers Dussel's call for the subaltern to claim equal status in the process of 'mutual and creative fecundation' or hybridity. Even if these conceptualizations, like Postcolonial Studies as a whole, have been criticized as systems that reify subalternity and victimization, it is clear that Dussel and Quijano's ideas provide the basis for the acceptance of a wide variety of singularities, and a politics of solidarity which would foster dignity for all subjects in revised structures of communal life.[6] In this restructuring, the body and its singularities, rather than being assimilated, segregated, or excluded, as is normally the case in widespread notions of community, would be the sign of community. It is this yearning to rewrite the body that conveys a desire for new forms of community.

The concept of community referenced here comes from Jean-Luc Nancy, for whom community, seen as communion, reveals the violence of views that are imposed from above, as is the case of liberal and neoliberal doctrines that purport to advocate for the greater good. Nancy explains that:

> [Par conséquent,] la communauté est la transcendance : mais la « transcendance », qui n'a plus de signification « sacrée », ne signifie rien d'autre, précisément, que la résistance à l'immanence (à la communion de tous ou à la passion exclusive d'un ou de quelques-uns: à toutes les formes et à toutes les violences de la subjectivité). (88)

> [As a consequence,] community is transcendence, but transcendence that has lost its sacred connotation and, as a matter of fact, does not mean anything other than resistance to immanence (to the idea of communion of everybody, to the select desires of a person or a group of persons, to all forms of violence associated with subjectivity).

Community, then, is resistance to processes of homogenization and an aperture towards particular traits that make up singularity. This idea is closely related to a questioning of the traditional nation-state and to the desire for new communal settings. As I have implied, and as Juan Duchesne Winter notes, Nancy's notion of community finds meaning outside of modernity's reasoning (41). For Nancy, community has not taken place. The projections of community imposed on historical social formations such as the Guayaki Indians, alongside Hegel's 'spirit of the people' or Christian notions of love (Nancy, 33–34) which nostalgically mourn something presumably lost, differ from Nancy's idea of community as a task in progress via the interactions of diverse singularities. Rather than hierarchical vertical interactions such as in centre/periphery models associated with the nation-state, this concept highlights horizontal exchanges. Such an 'inoperative' model, as Nancy names his project, contradicts a communal logic of fusion with its concomitant drive for stifling diversity which, as Nazism proved, may in fact be deadly (Nancy, 36). A desire for such an alternative model provides an explanation, not only for the strengthening of civil society and the social movements mentioned above, but also for cultural interventions, such as some of the films presented in this anthology, that give screen time and voice to minorities, 'non-normative' subjectivities, and counter-cinema filmic expressions, that is, those that as a rule are devalued by the film establishment.

A communal structure with transversal ways of interacting might also transcend national spaces, developing transnational flows as people are increasingly linked through the media, migration, corporate global capital, and commodity culture. Transnationalism in this sense, even though it takes hybridity into account, also seeks to highlight global flows in a multidimensional and multiply-inhabited social space, where, as Crang, Dwyer and Jackson point out, not everybody is equally touched by its effects (449–51). Such a definition allows for recognition of the various dimensions of transnationalism, which, beyond the diasporic, include the cultural and the economic. It also helps position films and filmmakers as they participate in relations of production, distribution, and consumption that contribute to the ongoing dialogue about the place of cinema in contemporary culture. This place is wrought, not only through direct or indirect thematic engagement with the theories about modernity and community outlined above, but also through an emphasis on cinematographic form which, to a certain extent, in its capacity to engage filmmakers, producers, and spectators in different types of discussions, can also be said to advance or question modernity and fixed ways of thinking.

The first part of this anthology, "Crisis of the Nation-State and Desire for Community," groups four essays that, from different perspectives and theories, question the nation-state and its related institutions. The centrality of the body and citizenship presents the opportunity to examine the breakdown of state, community, and the conventional family and to move towards a critical standpoint about social changes affecting and shaping the lives of the common citizen. In the first essay, "National Belonging in Juan José Campanella's *Luna de Avellaneda*," Rebecca L. Lee explores Juan José Campanella's film *Luna de Avellaneda* (2004) as an allegory for Argentina's 2001 economic crisis. Focusing on thematic content that centres on the preservation or demise of a local social club, Lee argues that the film narrates how the dual crisis of capitalism and the state is instrumental in fuelling new notions of national belonging. In Argentina, much as in Mexico and in other Latin American countries, the crisis led to increased citizen participation, which in this case took the form of *Asambleas Populares*. In these gatherings people displayed their dissatisfaction with neoliberalism and voiced their demands for social change.[7] The film thematizes these dynamics and the desire for community through the protagonist, Román (Ricardo Darín), and the character of Dalma (Micaela Moreno). Román's effort to resist privatization links capitalism to dehumanization and consumerism. Dalma functions as a symbol of the growing marginalization of the lower classes, which would normally not fulfill entry requirements to the social club. The protagonist's argument that in Avellaneda's social club Dalma "found a place" resonates as a call to arms for revised notions of community in the face of privatization. The club, then, in a move that evokes Nancy's idea of inoperative community, emplaces the desire for a break of social-class barriers and serves, even if momentarily, as a site which finds in Dalma's singularity its raison d'être. Thus the club signals the breakdown of the nation-state and provides a critique of neocolonial forms of economic subjection.[8]

In contrast to the first essay, "From National Allegory to Autobiography: Un-Pleasure and Other Family Pathologies in Two Films by Lucrecia Martel" by Paola Arboleda Ríos goes against the grain of allegorical readings. Yet Arboleda Ríos's interpretation also advances the need for community in ways that go beyond the thematic to accentuate the materiality of film. Her proposal that Lucrecia Martel's *The Swamp* (2001) and *The Holy Girl* (2004) consciously transform the national-allegorical into the subjective-autobiographical serves to underscore the importance of the body and personal experience in the production of identity. Besides questioning institutions such as the family, the Church and the medical establishment, Martel's autobiographical cinema highlights the important role of women as generators of diaries, memories, and self-reflexive narratives. At a thematic level, the family and other institutions are portrayed in the films as plagued by death, incest, destructive impulses, and unconscious desires. Martel's play with visual, auditory, and tactile stimuli draws attention to the body as a site that disrupts idealized views of typical nation-state institutions. The body appears in its singularity, displacing the nation-states' homogenizing and controlling discourses. This move may be seen as another instance of desire for community, via Martel's probing of current non-idyllic communal settings strategically played out in a hotel and around a pool. The pool and the hotel, like the social club in *Luna de Avellaneda*, function as heterotopic sites which, in order to be legible, must be allowed to function outside of modernity and in synchronization with singularity and plurality. Important for Arboleda Ríos's examination is the materiality of the cinematographic apparatus. Martel's films engage in a process of decolonization that not only disrupts mainstream film narration but also adopts Brechtian techniques of defamiliarization in the spirit of a long tradition of Latin American "digestive" appropriation of cultures, as Peter Hulme would say (416). These techniques, including unusual characterization, fragmented images, and an eye-catching camera work, are used to disavow identification and produce affect in audiences. The idea that films can puzzle spectators into thinking about alternative ways of imagining the world is thus enhanced by form.

Alternative ways of imagining the nation are also strongly called for in Peruvian director Francisco Lombardi's *Ojos que no ven* (2003). In the third essay of this section, "Bodily Representations: Disease and Rape in Francisco Lombardi's *Ojos que no ven*," Elizabeth Montes Garcés and Myriam Osorio show how the film establishes a metaphorical connection between disease, rape, and the state to portray the devastating effects of political corruption in the lives of regular citizens. If in the previous essays crises were connected to the violence inflicted by neo-liberal economic policies and the limitations of national institutions, in this chapter the breakdown of the nation-state is more crassly represented through state corruption and physical violence against citizens. Set in the year 2000 during Alberto Fujimori's second presidency, *Ojos que no ven* focuses on the Peruvian state and its pervasive corruption notoriously materialized in the now-infamous videotapes of presidential counsellor Vladimiro Montesinos engaging in acts of bribery and manipulation. From such high spheres, the sickness of the body politic seems to spread in the form of disease and rape to the body of common citizens who end up at the General Hospital. The hospital functions as a space where socio-temporal relations become embodied through injury due to physical acts of violence brought about by the state apparatus. More graphically than Campanella and Martel, Lombardi presents the body as a bloody site where power inscribes itself. Deploying a severely critical and pessimistic tone, the film portrays the complete collapse of government, politics, and the military, as well as the equally disturbing passivity of the common citizen. Although it does not seem to offer a way out of the situation, the film shows that to continue to preserve the system in question is to fall more and more into chaos and oppression. In an indirect way, the film's critique of current forms of government and politics implies a call for a new community of empowered citizens. Even if not explicitly suggested, an inoperative community of transversal exchanges, in the sense proposed by Nancy, would likely be more humane than the community of vertical relations depicted in *Ojos que no ven*.

A look back through film history suggests that the desire for community is contiguous to modernity and capitalist projects, arising as a potential alternative to their alienating structures. The fourth paper of this section, David William Foster's "Films by Day and Films by Night in São Paulo," examines the representation of São Paulo, an important financial centre in Brazil, through four films spanning from the 1960s to the 2000s. Similarly to what Isabel Arredondo does with respect to the representation of rape in chapter 7, Foster presents shifting views of the city through different decades. If in the three previous essays, the social club, the hotel with the pool, and the hospital function as sites in which modernity and traditional institutions are questioned, in Foster's article it is the whole city and urban life that come under scrutiny. Film samples, including Amácio Mazzaropi's comedy *O puritano da Rua Augusta* (1965) and Beto Brant's assassination thriller *O invasor* (2002), portray the city during the day as a dehumanized place where people only look out for themselves in a sometimes risky game to impose their own interests. In this environment, the city writes on the bodies of its citizens and is in turn written by them as hierarchical social-class structures are undone and rebuilt. Disaffection, social conflict, corruption, and cynical human relations are integral parts of urban life. In contrast, Wilson Barros's *Anjos da noite* (1987) toys with the idea that, at night, São Paulo offers a more humane approach to human topology. Foster argues that in this context, identities, sexual and otherwise, can be unstable in ways that present the night as an alternative universe to the city's hierarchically ordered daylight face. Although Foster is reluctant to draw conclusions, the status of São Paulo as a privileged site of capitalism is linked with social ills associated with the order and progress imposed by modernity. This seems to be countered by alternative ways of organizing relationships, as seen in *Anjos da noite*. In this film, the dis-order revealed in the panorama of lives portrayed by Barros turns night in the city into a sort of in-between time where carnival and sin reign, allowing the unspoken to be heard and the invisible to appear. Even if Barros does not seek to make a political statement, his representation of the city suggests that identity instability and singularity, such as envisioned by Nancy in his inoperative community project, offer more hope of transversal re-orderings than an established order governed by the logic of commerce and power. As the articles of this first section suggest, resistance to all forms of subjectification establishes a link between social relations in their specific timespace and contingent sociohistoric, economic, and cultural formations, including explicit physical locations, and the bodies that experience such relations. The following section of the book will clarify even more how forms of corporality are subjectified by social categories such as gender, sexuality, heterosexuality and the structures of representation.

In the second section of the book, the emphasis on the collapse of the nation-state and its institutions gives way to a more particular focus on diverse configurations of plurality and singularity. This part, "Sexuality, Rape and Representation," groups essays that emphasize the importance of corporality and singularity in terms of sexuality and gender. In the first essay, "Bodies So Close, and Yet So Far: Seeing Julián Hernández's *El cielo dividido* through Gilles Deleuze's Film Theory," Gerard Dapena relies on the analysis of sights, sounds, and textures to demonstrate how Hernández's 2006 film temporalizes the film image.[9] By stressing the materiality of film and the sensations to which spectators are subjected, Dapena shows how Hernández's corporeal cinema dialogues with Deleuze's ideas about the centrality of affect and the body. In unsettling ways reminiscent of Martel's cinema, Hernández explores the constitution of gay desire. As Dapena suggests this cinema of sensation and duration works to provoke spectators to imagine more affirmative modes of existence for gay men, and also to potentially make heterosexual viewers feel and think differently about homosexual desire. As in Martel's films, form is here enlisted as a decolonizing strategy in which singularity is visualized through depictions of the male body and the exploration of a range of emotions lived by the characters. Fluctuations within *El cielo dividido* invoke Duchesne Winter's principle of alliance for community building, which he uses to expand on Nancy's idea of the inoperative community. According to this principle, instincts, prejudices, suppositions, and quotidian ways of knowing help in the configuration of a system that allows for creativity and is not limited by modernity's social reasoning and disciplining (Duchesne Winter 51). Going back to Nancy, Hernández's film shows that spaces of intercommunication and affect are not sites of fusion and communion but places of dislocation in which singularities are defined and embraced (64–65). Both within and outside the film, the desire for community is projected onto sexuality as an indicator of plurality and singularity.

The second essay in this section also centres on a figure of sexual singularity, in this case the life experience of an intersex adolescent. In "Myth and the Monster of Intersex: Narrative Strategies of Otherness in Lucía Puenzo's *XXY*," Charlotte E. Gleghorn discusses the strategies by which Puenzo's *XXY* (2007) brings singularity to the fore. By historicizing the terms 'monster' and 'hermaphrodite,' Gleghorn lays bare the politics of representation of this film which, while attempting to inscribe the body of the intersex person in the visual realm, also reiterates this same body as mythical and monstrous. The film's cinematography seems to ally itself with a voyeuristic gaze that relegates Alex, the protagonist, to the realm of the other-worldly. However, its critical revision of modern medical discourses emphasizing sexual dimorphism serves to emplace the intersex subject as an autonomous corporality that defies gender and sexual classification. The protagonist's refusal of both hormonal therapy and surgical intervention shows how s/he challenges disciplining and controlling heterosexual structures. By assuming an 'in-between state,' Alex embodies a figure of ambiguity that not only questions the medical system but also the dominant system of representation. Surreptitiously imbued with the homogenizing drives of the nation-state and its 'operative' idea of community, the representation provided in the film puts in the forefront the tensions inherent in cultural and cinematographic treatments of singularity. The juxtaposition of image, myth, and discourse simultaneously shows the violence of representation that tries to discipline subjects into 'normalcy,' as discussed by Teresa de Lauretis (1987), as well as the continuous search for a narrative language, as Dussel would say, which could provide a way to reconstruct both particular histories and singular identities (2008, 343). This search is one of the common denominators of contemporary Latin American cinema and thus also constitutes a common thread that unites many of the essays in this anthology.

The next chapter, Isabel Arredondo's "Watching Rape in Mexican Cinema," continues the discussion of violence and representation by tracing depictions of rape in Mexican cinema. Beginning with Fernando de Fuentes' *Doña Bárbara* (1943) and Matilde Landeta's *La negra Angustias* (1949) and ending with Marisa Sistach's *Perfume de violetas: nadie te oye* (2000) and María Novaro's *Sin dejar huella* (2000), Arrendondo concludes that representations of rape, including those linking rape to tropes of a changing national ideology, are contingent upon the political and cultural agendas of specific interest groups. She argues that, since the 1970s, feminist filmmakers have developed visual and narrative strategies in order to intervene in wider public debates. From 2000 on, these filmmakers have been moved to question what Arredondo calls the post-feminist disappearance of women's solidarity and mutual support around rape. Both Novaro's and Sistach's films engage this issue by focusing on lower-class young women who are confronted with a patriarchal system in which rape is seen as women's fault. What is striking in these films is that patriarchal views are espoused both by men and women in a dynamic that renders women complicit with sexual brutality. Novaro's and Sistach's calls for solidarity and activism speak of a malfunctioning at the level of current 'operative' community settings. In these settings, as Drucilla Cornell has argued, women's bodies are often thought of as unequal to those of men and are thus not considered to deserve equivalent rights. Equivalency of rights at a par with singularity would seem to go hand in hand with Nancy's inoperative community and with Novaro's and Sistach's cautionary tales that seek to narrate rape against the backdrop of neoliberal realities, flawed justice systems, and public indifference. Conventional and new ways of representing the body corroborate the intrinsic relationship between ways of seeing, representation, and a heterosexual matrix that is still pervasive and tied to modernity. The last section of the book delves into how transnational global flows beyond fostering creativity through cultural exchanges also advocate for a continuous search, as projected by Nancy, in which representation and interpretation go hand in hand with reviewed meanings of cinema as an industry.

The desire for community that weaves through the essays of the first two sections of this book moves in the third part, "Visions of the Transnational," to the recognition of a global sense of interconnectedness. This is one of the senses of what Dussel calls creative fecundation which has found expression in many literary and cultural traditions in Latin America, from religious syncretisms to popular culture to music to painting, among other art forms, and which is seen here in Hernández and Martel's appropriation of 'European' strategies of defamiliarization, in Puenzo's use of myth, and in Mora Catlett's recourse to eclecticism. Beyond these important aesthetic and cultural hybridization processes, there are equally vital flows that further situate the desire for community with regard to the transnational as an arena of exchanges including concerns about cinema as an industry. Here cinema is understood not only through the content and form of specific films but also through attention to exhibition channels and consumption patterns. The transversalism of exchanges that characterizes Latin American cinema exposes those commercial and other spaces in which new production strategies, counter-cinemas, and emergent cinemas also find an opening in which to assert their singularity vis-à-vis mainstream national and international cinemas.

Hybridization and fecundation are strongly present in Keith John Richards's essay "A Shamanic Transmodernity: Juan Mora Catlett's *Eréndira Ikikunari*," for which the author draws from Dussel's notion of 'transmodernity' and Chilean filmmaker Raúl Ruiz's conception of 'shamanic cinema.' In Dussel's transmodern vein, Richards demonstrates that *Eréndira Ikikunari* (2006) adopts and resignifies autochthonous legend in Mexico, strategically deploying colonial imagery and non-indigenous sources in the restoration of cultural memory and identity. The film expresses a desire to create an updated and non-stereotyped native aesthetic, which leads Mora Catlett to make use of a wide range of visual and auditory sources, in keeping with Ruiz's notion of shamanic cinema. Akin to Deleuze's cinema of sensation, Ruiz proposes "a cinema capable of accounting, above all, for the varieties of experience in the sensible world" with an equally important role given to memory (quoted by Richards). Similar to what Hernández does in *El cielo dividido*, Mora Catlett orchestrates time and space to conjoin past, present, and pure imagination in order to arouse spectators into revaluating their assumptions about pre-Columbian and present-day native cultures. The materiality of film is emphasized to suggest ways of understanding historical and cultural circumstances beyond any question of faithful recreation. Such transversal eclecticism is a transcultural, transmodern, 'digestive,' and syncretic response that distinguishes this type of cinema from other

Latin American and Hollywood representations of indigenous peoples, and that purports to place indigenous singularity on equal terms with other contact cultures.

Such a search is not only the domain of feature films. Indigenous videomakers have also responded to the homogenizing discourses of mainstream cinema by exploring technologies for self-representation, as mentioned by Richards and discussed by Elissa J. Rashkin in "We Are Equal: Women and Video in Zapatista Chiapas." Rashkin concentrates on indigenous women's participation in the Zapatista movement as important for the development of an independent video sector in Mexico. In her analysis of the video *We Are Equal: Zapatista Women Speak* (2004), she points out that singularity calls for approaches that sometimes involve the symbolic suppression of identity in favour of strategic group identification. As Rashkin affirms, Chiapas women's identification may be less with the nation as such than with other categories, such as Maya, *indígena*, Zapatista, or simply "from below." This echoes Nancy's views of transversal and horizontal community formation, but Rashkin also draws on Néstor García Canclini's concept of multicontextuality, according to which the multiple contexts registered in and by the videos attest to the notion of identity as a collaborative work perpetually in progress. Rashkin analyzes strategies of horizontal transnational networking exemplified by Promedios, a binational partnership which seeks to train and support indigenous communities in the production and distribution of their own media. Although normally non-commercially profitable, the exhibition of indigenous videos not only has linked diverse indigenous groups, thus bypassing a Mexican cinemascape which has typically rendered the indigenous subject invisible, but also has created new channels of commodity exchange in which video products travel not only across groups but also on a South-North axis.

The third essay of this section deals with a non-mainstream cinematographic practice that made its way onto Argentine screens in the 1960s and 1970s. My essay, "Sexploitation, Space, and Lesbian Representation in Armando Bo's *Fuego*," argues that *Fuego* (1968), in its mixture of genre aesthetics and industrial mechanisms with transnational spatial business practices, reveals the ways in which representations of the female body very often respond to global stylizations. Referencing Henry Lefebvre's theory of space, this essay explores how, although to some extent Bo and

Isabel Sarli's sexploitation project created a space for the lesbian subject, this representation was highly regulated. The film's double play on lesbian (in)visibility epitomizes the instability of representation in which lesbianism is included as a strategy for audience enticement but is also represented as an ultimately non-viable option for the protagonist. Through Sarli's commodification as an erotic and transnationally marketable product, Bo and Sarli were able to move their films beyond national borders and onto the screens of the world, thus exemplifying the conjunction of genre with socio-economic and culturally conditioned aesthetic frameworks. This should not be taken only in a negative light since, as Rashkin also notes, images are produced, consumed, and used in various ways by audiences who constitute a dynamic social sphere. This particularly speaks of a set of spatial interactions by which counter-cinemas may sometimes obtain a transnational status as in the case of sexploitation. The marginalization of counter-cinemas and its cinematographic practices, despite the cult status that sexploitation currently enjoys among some audiences, implies the existence of a film canon that serves to silence competing projects. While it is hard to link Sarli's and Bo's films to a concerted effort or desire for community, it is clear that by engaging in alternative film practices, and by being successful in doing so, they questioned a hierarchical epistemological model of filmmaking and opened up the field for an acceptance of all sorts of film practices as meaningful and relevant.

In the final essay of the book, "At the Transnational Crossroads: Colombian Cinema and Its Search for a Film Industry," Juana Suárez situates contemporary Colombian cinema vis-à-vis the cinemas from Mexico, Brazil, and Argentina and explores the impact and implications of the 'ley de cine' or Film Law 814 passed in 2003. Using Françoise Lionnet and Shu-Mei Shih's discussions of minor transnationalism, as a space in which to produce culture outside of a local/global dichotomy, Suárez shows that Colombian filmmakers have embarked on a quest to solidify the national film industry and to break into the global market not only by rejecting or accepting Hollywood models. Cineastes like Patricia Cardoso and Rodrigo García have tried to make it in Hollywood, as the transnational flux offers directors the flexibility of filming in different geographic locations and directing in foreign countries. Others, like Felipe Martínez and Juan Felipe Orozco, exemplify an interest in reactivating less explored genres and/or venturing into film approaches less common in Colombia. Still others, such as Dago García, bring to the big screen well-worn television formulae to tap into a market of consumers weary of violence as a privileged topic in national cinema. Recent legislation seeking to consolidate Colombian cinema as an industry also informs the desire to open up spaces for a variety of genres and subjects. An engagement with thematic content has been accompanied by technical know-how to put Colombian cinema in the global map and to attract and affect local audiences. In keeping with the notion of minor transnationalism, Suárez shows that Colombian cinema interacts transversally with the cinemas of Argentina, Brazil, and Mexico, rather than with Hollywood, and employs strategies used locally and in the Pan-American context. These initiatives seem to take into account horizontal connections in a multidimensional or multicontextual space where various agents interact with existing film traditions, including Latin American ones, in the effort to build a viable industry.

Even if precarious, the questionings, identity emplacements, and exchanges described in this introduction denote a desire for community that implies a need for change, not only at the level of interrelations among citizens, but also at the level of systems like the film industry that might segregate and marginalize non-mainstream representational practices. I would like to emphasize that the threads that I have used to connect the essays included in this anthology have not been easy to weave together. There are as many common links between these articles as there are varied themes, methodologies, and theoretical approaches. This attests to the richness of Latin American cinemas, to the expansion of academic and critical awareness about these cinemas, and to the ever-changing conditions of Hispanic Film Studies. All of these circumstances allow for shifts in which counter-cinemas, art cinemas, lesser-known cinemas, as well as more mainstream ones, can, and probably should, be studied together as part and parcel of a shared cultural paradigm. In this paradigm, economics and politics mingle with aesthetic, social, and historical concerns, contributing to the representation of a wider array of subjectivities and an ever-growing spectrum of spaces and voices engaged in a search for community.

WORKS CITED

Barrow, Sarah. 2005. Images of Peru: A National Cinema in Crisis. In *Latin American Cinema: Essays on Modernity, Gender, and National Identity*. Ed. Stephanie Dennison and Lisa Shaw, 39–58. New York: MacFarland.

———. 2007. Peruvian Cinema and the Struggle for International Recognition: Case Study on *El destino no tiene favoritos*. In *Contemporary Latin American Cinema: Breaking into the Global Market*. Ed. Deborah Shaw, 173–89. Lanham, MD: Rowman & Littlefield.

Bartra, Roger. 1987. *La jaula de la melancolía: Identidad y metamorfosis del mexicano*. 2nd ed. Mexico D.F.: Editorial Grijalbo.

———. 1989. La crisis del nacionalismo en México. *Revista Mexicana de Sociología* 51, no. 3: 191–220.

Bermúdez Barrios, Nayibe. 2008. *Bolívar I am*: *Telenovela*, Performance, and Colombian National Identity. *Studies in Latin American Popular Culture* 27: 45–70.

Blackwell, Maylei. 2006. Weaving in the Spaces: indigenous Women's Organizing and the Politics of Scale in Mexico. In *Dissident Women: Gender and Cultural Politics in Chiapas*. Ed. Shannon Speed, R. Aída Hernández Castillo, and Lynn M Stephen, 115–54. Austin: University of Texas Press.

Brown, Stephen. 2002. Con discriminación y represión no hay democracia: The Lesbian and Gay Movement in Argentina. *Latin American Perspectives* 29, no.2: 119–38.

Carrier, Joseph M. 1989. Gay Liberation and Coming Out in Mexico. In *Gay and Lesbian Youth*. Ed. G. Herdt, 225–52. New York: Haworth Press.

Correa Restrepo, Julian David. 2003. Una Mirada regional que se hace universal. Foreword *Cuadernos de Cine Colombiano 3*. Bogotá: Cinemateca Distrital, 1–3.

Cornell, Drucilla. 1995.*The Imaginary Domain: Abortion, Pornography, and Sexual Harassment*. New York: Routledge.

Costello, Judith A. M. 2005. Politics and Popularity: The Current Mexican Cinema. *Review: Literature and Art of the Americas* 70 (38.1): 31–38.

Crang, Philip, Claire Dwyer, and Peter Jackson. 2003. Transnationalism and the Spaces of Commodity Culture. *Progress in Human Geography* 27, no. 4: 438–53.

Duchesne Winter, Juan. 2005. *Fugas incomunistas: Ensayos*. San Juan: Ediciones Vértigo.

Dussel, Enrique. 1995. *The Invention of the Americas: Eclipse of the Other and the Myth of Modernity*. Trans. Michael D. Barber. New York: Continuum.

———. 2008. Philosophy of Liberation, the Postmodern Debate, and Latin American Studies. In *Coloniality at Large: Latin America and the Postcolonial Debate*. Ed. Mabel Moraña, Enrique Dussel, and Carlos A. Jáuregi, 335–49. Durham, NC: Duke University Press.

Falicov, Tamara. 2007. *The Cinematic Tango: Contemporary Argentine Film*. London: Wallflower Press.

Franco, Jean. 1997. Nation as Imagined Community. In *Dangerous Liaisons: Gender, Nation and Postcolonial Perspectives.* Ed. Anne McClintock, Aamir Mufti, and Ella Shohat, 130–40. Minneapolis: University of Minnesota Press.

Goldman, Ilene S. 1997. Recent Colombian Cinema: Public Histories and Private Stories. In *Framing Latin American Cinema Contemporary Critical Perspectives*. Ed. Ann Marie Stock, 57–76. Minneapolis: University of Minnesota.

Gutiérrez, María Alejandra. 2004. Bountiful Rebound of Argentine Cinema. *Americas* 56: 24–29.

Hooker, Juliet. 2005. "Beloved Enemies": Race and Official Mestizo Nationalism in Nicaragua. *Latin American Research Review* 40, no. 3: 14–39.

Hulme, Peter. 2008. Postcolonial Theory and the Representation of Culture in the Americas. In *Coloniality at Large: Latin America and the Postcolonial Debate*. Ed. Mabel Moraña, Enrique Dussel, and Carlos A. Jáuregi, 388–95. Durham, NC: Duke University Press.

Johnson, Randal. 1984. *Cinema Novo x 5: Masters of Contemporary Brazilian Film*. Austin: University of Texas Press.

King, John. 1997. Andean Images: Bolivia, Ecuador and Peru. In *New Latin American Cinema: Studies of National Cinemas*, vol. 2. Ed. Michael T. Martin, 483–505. Detroit: Wayne State University Press.

Klor de Alva, Jorge. 1995. The Postcolonization of the (Latin) American Experience: A Reconsideration of 'Colonialism,' 'Postcolonialism,' and 'Mestizaje.' In *After Colonialism: Imperial Histories and Postcolonial Displacements*. Ed. Gyan Prakash, 241–75. Princeton, NJ: Princeton University Press.

Koshy, Susan. 2005. The Postmodern Subaltern: Globalization Theory and the Subject of Ethnic, Area, and Postcolonial Studies. In *Minor Transnationalism*. Ed. Françoise Lionnet and Shu-Mei Shih, 109–31. Durham, NC: Duke University Press.

Lauretis, Teresa de. 1987. The Violence of Rhetoric: Considerations on Representation and Gender. In *Technologies of Gender: Essays on Theory, Film, and Fiction*. 31–50. Bloomington: Indiana University Press.

Martin, Michael T. 1997. *New Latin American Cinema: Theory, Practices, and Transcontinental Articulations*, vols. 1 and 2. Detroit: Wayne State University Press.

Maybury-Lewis, David, ed. 2002. *The Politics of Ethnicity: Indigenous Peoples in Latin American States*. Cambridge, MA: Harvard University Press.

McClintock, Anne. 1997. 'No Longer in a Future Heaven': Gender, Race and Nationalism. In *Dangerous Liaisons: Gender, Nation and Postcolonial Perspectives*. Ed. Anne McClintock, Aamir Mufti, and Ella Shohat, 89–112. Minneapolis: University of Minnesota Press.

Mollett, Sharlene. 2006. Race and Natural Resource Conflicts in Honduras: The Miskito and Garifuna Struggle for Lasa Pulan. *Latin American Research Review* 41, no. 1: 76–101.

Monsiváis, Carlos. 1987. Muerte y resurrección del nacionalismo mexicano. *Nexos* 109: 13–22.

Nancy, Jean-Luc. 2004. *La communauté désœuvrée*. 4th ed. Paris: Christian Bourgois.

Pick, Zuzana M. 1993. *The New Latin American Cinema: A Continental Project*. Austin: University of Texas Press.

Podalsky, Laura. 1994. Negotiating Differences: National Cinemas and Co-Productions in Prerevolutionary Cuba. *Velvet Light Trap* 34: 59–70.

Pratt, Mary Louise. 2008. In the Neocolony: Destiny, Destination, and the Traffic in Meaning. In *Coloniality at Large: Latin America and the Postcolonial Debate*. Ed. Mabel Moraña, Enrique Dussel, and Carlos A. Jáuregi, 459–75. Durham, NC: Duke University Press.

Quijano, Aníbal. 2000. Colonialidad del Poder y Clasificacion Social. *Journal of World-Systems Research* 11, no. 2: 342–86. Special Issue: Festchrift for Immanuel Wallerstein – Part I.

Rangil, Viviana. 2005. *Otro punto de vista: mujer y cine en la Argentina*. Rosario: Beatriz Viterbo.

Rueda, María Helena. 2000. La letra vs. el cine en el imaginario cultural colombiano. In *Literatura y cultura: Narrativa colombiana del siglo XX*, vol. 3. Comp. María Mercedes Jaramillo, Betty Osorio, and Ángela Robledo, 462–86. Bogotá: Ministerio de Cultura.

Shannon Speed, R. Aída Hernández Castillo, and Lynn M Stephen. 2006. Introduction to *Dissident Women: Gender and Cultural Politics in Chiapas*. Ed. Shannon Speed, R. Aída Hernández Castillo, and Lynn M Stephen, 33–54. Austin: University of Texas Press.

Shaw, Deborah, ed. 2007. *Contemporary Latin American Cinema: Breaking into the Global Market*. Lanham, MD: Rowman & Littlefield.

Smith, Paul Julian. 2003. Transatlantic Traffic in Recent Mexican Film. *Journal of Latin America Cultural Studies* 12, no. 3: 389–400.

Stephen, Lynn. 2006. Epilogue to Rural Women's Grassroots Activism, 1980–2000: Reframing the Nation from Below. In *Sex in Revolution: Gender, Politics, and Power in Modern Mexico*. Ed. Jocelyn Olcott, Mary Kay Vaughan, and Gabriela Cano, 241–60. Durham, NC: Duke University Press.

Stock, Ann Marie. 2006. Migrancy and the Latin American Cinemascape: Towards a Post-National Critical Praxis. In *Transnational Cinema: The Film Reader*. Ed. Elizabeth Ezra and Terry Rowden, 157–65. London: Routledge.

Suárez, Pablo. 2003. Amidst Political Chaos, Social Instabillity and Economic Meltdown The New Argentine Cinema Continues to Bears Witness. Film Comment. *Buenos Aires Journal*, 11–13. http://www.filmlinc.com/fcm/9–10–2003/journal.htm (accessed April 10, 2008).

Thayer, Millie. 1997. Identity, Revolution, and Democracy: Lesbian Movements in Central America. *Social Problems* 44, no. 3: 386–407.

Troyan, Brett. 2008. Re-Imagining the "Indian" and the State: *Indigenismo* in Colombia, 1926–47. *Canadian Journal of Latin American and Caribbean Studies* 33, no. 65: 81–106.

Villalón, Roberta. 2007. Neoliberalism, Corruption, and Legacies of Contention: Argentina's Social Movements, 1993–2006. *Latin American Perspectives* 153 (34.2): 139–56.

Walsh, Catherine E. 2008. (Post)Coloniality in Ecuador: The Indigenous Movement's Practices and Politics of (Re)Signification and Decolonization. In *Coloniality at Large: Latin America and the Postcolonial Debate*. Ed. Mabel Moraña, Enrique Dussel, and Carlos A. Jáuregi, 506–18. Durham, NC: Duke University Press.

NOTES

1   See: Costello, Falicov, Gutiérrez, Rangil, Smith, and Pablo Suárez, among others. Deborah Shaw rightly notes that the term 'Latin American cinema' does not manage to include all of the cinemas from the region because some countries either do not make or cannot distribute their films and videos (Shaw 3). Also important is the fact that the term might not reflect geopolitical conditions of production and consumption (Stock 158).

2   For some notes on the state of Peruvian cinema, see Barrow and King. For information on Colombian cinema, see Bermúdez Barrios, Correa Restrepo, Goldman and Rueda.

3   The debates concerning 'modernity' as a term need not be rehearsed here. Suffice it to say that it is usually linked to the myth of European superiority over non-European cultures (Dussel 2008, 341).

The homogenizing and patriarchal features of *mestizaje* in national projects, particularly the Mexican one, have been discussed by authors such as Bartra, Franco, Monsiváis, and McClintock. More recently, Hooker and Mollett have noted the same *mestizo* undercurrent for Nicaraguan and Honduran nationalisms respectively. This does not mean that these discourses are monological but rather that certain strategies of legitimization are privileged and repeated to the exclusion of other perspectives.

4   For a recent critique of Klor de Alba, see Hulme.

5   For indigenous organizing, see Blackwell, Maybury-Lewis, Stephen, and Troyan. For gay and lesbian movements, consult Brown, Carrier, and Thayer. Although this discussion focuses on the limits of the nation-state, this does not mean that nation-states in Latin America have disappeared. With the advent of narcoterrorism and paramilitary branches of government, some nation-states in Latin America have increased their control over their populations through violence, state terrorism, and other strategies aimed at stifling citizens' dissent.

6   For a critique of Postcolonial Studies, see Juan Duchesne Winter (29), Mary Louise Pratt (462), and Susan Koshy (110).

7   As Mary Louise Pratt asserts, contemporary neoliberalism has not been able to hide its imperial character even if this was obscured for a time by the language of free trade and open markets (461). Pratt thus sees neoliberalism as a form of neo-colonialism.

8   I would like to acknowledge that Duchesne Winter's ideas on the working of community guided me in thinking about this film. See especially page 49 of his *Fugas incomunistas: Ensayos*. For more examples of attempts at community reorganization, among which 'clubes de trueque' see Villalón (148–49).

9   Dapena uses the term 'modernist' to refer to experimental techniques of film narration. This term should not be confused with the term 'modernity,' which expresses a teleological view of progress.

PART I: Crisis of the Nation-State and Desire for Community

NATIONAL BELONGING IN JUAN JOSÉ CAMPANELLA'S *LUNA DE AVELLANEDA*

Rebecca L. Lee[1]
University of Missouri, Kansas City

Juan José Campanella is arguably the best internationally known Argentine film director of his generation. His recent film *El secreto de sus ojos* [*The Secret in Their Eyes*] (2009) has received critical acclaim both at home and abroad and was recently presented for an Oscar nomination.[2] Described as an industrial auteur, a term used to designate a generation of directors who combine elements of mainstream Hollywood cinema with qualities normally attributed to independent filmmaking, Campanella is, in many ways, at the crossroads of the current debate surrounding Argentine national cinema.[3] Unlike the directors of the recent wave of film production known as New Argentine Cinema, Campanella attended film school in the United States and, after graduating from New York University's Tisch School of the Arts, went on to direct box office hits such as *El hijo de la novia* [*The Son of the Bride*] (2001) and numerous TV series (House, Law and Order, Criminal Intent) for American audiences.[4] Many film critics in Argentina dismiss his work as overly sentimental and melodramatic while triumphing the minimalist, open narrative, experimental style of directors such as Adrián Caetano, Adolfo Aristarain, and

Pablo Trapero.[5] These tensions between what has been broadly termed a high and low style of cinematic production draw into question the state's role in regulating culture – a subject of intense discussion in recent years as local theatres screening Argentine films have been displaced by transnational movie multiplexes showing Hollywood blockbusters.[6] In order to counter these global market forces and to foster a national cinema, the Argentine government implemented a law in 1995 to reinvigorate domestic film production. Law 24,377 mandates several measures to develop local filmmaking, such as subsidies, screen quotas, and the creation of a national public entity to regulate cinematography, the National Institute of Cinematography and Audiovisual Arts (INCAA).[7] Despite protectionist measures, many of these films have failed to attract significant domestic or international audiences. And although local film critics have widely lauded this new independent cinema, others argue that the lack of spectators, despite screen quotas and subsidies, undermines the fundamental premise of Law 24,377.[8]

Interestingly, the differences between industrial auteurs and new independent directors are, in some ways, diminishing. As first-time directors such as Trapero and Caetano gain recognition and commercial exposure, they too have begun partnering with global production companies, thus calling into the question the label "independent." Furthermore, films in recent years by both lesser-known and more prominent directors have coalesced around similar themes. The majority of these films recount the ills of globalization and have as their historical backdrop the experience of extreme economic hardship and political unrest that began in Argentina in the 1990s and reached its apex in 2001. In addition, both sets of directors, at some level or another, grapple with themes of subjectivity and displacement, the result of which are films that document the demise of the nation–state while aiding in its reconstruction.

Campanella's *Luna de Avellaneda* [*Moon of Avellaneda*] (2004) is representative of this blending of international cinematic trends with localized narratives. The film melds global and domestic concerns by focusing on communities devastated by Argentina's not-so-distant economic collapse. From the first scene, a crowd cheering as a man struggles to climb a soaped pole, *Luna de Avellaneda* signals to viewers the centrality of camaraderie to humanity.[9] Set in 2001 in the middle class town of Avellaneda, the film investigates the fate of a once vibrant social club, its recent decline, and the ensuing debate around saving what has been for more than a half century a centre for community gatherings and civic support. Club members, confronted by rising unemployment and a declining economy, face a difficult decision. Selling the club would assure the elimination of an institutional anchor within the Avellaneda community, but the foreign investor interested in the property has promised a new casino and two hundred jobs.

Undeniably, the relevance of the year 2001 is not lost on Argentines, who in that year witnessed a complete economic, political breakdown and the subsequent unraveling of local communities. When placed in historical context, Juan José Campanella's *Luna de Avellaneda* can be read as an allegory of this economic crisis. The film narrates the country's conflicted relationship to the neo-liberal policies, including a notable rise in foreign investment, the privatization of industries, and the implementation of austerity measures particularly at the level of social programming and education, enacted by Carlos Saúl Menem during his presidency (1989-99) and the abrupt departure from the economic boom often referred to as the "fiesta menemista."[10]

The film, however, goes beyond simply documenting the financial collapse and offers a portrait of the national psyche through a series of personal vignettes. Bordering at times on sentimental melodrama, *Luna de Avellaneda* explores the reconfiguration of citizenship and state responsibility and cites the dual crisis of capitalism and the state as instrumental in fuelling new notions of national belonging.[11] Returning continually to the theme of a community in peril, the film seeks to consolidate the nation by remembering the economic crisis as a moment of lost and then restored solidarity. Central to this analysis are questions about this new citizen activism that was born during the most devastating economic crisis in Argentine history and how this relates to the most notable creative peak in Argentine cinematic production.[12] How are we to understand, for example, the simultaneous rise of cultural production at the moment of complete societal, political, and economic breakdown?

A SYMBOL OF ANOTHER TIME

At the start of the film, the club is flourishing. Bursting membership roles and a full calendar of social events stand as testimony to the critical social function of the club within Argentine culture. In the film's first eight minutes, two evocative moments, both of which revolve around a celebratory festival of carnival games and entertainment, speak explicitly to the power of solidarity to community well-being. The first scene focuses on a crowd that has gathered beneath a soaped pole cheering enthusiastically for the latest contestant attempting to reach the top and ring a bell. Following the young man up the pole, the camera pans from a close-up of his face set in intense exertion to a nearby and brightly lit sign, "Luna de Avellaneda." The visual juxtaposition of the man and the sign together with the sounds of the encouraging spectators and joyful music symbolize the essential nature of the social club and foreshadow the ensuing narrative. The message is clear: communities matter.

Leaving no room for an alternative interpretation, the theme of solidarity is reiterated once again in the very next scene that is linked by the same poignant music. Multi-generation families dine and dance to a live band in a brightly lit auditorium. Children run about, and young couples, surrounded by close-knit families, engage in courting rituals. The action is momentarily interrupted as a small group winds its way to the front with a labouring pregnant woman in tow. Sensing the urgency of the situation, the audience jumps to the woman's aid and a club member, who is also a doctor, delivers the baby while the rest of the community sits in nervous anticipation. Eventually, the silence is broken by the newborn child's cries followed by explosive applause and celebration from the club's extended family.

The birth of a healthy baby boy as a figurative representation of Avellaneda's vitality quickly gives way, however, to images of hardship and decline. The camera transitions with a dissolve from the celebration to a middle-aged man standing in the same auditorium. Distinctive wall designs make the setting recognizable to the film viewers, but the space is now noticeably decrepit from years of neglect. The viewer quickly learns that the man whose hair has begun to grey is Román (Ricardo Darín) – the baby born amid the raucous ballroom celebration some four decades earlier. Times and fortunes have clearly changed. The music and decorations are gone. And the club is a tired institution badly in need of paint and repairs. Membership has declined, and many of those that do remain are unable to afford their dues. What keeps the club going is a handful of devoted members, including the film's protagonist, Román, the only lifetime member, an honour bestowed upon him the night he was born. A formidable activist in his youth, Román is now a taxi driver who works twelve to fourteen hours a day and spends whatever free time he has volunteering at the club. To some, the club is an antiquated institution that has outlived its usefulness. To Román, however, it is not just a place where local schoolchildren come to play basketball, learn ballet, and receive mentorship, but the foundation of a strong community.

Despite their best efforts to breathe life back into the social club, Román and others like him, find the club and the very notion of community shaken by a rapidly deteriorating economy. The local characters of the film, like the larger nation they represent, attempt to cope with the extreme aftershocks of a prolonged period of governmental corruption and mismanagement during its shift from a deeply statist economy toward a neo-liberal model. In 1999, for example, Argentina suffered a 4 per cent drop in the Gross National Product (GDP) and the country entered a recession that lasted more than three years. Argentina hit bottom in December of 2001 with a devastating institutional and financial collapse that spawned subsequent popular uprisings. Government corruption fed the decline, but especially troubling was a 1991 fiscal convertibility plan that pegged the Argentine peso to the U.S. dollar. One dramatic result was an overvalued peso and an imbalanced economy that was impossible to sustain. The ability of government officials, first under Menem, and later under Fernando de la Rúa, to maintain the façade of a healthy economy was coming to a rapid end. The predictable collapse devastated a large segment of the population as money once thought safely protected by the state was now held by bankrupt financial institutions.

More than just a crisis of economy or capitalism, however, Argentines suffered a fundamental loss of faith in their government and the state in general. The most explicit display of declining confidence came in the form of a large exodus of the nation's population. Believing that an end to the country's misery was nowhere near, local communities evaporated as scores of Argentines sought new opportunities elsewhere. More than a quarter of a million people, roughly six times the total number of emigrants in the period 1993–2000, left Argentina in the immediate wake of the 2001 collapse, the majority headed to Spain and Italy. The impact of this population loss was obviously considerable.[13] Particularly troubling were news reports about who was leaving. Between 2001 and 2003, a growing proportion of the skilled population emigrated, fuelling fears of a "brain drain" that, in turn, only further increased the flood of citizens looking for a better future elsewhere. The end result was a generalized view that the country had little hopes for recovery.

STRATEGIES OF SURVIVAL IN A GLOBALIZED WORLD

The economic disaster of 2001 was all–encompassing except for the select few able to profit from the suffering and financial hardship of others. It is against this historical backdrop that Campanella narrates the lives of his characters. In the film, Alejandro (Daniel Fanego) represents the national elites who participated in the privatization of state industries that led to the widespread insolvency of local businesses. A member of the social club since he was a child, Alejandro finds himself on the opposite side of the negotiation table when the club lands in financial trouble. When Alejandro enters the film, the club can barely pay its bills or their salaried staff, and it owes the city 40,000 pesos for not filing balance sheets between 1988 and 2001. A board meeting reveals just how dire the situation has become as they attempt to save money by turning off the lights during the halftime of the basketball game. Confronted with back taxes and a large fine, club board members seek out Alejandro, who works at the municipality, and ask for help. His only advice: sell. Like the elites he symbolizes and whom many Argentines believe were complicit in the government's mishandling of the economy, Alejandro does not see a community but a commodity that can be auctioned off to the highest bidder.

Unquestionably, the devaluing and displacement of communities is the central tragedy of the film. Against the backdrop of economic malaise, marriages erode, families bicker, kinship ties are strained, and many find themselves embroiled in crises. In stark contrast to the opening scenes of the film, now parents are stressed to the maximum under the demands of sustaining themselves and their families in the face of financial struggle. Román's own marriage is on the brink of collapse, as he and his wife, Verónica (Silvia Kutika), fight to maintain a semblance of respect for themselves and for one another during desperate times. The two find themselves repeatedly faced with the humiliation of their reduced financial circumstances and their plight reveals the degree to which economic difficulties have penetrated the lives of individuals. On one occasion, Roman cannot take his daughter to the doctor as a result of his failure to make the insurance payments. An even more poignant scene is illustrated by his inability to afford a bottle of cologne or a bouquet of flowers, both needed to woo back his estranged wife.

Further, the subtle details of Román's insurance conundrum point to the realities of life in a globalized society, most notably the privatization of basic services and the lack of a social safety net. In this new world order of neo-liberal economic reform and deepening austerity measures at the level of public funding, the average Argentine citizen is increasingly unable to compete in the marketplace. The economics of globalization clearly undercut Román's ability to afford simple luxuries such as cologne but such trends also reduce the range of products available to him.[14] After being shown several options and each time asking the salesperson for something less expensive, Román concedes that he cannot even afford a Taiwanese knock off of a designer American fragrance. He finally settles for a local product for 5 pesos. To his eventual shame, he realizes that his purchase, a perfect representation of industrial anemia in Argentina, does nothing to elevate his self-esteem. It has, instead, quite the opposite effect. The local cologne resembles the scent of a skunk and the all-pervasive smell lingers persistently like a sad, stale reminder of his and the nation's abject state.

As the film's narrative develops, nearly every character is leading an increasingly isolated, individualistic, and alienated existence. Román realizes he has become a stranger to his son Darío (Francisco Fernández de Rosa), whose life marches forward independent from that of his father, mother, and sister. In a vain attempt to maintain a living wage, Darío is forced to work double shifts without overtime compensation. Unable to participate in the championship finals for the club's basketball team for fear that he will lose his job, he has his apprehension confirmed when his boss lays him off in favour of less expensive immigrant labour. Darío's resulting anger is tempered, at least in part, by yet another scene of disempowerment. Yucatán, the pejorative and essentializing name that Darío's boss has given his replacement, submissively observes Darío's dismissal with his head cast downward. He is, undoubtedly, a symbol of the countless migrants who, out of desperation, unwittingly facilitate globalization's perpetual search for cheaper labour and resources to minimize costs and to maximize earnings.[15]

Emphasizing the true crisis of capitalism, director Campanella depicts a society in which people are dispensable and only money matters. More than capital gains, the result is a profound loss at the level of society as citizens witness their vulnerability deepen and their ability to act dwindle. The film, nevertheless, hints at pockets of resistance. Like the scores of Argentines who took to the streets in violent protest on 19 and 20 December 2001, Román and his son recapture some sense of solidarity when they react loudly and aggressively to Darío's dismissal by his employer, an act that ultimately lands them in jail.[16] Yet, despite this setback, the narrative does not assume an apologetic or tragic tone but is instead defiant, triumphant, gesturing toward a forgotten but not lost spirit of dignity and self-determination. The victory is short-lived, however, as the geopolitical forces prove too great for two lone revolutionaries.

In what is perhaps the most powerful scene of the film, Alejandro has bailed Román and his son out of jail and takes the opportunity to lord his power and authority by inviting himself into their home. Alejandro enters with entitlement and smug superiority while flirting unabashedly with Román's wife, Verónica. Shortly thereafter, Alejandro takes a seat at the dining room table across from Darío and literally usurps Román's position as master of his own household. Verónica attentively serves Alejandro coffee while Román becomes an awkward bystander without a place to sit – a displacement which is signaled by his positioning in the scene to the far left of the screen. That this part of the story takes place within Román's home only serves to heighten the degree to which domestic as well as international actors have penetrated and participated in the demise of the figurative national family.

Highlighting the intimacy of the situation and, therefore, level of violation which Alejandro has attained, Campanella chooses the bathroom as the setting for the film's climax. Román is in the shower, his wife sits on the toilet, and his son stands just inside the door. As the family grapples with maintaining unity in the face of adversity, Alejandro gazes voyeuristically from the threshold. Darío believes his only option is to migrate to Spain in search of work and challenges his father to provide a more persuasive alternative. As before, Alejandro offers his unsolicited and paternalistic recommendation that Darío come to work for him at City Hall, effectively inviting him to cross political lines and the ideological divide within the family.

In this scene, the protagonist finds himself utterly vulnerable, literally naked and emasculated by the fully clothed Alejandro who parades Román's disenfranchisement and loss of power in front of his family. Alejandro mocks Román's fall from political activist to ineffectual victim. A watershed moment that is marked by a close-up of the protagonist's tightly clenched fist, it is ironic that the film's antagonist provides the catalyst for Román's eventual return to empowerment. In the subsequent scene, he stands on the banks of the river that separates the shantytowns from the city and calls to Dalma (Micaela Moreno), the film's symbol of the growing marginalization of the forgotten lower classes.[17] At this juncture, Román assumes the emblematic helm not only of his destiny and that of his family, but of the Argentine nation as well.

DREAMS OF NATIONAL BELONGING

In *Luna de Avellaneda*, Dalma, a young girl from the shantytowns who dreams of becoming a ballerina, symbolizes the crisis of state responsibility that resulted from neo-liberal economic reforms enacted in Argentina in the 1990s.[18] Román's daughter has brought her friend to the social club so that she can participate in dance classes. Román attempts to explain to the two girls that Dalma, whose name loosely translates to "of the soul," cannot stay because she is unable to pay the membership fee. The diminutive stature of the girl, who lacks access to education and who is clearly suffering from hunger, in contrast to Román, who is seated across from her, provides a visual contrast to what is being said and the unlikely recipient of these words. Additionally, the fact the Dalma resides in a shantytown – the most visible marker of the extreme unequal distribution of wealth as a result of globalization – is significant.[19] Ultimately, the scene reveals a breakdown of civil society. The most critical victim is a lost generation of children, like Dalma, who cannot afford the luxury of dreams and security, both of which are cast as haphazard extravagancies and relics of a previous period.

The incongruent nature of an adult speaking to a child about the realities of globalization is punctuated by the introduction at this moment of Román's unlikely foil, a balding, marginally employed forty-year-old who still dreams of being a rock star. Amadeo (Eduardo Blanco) is the only character in the film that has visibly retained the positive hope of new love and still believes in the possibility that things will end happily. According to his love interest, Cristina (Valeria Bertuccelli), the somewhat reserved and emotionally guarded dance teacher, Amadeo metaphorically keeps "lighting matches," always optimistically expecting more where others expect less. He is, without doubt, the true dreamer of the story.

By contrast, the other characters embody the defeat of the common Argentine. Graciela (Mercedes Morán), for example, is an involuntary divorcee who spends the bulk of her time trying to elicit alimony payments from her husband who left her for another woman. At one point, Graciela finds herself lulled into a dream-like state during an expensive dinner with a handsome businessman who is head of a transnational corporation. He promises to take her to Paris to act as an interpreter but leaves her with the bill in the end. Having been swindled, Graciela laments her lapse in judgment and berates herself for having been so naïve as to think that she could have shared in the riches and benefits of elite society. She resumes her downtrodden role as she is left holding the literal purse of expenses incurred by the exploits of international business.

Not surprisingly, the depressed economic climate that national elites have just begun to feel and which the lower and middle classes have been experiencing for quite some time pushes people to desperate acts as camaraderie takes a back seat to financial survival. When faced with having her electricity cut off, a desperate Graciela resorts to deception. A board member of the social club, she is caught siphoning funds. Likewise, Román jockeys with fellow taxi cab drivers for a handful of fares in order to pay his telephone bill. Despite good intentions, the remaining members lapse in their payments and the ailing physical club itself becomes a sign of the deteriorated investment in local communities and, perhaps more importantly, a symbol of all those left behind.

Sadly, the fictional town of Avellaneda mirrors the reality of so many local communities that struggled to recover from the devastating blow of Argentina's failed economy. There was, moreover, a general sentiment that the administration had not acted in the best interest of the majority of Argentines and that myopic solutions to retain the privileges of the upper echelons of society had been set forth while the less fortunate footed the bill.

In the aftermath of the economic collapse in 2001 and in response to the *corralito*, a partial freeze on bank accounts to shore up the Argentine peso, entire families roamed the streets at night, rummaging through dumpsters for recyclable scraps with their bare hands. With makeshift carts, scores of abruptly unemployed Argentines became scavengers seeking bits of paper, plastic, glass, and cardboard to resell at a rate of 0.42 centavos (0.12 U.S. cents) a kilo. In a true sign of desperation, reconditioned scrap metal became big business. Vandals stole bronze plaques on commemorative statues and other historical monuments as well as copper cables from telephone lines and aluminum from the electronic circuitry of traffic lights.[20]

Perhaps most troubling, despite small attempts at recovery, the severity of the situation persisted. Once referred to as the richest nation in South America, Argentina fell into its worst slump in recent history.[21] Between June 2001 and June 2002, Argentina's GDP fell by 13.5 per cent, dramatically affecting employment and incomes. In response, poverty rose sharply, and, as of September 2002, 19 million of the country's total population of 35 million earned less than the U.S.-dollar equivalent of $190 per month while another 8.4 million were destitute, subsisting on less than $83 per month. In primary and secondary schools, there were widespread reports of children suffering from malnutrition with many depending upon school services to provide their only meal of the day. In some towns, people were reduced to eating fried frogs and rodents as their principal source of daily sustenance. And although members of the lower classes, like Dalma, endured the most severe reduced circumstances, every level of society was affected.[22]

GLOBAL ECONOMIES/LOCAL REALITIES

Having learned that his wife is having an affair, Román seeks shelter and a place to sleep at the club. In the process of clearing a space to form a makeshift bed, he stumbles upon the remnants – signs, bells, loudspeakers – from the carnival that began the film and marked the day of his birth. Surveying the artifacts of a forgotten era, Román finds inspiration to salvage the club from its onerous debt by staging a festival and, in doing so, attempts to restore the cohesion and prosperity of an earlier time.

A reincarnation of past glory proves futile. In contrast to the original affair and its vibrant, potent images of harmony, lightheartedness, and affluence, the modern-day festival is a hollow recreation, lacking in both attendance and vitality. The scene with the soaped pole repeats itself, only this time it is a lesson in complacency and resignation. No group gathers to cheer on the contestant, who instead finds himself alone in an unsuccessful struggle to reach the top. The solidarity that once existed has been weakened by economic woes. The festive atmosphere of possibility is replaced with a new reality as parents counsel their children in the virtues of self-denial. Graciela, for example, repeatedly reminds her son Bruno that the only joy he can derive from the situation is his non-active, non-cost-incurring participation. Unlike the children who attended the carnival that opens the film, he is an impotent observer of a scene to which he has been denied full access. Disappointment has taken the place of childlike wonderment as even the carnival ultimately serves only to remind Bruno of his lack of money and the foregone conclusion of his optionless future.

Compounding the tragic tone of the event is Amadeo's own fall from grace that takes the form of him getting drunk, after having sworn sobriety to his now girlfriend Cristina, and missing the dance piece she has choreographed. She finds him hunched over and passed out next to a bush outside the fairgrounds. The betrayal of his promise and Cristina's realization of having misplaced her faith in humanity yet again cast a dark and ominous shadow over the narrative. In this sequence, the lone bastion of eternal hope in the film, embodied in Amadeo's unrelenting optimism and his growing love for Cristina is lost.

At the moment of Amadeo's failure, however, Dalma's star begins to rise. The little girl from the shantytown dances proudly on the stage before an attentive audience – a scene that Román observes with an expression of self-satisfaction. Yet, despite efforts to the contrary, the carnival does not yield the desired result and the board succeeds in raising only a small portion of the total amount needed to repay the debt. According to Don Aquiles (José Luis López Vázquez), the town's patriarch and founding member of the club, "la gente quiere pero no puede" [not everybody can keep up with the Joneses].[23] Having exhausted the alternatives, an assembly is called to determine the fate of the social club.

Alejandro, who symbolically represents the interests of national elites, and Román, who embodies the plight of the common Argentine, square off in a public debate in the same auditorium in which the film begins. Amid peeling paint and under a leaking roof, Alejandro reiterates the initiative to sell in order to pay off the debt, in effect allegorizing the situation of the club to that of the nation by arguing that "son los buenos negocios que tiran un país para arriba." ["Good business deals are what move a country forward."] To his mind, the preservation of the club and community is a form of misplaced romanticism and has no place in the modern world. Urging the members not to be foolhardy, he presses them to recognize "un buen negocio" [a good deal]. From Alejandro's perspective, times have changed and Avellaneda, like Argentina, is no longer a town of thriving families with well-paying factory jobs but a desolate backwater.

What Alejandro's speech fails to note, however, is the source of this social and economic decline. Several club members rise to explain how their family businesses and industries have slowly been whittled away by the infusion of transnational capital and the subsequent liquidation of the country. A father laments the loss of his butcher shop, named after his two daughters, but sold, likely to foreign investors, and then reconditioned as Laughing Cow Incorporated. Similarly, in the last decade, the many factories that used to fuel the local economy and were a source of jobs have been sold off and closed in a series of international corporate mergers and acquisitions. And although Alejandro does not say it explicitly, it is likely that he knows, signified by his discomfort in having Dalma gaze upon him as he speaks, that the result of selling will surely be the demise of the community rather than its renewal.

In contrast to Alejandro's suggestion that there is nothing left to save, Román counters with the example of Dalma, for it is only in the club that she "encontró un lugar" ["found a place"]. Román calls upon others to recognize not only their ability but also their responsibility to act. Through their complacency and willingness to settle for less, the members have essentially sealed their own fate. In the words of the protagonist, "Cada vez queremos menos, cada vez tenemos menos." [By always settling for less, we always end up having less.] The club, however, appears destined to be yet another casualty in the overwhelming force of globalization. Despite Román's best efforts to persuade the members to band together, to have pride in their ability to be effective producers, to "crear algo," ["to create something,"] the promise of new jobs, although unlikely to materialize, wins out over the preservation of community and the futures of children like Dalma. In a tally of 33–26, the members vote to sell the club to a private investor.

The club's decision can be read figuratively as the Argentine government's own choice, albeit at the behest of the International Monetary Fund, to repay the external debt at the expense of domestic infrastructure and the average citizen. The belief that the relatively short-term implementation of neo-liberal reform measures would produce a long-term pay-off either in the form of jobs or the increased wealth of all individuals was what essentially facilitated the complete mortgaging of Argentina and its citizens. Detractors of neoliberalism have questioned its long-term efficacy and ability to improve the living standards of an entire population by arguing "these economic reforms tend to be most concentrated among social groups that already have had access to education and capital, while few benefits have accrued to the poor and those with limited education." (Kent, 337) Despite, for example, Argentina's increase in overall wealth during the 1990s, unemployment remained steady at roughly 20 per cent. During that ten-year period, moreover, the top 20 per cent of the population experienced an increase in their annual incomes while the rest of the nation underwent a visible economic decline. To be sure, the devastating disintegration of Argentina's economy and social fabric in recent years point to this simultaneous rise in GDP and social inequity as an unsustainable venture.

RECONFIGURING CITIZENSHIP AND STATE RESPONSIBILITY

At the close of the film, Román and Verónica begin the symbolic journey back towards life as a couple, only this time their relationship bears the scars of survival. In all, there is a strong suggestion that, in fact, times have changed. The final scenes depict the protagonist and his family together with their friends sharing a farewell meal. Darío and his girlfriend, Yanina (Sofía Bertolotto), both symbols of a lost generation, are scheduled to leave on a flight to Spain, believing that Argentina holds nothing of value and no potential prospects of employment.[24] Román and his wife have plans to sell their house and to follow in the footsteps of their son.

When Román proposes a toast to the departure of Darío and Yanina and to his own, Emilio (Atilio Pozzobón), one of the core members of the club, is unwilling to oblige, stating that he refuses to celebrate the dissolution of their extended community.[25] Román, as others before him, feels justified in his decision to leave and to abandon the hope of founding a new social institution, declaring that he cannot continue in vain. He defends his right to emigrate and blames the thirty-three who voted against saving the club. In response, Amadeo, forever the spoiler, asks, "Y los otros veintiséis?" ["And the other twenty-six?"], to which Román replies that in this new era the only responsibility he has is to himself and his immediate family.

Campanella does not, however, allow the story to end there. Amadeo and Cristina have made up, both acknowledging the sweet yet arduous and sometimes uncertain path toward effecting change. Even more significant, Cristina is pregnant, essentially bringing the film's narrative full circle and foreshadowing the birth of a new national family. Also, as Darío and his girlfriend prepare to depart, Román searches for a replacement suitcase and happens upon his forgotten lifetime membership card tucked away on a dusty shelf in the garage. The discovery serves as a reminder of the integral aspect of strong community institutions to society and prompts Román to ask Amadeo how to go about founding a new club, to which Amadeo, having embarked on his own uncertain path toward reform and the reconstitution of his relationship with Cristina, says, "Debemos averiguar." ["We should find out."]. As the ending to *Luna de Avellaneda* suggests, state responsibility is only part of the equation and Argentines themselves need to play a role in a solution to the crisis of capitalism.

Argentines did just this in the popular uprisings of 19 and 20 December 2001. In the weeks and months following these protests, a majority sought to renegotiate the terms of citizenship and state responsibility through a series of mass demonstrations. These *Asambleas Populares* galvanized and gave voice to the millions of Argentines who had suffered under the policies of neoliberal economic reform.[26] Among the demands were the nationalization of key industries, the deferment of external debt repayment, the re-fortification of social institutions, and the prosecution of government corruption.

The election of Néstor Kirchener to the presidency and his landmark decision to focus first on domestic infrastructure and to postpone payments to the World Bank constituted a massive reconfiguration of Argentine governance. In forcing the implementation of critical changes, Argentines did more than just actively respond to an economic crisis. By demanding that their voices be heard they had essentially fuelled new notions of national belonging.

Through an arguably utopian view of the past, Campanella effectively critiques the conditions of neoliberalism that not only encourage the exodus of wealth and resources from the nation but also produce increasingly fractured societies. *Luna de Avellaneda*, moreover, alludes to a pivotal moment in Argentine history in which civil resistance sought to trump institutional and governmental power. Beyond indirect documentation of an event, however, the film is also a reminder that the struggle is far from over. Indeed, Roman's story is more than just an affirmation of the innumerable Argentines who rose up in protest, it is a call to arms for generations to come.

WORKS CITED

Augé, Clare. 2002. Argentina: life after bankruptcy. September. http://monde-diplo.com/2002/09/13argentina (accessed February 6, 2008).

Bernades, Horacio, Diego Lerer, and Sergio Wolf, eds. 2002. *El nuevo cine argentino: Temas, autores y estilos de una renovación.* Buenos Aires: FIPRESCI.

Burbach, Roger. 2002. Throw Them All Out: Argentina's Grassroots Rebellion. *NACLA* 36, no. 1: 38–42.

Chant, Sylvia. 2007. *Gender, Generation and Poverty*. Cheltenham, UK, and Northhampton, MA: Edward Elgar Publishing.

Coscia, Jorge. 2005. Cuota de pantalla, un paso esencial. In *El estado y el cine argentino*, 19–23. Santa Fe: Instituto Superior de Cine y Artes Audiovisuales de Santa Fe.

Evans, Leslie. 2003. The Crisis in Argentina. April. http://www.international. ucla.edu/article.asp?parentid=3566 (accessed March 13, 2008).

Faiola, Anthony. 2002. Despair in Once-Proud Argentina. *Washington Post*, 6 August.

Falicov, Tamara. 2007. Young Filmmakers and the New Independent Argentine Cinema. Chap. 4 in *Cinematic Tango: Contemporary Argentine Film*. London: Wallflower Press.

Faux, Jeff, and Larry Mishel. 2000. Inequality and the Global Economy. In *Global Capitalism*. Ed. Will Hutton and Anthony Giddens, 93–111. New York: New Press.

Galeano, Eduardo. 1997. *Open Veins of Latin America*. New York: Monthly Review Press.

García Canclini, Nestor. 1993. Habrá cine latinoamericano en el año 2000? *Jornada Semanal* 193 (February 17): 27–33.

Godoy, Lorena. 2004. *Understanding Poverty from a Gender Perspective*. Santiago, Chile: United Nations Publications.

Kent, Robert B. 2003. *Latin America: Regions and Peoples*. New York: Guilford Press.

Krauss, Clifford. 1999. Argentina Looks for a Way to Stem Illegal Immigrants. *New York Times*, 18 February.

La Nación. 2001. Serios disturbios en Plaza de Mayo. 19 December.

Mason, Andrew D., and Elizabeth M. King. 2001. *Engendering Development through Gender Equality in Rights, Resources and Voice*. New York: Oxford University Press.

Page, Daniela. 2002. La emigración y los jóvenes. *La nación*, 14 June.

Page, Joanna. 2009. *Crisis and Capitalism in Contemporary Argentine Cinema*. Durham, NC: Duke University Press.

Plaza, Mariano Elías. 2002. La juventud ante una opción difícil. *La nación*, 14 June.

Poblete, Juan. 2004. New National Cinemas in a Transnational Age. *Discourse* 26, nos. 1/2: 214–34.

Repic, Jaka. 2006. Las migraciones invisibles: migración transnacional entre Argentina y Europa. *Revista de la Facultad de Ciencias Sociales y Jurídicas* 1, no. 1: 233–52.

Rocha, Carolina. 2009. Contemporary Argentine Cinema during Neoliberalism. *Hispania* 92, no. 4: 824–34.

Rock, David. 1987. *Argentina: 1516–1987*. Berkeley: University of California Press.

Rosaldo, Renato. 1994. Cultural citizenship in San Jose, California. *PoLAR* 17, no. 2: 57–64.

Svampa, Maristella. 2005. *La sociedad excluyente: La Argentina bajo el signo del neo-liberalismo*. Buenos Aires: Taurus.

Tranchini, Elina. 2008. Tensión y globalización en las formas de representación del cine argentino contemporáneo. In *El cine argentino de hoy: entre el arte y la política*. Ed. Viviana Rangil, 119–35. Buenos Aires: Biblos.

Vales, Laura. 2002. Política desde la base. *Página/12*, 6 January.

Villalón, Roberta. 2007. Neoliberalism, Corruption, and Legacies of Contention: Argentina's Social Movements, 1993–2006. *Latin American Perspectives* 153 (34.2): 139–56.

FILMS

El abrazo partido. Directed by Daniel Burman. Distribution Company, 2004.

Bolivia. Directed by Adrián Caetano. Fundación PROA, 2001.

El bonaerense. Directed by Pablo Trapero. Argentina Video Home, 2002.

Buena vida delivery. Directed by Leonardo Di Cesare. Distribution Company, 2004.

El hijo de la novia. Directed by Juan José Campanella. Argentina Video Home, 2002.

Luna de Avellaneda. Directed by Juan José Campanella. 2004. DVD. Argentina Home Video, 2005.

Un oso rojo. Directed by Adrián Caetano. Distribution Company, 2002.

El secreto de sus ojos. Directed by Juan José Campanella. Distribution Company, 2009.

NOTES

1   I would like to thank John Herron, Viviana Grieco, Joy Renjilian-Burgy, my fellow conference panelists at the 2008 meeting of the AATSP and the anonymous reviewers for their comments on an earlier version of this essay.

2   *El secreto de sus ojos* has had over two and a half million viewers in Argentina alone. "El secreto de sus ojos" winner of the 2010 Academy Award for Best Foreign Film "is the sixth Argentine movie nominated to an Oscar. Previous ones include Sergio Renán's "La tregua" (1974), María Luisa Bemberg's "Camila" (1984), Luis Puenzo's "La historia oficial" (1985), Carlos Saura 's "Tango" (1998), and Campanella's "El hijo de la novia." See Clarin. com   http://www.clarin.com/diario/2010/03/06/um/m-02153638.htm (accessed March 6, 2010).

3   The blending of elements of mainstream Hollywood cinema such as big budgets, high technical standards, story lines with broad appeal and an ability to attract large audiences with qualities normally attributed to independent cinema such as relatively quick production and realization, freer scripts, and more experimental style is characteristic of industrial auteurs. For a close analysis of this blending of a Hollywood aesthetic with more vernacular and regional forms, see Juan Poblete, "New National Cinemas in a Transnational Age."

4   For a comprehensive list of the most recognized films as well as further discussion of New Argentine Cinema, see Horacio Bernadés, Diego Lerer, and Sergio Wolf, *Nuevo cine argentino: Temas, autores, estilos de una renovación.*

5   Although local film critics have not always looked favourably upon Campanella's work, *El hijo de la novia* (2001) and *Luna de avellaneda* (2004) were well received by domestic audiences with 1.2 and 1.26 million spectators respectively at the end of a three-month run. Falicov, 154.

6   For further discussion on the role of the state in promoting cultural production and mitigating market forces, see Nestor García Canclini, "¿Habrá cine latinoamericano en el año 2000?"

7   Jorge Coscia was a prominent supporter of these protectionist measures early on and argued that screen quotas would help level the playing field between national cinema and Hollywood blockbusters. See "Cuota de pantalla, un paso esencial."

8   Carolina Rocha utilizes data from the Argentine Union of the Cinematographic Industry (SICA) to measure the effects of Law 24,377 in her article "Contemporary Argentine Cinema During Neoliberalism" and argues that, although the law has helped increase national production, it has not actually resulted in higher film consumption by local audiences.

9   Elina Tranchini writes, "Las historias de los films de los últimos cinco años reconocen el fortalecimiento de la sociedad civil occurido en la Argentina.... Esta politicización operó activando la memoria social y la movilización local y comunitaria, la reconstrucción de los lazos sociales, la solidaridad y una cultura cívica orientada hacia intereses comunitarios" (125).

10   Pablo Trapero's *El bonaerense* (2002) and Adrián Caetano's *Un oso rojo* (2002) are two other Argentine films in which the 2001 economic crisis serves as a historical backdrop. The financial collapse not only impacted the content of film production during this time but the ability of directors to finance their films. The film industry in Argentina and many directors were forced to contend with dramatic spending cutbacks at the exact moment when Argentine film seemed to be taking off internationally. The devaluation of the Argentine peso resulted in a steep increase in the cost to produce a film. However, many directors such as Trapero, Caetano, Campanella, and Fabian Bielinksy were somewhat insulated from the crisis as a result of co-production financing from countries such as the United States, Spain, and France. For more on this, see Tamara Falicov (115–50).

11   Tamara Falicov has argued that directors of the New Independent Argentine Cinema like Campanella, Adrián Caetano (*Bolivia*, 2001*)*, and Daniel Burman (*El abrazo partido*, 2004) have sought "to expand the notion of Argentine citizenship to include subjects and characters who have traditionally been invisible or excluded from Argentine screens" (133).

12   Ironically, the transnational flow of capital and collapse of the Argentine peso that many of these directors thematize in their work was the very thing that made production of many of these films possible. In *Crisis and Capitalism in Contemporary Argentine Film*, Joanna Page analyzes the surge of cinematic production in Argentina that began in the mid-1990s and investigates the meanings and "conflicts

between meanings" arising from the circulation of Argentine films within the same global economy they so often critique (4).

13   Referred to as *jus sanguinis*, Argentines of Italian descent are eligible for dual citizenship if a parent or grandparent is Italian born. Many European countries, such as Spain, have this same policy of dual citizenship. This exodus of Argentines with European ancestry is a recurrent theme in *El abrazo partido* (Burman 2004) and *Buena Vida Delivery* (Di Cesare 2003).

14   Throughout this essay I use the term 'globalization' to describe the unregulated capital and trade flows that have contributed to the rise of social inequality, the withering of local industries, and the increased disenfranchisement of the less fortunate. See Jeff Faux and Larry Mishel (93–111).

15   Caetano also dramatized this influx of illegal immigrants in his film *Bolivia*. For more on migration from Peru and Bolivia into Argentina, see Clifford Krauss.

16   See *La nación* ("Serios disturbios en Plaza de Mayo").

17   Neither the stark divide between rich and poor nor the shantytowns known as *barrios miseria* are recent developments in Argentina. In *Open Veins of Latin America*, Eduardo Galeano traces the historical origins of this deep economic disparity and documents the ways in which the complicity of Latin American elites and their subservience to foreign powers have combined to create increasingly unequal capitalist societies in the region (205–19).

18   It is significant that Campanella chose a girl to represent the perils and hardship

of neo-liberal economic reform. The World Bank published a report in 2001 that documents the ways in which poverty exacerbates gender disparities. See Andrew D. Mason and Elizabeth M. King (31–72). For more on the feminization of poverty in Latin America, see Lorena Godoy (9–17) and Sylvia Chant (78–124).

19   Anthropologist Renato Rosaldo has written widely on the issue of cultural citizenship and challenges the idea that citizenship is simply a matter of having the proper legal documents. The term 'cultural citizenship' focuses on how belonging is enacted and constituted in everyday practices of inclusion and exclusion (57–64).

20   See Clare Augé.

21   In his book *Argentina: 1516–1987*, historian David Rock describes Argentina as one of the most prosperous countries in the world in the early twentieth century (162).

22   See Leslie Evans.

23   Proverbs such as "Quiero y no puedo" and "Tanto tienes, tanto vales" [if you can pay, you can stay] are alluded to indirectly throughout the movie.

24   Campanella is also a product of displacement, having resided outside Argentina for an extended period of time. He lived in the United States while studying film at the Tisch School at New York University and directing episodes of *Law and Order*. He returns to Argentina periodically to make feature films. One of his best known films is *El hijo de la novia* (2001). For more on the exodus of Argentine youth after 2001, see Mariano Elías Plaza and Daniela Page.

25   For a discussion regarding how transnational migration after Argentina's 2001 economic collapse has contributed to redefinitions of national belonging, see Jaka Repic.

26   Many Argentines saw the protests as a way of realizing their political power and connecting with local communities. See Laura Vales. For a detailed account of alternative means of dissent and organization, see also Roberta Villalón.

FROM NATIONAL ALLEGORY TO AUTOBIOGRAPHY: UN-PLEASURE AND OTHER FAMILY PATHOLOGIES IN TWO FILMS BY LUCRECIA MARTEL

Paola Arboleda Ríos
University of Florida

¿No deberíamos intentar establecer un pacto entre nosotros, para organizar este mundo del modo que nos parezca mejor para la felicidad de todos, sin intentar hacernos iguales? En el fondo me parece un mejor camino que el "no hemos venido a liberar a los esclavos, sino a hacerlos buenos" que dice San Pablo. Yo creo que es hora de liberar a los esclavos (Quoted by Marques).

[Shouldn't we try to establish a pact between us, in order to organize this world in the best possible way? A way in which we all could achieve happiness without trying to make everybody be the same? Deep inside I think this is a better path than the one proposed by Saint Paul: "we have not come to free the slaves, but to make them good." I think it is time to free the slaves.]

FROM THE NATIONAL TO THE SELF

In the wake of Roland Barthes' famous 1968 declaration of the death of the author, feminist scholars have theorized the return of issues of authorship, both in literature (Bruss, Brodzki and Schenck, Kosta, Smith and Watson) and in film studies (Maule, Egan, Portuges, and Gabara). These scholars have demonstrated that 'woman,' as the "autobiographical subject," differs from 'man,' the ideal of bourgeois humanism, who was considered a truth-finder, the essence of the text, and the centre of the world (Smith, 266). The objective of this paper is to explore the meanings of the shift from a national–allegorical to a subjective-autobiographical paradigm in the work of Argentinean director Lucrecia Martel and to recognize her search for agency in a historically patriarchal and profoundly *machista* society.[1]

Questioning Fredric Jameson's hypothesis that all texts that have been produced in what he defines as the "Third World" are "necessarily allegorical" (Jameson, 320), and drawing upon authors such as Jean Franco, Anne McClintock, and Doris Sommer, who have shed light on the patriarchal character of nationalism(s), this essay proposes that Martel's feature films, like those of other Latin American women directors, demonstrate discursive and structural ruptures with the national allegory paradigm.[2] These productions underscore the need experienced by some directors and writers from the 'Third World,' particularly women, to depart dialectically from the allegorical.[3] This goal is achieved by transforming the emphasis of their narrations. Authors and directors like Lucrecia Martel have demonstrated that they are capable of telling personal stories, "libidinal" ones as Jameson would call them, as alternatives to exclusively allegorical/nationalist ones.

Two types of re-formulation will be discussed in relation to Martel's productions: cinematographic technique and narrative content. I will demonstrate how both films use the same strategy of *defamiliarization* (*estrangement* or *alienation*) as proposed by Victor Shklovsky (1917) and Bertolt Brecht (1964).[4] In *The Swamp* [*La Ciénaga*, 2001], the allegorical content is superseded by its own defamiliarizing strategies. The same happens in *The Holy Girl* [*La niña santa*, 2004], through autobiography and self-disclosure. Both films disturb the "tutor-code of classical cinema" and break the pleasure principle creating texts that have been described by some critics as a Faulknerian affair (Seger), a reminder of Chekhov, Dostoyevsky and Buñuel (Schumann), and by most viewers as "difficult to watch."[5] The variation of emphasis in two films by the same director might help us to figure out if perhaps the split between the allegorical and the personal is in fact less pervasive than most of its theorizations.

Lucrecia Martel, who defines herself as a "protofeminist," is part of a younger generation of Argentinean authors and filmmakers who offer a counterpoint, a re-interpretation of the 'national/allegorical.'[6] Along with Martín Rejtman (*Rapado*, 1991), Esteban Sapir (*Picado fino*, 1993), Pablo Trapero (*Mundo grúa*, 1999), Bruno Stagnaro and Adrián Caetano (*Pizza, birra, faso*, 1998), she belongs to a group that has been linked with the 'New Argentinean Cinema.' The group's films are mostly low-budget and independent productions with a focus on personal and intimate stories that look at the country without limiting their narrative potential to political conflicts or ideological interpretations. These filmmakers were not direct victims of persecution by the state terrorism of the Dirty War (1976–83), and their films are not politically 'militant' or openly 'revolutionary,' as were most Argentinean and Latin American productions of the "New Latin American Cinema" of the 1960s, 1970s, and even the 1980s.[7] Although in some of their public commentaries and within the subtexts of some of their films it is possible to see re-evaluations and reflections about the outcomes of this dark era in Argentina's history, their narratives are usually very personal. Works such as Lucrecia Martel's demonstrate that the 'human' is not universal. Moreover, Martel's films reveal that the gaze can be transformed, and that autobiography, particularly as an experience lived by and through the body, has a key role in this cinematographic, social, cultural and, gendered (r)evolution.[8]

BEYOND ALLEGORY: DEFAMILIARIZATION AND DOMESTIC PATHOLOGIES IN *THE SWAMP*

Me interesa que mis películas no se vayan tan rápido de la cabeza como las del cine comercial, aunque las odiés. Quiero lo opuesto a la comida chatarra, donde tenés que masticar rápido porque si apelás a la lentitud te das cuenta de que es una mierda (Interview with Juárez).

[Even if people hate them, I am interested in making my films stay in the spectator's head longer than is the case with commercial cinema. I want the opposite of junk-food, which you have to chew fast because if you slow down you realize it is shit.]

Allegory has been one of the interpretive tools preferred by many critics in order to read and analyze texts within and from Latin America and to establish connections between 'the nation' and its cultural products. As Jean Franco and Doris Sommer have asserted, allegories of nation (of patriarchal nations) constituted key elements in Latin American literature and art during the nineteenth century. They served the purpose of supporting nationalist campaigns and maintaining androcentric ideals and heteronormative archetypes. In order to achieve an effective revaluation of the role of women in society and in the film industry within a phallocentric economy, feminists have emphasized the necessity of *denaturalizing* the apparently natural order created by the dominant ideology, including essentialist notions of femininity, and binary models of thinking.[9]

As I mentioned above, aspects of Lucrecia Martel's filmic texts contradict some of the rules of what Daniel Dayan has theorized as the "tutor-code" of classical cinema. Martel proposes a different system of enunciation, her own microcosm of visual meaning(s), a different kind of suture and "a new kind of cinematic pleasure," in which the spectators are alienated from the diegesis but not from the text, as Cynthia Baron has argued for another context (22).[10] *The Swamp* forces the spectator to adopt an estranged gaze, to feel unease in the theatre. Mysteriously and deliberately, Martel "inflicts" thinking on her viewers.

The opening sequence of the film allows a simultaneous reading of its allegorical content and the denaturalizing elements of Martel's cinematography. The sound of thunder and the chirping of birds are heard over a black background followed by a close-up of red peppers aligned in a terrace. The intensity of their colour creates a sharp contrast with the deep grey sky of the background. Credits appear in fonts that seem to melt on the screen while the sound of thunder and an eerie melody keep building suspense. Without transitional shots, the close-up of the red peppers is followed by another close frame in which a table, dirty from spilled wine, is surrounded by half-empty glasses. A shaky female hand tries to pour some wine and spills more outside than inside the glass, revealing a probable intoxication. The hand adds ice and grabs the glass, whose vibration duplicates the sound of a bell. The camera follows the trembling hand for a couple of seconds and a cut introduces a middle-aged woman, Mecha (Graciela Borges), wearing sunglasses in spite of the gloomy sky. More credits are introduced against a metallic sound as of chains being dragged. A series of images of male and female middle-aged torsos highlight drunk and sleepy bodies holding wine glasses and cigars, as old and rusty sun chairs are pulled. More shots cut out between the neck and the hips. Faces are not seen clearly and the slowness of the bodies' movement is almost unbearable. A few images later a pool with green rotten water appears in the screen. Mecha falls down into it and the storm finally starts.

This sequence reveals that we are in front of a complex cinematic style and a non-conventional narrative technique. *The Swamp* can be described as a collection of dead moments in which, apparently, nothing happens. Furthermore, Lucrecia Martel's persistent use of close-ups and framing of torsos, the lack of establishing shots, a hand-held camera and the few sounds that we are forced to pay attention to while the screen fades to black can be read in an allegorical manner but also have the strategic potential to achieve defamiliarization. Time is of the utmost importance in almost each sequence of the film, as spectators experience how slowly and painfully it can pass for some people, while for others it can bring the sudden loss of life.

The Swamp deals, in an allegorical manner, with the social effects of the economic disasters Argentina has faced since the late 1990s: the corporate takeover of the finances of the State, the privatization of the social security system, corruption at high levels, including the judicial system, excessive presidential expenses, high salaries of government employees, and permanent tax frauds. These economic failures led Argentina to national bankruptcy. According to Stephen J. Greenblatt, "allegory emerges in situations of misfortune, episodes in which a formerly strong power (theological, domestic, political) is in danger of being erased" (viii). In *The Swamp* Martel speaks about an inert generation on the verge of drowning in indolence and of a country as corrupt and broken-down as Mecha's farm *La Mandrágora*, in whose rotten pool the protagonist and her friends lie around on grey, humid, summer days drinking themselves to death. The matron herself is an alcoholic and her house, as everything around her, is crumbling; old bourgeois structures and family traditions are falling apart. Mecha has a useless, alcoholic, and unfaithful husband (Martin Adjemián), four lethargic children, and a pepper-producing farm with a pool filled with putrid water. Mecha's narrative counterpart is represented in her cousin, Tali (Mercedes Morán), who also has four children. Tali feels trapped in a marriage with a hard-working man and loving father whose house is too small for a pool in which to pass the summer's sweltering days. In one of their incoherent conversations, and using the excuse of buying school supplies for the children, the two women decide to make a trip to Bolivia to temporarily escape from their decadent realities. However, their lack of determination does not allow them to travel. Beside Mecha's pool, the two women are united by two accidents as tragedy unfolds with the storm that has been announced.

This is the image of an impoverished bourgeoisie that has lost its privileges and now survives by inertia, blaming everything and everybody else for their problems and their nonsensical existence. As we see during the film, the indigenous Others are the ones that especially bear the brunt of this blame. Although the young maid Isabel (Andrea López) maintains the little order that exists in *La Mandrágora*, she is permanently reminded of her lower-class status, which seems to be equated with thieving. Every time Mecha and Isabel appear in the same sequence, the girl gets blamed for the disappearance of the houses' towels. The essentializing '*they*' is used to align Isabel with *los collas*, or indigenous people, in a move that associates Otherness with dishonesty. Also, in a strange scene, while hunting in *el cerro*, the hill close to *La Mandrágora*, Joaquín (Diego Baenas) one of Mecha's sons who lost an eye in a hunting accident, commands some indigenous children not to caress the dogs because the animals might "get ruined." The meaning of this soon becomes clear. Once Joaquín sends the kids to get his hunting prey, he starts stroking one of the animals as he struggles to lift its tail violently. Mecha's son wants to verify if the dog has been sexually abused by the indigenous children. Joaquín also advices his

FIG. 1. MECHA (GRACIELA BORGES) AND GREGORIO (MARTÍN ADJEMIÁN)
DRINKING NEXT TO LA MANDRÁGORA'S POOL OF ROTTEN WATER
(COURTESY LITA STANTIC PRODUCTIONS AND LUCRECIA MARTEL).

hunting friend Martín (Franco Veneranda) to beware of *them*. He notes
that "they live all together in the same house. The father, the mother,
the grandmother, the grandfather, the cat, the dog, the grandmother....
Didn't you see that they fondle it [the dog]? They are all day caressing it."
What is even more striking in this sequence is that Joaquín seems to be
unaware that his description of *los collas* seems to depict his own family's
lifestyle.

As implied by Joaquín, interactions in *The Swamp* challenge the status
quo through a series of sensually suggestive situations in which the summer's heat conflates with a certain 'bucolic' boredom. Brothers and sisters
sleep together, girls in need of motherly love fall in love with other girls
as seen in Momi's (Sofia Bertolotto) doting on Isabel and her implied
defiance of the "heterosexual matrix."[11] The humidity is oppressive and
almost unbearable; everybody sweats and shares a bed in Mecha's country

FIG. 2. Momi (Sofía Bertolotto) and Isabel (Andrea López), the family's maid, sharing a bed as their daily afternoon ritual (courtesy Lita Stantic Productions and Lucrecia Martel).

house. *The Swamp* is permeated by a feeling of constant unease that talks about the loss of traditions and the absence of parenting. As Sara Cooper comments, the family has been an inexhaustible topic in Hispanic film and literature since their beginnings, during every literary movement in Spain and Latin America, and within the increasingly visible work by North-American-born or immigrant Latino/as (2). The possibility of a certain kind of subversive perversion that Cooper references with relation to the Spanish or Latino family alerts us to a reading beyond the allegorical and towards one of the most important instances of 'alienation' and/ or 'estrangement' in the work of Lucrecia Martel: the denaturalization of the family and family relations.

It is specifically the 'natural' subordination of woman to man, as well as that of child to adult that is challenged in Martel's film as a kind

Fig. 3. Mecha (Graciela Borges) and her son José (Juan Cruz Bordeu) together in bed, while the mother heals from the pool accident (courtesy Lita Stantic Productions and Lucrecia Martel).

of family and social pathology. In *The Swamp*, the children are apparently under the control of the adults, as they live with their parents; yet, as a disconcerting example of Martel's dynamic, and filtered by a very distressing use of the camera and its gaze, we see a constant depiction of children who are 'in charge.' Christian Gundermann has asserted that the directors of the New Argentinean Cinema, including Martel, seem to share "an obsession with the gaze" and with what he calls "loose objects" or elements that are not connected with the diegesis or the plot in a traditional manner. In *The Swamp*, the lack of control of the gaze sheds light on Gundermann's notion of loose objects as "the broken residue of a society that once was productive but is no longer because it has been dismantled, put out of work" (242). Similarly, more than a male or a female gaze, in Martel's film we see through a disjointed gaze. Moreover, this gaze does not belong exclusively to any one character, being fragmented and shared by all the young protagonists. Their solitude reflects the adults' spiritual dejection. These children occupy an ambiguous position: they keep track of their vaccinations, take care of their younger siblings, cook, clean, drive, and even act as nurses as they help and save the adults. However, the children in this film are also alone, afraid of the dark, fearful of old men who dye their hair, and, most of all, terrified of dogs that could turn out to be African rats.

This sense of fracture is further explored in *The Swamp* as the film's narrative force does not fall exclusively onto any one of the protagonists. Instead, as suggested in Brecht's theorizations about epic theatre, and as a further defamiliarizing element, narrative force is dispersed and divided between the characters. As is well known, the epic theatre avoids creating too much closeness between the character and the viewer. This contradicts what commercial Hollywood cinema defines as "character-centered causality," which privileges "plots that tend to focus on a central character, with clearly delineated psychological traits, whose desires motivate the action, setting off a chain of cause and effect" (Fabe, 15). As Brecht argues: "the epic theatre avoids creating too much closeness between the character and the viewer. As the play develops, they should not approach one another but separate. Not all the secrets of the character must be revealed. The element of terror, necessary in all recognition, must be preserved" (71). In *The Swamp* there is not a hero or a heroine, and it is very difficult to establish who the protagonist is. It is not clear if it is Tali, Mecha, or their children, Momi, Marianita (Maria Micol Ellero), Luciano (Sebastián Montagna). It is not obvious if it is the swamp or the humidity. It is not evident either if it might be the pool, a critical element in both *The Swamp* and *The Holy Girl*, and which functions as a location representing that "private paradise" the director "hates" because it celebrates the absurd way of life of useless bourgeoisies.[12]

Considering that Mecha and Tali are the mothers of the two families of the story, one might say that they are the focal points and that the film revolves around them. However, this conclusion would be a product of our patriarchally-trained perception. The traditional trope of mother as homeland, as 'the centre,' does not operate in these two Martel' films, and if it is quoted it is only in ironical ways. These two mothers are close to dying from apathy, loneliness, and neglect. Moreover, there is no Aristotelian structure that requires a hero.[13] Other than surviving one more summer or escaping to Bolivia, there are no goals to achieve. The director does not give us the necessary clues in order to establish who the good or bad characters are, who represents virtue and who is in charge of recreating the undesirable in humanity. The characters depend too much on each other and on their interactions. They are always together. There is not a scene in which only one actor's performance dominates. There are not interior monologues or stream of consciousness. Conversations are always taking place in and around beds. Before Mecha's accident, Momi and Isabel are sleeping together; when Isabel wakes up, Momi gets in bed with her sister Verónica (Leonora Valcarce) and confesses her feelings for Isabel. In a different scene, Verónica sleeps with his brother José (Juan Cruz Bordeu); after that José sleeps with his mother, Mecha, while she asks her husband to sleep in another room.

Desire and death are permanently lurking around in *The Swamp*, and in an alienating way they are always close to the children's games and visible in the scars on their faces. Tali's son Luciano's permanent contact with death at his young age of eight or nine years is one of Martel's most striking challenges to the idea of the young as the pure and innocent that should not be touched by fate. Holding his breath and playing dead after his little sister shouts "dead, dead, dead, Luciano you are dead" are two of Luciano's favourite games. He also cuts his leg and has to be taken to the hospital. In this particular sequence, his blood is seen flowing next to a dead rabbit on the kitchen counter. In another scene during a hunting outing, the children are fascinated to find a cow that is drowning. While the older kids decide if they should kill the cow, they also point their guns at Luciano. A shot is heard over an image of a grey sky. For a couple of seconds the spectator does not know who they decided to shoot. Although Luciano is not killed by his cousins, the film does end with a fatal accident in which he is involved.

Martel has argued that she is interested in portraying a reality in which nature is not romanticized but is the site of constant struggle. In her first feature film, nature interlocks with life and death, and desire and violence are part of the children's realities to achieve *denaturalizing* effects. Martel's immense capacity for representing the perversions society tries to hide, such as negative impulses, unconscious desires, life and death instincts, is one of the fundamental reasons for the discomfort provoked by her films. In *The Swamp* Martel questions the role of the family in the building of the Argentinean nation and invites us to consider the social constructedness of the family's rules, boundaries, and "normality."[14] The allegorical has a place in this film as a twisted element that is superseded by a lack of a clear connection between cause and effect and which is enhanced by the defamiliarizing strategies explored, including narrative ones. In *The Holy Girl*, Martel's representation of reality becomes even more disturbing when we see it portrayed by young girls.

UN/FAMILIAR FICTIONS: GIRLS, MONSTERS AND THE SELF IN *THE HOLY GIRL*

> I know what it is to be a teenager, you feel like you are the super-powerful girl and you are also very much into mysticism, religious and mystical subjects. Above all, I passionately devoted myself to all those things. They [teenagers] have an idea of a personal relationship with God and that makes them extremely powerful people.[15]

In spite of the difficulty of translating literary autobiographical theory to cinema studies, women filmmakers and scholars have produced and studied, respectively, a few examples of the 'I/woman,' even if narrated in the third person. They have also been preoccupied with re-evaluating the substantial range of possibilities that the genre presents to the feminine subject such as validating personal experience, memories, and desire, and, at the same time, giving a voice to formerly silenced individuals, re-inscribing women into history, recuperating a sense of agency, and de/constructing identities.[16]

Although the purpose of this essay is not to determine whether autobiography can be considered a 'genre' or a 'figure' for reading and interpreting texts, I do wish to emphasize the relevance of re-formulating autobiography, not in the strict sense envisioned by Philipe Lejeune, nor in the loose and almost 'unimportant' way of reading suggested Paul de Man, but rather as the deliberate and conscious act of telling personal stories, re-creating journals, letters, testimonies, confessions, even if some degree of fiction is involved.[17] I would add, as many feminists have argued before, that every autobiographical act allows memory and desire to merge in a macabre game played by and against the subject who searches for and shares her process of self-discovery and redefinition.

In her essay "Women and Diaries: Gender and Genre" Valerie Raoul describes the conventions of autobiography as follows: "Autobiography is a life-*story*, addressed to an audience, whether it be the author's own children or the general public. It is frequently a form of self-justification, apology or example (to follow or to avoid), with rhetorical ends dependent on its reception by an audience" (60). Although *The Holy Girl* does not comply with all the conventions discussed by Raoul, it does feature multiple aspects and angles taken from the director's life which serve to strengthen its 'self-narrative' character. These include Salta, Martel's hometown, where she spent her childhood and teenage years; her religious activism with a group named Acción Católica [Catholic Action]; her encounter with Dr. Jano; and her interest in what she has called the "internal sensuality within the family."[18] Martel has stated in many interviews that *The Holy Girl* is an 'autobiographical film.' She has explained:

> Teníamos catorce o quince años. El mundo tenía la medida exacta de nuestras pasiones. La intensidad de las ideas religiosas y el descubrimiento del deseo sexual nos hacía voraces [...] Estábamos alertas porque teníamos una misión santa, pero no sabíamos cuál era. Cada casa, cada pasillo, cada habitación, cada gesto, cada palabra, necesitaba de nuestra vigilia. El mundo era monstruosamente bello. Fue entonces cuando conocí al Dr. Jano (Quoted in Sartora).

> [We were fourteen or fifteen years old. The world had the exact measurements of our passions. The intensity of religious ideas and the discovery of sexual desire made us voracious. We were relentless in our secret plans [...] Every house, every hall, every room, every gesture, every word, needed our vigilance. The world was monstrously beautiful. It was then that I met Dr. Jano.]

Martel has also emphasized the importance that her own diaries, as efforts of self-reflexivity and self-narration, and childhood memories have had in her films:

> I write by collecting, putting together bits of memories, diaries, images. It's difficult to say exactly where you start it because it is like a state of mind [...] I used to go on house visits with my granny, and the conversations we would have were a huge influence. Especially the structure of conversations which you don't know the direction it's going to take (Interview with Skye).

Although the diaries as well as the remembered interactions between older and younger women could be seen as simple affairs, as unimportant moments in one's life, they are related in a very particular way to the autobiographical character of Martel's films and possibly, as Raoul explains for another context, to the *malaise* effect that these create for viewers. Commenting on the calculated elimination of diaries from Alain Girard's study of autobiography, Raoul asserts that:

> The reason for this elimination is related to the particular type of malaise found in women's journals. Torn between writing their lives and living their lives as women, women's diaries frequently become uninteresting (from a canonic male point of view) because they conform too closely to the diary norm. The "*quotidien*," the banal elements of everyday life central to the regular (diurnal, "*journalier*") recording of existence, tend to take over in any woman's life. (61)

The Holy Girl is, precisely, a film about apparently ordinary individuals. Yet, at the same time, it could be described as a wicked symphony interpreted by regular, mortal and imperfect beings full of fear, and, of course, full of sin. This is what produces what Raoul calls the *malaise* effect. As stated above, Martel's immense capacity for representing perversions is one of the fundamental reasons for the discomfort provoked by her films. In *The Holy Girl*, Martel's realities become troubling when we see them represented through young girls who might be expected to be holy, and who want to be holy in the most Catholic sense. Their specific experiences transcend the allegorical by means of the autobiographical and the weight given to the body.

Amalia (María Alche) and Josefina (Julieta Zylberberg) are two adolescents who, in the midst of their search for identity and transcendence, join a Catholic group. They find a promising path for self-knowledge, as well as what they consider guidance in finding their mission in the world. Amalia discovers that her calling, her mission, is to save Dr. Jano (Carlos Belloso), a prestigious ear, nose, and throat specialist. This married man rubs himself against Amalia in a public place and also demonstrates interest in Amalia's mother Helena (Mercedes Morán), who owns the hotel in which an otorhinolaryngology congress is taking place. In fact, as a retired diver Helena suffers from a problem in her ears and it is precisely this condition that Dr. Jano uses as an excuse to get closer to her. From its first sequence, the film presents us with the interlocking of sexuality and religiosity: we see the girls singing a religious song in their church group and, at the same time, we hear them talk about the sexual encounters between their young and beautiful instructor and an older man. Martel introduces us immediately to the teenagers' concerns: spirituality and their own sexual awakening.

Although Martel has not spoken publicly about her use of the word "holy" in her film, she has frequently emphasized in interviews her personal connection to Catholicism. The director says that she is interested in Catholicism because "it is my religion, where I learned a way of thinking, a system of thought" in which beliefs are revealed as certainties.[19] *The Holy Girl* also reflects Martel's interest in the authority figures that society imposes arbitrarily, not only on the young, but on all those who do not possess the means to defend themselves. According to Martel, men like Dr. Jano represent the monsters that we have all met sometimes, or even the monsters we all have inside. She states: "I sincerely believe that mankind is like a monster [...] the monster is also the doctor in *The Holy Girl*, the authority in front of which one has to strip down."[20] She insists on a close relation between medicine, the monstrous, and holiness:

> There is something between medicine and holiness that interests me. The sick bodies and the healthy bodies. [...] The saints sick from saintliness and their miraculous cures. [...]

The sick so sick that they look like monsters [...] Monsters have mutated with time and then came the degenerate ones; those without the Aryan standards, the serial killers dressed in human skin, the poor in general who represent a menace with their monstrous needs. We are a monstrous species that betrays all that is foreseeable.[21]

In her films, Martel awakens the monsters but does not make them return to their places of reclusion. This is particularly *alienating* and in many different ways terribly frightening. It also corresponds to one of the goals of the Brechtian epic theatre: the re-awakening of the senses. Sensual suggestion is one of *The Holy Girl*'s most important narrative strategies. The film forces us to pay close attention to visual, auditory, and tactile stimuli, and to constant references to the senses: a hotel that is permanently deodorized, a pool that smells like flowers, a gathering of doctors [monsters?] who specialize in problems of the sensory organs. There are also very close frames of Amalia's hands travelling slowly over the walls and objects around the hotel, usually while she follows Dr. Jano or thinks about how to save him.

As mentioned in relation to *The Swamp*, Martel's films very skilfully subvert the conventions of mainstream Hollywood film narrative by using extremely close shots and odd angles, open-ended narration, soft focus, very dark lighting, and a camera that, without travelling shots, without the use of a dolly, and without technical complexity, acquires a sense of mobility that almost transforms it into a character. Martel has said of her use of the camera:

La cámara es un personaje con el que me siento muy iden-tificada [...] aunque no es ningún personaje en particular, la cámara es alguien. Tanto en *La ciénaga* como en *La niña santa*, el personaje que observa es menor que un adolescente y tiene una curiosidad que le permite suspender el juicio moral.

[The camera is a character with whom I identify a lot. [...] although it is not a particular character, the camera is some-body. Both in *The Swamp* and in *The Holy Girl*, the character that looks is younger than an adolescent and has a curiosity

Fig. 4. Amalia (María Alche) hides while she follows and stares obsessively at Dr. Jano (Carlos Belloso) when he is swimming.

Fig. 5. Amalia (María Alche) looking at Dr. Jano while he sleeps.

that allows him/her to suspend moral judgment.] (Quoted in Oubiña, 65)

Some of these techniques render Martel's films "difficult to watch" for many viewers, a difficulty compounded by the fact that some of the clues about the autobiographical character of the film are extradiegetic and only appear in interviews, press releases, and internet sites. Yet rather than dwell on the films' "difficulty," I would assert that the *alienating and denaturalizing* techniques discussed here and earlier stimulate a different and almost uncomfortable level of understanding and empathy between spectator and character. Instead of presenting a model of "identificatory fictions," as described by Veronica Hollinger (304), and deepening the dichotomy between the feminine and the masculine, the North and the South, the East and the West, the director opens up the possibilities for reinterpretation and resistance, for the deconstruction of limiting borders and structures. *The Holy Girl* is a film that evolves in polyphonic ways and raises concerns related to gender, homo/sexuality, girlhood/identity, family relations, incest, and the pursuit of a certain feminine sexual self-determination that, from a Freudian perspective, could be considered "perverse."[22] Catherine Driscoll contends that discourses about girls and girlhood are marginalized within social and cultural studies (235).[23] I would suggest that Martel's films and extratextual assertions indicate her awareness of the necessity of opening up discussions around adolescence and particularly girls' sexual awakening and that this is one of the reasons that motivates the director's privileging of self-disclosure and autobiographical fiction above political or nationalist concerns.

Feminist autobiographer and theorist Shirley Neuman has argued that "women's autobiographical theory in particular takes up the body as a source of knowledge" (6). Perhaps one of the most interesting aspects of *The Holy Girl* is the girls' relation to their bodies; they appear to have more control over them than over their ideas, thoughts, and goals. They masturbate, they practice anal sex in order to remain "virgins" until the day they marry, and they swim in only their underwear in the hotel's pool, even as their minds get lost and confused between prayers and dogmatic ideas about morality and salvation. The body is definitively a protagonist of *The Holy Girl*. Its critical role is directly connected to Martel's "open" portrayal of girls' sexual curiosity and awakening. For the

From National Allegory to Autobiography

Argentinean director, sexuality is fluid, malleable, "a children's game," in which apparently the adults no longer participate.

MARTEL'S FILMS AND THE BODY

> Subjectivity is not, after all, an out of body experience. The 'autobiographical subject' of bourgeois humanism may have emerged as a unitary, essentialized 'self,' somehow locally and universally operative irrespective of or despite the bodily surround [...] but current notions of the constitution of the subject anchor subjectivity very much in the body. – Sidonie Smith

Sidonie Smith has noted the inevitable connection between subjectivity, women's autobiographies and the 'body,' bodily experiences and physical desires (266). According to Martel, the idea for the script of *The Holy Girl* also started as a physical experience, beginning with the memory of a hotel she used to visit with her family as a child. This hotel was very similar to *El Termas*, where the film takes place. "We'd walk around the spa," Martel explains, "and without having a very precise sense of it, there was something very erotic about that place [...] the whole architecture was conceived around the body. So I started writing this story when I was remembering this hotel" (Anderson). In a way, that is very relevant to Martel's movie, as *The Holy Girl* is a film about the *senses*, a story about personal, libidinal, and/or subjective experiences. Smith explores the politics of autobiographical skins and asks: "what does skin have to do with autobiography and autobiography with skin? Much I think – as the body of the text, the body of the narrator, the body of the narrated, the cultural body, and the body politic all merge in skins of meanings" (266). In the work of Martel, the relation between autobiography and skin is clearly "palpable." Not only does she narrate through her own memory, but it seems that her ability for remembering is pervasively intertwined with a wide range of sensations which involve young girls' bodies in multiple ways: young bodies that desire for the first time, kiss for the first time, feel themselves, and are unexpectedly rubbed by older bodies that, wishing to be touched, approach the forbidden and initiate "inappropriate" contacts. Both Amalia and Josefina are caressed inappropriately: Amalia by Dr. Jano and Josefina by her cousin. As a consequence their sexualities awaken, and it is precisely then when they start to 'touch' the lives of everyone around them.

The body is also another opportunity for filmic *denaturalization*. The depiction of anal intercourse between Josefina and her cousin is perhaps one of the most disturbing instances of alienation in the film, particularly if one considers that, as Gwendolyn Foster argues, visual representations of anal and oral sex, like those of frontal male nudity, are taboo images rarely seen in mainstream films directed by either men or women (113). From a feminist perspective, what is even more important is that "an active female sexuality disrupts the basis of gender identification" (Foster, 112). Foster asserts that starting in the eighteenth century, women were defined as the passionless sex and reminds us that doctors used women's bodies as a "battleground for redefining the ancient, intimate, fundamental social relation: that of woman to man" (150). Martel not only portrays sexually active women but also dares to portray sexually active girls: girls who believe in God, who go to church and pray.

Incest, or something very close to it, is a recurrent topic in Martel's films. The director has stated:

> I am marked by the experience of a numerous family and by the idea of the private space that can be invaded without bad intentions: that is, when a lot of people live in a house you have to learn to deal with that. [...] I am attracted to the family's internal sensuality. There are incestuous desires that flow in the family and they are the most normal thing in the world. It is common when two or three people are living together. These are difficult things to say because it looks like I am proposing that everything be complete chaos; but I do not agree with it being so terrible. I think it is one more possibility of the human (Quoted in Enriquez).

There is an interesting scene in which Helena, Amalia's mother, and her brother Freddy (Alejandro Urdapilleta), although she usually calls him

Alfredito, little Alfredo, lie in bed together, in a dark room, while she caresses her head and admires his "beautiful" hands. In fact, she argues, they are "like a doctor's hands." Helena's relationship with her brother is suggestively incestuous and very immature at the same time. Helena and Freddy behave like two abandoned children playing to be adults. Helena thinks she is the one who takes care of the hotel they own, but it is really her aunt, Mirta, (Marta Lubos) who does all the work. Her brother has two children he has not seen in years and he is not brave enough to re-establish contact with them; he also prefers to knock on her sister's door and sleep with her, instead of asking Mirta for new keys to his own room. Within their infantile everyday life, incestuous situations are repeatedly insinuated.

References to fever and to incipient forms of illness are also important elements in the construction of Martel's defamiliarizing world of the senses. Amalia gets a fever masturbating in her room upon coming back from the swimming pool. Martel has noted that in her film, fever is a physical symptom because it is related to desire and to religious ecstasy, that is, it is the "hot body." The director has also stated that when she writes she usually starts with an illness. Instead of being something negative, Martel believes that "la enfermedad tiene algo maravilloso, que es la desactivación de la percepción domesticada" ["illness has something wonderful, which is the de-activation of the domesticated perception"] (Quoted in Enriquez).

The de-activation of domesticated perception in *The Holy Girl* is achieved through its challenge to the voyeuristic male gaze. Amalia follows Dr. Jano, watches him closely, gets into his room and his life. As Judith Butler suggests, "if the body is synecdochal for the social system per se or a site in which open systems converge, then any kind of unregulated permeability constitutes a site of pollution and endangerment" (quoted in Tasker, 32). The representation of the male body for the scopophilic gaze of the female or the homosexual male is unconsciously recognized as a dangerous trope of unregulated desire, one that is rarely broken by films that follow the conventions of Hollywood cinema. Using extremely close shots, odd camera angles, and a minimal amount of sound, Martel deploys what I would like to call an 'interpellating' camera, which presents a very different cinematographic gaze: a feminine look, from Latin America, and from the self. She provides the perspective of a voyeuristic

Fig. 6. Close up of Amalia's (María Alche) intense gazing (courtesy Lita Stantic Productions and Lucrecia Martel).

girlhood, a sexually active one, and even more importantly, one that is far from *holy*; but she does not attempt to polarize and institute the 'queer' or the homosexual as a new or correct norm in her filmic universe. Fluidity is the key concept in Martel's world.

CONCLUDING REMARKS

> [...] there is no third world without its first world, no first world without its third.[24] – Trinh T. Minh-ha

Deaestheticization, *denaturalization*, and *alienation* are interpretive tools that allow us to uncover the ways in which Lucrecia Martel's creative proposal is pervasively enhanced by personal experience, memories, diaries, and desire. She makes us think about our own personal pathologies, their patriarchal construction, as well as the dynamics of Argentinean society. At the same time, she explores and re-creates possibilities for visually narrating a life in the feminine; conveying identity and agency from the "Third World" and from a woman's perspective. If, as Julia Kristeva suggests, "true dissidence today is perhaps simply what it has always been: *'thought'*" (1986, 299) and if thought has not historically been considered women's domain, then filmmaking by women of colour, queer feminists, and women from the "Third World" who use strategies such as *deaestheticization* and *alienation* in order to wake up the spectators is visual evidence of the existence of a contemporary kind of dissidence engaged in creative activity. Lucretia Martel, I propose, is an intellectual who is distant in time from the one proposed by Kristeva but very close in her persistent effort to question, dismantle. and rebel against political, patriarchal, and ideological powers.

WORKS CITED

Anderson, Jeffrey M. 2005. Interview With Lucrecia Martel. The Nature of Water. *Combustible Celluloid*. http://www.combustiblecelluloid.com/interviews/martel.shtml (accessed April 15, 2006).

Barnet, Sylvan, Morton Berman, and William Burtol. 1971. *A Dictionary of Literary, Dramatic and Cinematic Terms*. 2nd ed. Boston: Little Brown and Co.

Baron, Cynthia. 1998. The *Player's* Parody of Hollywood. A Different Kind of Suture. In *Postmodernism in the Cinema*. Ed. Cristina Degli-Esposti, 21–44. Papers from a conference held in 1994 at Kent University. Kent: Berham Books.

Barthes, Roland. 1977. The Death of the Author In *Image, Music, Text*. Ed. and trans. Stephen Heath, 143–48. New York: Hill and Wang.

Bordwell, David, Janet Staiger, and Kristin Thompson. 1985. *The Classical Hollywood Cinema: Film Style and Mode of Production to 1960*. New York: Columbia University Press.

Brecht, Bertolt. 1964. *Brecht on Theatre. The Development of an Aesthetic*. Ed. and trans. John Willett. New York: Hill and Wang.

Brodzki, Bella, and Celeste Schenck. 1988. Introduction to In *Life/Lines: Theorizing Women's Autobiography*. Ed. Bella Brodzki and Celeste Schenck, 1–18. Ithaca, NY: Cornell University Press.

Brunsdon, Charlotte. 1987. *Films for Women. London:* BFI.

Bruss, Elizabeth W. 1980. Eye for I: Making and Unmaking of Autobiography in Film. In *Autobiography: Essays Theoretical and Critical.* Ed. James Olney, 321–42. Princeton, NJ: Princeton University Press.

Butler, Judith. 1990. *Gender Trouble: Feminism and the Subversion of Identity.* New York: Routledge.

Cooper, Sara E. 2004. Introduction to *The Ties That Bind. Questioning Family Dynamics and Family Discourse in Hispanic Literature.* Ed. Sara E. Cooper. 1–42. Lanham, MD: University Press of America.

Dayan, Daniel. 1974. The Tutor-Code of Classical Cinema. In *Film Theory and Criticism: Introductory Readings.* Ed. Leo Braudy and Marshall Cohen, 118–29. 5th ed. New York: Oxford University Press.

"Desde los 18 Me Siento Vieja. Una Entrevista con Lucrecia Martel." 2004. *El Clarín.* February 3. Suplemento Mujer. http://www.clarin.com/suplementos/mujer/2004/03/02/m-00401.htm (accessed July 10, 2006).

Driscoll, Catherine. 2002. *Girls: Feminine Adolescence in Popular Culture and Cultural Theory.* New York: Columbia University Press.

Eakin, Paul John. 1985. *Fictions in Autobiography: Studies in the Art of Self Invention.* Princeton, NJ: Princeton University Press.

Egan, Susana. 1999. *Mirror Talk: Genres of Crisis in Contemporary Autobiography.* Chapel Hill: University of North Carolina Press.

———. 1994. Encounters in Camera: Autobiography as Interaction. *Modern Fiction Studies* 40, no. 3: 593–618. Purdue Research Foundation.

Enriquez, Mariana. 2004. "Ese Oscuro Objeto Deseo." *Página 12 Web.* Buenos Aires: Radar. http://www.pagina12.com.ar/diario/suplementos/radar/9-1390-2004-05-02.html (accessed July 6, 2006).

Fabe, Marilyn. 2004.*Closely Watched Films: An Introduction to the Art of Narrative Film Technique.* Berkeley: University of California Press.

Falicov, Tamara. 2007. *The Cinematic Tango: Contemporary Argentine Film.* London: Wallflower Press.

Fineman, Joel. 1980. The Structure of Allegorical Desire. In *Allegory and Representation: Selected Papers from the English Institute, 1979–80.* New Series, no. 5. ed. Stephen J. Greenblatt, 26–60. Baltimore: Johns Hopkins University Press.

Fletcher, Angus. 2003. Allegory in Literary History. *The Dictionary of the History of Ideas.* Maintained by: The Electronic Text Center at the University of Virginia Library – the Gale Group (Vol. 1, 41–48) http://etext.lib.virginia.edu/cgi-local/DHI/dhi.cgi?id=dv1-07 (accessed July 6, 2006).

Fonseca, Alberto. 2004. *Against the World, Against Life: The Use and Abuse of the Autobiographical Genre in the Works of Fernando Vallejo*. MA thesis Arts in History. Virginia Polytechnic Institute and State University.

Foster, Gwendolyn. 1999. *Captive Bodies, Postcolonial Subjectivities in the Cinema*. Albany: State University of New York Press.

Franco, Jean. 1989. *Plotting Women: Gender and Representation in Mexico*. New York: Columbia University Press.

———. 1997. Nation as Imagined Community. In *Dangerous Liaisons: Gender, Nation, and Postcolonial Perspectives*. Ed. Anne McClintock, Aamir Mufti, and Ella Shohat, 130–40. Minneapolis: University of Minnesota Press.

Freud, Sigmund. 1953 [1905]. Three Essays on the Theory of Sexuality. In *Standard Edition*, vol. 7. London: Hogarth Press and the Institute of Psycho-Analysis.

Gabara, Rachel. 2003. Mixing Impossible Genres: David Achkar and African Autobiographical Documentary. In *New Literary History* 34, no. 2: 331–52.

———. 2005. Screening Autobiography. *French Cultural Studies* 16, no. 1: 55–72.

———. 2006. *From Split to Screen Selves. French and Francophone Autobiography in Third Person*. Stanford: Stanford University Press.

Gledhill, Christine. 2000. Rethinking Gender. In *Reinventing Film Studies*. Ed. Christine Gledhill and Linda Williams, 221–43. London: Oxford University Press.

Greenblatt, Stephen J. 1980. Preface to *Allegory and Representation*. Selected Papers from the English Institute, 1979–80. New Series, no. 5. Ed. Stephen J. Greenblatt, vii–xiii. Baltimore: Johns Hopkins University Press.

Gundermann, Christian. 2005. The Stark Gaze of the New Argentine Cinema. *Journal of Latin American Cultural Studies* 14, no. 3: 241–61.

Hardon, John A., S.J. 1999. "Holiness." *The Modern Catholic Dictionary*. The Real Presence Association. http://www.therealpresence.org/cgi-bin/getdefinition.pl (accessed July 10, 2006).

Hart, Stephen. 2002. Bemberg Winks and Camila Sighs: Melodramatic Encryption in *Camila. Revista Canadiense de Estudios Hispánicos* (XXVII. 1). ed. Rita De Grandis. 76–85.

Hollinger, Veronica. 2002. (Re)reading Queerly: Science Fiction, Feminism and the Defamiliarization of Gender. In *Reload.: Rethinking Women and Cyberculture*. Ed. Mary Flanagan and Austin Booth, 302–20. Cambridge, MA: MIT Press.

hooks, bell. 1996. *Reel to Real: Race, Sex and Class at the Movies*. New York: Routledge.

"Interview with Lucrecia Martel." 2004. *La Niña Santa*. Official Web Site. http://www.laninasanta.com/interview.html (accessed July 12, 2006).

Jameson, Frederic. 2000. Third World Literature in the Era of Multinational Capitalism. In *The Jameson Reader*. Ed. Michael Hardt and Kathi Weeks, 315–40. Oxford: Blackwell.

Johnston, Claire. 1973. Women's Cinema as Counter-Cinema. *Notes on Women's Cinema*. London: Society for Education in Film and Television.

———. 1975. *The Work of Dorothy Arzner: Toward a Feminist Cinema*. London: British Film Institute.

Juárez, Carlos. 2004. Entrevista con Lucrecia Martel. Desdomesticar la Percepción. *Revista Teína*. No. 6. Oct.-Nov.-Dic. La Familia. http://www.revistateina.org/teina6/cine4.htm (accessed July 6, 2006).

Kaplan, Caren. 1998. Resisting Autobiography Out-Law Genres and Transnational Feminist Subjects. In *Women, Autobiography, Theory: A Reader*. Ed. Sidonie Smith and Julia Watson, 115–38. Madison: University of Wisconsin Press.

Kosta, Barbara. 1994. *Recasting Autobiography: Women's Counterfictions in Contemporary German Literature and Film*. Ithaca: Cornell University Press.

Kristeva, Julia. 1986. A New Type of Intellectual: The Dissident. In *The Kristeva Reader*. ed. Toril Moi, 292–300. Trans. Seán Hand. New York: Columbia University Press.

Lauretis, Teresa de. 1987. *Technologies of Gender: Essays on Theory, Film, and Fiction*. Bloomington: Indiana University Press.

Lejeune, Philippe. 1975. *Le pacte autobiographique*. París: Seuil.

de Man, Paul. 1984. Autobiography as Defacement. Chap. 5 in *The Rhetoric of Romanticism*. New York: Columbia University Press.

Marques, Leandro. 2004. "Niñas, Doctores, Tabúes." *La Butaca. Revista de Cine*. http://www.labutaca.net/films/26/laninasanta2.htm (accessed July 10, 2006).

Martin, Michael T. 1997. New Latin American Cinema. In *Contemporary Film and Television Series*. Ed. Michael T. Martin, vol. 1. Detroit: Wayne State University Press.

Martins, Laura. 2007. Bodies at Risk: On the State of Exception. (Lucrecia Martel's *La ciénaga [The Swamp]*). In *Argentinean Cultural Production During the Neoliberal Years (1989–2201)*. Ed. Hugo Hortiguera and Carolina Rocha, 205–15. Lewiston, NY: Edwin Mellen Press.

Maule, Rosanna. 1998. De-Authorizing the Auteur: Postmodern Politics of Interpellation in Contemporary European Cinema. In *Postmodernism in the Cinema*. Ed.Cristina Degli-Esposti, 113–30. New York: Berghahn Books.

McClintock, Anne. 1997. No Longer in Future Heaven. Gender, Race and Nationalism. In *Dangerous Liaisons: Gender, Nation and Postcolonial Perspectives*. Ed. Anne McClintock, Aamir Mufti, and Ella Shohat, 89–112. Minneapolis: University of Minnesota Press.

Metz, Christian. 1975. The Imaginary Signifier. *Screen* 16, no. 2: 14–76.

Mulvey, Laura. 1989. *Visual and Other Pleasures*. Bloomington: Indiana University Press.

Neuman, Shirley. 1989. An Appearance Walking in a Forest the Sexes Burn. Autobiography and the Construction of the Feminine Body. *Signature* 2: 1–26.

Oubiña, David. 2006. *Estudio Crítico Sobre la Ciénaga.Entrevista a Lucrecia Martel*. Buenos Aires: Picnic Editorial.

Popick, Jon. 2001. "La Cienaga." http://www.sick-boy.com/lacienaga.htm (accessed July 10, 2006).

Portuges, Catherine. 1988. Seeing Subjects: Women Directors and Cinematic Autobiography. In *Life/Lines: Theorizing Women's Autobiography*. Ed. Bella Brodzki and Celeste Schenck, 338–50. Ithaca: Cornell University Press.

Raoul, Valerie. 1989. Women and Diaries: Gender and Genre. *Mosaic* 22, no. 3: 57–65.

Sartora, Josefina. "La Niña Santa." *Cineismo*. http://www.cineismo.com/criticas/nina-santa-la.htm (accessed July 6, 2006).

Schumann, Howard. 2002. "Moody, Sensual, and Atmospheric." *Internet Movie Database*. http://www.imdb.com/title/tt0240419/usercomments (accessed December 30, 2005).

Seger, Michael. 2001. "La Ciénaga (The Swamp, 2001)." *The R & R Film Reviews*. http://www.peanut.org/mike/text/cienaga.htm (accessed December 30, 2005).

Shklovsky, Victor. 1988 [1917]. Art as Technique. Trans. Lee T. Lemon and Marion J. Reis. Reprinted in David Lodge, *Modern Criticism and Theory: A Reader*, 16–30. London: Longmans.

Shuman, Mark D. 1997. Depicting the Post in Argentine Films: Family, Drama and Historical Debate in *Miss Mary* and *The Official Story*. In *Based on a True Story: Latin American History at the Movies*. Ed. Donald F. Stevens, 173–200. Wilmington: Scholarly Resources.

Silverman, Kaja. 1983. *The Subject of Semiotics*. New York: Oxford University Press.

Skye, Sherwin. 2005. "La Niña Santa Interview. Director Lucrecia Martel Confesses." *Collective*. http://www.bbc.co.uk/dna/collective/A3609993 (accessed July 6, 2006).

Smith, Sidonie. 1994. Identity's Body. In *Autobiography and Postmodernism*. Ed. Kathleen Ashley, Leigh Gilmore, and General Peters, 130–66. Amherst: University of Massachusetts Press.

Smith, Sidonie, and Julia Watson. 1996. *Getting a Life: Everyday Uses of Autobiography*. Minneapolis: University of Minnesota Press.

Sommer, Doris. 1991. *Foundational Fictions: The National Romances of Latin America*. Berkeley: University of California Press.

———. 1998. The Politics of Allegory. A New Understanding of Agency. In *Gendered Agents. Women and Institutional Knowledge*. Ed. Silvestra Marianello and Paul A. Bove, 323–48. Durham, NC: Duke University Press.

Stephens, Sonya. 2000. Unfamiliarity and Defamiliarization: Teaching *Les Fleurs du Mal* with *The Petits Poemes en Prose*. In *Approaches to Teaching Baudelaire's Flowers of Evil*. Ed. Laurence M. Porter, 93–99. New York: Modern Language Association of America.

Tasker, Ivonne. 1998. *Working Girls. Gender and Sexuality in Popular Cinema*. London: Routledge.

"Tenemos el mundo que hemos querido, no el único posible." 2005. *La Ventana*. http://laventana.casa.cult.cu/modules.php?name=News&file=article&s id=2587 (accessed July 11, 2006).

FILMS

La ciénaga. Directed by Lucrecia Martel. Transeuropa Video Entertainment, 2001.

Mundo grúa. Directed by Pablo Trapero. Lita Stantic Producciones, 1999.

La niña santa. Directed by Lucrecia Martel. Transeuropa Video Entertainment, 2004.

Picado fino. Directed by Esteban Sapir. 5600 Film, 1996.

Pizza, birra, faso. Directed by Adrián Caetano and Bruno Stagnaro. Palo y a la Bolsa Cine, 1998.

Rapado. Directed by Martín Rejtman. Martín Rejtman, 1991.

NOTES

1   The notion of allegory as an interpretive strategy implies that "no single literal meaning can stand alone, but that a valid utterance must possess a transcendent meaning as well, a symbolic surplus beyond the literal level" (Fletcher, 41).

2   According to Jameson, all Third World texts carry an inevitable political subtext that First World texts do not necessarily have. This is so, he argues, because Third World cultural productions do not reflect a clear separation between the public and the private, or between the poetic and the political, like First World texts do.

3   The films of Latin American women directors like Marta Rodríguez (Colombia), Tara Amaral (Brazil), Ximena Cuevas (Mexico), Margot Benacerraf (Venezuela), Marcela Fernández Violante (Mexico), Carla Camurati (Brazil), Ana Polak (Argentina), and Marianne Eyde (Norway-Peru), like those of Martel, can also be seen as challenging the national allegory paradigm.

4   In his essay *Art as Technique*, Shklovsky contends that habituation to the quotidian and the over-automatization of objects makes people live their lives unconsciously, almost as if they never existed. He asserts that this "habituation devours works, clothes, furniture, one's wife and the fear of war," and that the role of art is precisely to wake up human beings from this lethargy, to detach objects from the automatism of perception (7). He contends that the objective of art must be: "to impart the sensations of things as they are perceived and not as they are known.

The technique of art is to make objects *unfamiliar;* to make forms difficult, to increase the difficulty and the length of perception because the process of perception is an aesthetic end in itself and must be prolonged. *Art is a way of experiencing the artfulness of an object: the object is not important*" (7–8).

Brecht describes as *witchcraft* the effect that a "*Gesamtkunstwerk*" or "integrated work of art" has on the spectators. This effect is achieved in a theatre when the sound, acting, and the general production of the play are merged, creating a hypnotic effect and reducing viewers to a state of "idiocy." Brecht argues: "The process of fusion extends to the spectator, who gets thrown into the melting pot too and becomes a passive (suffering) part of the total work of art. Witchcraft of this sort must of course be fought against. Whatever is intended to produce hypnosis is likely to induce sordid intoxication or create fog, and has to be given up. *Words, music and setting must become more independent of one another*" (38). Instead of sharing an experience, the spectator must confront or question what he or she observes. Defamiliarization was later adapted by feminist scholars such as Laura Mulvey, Kaja Silverman, Teresa de Lauretis, and Cynthia Baron, among others.

5   Taking the classic narrative film and its "magic" style as her site of analysis, Mulvey emphasizes its skilled and satisfying manipulation of visual pleasure and points out how: "the unchallenged mainstream film coded the erotic into the language of the dominant patriarchal order [...] through these codes the alienated subject, torn in his imaginary

memory by a sense of loss, by the terror of potential lack in fantasy, came near to finding a glimpse of satisfaction: through its formal beauty and its play on his own formative obsessions" (16). Mulvey contends that the only way we can attack pleasure as a manifestation of patriarchal oppression is through the rejection of coercive forms that prevent meanings from transcending the "male gaze," at the same time daring to break with normal pleasurable expectations in order to conceive a new language of desire.

According to critics in the online publication *Planet Sick Boy*, "Lucrecia Martel's directorial debut, a Berlin Film Festival winner, is a terrific picture, even though it's pretty difficult to watch [...] Martel's fly-on-the-wall style might remind some of the *Dogme 95* aesthetic, and it's a real shock to learn that most of *La Ciénaga*'s acting talent had no acting experience, especially the kids, who were just residents of the villages where Martel filmed. It's a gritty, accomplished work that will ultimately pay off if you can sort out the characters and their stories" (Popick). See also Marques.

6   See "Desde los 18 Me Siento Vieja. Una Entrevista con Lucrecia Martel." *El Clarín*. February 3, 2004. Suplemento Mujer. http://www.clarin.com/suplementos/mujer/2004/03/02/m-00401.htm (accessed July 10, 2006).

7   Some of the most important directors and theorists from the New Latin American Cinema movement were the Argentineans Fernando Solanas and Octavio Getino ("Towards a Third Cinema") and Fernando Birri ("Cinema and Underdevelopment"), the Bolivian Jorge Sanjines, the Brazilian Glauber Rocha ("An Esthetic of Hunger"), and the Cubans Tomas Gutierrez Alea ("The Viewer's Dialectic") and Julio García Espinosa ("For an Imperfect Cinema"). See Martin.

8   Laura Mulvey contends that "in a world ordered by sexual imbalance, pleasure in looking has been also divided into the dichotomies active/male and passive/female. The female figure is styled according to the fantasy projected by the male gaze. In their traditional exhibitionist role, women are simultaneously looked at and displayed, with their appearance coded for strong visual and erotic impact so that they can be said to connote to-be-looked-at-ness. Mainstream film neatly combines spectacle and narrative" (19).

9   Drawing on structuralist/semiotic, ideological, and psychoanalytic formulations, theorists such as Pam Cook, Claire Johnston, Laura Mulvey, Teresa de Lauretis, Marjorie Rosen, E. Ann Kaplan, and Molly Haskell, and more recently post-structuralist and deconstructive scholars like Trinh T. Minh-ha, have all analyzed cinematographic representations of femininity. These authors have concluded that these representations are usually related to stereotypical portrayals of women as passive/submissive/object-to-be-looked-at, which may be challenged by the work of women behind the camera as producers, writers, and directors. They have realized that, as in most human artistic expression, but maybe most importantly within the collective consciousness of Western society, women still occupy marginal spaces and their achievements and contributions have been almost completely erased from the historical accounts of the ruling apparatus.

10 Kaja Silverman notes that, since Christian Metz first defined the film screen as "that *other mirror*" (Metz, 4), film scholars have used the psychoanalytic idea of suture in order to designate "the procedures by means of which cinematic texts confer subjectivity on their viewers" (Silverman, 195). Rachel Gabara describes the concept of suture as "the shot/reverse shot operation, which allows the subject to see from the point of view of the camera's gaze [...] the cinematic spectator experiences the *jouissance* of plenitude in the first shot of such a sequence, before the unpleasant realization that what they see is bounded by the gaze of an absent other, who has everything that the viewing subject lacks" (2003, 343).

11 Judith Butler explains that the "heterosexual matrix" is "a hegemonic discursive/epistemic model of gender intelligibility that assumes that for bodies to adhere and make sense there must be a stable sex expressed through a stable gender [...] that is oppositionally and hierarchically defined, through the compulsory practice of heterosexuality" (151).

12 See "Tenemos el mundo que hemos querido, no el único posible." 2005. *La Ventana*. http://laventana.casa.cult.cu/modules.php?name=News&file=article&sid=2587 (accessed July 11, 2006).

13 Brecht argues that "the Aristotelian aesthetics call for an impact that flattens out all social and other distinctions between individuals [...] they manage to flatten out class conflicts in this way, although the individuals themselves are becoming increasingly aware of class differences. The same result is achieved even when class conflicts are the subject of such plays and even in cases where they take sides for a particular class. A collective entity is created in the auditorium for the *duration of the entertainment*, on the basis of the 'common humanity' shared by all spectators alike. Non-Aristotelian drama [...] is not interested in the establishment of such an entity, it divides its audience" (Brecht, 60).

14 Ann McClintock asks, particularly of feminists, if the iconography of the family can be retained as the figure for national unity or if an alternative, radical iconography must be developed (McClintock, 109).

15 Director's statement in the additional features included in the DVD version of *La niña santa*.

16 Women scholars such as Catherine Portuges, Brodzki and Schenck, Susanna Egan, Barbara Kosta, and Rachel Gabara (2006) have recognized the relevance of feminine cinematographic autobiographies, even, and especially, if they do not comply with the formal requirements of the literary autobiographical genre.

17 It is important to recognize, as Gledhill and others have demonstrated, that genres are fictional worlds constructed by a series of conventions that define their boundaries (Gledhill, 238). The concept of genre is permanently changing and evolving and is always subject to the culture and the historical moment in which it is elaborated. But also, as Gledhill concludes, genres are as marked by history as they are dialogic; they are and will be permanently questioned, contested and redefined.

Leading theorists of literary autobiography like James Olney, Philippe Lejeune, and Paul De Man have postulated the "equation author=narrator=character"

(Fonseca, ii) and have argued that "autobiographical hybrids" do not exist because autobiography is not a question of degree, because autobiography is all or nothing, [it] "lends itself poorly to generic definition," and [it] "veils a defacement of the mind of which it is itself the cause" (Lejeune, 25; de Man, 81).

18   See Enriquez.

19   *The Modern Catholic Dictionary* defines the concept of 'holiness' as "being separated from the secular or profane, or dedication to God's service." The holy character of God is related to his separation from evil. Humans can be holy through their relation to God, which can be subjective (divine possession and the practice of moral virtue) or objective (formal, exclusive consecration to the service of God, as in the case of nuns and priests) (Hardon).

20   See "Desde los 18 Me Siento Vieja. Una Entrevista con Lucrecia Martel."

21   "Interview with Lucrecia Martel." *La Niña Santa* (2004).

22   Sigmund Freud defined perversion as: "The pursuit of 'abnormal' sexual objects without repression." He listed five ways in which an individual is perverse or "differs from the normal": having intercourse with animals, overstepping the barrier against disgust, incest, homosexuality, and transference of the part played by the genitals to other organs and areas of the body (74).

23   Driscoll notes that "'GIRL' indicates uncertain narratives about identity development and social position [...] girls are marginal to narratives about culture and yet, central to them" (235).

24   Quoted in Gabara (2006), xiv.

BODILY REPRESENTATIONS: DISEASE AND RAPE IN FRANCISCO LOMBARDI'S *OJOS QUE NO VEN*

Elizabeth Montes Garcés
University of Calgary

Myriam Osorio
Memorial University of Newfoundland

Francisco Lombardi is one of the most important contemporary Peruvian film directors. To date, Lombardi has made thirteen feature films and dozens of documentaries on several aspects of Peruvian society, ranging from human exploitation and greed to fanaticism to the role of the media in shaping public opinion.[1] In his eleventh feature film, *Ojos que no ven* (2003), Lombardi examines political corruption during the last days of Alberto Fujimori's second presidency in 2000. Set during the political crisis caused by the "vladivideos," a series of tapes of presidential counsellor Vladimiro Montesinos bribing industrialists, military officers, politicians from the opposition, and TV producers, the film consists of six interrelated stories that reveal the widespread corruption affecting all government spheres.

During his first term as president (1990–95), Fujimori focused efforts on fighting both hyperinflation and the leftist insurgency of the Shining Path and the Revolutionary Movement Tupac Amaru (MRTA). His close alliance with the military forces bore fruit with the capture of Abimael Guzmán, the leader of Shining Path, in 1992, and the termination of the 126-day-siege of the Japanese Embassy in Lima by the MRTA in September of the same year. Capitalizing on these successes, Fujimori was able to win the 1995 elections for a second term in office until 2000, when constitutional stipulations required that he step down and call an election. Fujimori ran for the presidency a third time and was elected on May 28, 2000, amidst rumors of fraud. After four months in power, the "vladivideos" were released on television, causing a major political crisis that ended with the sudden departure of Fujimori to Japan, and the arrest of Vladimiro Montesinos.[2]

Drawing on the concepts of paradigmatic and syntagmatic metaphors proposed by Christian Metz in *The Imaginary Signifier: Psychoanalysis and the Cinema* (1982), this article explores the ways in which *Ojos que no ven* uses such metaphors to portray the devastating effect of political corruption on the lives of regular citizens. Although the two concepts derive from the linguistic theories of language similarity and contiguity proposed by Roman Jakobson, Metz's reconceptualization of the terms for the study of film seems to us very useful for the analysis of *Ojos que no ven*. In particular, Metz considers "two different semantic lines" along which a stretch of discourse may develop: "one topic may lead to another either through their similarity [belonging to the same paradigm] or their contiguity [belonging to the same syntagm]" (69). Metaphor, thus, creates a relationship that consists in the qualities that objects are thought to share, no matter how unrelated they may be. According to Metz, syntagmatic metaphors function as filmic elements "which are both present in the chain [of sequences]" and "are associated by resemblance or by contrast." These elements may include, among others, "two images, two motifs in the same image, two whole sequences." In contrast, metaphors can be presented paradigmatically when two images are associated, "but they are presented as the terms of an alternative; in the film sequence, one replaces the other, while simultaneously evoking it" (Metz, 189). *Ojos que no ven* effectively illustrates both types of metaphors through male characters suffering from serious diseases and female characters sustaining the injuries of extreme violence as victims of rape. While in some sequences Lombardi alternates images of diseased or violated bodies with the "vladivideos," in others, images of injured or raped female bodies stand in place of the violence inflicted on Peruvian society by a repressive government. The signifying power of these metaphors is heightened by several cinematic techniques such as the use of light, the angles, the types of shots, and the composition.

From its very beginning, *Ojos que no ven* links the corruption of the Peruvian state with illnesses suffered by many characters of the film. The first sequence focuses on two old men of opposing political persuasions, the "fujimorista" Don Lucho (Carlos Gassols) and the "aprista" Don Víctor (Jorge Rodríguez Paz), watching the release of the first "vladivideo" from their hospital beds. The video shows Montesinos paying Congressman Alberto Kouri US$15,000 to switch his alliance to the government party. As they watch, the camera tells the audience that the two men are at the General Hospital in Lima. Lucho is afflicted with a respiratory problem while Víctor suffers from phlebitis, a blockage of the veins on his left leg. By juxtaposing the images of the two sick men with the images of the "vladivideo," this sequence reveals itself as a clear example of a metaphor presented syntagmatically, showing the viewers, through similarity, the link between illness and corruption.

Illnesses, as Susan Sontag has remarked, have been used as metaphors of corruption in the body politic. According to Sontag, "Illnesses have always been used as a metaphor to enliven charges that a society was corrupt or unjust" (72). Sontag further develops this idea by arguing that in modern times as a result of "a profound disequilibrium between individual and society, with society conceived as the individual's adversary, disease metaphors are used to judge society not as out of balance but as repressive" (73). Although Sontag's elaboration seeks to dissolve the connection between disease and corruption, Lombardi's film, on the contrary, aims at maintaining it. That is the reason why in *Ojos que no ven*, Lombardi uses both syntagmatic and paradigmatic metaphors. Most of the characters end up at the General Hospital because they are either sick or are victims of an act of repressive violence resulting in serious bodily injuries. Both the sick and the injured are present in the film as well to portray metaphorically the state corruption in the Peruvian nation. The former are represented by Don Lucho and Don Víctor but also by

Gonzalo del Solar (Paul Vega), a successful TV reporter whose facial skin breakout is diagnosed as aggressive skin cancer. The latter are depicted by two women: Elena Polanco (Patricia Pereyra), who loses her unborn child after being run over by Colonel Héctor Revoredo (Gianfranco Brero), and Mercedes Lobatón (Melania Urbina), a sixteen-year-old girl who is raped by Federico Peñaflor (Gustavo Bueno), a corrupt lawyer working for Vladimiro Montesinos.

Nelson Carro (2003) has effectively summarized the link between corruption and disease in his critical review of the film when he states:

> No hay posibilidad de final feliz: amputación, cáncer ful-minante, aborto, violación, asesinato, misoginia [...] El de-terioro social y político encuentra su reflejo en todos esos seres enfermos que no por accidente circulan alrededor de un hos-pital.

> [There is no possibility of a happy ending: amputation, lethal cancer, abortion, rape, assassination, misogyny [...] Social and political deterioration is reflected in all of these sick individ-uals that, not by accident, inhabit a hospital.]

Illness as a metaphor of corruption is not only a structural device that links the six stories together; it also serves as a strategy to produce the atmosphere of confinement and despair that characterize the entire film. This confinement is further reinforced on the screen through a series of carefully crafted sequences. In what follows, we will analyze in detail key sequences by addressing the similarities of apparently opposite elements.

The initial scenes catch the viewers' attention by reproducing the continuous "vladivideos" news releases by Gonzalo del Solar, a TV an-chor who is well-known in Peru's entertainment business and who is obsessed with his appearance. In one of these sequences, Víctor, Lucho, and some of the medical staff at the General Hospital see a healthy and handsome Gonzalo on the TV screen in a medium shot at an eye-level angle and lit in high key. The bright and even illumination of Gonzalo's well-dressed upper body at a modern TV studio contrasts sharply with the full shot of Víctor, lit in low key and surrounded by shadows and darkness. Thus, illumination and the angles from which the characters are photographed play key roles in establishing the contrast between light and dark, the show-business world and the hospital, health, and illness. The shadows that surround Victor suggest that the life of this old, sick and destitute individual is not worth very much and his poor health is unlikely to improve. Similarly, Lombardi establishes a connection between the sick condition of Lucho and Fujimori's turn in the presidency. Although the film does not offer many details of Lucho's illness, the audience is made aware that this man, suffering a terminal diagnosis, has a few months to live. Just as Víctor, who is unlikely to recover, and as Lucho, who is connected to an oxygen tank unable to breathe on his own, Peru is asphyxiating under the corruption exercised by the Fujimori-Montesinos duo.

Furthermore, the images of Lucho and Victor's ordeal suggest that a binary opposition is at work. In their elaboration of Metz's theory on metaphor, Stephen Cohan and Linda Shires explain that a binary opposition occurs when "both terms are present in the segment, so these two signifiers and their signifieds are syntagmatically set in opposition" (37). Lucho's and Víctor's beds are located on the right- and left-hand sides of the screen, signifying Lucho's and Victor's political alliances with the left-wing "Aprista" and the political right "Fujimorista" parties of Peru. In doing so, Lombardi illustrates both aspects of the metaphorical relationship in one segment as Lucho and Víctor are at once distanced by ideology and united by illness. These characters' fanaticism blinds them from seeing what political corruption is doing to regular people in Peru. Don Lucho takes lightly Víctor's complaint that the Fujimori government has left him penniless because the authorities have denied him his right to an old age pension. Don Víctor, however, is disappointed that after years of loyalty to the Aprista party, they have turned down his request for the orthopedic aid he needs to replace his amputated limb.[3] The juxtaposition offered in this sequence is used to show the audience the disintegration of the government apparatus, the futility of the characters' loyalty to political parties, and the devastating impact of corruption in the lives of common citizens. As a reminder of the forces that cause this disruption, an important element of this sequence's *mise-en-scène* is the "vladivideo" itself. Shot from an oblique angle and with an extremely poor illumination, this video depicts Vladimiro Montesinos on the far right-hand side of the screen handing money to Senator Kouri. The tension represented by this shot is thus connected in the movie to the despair and potential loss of life of Victor and Lucho.

By interweaving film and video images with takes captured at the TV studio, Lombardi gives more prominence to the link between illness and corruption explored above. Beyond the escalation of Víctor's phlebitis and Lucho's respiratory problems, this is achieved through the advance of the TV anchor's skin cancer. Gonzalo's daily broadcasts are presented as a syntagmatic metaphor in which two contiguous images are linked by contrast. In one of his ground-breaking reports, the famous anchor announces the exhumation of the bodies of several peasants, apparently assassinated by the military forces in Ayacucho for their presumed ties with the Shining Path. Gonzalo also covers a press conference in which Fujimori reveals details about the astronomical amount of money Montesinos held in a Swiss bank account. In spite of the fact that Fujimori turns his back on Montesinos by firing him and portraying him as a dishonest man who had infiltrated the government, the images of the "vladivideos" mingle with that of Fujimori. The spectatorship of *Ojos que no ven* is presented with simultaneous images of unmarked mass graves and murky deals to make them realize that the Fujimori government and its officials are not only corrupt but are also implicated in extreme violence to maintain the status quo.

The progression of Gonzalo's disease runs parallel to the increasing revelations of the obscure dealings of the Fujimori government. In one sequence, Gonzalo examines and touches a dark spot on his face while sitting in front of the mirror in his dressing room. Angélica (Tatiana Astengo), his make-up artist, unsuccessfully tries to cover the blemish with cosmetics. Angélica's efforts to conceal the spot so that shooting can continue mirror Fujimori's government pains at covering up information that might incriminate the president. As in the previous sequence with Lucho and Víctor, the illness metaphor is presented syntagmatically, as both elements of the comparison, namely the melanoma spot on Gonzalo's face and the exorbitant amounts of money stolen by Montesinos, are present in the same segment.

Since the best melanoma specialist, Dr. Viadurre (Carlos Tuccio), has his practice at the General Hospital, Gonzalo, as Víctor and Lucho, also ends up there. Lombardi uses a paradigmatic metaphor to show how the anchorman's body stands in place of the weakening corpus of the nation.

FIG. 1. THE OLD MEN: DON LUCHO (CARLOS GASSOLS) AND DON VÍCTOR
(JORGE RODRÍGUEZ PAZ). PHOTO BY TEODORO DELGADO (COURTESY OF
FRANCISCO LOMBARDI).

The doctor's description of the way the tumour developed on Gonzalo's
face doubles as a description of the manner in which the corruption of
Fujimori's government wreaks havoc in the fibres of the social tissue.
As the doctor tells Gonzalo, "Esos nódulos avanzan con mucha rapidez.
Invaden la dermis casi desde el inicio. Es casi imposible diagnosticarlos a
tiempo." ["Those nodules develop very quickly. They invade the dermis
from its roots. It is impossible to diagnose them in time."] Just as Gonzalo's melanoma spread quietly, so did the cancer of corruption stealthily
permeate and take root in Peruvian society.

As a matter of fact, the extreme close-ups used in this sequence transform the tumor itself into a synecdoche not only of the sick body of its
host but also the State. Discussing Jakobson's ideas on the synecdochic
nature of the close-up, Metz praises Jakobson's idea that "one of the basic
characteristics of the cinema is that it transforms the object into a sign"
(194). This transformation is accomplished by "selectively representing
one part of the object [...] thereby choosing the meaning one wants to
give it over and above this representation" (195). Because of the many

Fig. 2. Gonzalo's (Paul Vega) image in the mirror. Photo by Teodoro Delgado (courtesy of Francisco Lombardi).

close-ups, Gonzalo's face and his prominent tumor are emphasized and magnified. Gonzalo's decaying body that might be considered a sign of his indifference to the disturbing events that he reports also represents an ailing nation-state that is indifferent to the common citizens' suffering. As the surgeon implies, health can only be restored through the removal of the malignancy.

The sequence in which Gonzalo's surgery takes place is used in the film to emphasize the sense of total powerlessness the character experiences as he confronts his disease. Shot from a combination of low and high angles the sequence in the operating-room shows doctor Viadurre removing the tumor on Gonzalo's left cheek. The dialogue between Gonzalo and the surgeon, combined with the low angle in which this sequence is predominantly shot, effectively convey the transformation of Gonzalo from one of the most influential personalities in Peru to a helpless individual who surrenders to Dr. Vidaurre's knowledge and skill. The high angle used in the last takes of this sequence conveys such a sense of weakness and fear. By showing Gonzalo lying helpless on the operating table, the audience is made further aware that his life as a TV anchor is in jeopardy because his face will be permanently disfigured. Metaphorically speaking, the vulnerable situation in which Gonzalo finds himself reflects the helplessness many Peruvians experience when facing the corruption and abuse of State leaders, as will be seen more clearly when we address the representation of female characters in this film.

One of the last sequences of *Ojos que no ven* depicts the appalling effects of cancer in Gonzalo's life. Completely alone, Gonzalo sits in front of a TV camera to explain the reasons for his absence from the TV studios on a program called "Let's Talk Clearly." After he starts talking, however, his words are interrupted by his tears. The medium shot of Gonzalo's face is reminiscent of the first sequence of the film in which he announced the release of the first "vladivideo." However, while that sequence was shot in high key, this one shows Gonzalo in low key, creating a shadow over the left side of his face. Shortly thereafter, the light is slowly switched to high key and the audience is able to see not just his healthy right cheek, but his left cheek bearing the grotesque scar from the surgery. The medium shot then turns into a long shot of Gonzalo sitting in a leather chair in his apartment. The irony of Gonzalo's stating that he wishes to be seen in the open is thus revealed to the audience, as the anchorman has instead chosen to isolate himself by staying behind closed doors. This move to shun the eyes of the public to protect his image illustrates the title of the film. More specifically, Gonzalo has avoided taking a real interest in what is happening in Peru even though as a journalist he has first-hand knowledge of events. This stance personifies the popular saying "Ojos que no ven, corazón que no siente" ["What the eye doesn't see, the heart does not feel"] to which the title of the film, *Ojos que no ven*, refers. By adopting a cynical stance, Gonzalo projects the idea that political corruption does not have any real impact on his life. Likewise, just as Gonzalo did not want to accept the possibility that the scar on his face might be cancerous, Peruvians were in a state of denial, for example, regarding the massacre of hundreds of students and peasants perpetrated by the "Grupo Colina" and the manipulations of Vladimiro Montesinos.[4] As is well known, during the decade of Fujimori's rule, Peruvian people were led to believe that the government was just and that extreme violence and consolidation of power were necessary measures for remedying insurgency and the economic collapse. It seems plausible to assume that

Peruvians refused to see that the State had transformed itself into a corrupt and violent apparatus that sought to perpetuate the power of Fujimori and his supporters at the expense of the lives and freedom of speech of most civilians. As seen in the film, all the characters express an inability to react to their circumstances while being constantly bombarded with additional revelations of the corruption and abuse of Fujimori's government. That Peruvians refused to believe that their government was capable of such corruption is best illustrated by Lucho, who always defends "El chino" Fujimori, whose nickname roughly translates to Chinaman in reference to the president's East Asian descent. Lucho trusts that Fujimori is doing all he can to bring Vladimiro Montesinos and his cronies to justice.[5]

While male bodies are represented in Lombardi's film as suffering from terminal diseases, it is the female bodies that endure directly the repression of the state apparatus through the rape perpetrated by the secret police and high-ranking officials associated with Montesinos. Allied to disease, rape parallels the suffocating atmosphere suggested by Lucho's lung disease as well as the rampant repression in Peru at the time depicted. This entrapment translates into the reasons why *Ojos que no ven* reproduces a filmic discourse that promotes, as Susan Hayward has discussed, "a gendered proscription of agency and power. Implicitly, agency becomes naturalized as male, and the very real concept of rape is used in an abstract, but also extremely concrete way to keep that proscription in place" (98). The cases of Mercedes Lobatón and Elena Polanco bring rape to the fore in order to illustrate the lack of agency and the lack of justice they both suffer.

Mercedes Lobatón is the victim of Federico Peñaflor, a corrupt lawyer working for Montesinos. Mercedes is only sixteen years old, and she lives with her father and her maternal grandfather, Don Víctor.[6] Her father (Ismael Contreras) is a low profile figure who is hired by Peñaflor and the members of Montesinos' secret police to cause disruption in "La marcha de los cuatro Suyos" ["The Rally of the Four 'Suyos'"], a political anti-Fujimori rally lead by opposition politicians including Alejandro Toledo. When a TV reporter reveals that Montesinos had infiltrated the rally to manipulate public opinion against Toledo as a way to secure Fujimori's third term in office, the government arrests Mercedes' father for his involvement in Montesinos' plan.

Fig. 3. Gonzalo's (Paul Vega) TV show. Photo by Teodoro Delgado (courtesy of Francisco Lombardi).

Following her father's advice, Mercedes runs to seek help from Federico Peñaflor, who, treacherously acting as a disinterested father figure, promises Mercedes the help that she desperately needs. He bribes a judge for the release of her father and gives her money to buy medicine for her ailing grandfather. Peñaflor thus gains Mercedes' gratitude and no small measure of control over her. The unequal distribution of power and the tension that surrounds each and every encounter between these two characters suggests to the viewer that this man can and will take advantage of his position. To emphasize the dramatic overtones of this sequence, the 'seduction' occurs when Peñaflor is feeling the pressures of his involvement with Montesinos. The night before his attempted escape to the United States, Peñaflor invites Mercedes to his office where he drugs her drink and rapes her.[7] This segment, once again, makes present the title of the film as the young woman is raped in her sleep and is unable to see or do anything.

The images of Mercedes' rape have enormous symbolic value because they translate into a paradigmatic metaphor that once again points to the corruption in government spheres. This metaphor is of particular relevance for its representation of women as the unaware and helpless victims of a ransacking. In this particular sequence, Mercedes is turned into a sign that stands for a victimized collectivity while the perpetrators of the crime assume they will remain untouched. At the same time, the sequence exposes the misogyny that characterized Fujimori's regime. As in previous scenes, the use of a combination of angles and illumination play a key role in the composition of the sequence. When Mercedes arrives at Peñaflor's office, the room is lit in high key, portraying a well-illuminated workplace. Peñaflor invites Mercedes to sit down while he prepares her a drink. As she sits down, an extremely low angle and the perspective from which she looks at the lawyer suggest the power Peñaflor has over her. Peñaflor informs Mercedes that her father will soon be released and he asks her to celebrate by drinking a glass of wine in which he has put a tranquillizer. The background music Peñaflor plays from the opera *L'Elisir d'amore* by Gaetano Donizetti becomes an ironic setting for what is about to occur. When Mercedes finishes her drink but feels sick and lies down on the sofa, Peñaflor closes the blinds and tells Mercedes to relax. This contrasting shot of Peñaflor's office now illuminated in low key with diffused shadows references the title of the film. Penaflor's wants to make sure no one can see while he is committing the despicable crime of rape.

In using the image of the female virgin that is sacrificed to a male misogynist, Lombardi reaffirms a literary and cultural Latin American tradition of representing the nation as a female body raped by a powerful male figure.[8] As Doris Sommer has discussed, the close association between nation and woman characterizes nineteenth-century novels (172).[9] In the twentieth century, the famous Boom authors did not escape this metaphor. In novels such as Carlos Fuentes' *La muerte de Artemio Cruz*, rape is a prevailing image for the representation of women and the nation. Fuentes' novel on the Mexican revolution proposes that the new nation can be created as the union between the revolutionary Artemio and the faithful "soldadera" Regina, but their union is represented as a rape. This might imply that the future of the nation as a romantic fiction must be aborted in favour of a marriage based on political and economic benefits. Essays also address a connection between rape, women, and the nation. In Octavio Paz's *The Labyrinth of Solitude*, the Mexican poet asserts that

Fig. 4. Unconscious Mercedes (Melania Urbina). Photo by Teodoro Delgado (courtesy of Francisco Lombardi).

contemporary Mexicans are the result of the rape committed by the Spanish conqueror of both Malinche and the Mexican nation. In film studies this link has also been established, for example, by Julianne Burton-Carvajal, who analyzes Latin American films and their representation of rape. According to Burton-Carvajal, films such as *Doña Bárbara* (1943), *La negra Angustias* (1949), *Él* (1952), *Lucía 1895* (1968), *The Other Francisco* (1974), and *Up to Certain Point* (1984) display a number of (anti) foundational features, such as rape, prostitution, incest, sterilization, and orphanhood, to do away with the idea of idyllic heterosexual romance as a formula to represent the nation (262). There is, however, a significant difference in Lombardi's films. In contrast to those films in which rape is not shown on the screen but rather through its consequences, *Ojos que no ven* exposes it.

In the last scenes of the film, Peñaflor throws Mercedes into the arms of a hospital worker and gives him a handful of dollars to avoid any kind of responsibility. Like her grandfather Víctor, Mercedes becomes another sick patient at the General Hospital. A full shot of the hospital ward taken from a high angle shows Mercedes as a minute figure lying on her bed, crying and whispering that she wants to denounce Peñaflor, while all the other patients watch a TV report of his arrest for his involvement with Montesinos. Mercedes' quiet voice and withdrawn attitude lead spectators to believe that Peñaflor will never be charged for her rape: no one has seen it so no one can corroborate or deny it. Thus in Francisco Lombardi's *Ojos que no ven*, Mercedes' characterization as innocent, lonely, and submissive places women and, by extension, the nation in a position of victimization and powerlessness: Mercedes, like the judicial system, lacks the resources to respond to the crime of her aggressor.

This link is significant, as Lombardi equates the portrayal of abused women with a representation of the nation in the story of Elena Polanco, the wife of a forensic anthropologist. Elena is presented as a fragile housewife who is being watched by Chauca (Carlos Alcántara) and Pareja ((Ricardo Mejía), two small but devious individuals that work for the secret police. A full shot of Elena knitting in her softly illuminated bedroom highlights her pregnancy. Her husband, Antonio Polanco (Miguel Iza), works for a human rights organization that is exhuming the bodies of several peasants apparently killed by members of the "Grupo Colina." As a result, he is being followed by Chauca and Pareja, who expect his return to Lima to kill him. Elena's image in the calmness of her house is then sharply contrasted with a high-angle medium shot of her peering through a window at Chauca and Pareja. The sequence, then, emphasizes Elena's fear as the two men continue their surveillance in spite of Fujimori's public announcement that the secret service has been dismantled.

In a scene that foreshadows the loss of their baby and the tragic death of this couple, the camera focuses on the archeological site in Ayacucho where Antonio is digging a skull from a mass grave. The high-angle close-up of two hands looking for the human bones shifts to a full shot in which an indigenous woman starts crying upon seeing the remains Antonio has found, as she believes them to be the remains of her son. The high angle reiterates the powerlessness of ordinary people who are being killed by the "Grupo Colina" and of those who are afraid to speak out to demand justice. In this particular sequence, the images of the fragmented bodies lying on the ground work as a paradigmatic metaphor of the abuse and violence exercised by a repressive government. This scene is juxtaposed to another in which Elena phones Antonio to inform

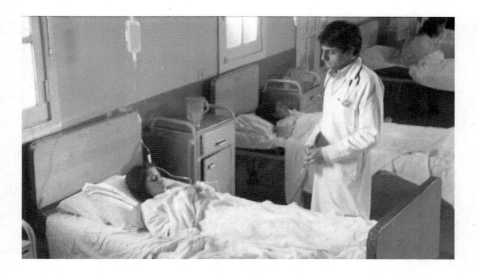

Fig. 5. Mercedes (Melania Urbina) at the General Hospital. Photo by Teodoro Delgado (courtesy of Francisco Lombardi).

him of the constant death threats she receives. Antonio tries to calm Elena down, naively believing that the situation will change with the collapse of Fujimori's regime. However, Antonio's reassuring words are undermined by a panoramic view of the barren area where he works, suggesting that he is rather alone in his fight against injustice. These two scenes are linked by contiguity and work as syntagmatic metaphors for the sense of powerlessness against the threats, although Antonio is less pessimistic than Elena. In another example of potentially damaging ignorance as suggested by the film's title, Antonio does not seem to appreciate the imminent danger surrounding himself and his wife. In fact, both of them become victims of a repressive government that tries to cover up its mistakes by all means possible.

After obsessively surveying Elena's house, Pareja breaks in and rapes her viciously. Although the atmosphere and circumstances of this assault are different from those of Mercedes' rape, the two are connected by the techniques used to depict them. Once again, a combination of takes illuminated in low key creates a dreary ambiance for Pareja's attack on Elena. After another tense telephone conversation with her husband, Elena hears broken glass falling to the floor. She goes downstairs to investigate and it is here in the shadowy semi-darkness of her own living room that Pareja rapes her violently, despite her desperate cries for help. The high angle in this scene serves to emphasize the power Pareja has over Elena and her inability to defend herself from her assailant.

Disoriented and unable to cope with the physical and emotional pain of the crime inflicted upon her, Elena hastily leaves the house the next morning and runs frantically along the highway only to be run over by another member of Fujimori's government. Colonel Héctor Revoredo (Gianfranco Brero), upset because he is forced to retire when he is about to be promoted, takes to the road in his car hoping to forget about the failure of his military career. He is so engrossed in his thoughts that he hits Elena. The sequence of the accident is created by a combination of extreme close-ups of the colonel with full shots of Elena running frantically in the middle of the highway. While Elena's lack of direction points to the dangerous uncertainty facing the country, her injured body serves as a paradigmatic metaphor of the scarred body of the nation. In turn Revoredo's aggression and clumsy movements as he turns the steering wheel erratically are symbolic of the inevitable collapse of the government apparatus.

During the following scenes, the audience is presented with a full image of Elena's injured body. A close-up taken from a high angle shows her lying unconscious on the pavement as blood trickles from her mouth. Revoredo rushes her to the General Hospital. The next close-up shows Revoredo holding Elena's injured body at the hospital's entrance, an image that can very easily be read as the bloody hands of the military holding the injured body of the nation.

It is evident that all the scenes related to the violence perpetrated against Mercedes and Elena follow the pattern proposed by Metz for a paradigmatic metaphor. This metaphor associates the damage inflicted on the female bodies with the corruption inflicted by Fujimori's government on the body of the Peruvian nation. Elena is perhaps the biggest casualty in this film as she has yet to suffer the devastating effect of the acts of violence committed by Pareja. Once Antonio returns to his house in Lima, Pareja shoots and kills him instantly. Meanwhile, Elena is kidnapped by Revoredo, who takes her to his beach house. There she falls into a deep depression at the loss of her unborn baby. Elena also finds out that her husband has been killed and his body has been found in a dump. This devastating intrusion of the Fujimori regime proves to be unbearable for Elena, who decides to commit suicide by drowning in the ocean. Thus the scene of the beautiful sunny morning that introduces the sequence of Elena at the beach house turns into a dark affair. Like Mercedes, she is portrayed as nothing more than a body on which members of Fujimori's repressive system inflicts deadly injuries. The films' metaphors demonstrate that women and men are not the only victims of the violence inflicted by government officials. Even unborn generations of Peruvians are not spared.

Metz's theory on metaphor effectively illustrates how Lombardi turns to corporeal imaging to represent the corruption of the State in *Ojos que no ven*. He uses illness and rape as a way to represent injustice in the body politic. In the scenes depicting rape, the use of high angles demonstrates the power of the male assailants and the inability of the victims to escape. Through their representation as victims of rape, physical assault, and suicide, women are devoid of any sense of agency. Women's injured bodies, as well as the ailing and decaying bodies of the men in the film, are therefore equated with the body of a nation that doesn't see any possibility of responding to an overwhelming and violent State apparatus. In the final analysis, the Fujimori regime had several features: a popular president, a corrupt government apparatus, and a huge collection of casualties of repression. Francisco Lombardi's film refers to all three aspects but highlights the human toll that has been consistently ignored and left unspoken. Perhaps the poor reception of the film in Peru had to do with the massive unwillingness to see and recognize the atrocities committed by a government that seemed to be effectively handling the economy and controlling the rampant insurgency that prevailed before the Fujimori years. The staged sense of order and stability promoted by Fujimori was so dear to a significant number of Peruvians that they were willing to pay for their blindness with the life of its citizens and the sanity of the nation.

Fig. 6. Elena Polanco's (Patricia Pereyra) suicide. Photo by Teodoro Delgado (courtesy of Francisco Lombardi).

WORKS CITED

Bedoya, Ricardo.1988. Encuentro de lobos. *Si*, 51–53.

———. 1997. Entre fauces y colmillos: las películas de Lombardi. *Huesca: Festival de Cine de Huesca.*

———. 1997. *Un cine rencontrado: las películas peruanas.* Lima: Universidad de Lima.

Burton-Carvajal, Julianne. 1993. Regarding Rape: Fictions of Origin and Film Spectatorship. In *Mediating Two Worlds: Cinematic Encounters in the Americas.* Ed. John King, Ana M. López, and Manuel Alvarado, 258–68. London: British Film Institute.

Cameron, Maxwell. 2006. Endogenous Regime Breakdown: The Vladivideo and the Fall of Peru's Fujimori. In *The Fujimori Legacy: The Rise of Electoral Authoritarianism in Peru.* Ed. Julio Carrión, 268–93. University Park: Pennsylvania State University Press.

Cameron, Maxwell A., and Philip Maurceri, eds. 1997. *The Peruvian Labyrinth: Polity, Society, Economy.* University Park: Pennsylvania State University Press.

Carrión, Julio, ed. 2006. *The Fujimori Legacy: The Rise of Electoral Authoritarianism in Peru*. University Park: Pennsylvania State University Press.

Carro, Nelson. 2003. Miradas a una sociedad enferma: *Ojos que no ven. El ojo que piensa: Revista virtual de cine iberoamericano* 5, no. 3. http://www.elojoquepiensa.udg.mx/espanol/numero05/cinejournal/06_ojosquenoven.html (accessed February 20, 2007).

Castro, Pércio B. de. 2000. Gritemos a plenos pulmones y contémoslo a todos: revelando secretos en *No se lo digas a nadie* de Jayme Bayly y Francisco Lombardi. In *Cine-Lit 2000: Essays on Hispanic Film and Fiction*. Ed. George-Cabello Castellet, Jaime Martí Olivella, and Guy Wood, 48–59. Portland: Oregon State University.

Cohan, Steven, and Linda Shires. 1988. *Telling Stories: A Theoretical Analysis of Narrative Fiction*. London: Routledge.

Conaghan, Catherine M. 2005. *Fujimori's Peru: Deception in the Public Sphere*. Pittsburgh: University of Pittsburgh Press.

Crabtree, John. 2001. The Collapse of Fujimorismo: Authoritarianism and its Limits. *Bulletin of Latin American Research* 20, no. 3: 287–303.

Fuentes, Carlos. 1965. *La muerte de Artemio Cruz*. Mexico D.F.: Fondo de Cultura Económica.

Galleno, Lucía Angela Jesús. 2001. *Los años de la violencia en el Perú: Cultura y representación*. PhD diss., University of California at Berkeley.

Giannetti, Louis, and Jim Leach. 1996. *Understanding Movies*. Scarborough, ON: Prentice Hall Allyn and Bacon Canada.

Hart, Stephen. 2005. 'Slick grit': auteurship versus mimicry in three films by Francisco Lombardi. *New Cinemas: Journal of Contemporary Film* 3, no. 3: 159–67.

Hayward, Susan. 2000. Framing National Cinemas. In *Cinema and Nation*. Ed. Mette Hjort and Scott MacKenzie, 88–102. London: Routledge.

Jakobson, Roman. 1956. [1971]. Two Aspects of Language and Two Types of Aphasic Disturbances. In *Fundamentals of Language*. Ed. Roman Jakobson and Morris Halle, 69–96. 2nd ed, rev. The Hague: Mouton.

Levitsky, Steven, and Maxwell A. Cameron. 2003. Democracy without Parties? Political Parties and Regime Change in Fujimori's Peru. *Latin American Politics and Society* 45, no. 3: 1–33.

Metz, Christian. 1982. *The Imaginary Signifier: Psychoanalysis and the Cinema*. Trans. Celia Britton, Annwyl Williams, Ben Brewster, and Alfred Guzzetti. Bloomington: Indiana University Press.

Middents, Jeffrey. 2009. *Writing National Cinema: Film Journals and Film Culture in Peru*. Hanover, NH: Dartmouth College Press.

Paz, Octavio. 1959. *El laberinto de la soledad*. Mexico D.F.: Fondo de Cultura Económica.

Sommer, Doris. 1991. *Foundational Fictions: The National Romances of Latin America*. Berkeley: University of California Press.

Sontag, Susan. 1989. *Illness as Metaphor and Aids and its Metaphors*. New York: Anchor.

FILMS

La boca del lobo. Directed by Francisco Lombardi. Cinevista, 1988.

La ciudad y los perros. Directed by Francisco Lombardi. Cinevista, 1985.

Mariposa negra. Directed by Francisco Lombardi. Sherlock Films Sl, 2006.

No se lo digas a nadie. Directed by Francisco Lombardi. DVD. Picture This! Home Video, 1998.

Ojos que no ven. Directed by Francisco Lombardi. Incacine S.A.C., 2003.

Pantaleón y las visitadoras. Directed by Francisco Lombardi. Artistas Argentinos Asociados, 2000.

Tinta roja. Directed by Francisco Lombardi. Alta Films, 2000.

Viridiana. Directed by Luis Buñuel. Kingsley-International Pictures, 1961.

NOTES

1   His most successful films have been his adaptations of novels by Latin American writers such as Mario Vargas Llosa (*La ciudad y los perros* 1985, *Pantaleón y las visitadoras*, 2000), Alberto Fuget (*Tinta roja*, 2000), and Alonso Cueto (*Mariposa negra*, 2006). Despite this success, Lombardi's films have yet to be the subject of a comprehensive study. There are, however, a few publications, such as Stephen Hart's analysis of *La ciudad y los perros, Pantaleón y las visitadoras* and *No se lo digas a nadie* (1998) and Percio Castro's article also on *No se lo digas a nadie*. Lucía Angela Jesús Galleno examined the representation of violence in Peru through an analysis of literature and film, including *La boca del lobo* (1988) in her unpublished dissertation. Recently Jeffrey Middents published a book on film culture in Peru based on an analysis of the impact of the film publication *Hablemos de cine*. In his book, Middents devotes one chapter to the Lombardi generation in which he explains the difference of perspective and cinematic technique in the two trends that made up the so-called national cinema in Peru: the peasant-like films coming from the Cuzco school of directors like Federico García, and the urban and more commercial films coming from the Lima directors such as Francisco Lombardi. Since *Ojos que no ven* was only released in 2004, it has received scant critical attention. We hope, therefore, that this article contributes to the analysis and discussion of this important film.

2   For further discussion and analysis of the Fujimori regime, see, for example, Maxwell Cameron's article "Endogenous Regime Breakdown:

The Vladivideo and the Fall of Peru's Fujimori" (2006) and his book *The Peruvian Labyrinth* (1997), edited with Philip Mauceri.

3   One of the key topics for Lombardi is fanaticism. In *La boca del lobo* (1988), Lombardi depicts how indigenous populations are caught up in the middle of a war between two groups of fanatics: the followers of the Maoist group Shining Path, and the Peruvian army. Both use the same tactics to take over the country but in the end the inhabitants of the highlands are the victims of the massacre perpetrated by these antagonistic forces. In *Ojos que no ven* (2003), only until Lucho and Víctor finally realize at the end of the film that they themselves are victims of corrupt governments, do they give up their political affiliations.

4   "Grupo Colina" was a Peruvian paramilitary death squad that was active from 1990 until 1994, during the administration of Alberto Fujimori. The group is known for committing several human rights abuses, including the La Cantuta massacre and the Santa massacre, as well as the murder of journalist Pedro Yauri. For further information on this subject, see Catherine M. Conaghan's book, *Fujimori's Perú: Deception in the Public Sphere*, and Julio Carrión's volume, *The Fujimori Legacy: The Rise of Electoral Authoritarianism in Peru*.

5   Interestingly enough, when Lombardi's film was released in 2003, three years after the "Vladivideos" crisis, the response of the viewing public was not positive. In "Miradas a una sociedad enferma: *Ojos que no ven*" Nelson

Carro states that "Para sorpresa de Lombardi, *Ojos que no ven* recibió una mala respuesta de público en Perú." [To Lombardi's surprise, *Ojos que no ven* received a negative response from the public.] See http://www.elojoque-piensa.udg.mx/espanol/numero05/cinejournal/06_ojosquenoven.htm. The reasons for this response can be attributed to a multiplicity of factors that go beyond the scope of this paper.

6   Víctor Alcántara, the APRA follower who is a patient at the General Hospital, is Mercedes' grandfather and her only real support in life. While Mercedes first appears in the General Hospital as a visitor, by the end of this film she too becomes a patient.

7   This scene bears a resemblance to Luis Bunuel's *Viridiana* (1961), except that Viridiana's uncle is apparently unable to consummate his desire to rape her.

8   In the first scenes of the film, Peña-flor is shown spying on teenage girls at the entrance of a high school. He is obsessed with the idea of deflowering virgins and dominating them. In order to relieve his sexual urge, he goes to a brothel where he makes a prostitute dress up as a student. When she tries to seduce him by talking to him as if he were a professor, he interrupts her and possesses her violently, demonstrating that his fantasy requires women to surrender to male power.

9   As Sommer (172) has argued, "Foundational Fictions" such as Jorge Isaacs's *María* and José Marmol's *Amalia*, written in the wake of national independence, were typically allegorical romances of the nation-building process. These novels draw direct links in one way or another between the nation and the women they portray. In the twentieth century, the famous Boom authors also used this metaphor.

FILMS BY DAY AND FILMS BY NIGHT IN SÃO PAULO

David William Foster
Arizona State University

Of the approximately 18,000 films that have been produced in Brazil in 110 years of filmmaking, it is impossible to determine how many are devoted to São Paulo. However, it is safe to assume that, because of its greater profile in national and international imaginaries, Rio de Janeiro far surpasses São Paulo in filmic representations, especially if one insists on a direct correlation between the city and the plot of the film and not just the presence of a circumstantial locale. São Paulo is an important venue for Brazilian filmmaking, and it is also the site of many important film festivals, including the São Paulo International Film Festival, which dates from 1990. Yet it is undeniable that the presence of São Paulo in Brazilian fiction is not matched – at least in terms of the central core of Brazilian cinema – by an equal degree of interest for filmmakers. That does not mean, however, that there have not been some remarkable films that incorporate a significant interpretive interest in the city. This essay will examine four of those films with respects to the role of São Paolo as an industrial and financial centre and the concomitant social divisions and ramifications that stem from this status.[1]

FIG. 1. POSTER OF RUDOLF REX LUSTIG'S 1929 *SÃO PAULO, SINFONIA DA METRÓ-POLE.*

SÃO PAULO, S.A. ([SÃO PAULO, INC.], 1965)

Luís Sérgio Person (1936–67) is one of the names most associated with a
Brazilian filmmaking rooted in the social realities of São Paulo. Although
Person died young and left only a handful of feature-length films, his
São Paulo, S.A. (1965) is considered one of the key films associated with
the city, revealing very much of the influence of Italian neorealism and
anticipating the social concerns of the Cinema Novo, whose first manifestations are associated with the year 1965.[2] Critics are in agreement that
São Paulo, S.A. is thematically important because of the representation it
affords, through the main character, Carlos (Walmor Chagas), of the development of the automotive industry in that city between 1957 and 1961
(Bernardet; Catani). This is a period in which the capitalist development
of Brazil, centred in São Paulo, expands enormously, in part because of
Brazil's alliance with the United States during World War II.[3] This is, in
short, a period of a considerable amount of Americanization in Brazilian life, and the automobile is, despite the fact that German imports also
figure in the film, an essential icon of U.S. postwar dominance.[4]

The setting of Person's film is, consequently, firmly anchored in the
Brazilian professional class, at least that segment of it relating to the country's industrialization. In a typical neorealist fashion, Person correlates
the psychological vicissitudes of Carlos's life, namely his perennial rest-
lessness, his inability to relate emotionally, and his dissatisfaction with
the model of bourgeois life he has attained, with the alienation, viewed
very much in Marxian terms, which industrial capitalism exacts from
the individual who supinely accepts participation in the system. Carlos
is something like a Brazilian "man in the grey flannel suit," someone for
whom a fully emotional and sentient human existence is incompatible
with the depersonalizing routine of corporate life.[5]

Carlos is portrayed in unsympathetic terms in the film, and on no
occasion is the viewer invited to regard him as a tragic victim of the system. Indeed, his determined, although apparently unconscious, mistreat-
ment of those around him, including his long-suffering wife, is shown as
character failings on his part. *São Paulo, S.A.* is driven by a voluntaristic
notion of human experience whereby the central problem is Carlos's inability to take charge of his own life and live fully as human being in

order to overcome his debilitating alienation. Jean-Claude Bernardet sees Carlos as illustrating a "failure to choose" (286). Moreover, "Carlos, who is guided only by the opportunities that society offers him, who chooses neither for himself nor for others, who has neither idea or action with which to oppose the situation, who is capable only of flight, is ripe for fascism" (Bernardet, 288). It might be inaccurate to describe as fascistic the unquestionably authoritarian and tyrannical military governments, any one of them or all of them collectively, that held power in Brazil between 1964 and 1985. Yet, there is little question that Person's film, released the year after the military came to power, can sustain an interpretation of a Brazilian bourgeoisie that ensured the military's imposition of a dictatorship grounded in large measure on the promises of an enduring capitalism, industrialization, and the status quo.

If Carlos develops his investment in the status quo and by the end of the film has consolidated a life of bourgeois alienation, the film turns in part on his attempt to revolt, only to ultimately reintegrate himself within the system. Although São Paulo is constantly present as part of the backdrop of the film, as much in terms of the material reality of the cityscape as in terms of the texture of the everyday life of the social class to which Carlos belongs, it is the occasion of his brief and frustrated revolt against his chosen destiny that provides for the film's greatest display of the city. It is as though when Carlos goes about the routine of his alienated life, the city, in all of its successful dimensions, is only there as an incidental arena for the tribulations of his personal story. But when he assumes, however briefly, a sense of nonconformity that leads to a fleeting rebellion against the life path he has chosen, the city bulks large, not as part of an allegorical representation of the forces of modern capitalism that Carlos might resist, but rather as a directly experienced social environment that he now inhabits dialectically, instead of the inert backdrop of his passive circumstances. Especially effective in this regard is the opening scene of the film, in which Carlos is seen engaged in a violent fight with his wife (Eva Wilma). They argue, and he ends up sending the contents of a dining table crashing to the floor. As they struggle, he eventually slapping her and throwing her to the ground, the camera captures the moment through the sliding glass door of the balcony of their well-appointed high-rise apartment: their voices are muffled, but the surrounding buildings of the city are deftly mirrored in the glass of the door.

As Carlos stalks out of the room and out of the apartment and while the credits roll, the camera swings to record in varying degrees of proximity the buildings, icons of São Paulo capitalism, that hem the characters in. At other moments in the film the camera dwells on the city's industrial establishments, of which the automotive industry is only a part. As Carlos's employer at one point indicates, "São Paulo is the engine of Brazil. [...] São Paulo is growing and will not cease to continue to grow."

The foregrounding of the city's presence is never more evident than on those occasions when Carlos wanders the streets of the city, thus engaging in a form of physical contact no matter how disconnected from it he may be. Moving through the city in an automatized fashion, his face characterized by a vacant stare, Carlos's random *dérivés* oblige him to negotiate his physical surroundings, some of which he may be experiencing for the first time. One is reminded how the culture of the car frees the individual from the imperative to negotiate the city in an immediately physical sense: it is one thing to experience the city from the sidewalk through the soles of your feet and shoes; it is quite another to do so in the privileged space of the street thanks to the mediation of the automotive machine.

The opening scene of the film is repeated at the end, and this time we hear Carlos explain his decision to "dar o fora," to flee. Once again we see the buildings of the city reflected in the glass windows of the apartment, although this time the camera pans to those buildings as silent, monumental witnesses to Carlos's impetuous attempt to renounce the system in which he is enmeshed. Rejecting the humble Volkswagen that he has been accustomed to driving in the city, Carlos steals an upscale Karmann-Ghia.[6] As he speeds through the urban streets toward the coast, he energetically declares good-bye to the city. Yet his escape is short-lived. As he awakens in the car parked on a bluff, he suddenly bolts from the car, abandoning it with the door open, and hitches a ride with a trucker on his way to São Paulo. As the truck passes through the industrial outskirts of the city, Carlos enters into a sort of trance in which he mumbles repeatedly that one must start all over again, all over again a thousand times. As we hear him utter this statement, in a tone of despair, the camera focuses on successive waves of individuals that wash over one another as they rush across one of the symbols of modernity of capitalist São Paulo, the Viaduto do Chá (the Tea Viaduct), which was originally constructed to connect the northern outskirts of the city to the central core, the working class to the financial class. Modernity here being linked with capitalism, industrialization, and the status quo, the implication is clearly that Carlos will once more submit to the crushing dynamic of the city.

O PURITANO DA RUA AUGUSTA (*[THE AUGUSTA STREET PURITAN]*, 1965)

It is difficult to argue that Amácio Mazzaropi (1912–81), who made over thirty films between 1952 and 1980, should be denied a secure place in Brazilian film history. Yet this seems, with notable exceptions, to be the case. Perhaps it was because Mazzaropi's comedies, with their broad parodies and slapstick situations, went against the committed leftist and Italian neorealist-inspired grain of Brazil's Cinema Novo, an *auteur* movement that brought indisputable prestige to Brazilian culture and its film industry. The simple fact, however, is that Mazzaropi figures only sporadically in registries of Latin American and Brazilian cinema.[7] Eva Paulino Bueno has published an important monograph in which she sets out to demonstrate that Mazzaropi, especially with his hick persona, in the character of Jeca Tatu, more realistically captures the social tensions of São Paulo at mid-century than do the often pretentious texts of the Cinema Novo.[8]

Because of the ongoing internal immigration in the province of São Paulo, the movement from the despair of rural life to the promise of the metropolis/megalopolis, Mazzaropi's Jeca Tatu is an iconic figure of the pathos of adjustment to the city. This character represents the conflict between traditionalism and modernity, the travails of attempting to make it in a hostile urban environment that is frequently more daunting than the relentless misery of the countryside, and the attempt to make sense of a city life that often seems essentially incomprehensible. As Bueno demonstrates, Mazzaropi's Jeca Tatu films, taken as a whole, are invaluable to an understanding of the internal migration that accompanied the emergence of modern São Paulo. As in the case of other major urban centres in the Americas, there continues to be a directly proportional relationship between the degree of commercial, financial, and industrial importance of the city and the degree to which it draws in — sucks in, many would insist — the rural poor, both from the immediate surrounding province and from the country as a whole. It is an internal migration that complements the history of foreign immigration into the city, and Mazzaropi's films address the overwhelming confusion and disorientation of the new urban dweller.

As important as the Jeca Tatu films are with regard to the transformation of the country mouse into the city rat, I wish here to focus on somewhat of an exceptional text in the Mazzaropi filmography, *O puritano da Rua Augusta* (1965), a film that stands almost midway in the director's overall production. The Rua Augusta is a major street that traverses the Jardins residential district of southwest central São Paulo as it descends approximately twenty blocks from the dominant ridge, and dominant financial locus, that is the Avenida Paulista, one of the major thoroughfares of the central core of the city. In its day, the Rua Augusta was both a major commercial avenue and the site of solid middle-class residences. Today, although the Jardins remain a privileged residential area of the city, the Rua Augusta has become a tacky and often tawdry commercial strip along which businesses of some social standing, such as a branch of the famous Brazilian perfumerie O Boticário, are more the exception than the rule. One of the more notorious current businesses is a shop that specializes in the tools of the trade for the city's large force of prostitutes. However, during the mid-sixties when Mazzaropi's film takes place, the Rua Augusta was an icon of the city's modernity, whose commercial and residential addresses were evoked by those who were at home in the city and felt themselves to be an integral part of it.

In *O puritano da Rua Augusta*, the plot turns on the degree to which Punduroso (Amácio Mazzaropi), a play on *pundonoroso*, which means "characterized by dignity, honor, and discretion," will be able to convince his family to return to traditional Catholic moral beliefs to which the careless exposition of the body, the pursuit of sensual pleasure, and the repudiation of whatever might be considered old-fashioned are inimical. Punduroso's family, in short, is committed to the frenetic modernity and the sexual liberation of the 1960s as they arrive in urban Brazil and are taken up by his young-adult children. The latter live in São Paulo, while Punduroso lives outside the city, where he administers the family's interests, the source of the wealth that enables the urban life-style of his wife and children. In addition, Punduroso also has a factory in the city, of which his sons are nominally in charge. The juxtaposition here is a familiar one for certain Latin American families of wealth: the source of that wealth may lie outside the city, for example, in the vast ranches of Argentina and agricultural installations of Brazil, but in this case also the suburban industrial sector, the so-called ABC, of São Paulo. It is this wealth that moves through the financial centre and that enables the family to have either a permanent residence commensurate with its economic, and therefore social, standing or, a least, an in-town *pied-à-terre* where they can partake of the trappings of modernity that their wealth fuels and is in turn fuelled by, in the reciprocal fashion of capitalism. Three decades after Hildegard Rosenthal's camera captured the announcement on the side of a São Paulo trolley, to the effect that the city was the major industrial centre of Latin America, Punduroso's family universe testifies to the sustained expansion of that assertion.[9]

O puritano da Rua Augusta opens with an extensive travelling shot, as Punduroso and his family traverse the central core of the city in their chauffeur-driven American car. As they descend the Rua Augusta and arrive at their comfortable home — the modern appointments of the city are much in evidence in this sequence — the first thing that Punduroso spies is a classical nude statue in the entrance to his house: herein begins a series of unpleasant discoveries by Punduroso of the extent to which his own family has strayed from honorable domestic dignity in exchange for the São Paulo of rock-and-roll.[10] Mazzaropi plays his main character both as a man of conventional dignity (suit, overcoat, fedora, and rolled umbrella), but also as a hopelessly disjointed hick: literally, his character stumbles all over the place, apparently ill at ease in the refined urban environment.[11] After pulling one of his mother-in-law's housedresses over the naked statue, he returns to contemplate the maid, played as is the chauffeur by an Afro-Brazilian, decked out in pants so tight that Punduroso insists they must be glued on. When he orders her to return to her customary servant's uniform, she reacts huffily by saying "not on your life." As he announces to his children that he has decided to take up residence in São Paulo, the shocks multiply before Punduroso's appalled eyes, until the culminating moment of a house party organized by his children and their friends in the best "rock around the clock" fashion.

Punduroso's opposition to modernity is not merely a disgruntled or passive one. The title of the film refers to his active involvement with a group of religious zealots who preach their moral Puritanism in public. One of the delightful aspects of this film is the counterpoint between two value systems that occurs, not just in a limited domestic space, but in the public sphere in which the lived environment of the city and its citizens are materially represented in the film. This counterpoint extends to the use of music in the film: the religious hymns of Punduroso's companions in moral decency are juxtaposed with the rock-and-roll and other modern contemporary enthusiasms of his children, who always seem to be carrying LP record albums around.

After a series of setbacks in his puritanical campaign against modernity, Punduroso pretends to join them because he cannot beat them. He promises to stop scolding them for their tastes and begins to affect an imitation of them, including a hippy look. This whole set-up is as preposterous as his original efforts at restoring decency, but it does provide the film with a full array of Mazzaropi's typically quirky slapstick of the sort that is carried over from one film to another, so that the film is less about its ostensible theme and mostly a vehicle for the main character's comic persona. The confusion Punduroso's charade provokes, including the near break-up of his marriage to a young wife who seems closer in age to his young adult children than to him, his confinement to an insane asylum, and his daughter's incarceration in a convent, requires no extensive detail here, in part because it is more comically situational than narratively coherent. Suffice it to say that, in the end, some sort of equilibrium is established, based on the principle that all fanaticism and excess are bad for the cohesion of human social existence. Bueno underscores the social equilibrium espoused by the film (3–4). A strongly endorsed social equilibrium – a live-and-let live attitude – is often touted as a Brazilian national trait. This may not constitute any brilliant ethical discovery on Mazzaropi's part, but in moving his slapstick comedy toward a resolution needed to conclude the film, *O puritano da Rua Augusta* provides some excellent snapshots of São Paulo in the mid-1960s, ones that are less off-putting than the images of the dour *São Paulo, S.A.*

O INVASOR ([THE INVADER], 2002)

Brazilian films of social violence have been typically associated with Rio de Janeiro, a city that, because of its enormous importance as a tourist centre, is particularly concerned about public security. Recent films like *Cidade de Deus* [*City of God*] (Fernando Meirelles and Kátia Lund, 2002), *Ônibus 174* [*Bus 174*] (José Padilha and Felipe Lacerda, 2002), and *Tropa de elite* [*Elite Squad*] (José Padilha, 2007) are typical examples that have provoked as much controversy over their aestheticization of violence, which includes the way in which filmed violence panders to a certain range of spectator desire, as they have with respect to "selling" a particular vision of Brazil and, by extension, Latin American and other so-called Third-World societies, as uniquely violent and therefore irremediably resistant to civilized life. *Cidade de Deus* focuses on the violence generated in Rio's slums by drug trafficking and is singular for inscribing within the filmic text the question of the aestheticization of violence in the development of the photographic career of the main character, a career based on recording with the camera the violence of his surroundings. *Ônibus 174* depicts a bus hijacking gone awry, with the major emphasis falling on the aggressive approach of the police, who are more a threat to public safety than the hijackers themselves. A moral point of the film as true-life documentary is that the police will ensure that no suspect taken into captivity will arrive at the stationhouse alive. *Tropa de elite* also deals with police brutality and the indiscriminate violence the police inflict on bystanders. If the elite troop is intended to counter the corruption of the regular police, it becomes in turn an even more efficient instrument of corruption, enhancing exponentially, so to speak, the violence of the regular police. This culture of extreme violence, while abhorrent to some, was met by many audiences with enthusiasm. In fact, the film's rhetoric was designed to ensure approval of the activities and the conduct of the elite squad, whose struggle for survival is glorified by the film. The double violence the elite squad must confront, from drug dealers and from the regular police, mutes interest in the ways in which they duplicate the barbarism of their foes.

The filmic emphasis on Rio is unquestionably tied to the greater overall visibility of Brazil's former capital, which enjoys a fully rounded imaginary both within Brazil and internationally. It would be difficult to believe, however, that there is any lesser level of social violence in São Paulo, including the benchmark phenomenon of the drug trade. There is certainly an immense bibliography of fictional writing and dramatic production that focuses on issues of marginalization and criminality in that city and concomitant corrupt police institutions. What have not been prominent are filmic representations of the same degree of intensity and scope as those that have focused on Rio. São Paulo holds few attractions for the casual tourist, and the large international financial and commercial community that frequents the city moves in a security bubble that insulates it from the everyday issues of the city.[12] Lacking any notable role in an international imaginary regarding Brazil, a Brazilian film production that inevitably must aspire to an international market in order to survive mostly chooses to ignore São Paulo.

Beto Brant's (1965–) *O invasor* is a remarkable exception, and it is important to note from the outset that it does not focus on the slums, does not follow the activities of drug dealers, and does not showcase the blood and gore of police brutality. In fact, the police only figure briefly at the end of the film. Rather, and as befits São Paulo's national and international role, the film tells the story of a business operation, one that is firmly linked to the huckster developmental mentality of the city. This mentality is characterized by financial overextension, blatant displays of consumerism, and a *modus operandi* that is deeply complicitous with the corruption and corner-cutting that grease Brazilian business.[13] Specifically, two members of a business partnership who run a construction firm, the signature enterprise in a city driven by the need to reduplicate itself ceaselessly in urban monoliths, decide to do away with their third partner in order to assume his assets and cover their own shoddy dealings. They hire a hit man, who successfully carries out his assignment. Brant's assassination thriller becomes a horror flick when Anísio, the hit man, played with eerie efficiency by rock musician Paulo Miklos, decides that he wants to pursue a relationship with the punk-style daughter of his victim, probably more out of erotic desire than as means to get to her wealth. He also wants, as a corollary of his active "participation" in the partnership, to take over the business. This involves "invading" a corporative body, both in terms of the business and its associated social institutions, such as the family. Since Anísio would normally be socially and economically excluded from this social milieu, the two remaining partners, understandably, do not desire his further association.

The "rightful order" of the universe is restored at the conclusion of the film, but it is clear that Anísio will now play some role in it. The horror of what should have been a straightforward narrative of a routine partnership restructuring, thanks to the resources of the social system on which São Paulo is grounded, such as easy access to hit men and the assurance of police indifference, arises when Anísio blatantly asserts his decision to violate the social structure and challenge the financial and therefore social security of his one-time employers.[14] In addition, there is the adjunct horror for the spectator in the assertion that someone like Anísio can, in fact, lay a viable claim to the system that he has "serviced," according to the euphemism used in the film. Part of the texture of the film involves the astonishment and, initially, the immobility of the surviving partners in view of the hit man's demand. It is as though he were speaking a foreign language, since the partners are simply bereft of any horizon of intelligibility such that they might grasp what he is getting at. There is a grim humor in all this, even when the spectator has no reason to believe that the reigning social dynamic of São Paulo is any less resistant to assault than the dense array of urban monoliths that are its icons.

The title of the film is a crucial irony with respect to the functioning of the São Paulo social dynamic. Throughout the film, the designation clearly refers to the fashion in which Anísio invades the realms of the social order that should be closed to him, and that he is invading or trespassing.[15] Yet the film opens with an invasion of his social space by the two partners seeking a hit man. Significantly, the film withholds the appearance on screen of the potential hit man. Indeed, we don't see his face until almost a third of the way into the film, after he has completed his "service" and arrives at the partners' office to begin new negotiations with them. Even though we have yet to see him, the two partners recognize him. Before this appearance, we first see the incursion of the two prosperously dressed businessmen, in their expensive car, into the marginal urban space in which Anísio customarily dwells. Throughout the film, there is an eloquent juxtaposition between the exterior spaces of São Paulo, predominantly characterized by a vertiginous jumble of people, vehicles, and street life in general, including screeching traffic, and the double cocoon that the prosperous create for themselves in their workplaces and in their residences and associated refuges, such as fancy restaurants, clubs, boutiques, and the like. In fact, as soon as the two accomplices forward the hit man the money he demands in the ratty bar where they meet, they go off to celebrate at an exclusive gentleman's club. This sort of unsubtle juxtaposition sets the film's narrative up in terms of customary expectations of the social dynamic, which will subsequently be challenged by the outrageous demands Anísio will later make.

If Anísio encounters resistance in his invasion of the workplace of the construction company, he receives a ready reception from the daughter of his murder victims (as it turns out, he has also killed the third businessman's wife). Marina (Mariana Ximenes), the daughter, whose nonchalant ennui leaves her open to the hit man's feral advances, accompanies Anísio in his tour through a city that he is beginning to feel might have something to offer him. As he confesses to her, he always thought the talk of palaces was so much bullshit, and here we see him making himself comfortable in her palatial life. This process allows the camera to portray the details of the life of the privileged in São Paulo, while at the same time it juxtaposes scenes of the marginal spaces to which Anísio had been consigned. For Marina, it is just so much slumming, a world that she cannot be forced to inhabit, but which is interesting as a change of scene. It is Anísio's São Paulo, but also the one he has every intention of renouncing in favour of the social ascendance he thinks lies before him. What is particularly interesting in this sequence is the use of nonprofessional actors drawn from the social milieu Anísio is attempting to abandon, in contrast to the polished professional actors of the world to which he aspires. Filmically, this renders the separation between the worlds in stark dimensions that reinforce the obvious material differences the camera can capture so well. Moreover, such differences are highlighted by erratic camera movements and the heavy rock that suggests the nitty-gritty of marginal social existence.

Meanwhile, things are not working out between the two surviving partners, and one begins to betray the other with, it appears, the connivance of Anísio. The betrayed partner begins to fall apart psychologically, and we see him careening through the São Paulo nightscape, as the rap music on the soundtrack speaks of "suicide capitalism."[16] As the film draws to an unresolved conclusion, he goes to the police, but they only turn him over to his other partner, who is in the company of Anísio. One assumes that the latter two will kill the former, but it is not completely clear whether Anísio will retain his newfound place in the palace or will disappear in the second, impending administrative readjustment. In the course of expounding in detail on the dirty police-abetted dealings of the São Paulo financial and commercial establishment, Brant makes effective use of the backdrop of the city itself, deftly paralleling, juxtaposing, and intersecting the realms of the privileged and the realms of their servants, with the latter ever ready to makes use of the arms of the privileged in order to usurp their power.

ANJOS DA NOITE (*[ANGELS OF THE NIGHT]*, 1987)

Brazil's Rio de Janeiro-based Cinema Novo emerged at the end of the 1950s and came to fruition in the early 1960s, unquestionably as part of the radical populism that was a part of the political and social culture of the day. Although very much inspired by leftist politics and left-wing cinematographic movements in Europe, especially those that opposed the unrelenting commercialism of Hollywood and its foreign imitators, Cinema Novo was able to continue to have a measure of continuity after the right-wing military coup of 1964, perhaps because it never much appealed to the masses, remaining a program of filmmaking by and for intellectuals, and also perhaps because it brought much international attention, and presumably some foreign cash, to Brazilian culture.[17] As antidemocratic tyranny began to wane in Brazil in the late 1970s, with an institutional transition to democracy in 1985, the major names of the Cinema Novo and a subsequent generation they inspired were integral components in the more universally appealing yet strongly socially committed filmmaking that has attracted so much international attention in the past twenty-five years. The filmography of Cinema Novo is often associated with rural themes, the misery of life in many parts of the countryside and the ensuing migration of peasants to Brazil's major cities, as abiding cultural motifs. However, there is an important inventory of urban-focused titles as well.

Although the Cinema Novo in its original form had little interest in the city of São Paulo, Luís Sérgio Person's *São Paulo, S.A.*, discussed above, has been considered part of a "second wave" of Cinema Novo that includes representations of the country's largest city. Yet, it is not until the return to democracy and the sort of social analysis film that came with it that we can point to major films set in São Paulo that deal with social issues. These films represent an analysis that is far more varied and not as politically homogeneous as the films of the Cinema Novo; they are also not above reifying social types or ignoring political implications, or, for that matter, even offering happy endings of a sort. Overall, these films are more interested in portraying the complexities of urban life, including a full array of details concerning the marginal and the previously unspoken, than they are in contributing to dogmatic positions.

Anjos da noite (1987) by Wilson Barros (1948–1992) shows vividly the break with the conventions of the original Rio de Janeiro-based Cinema Novo in the carnivalesque and pastiche nature of the plot, the many instances of metacinematographic self-reflexivity, and the inclusion of abundant U.S. popular culture references, including a Fred Astaire and Cyd Charisse-style dance sequence under the night-time glare from downtown buildings, cars, and streetlamps.[18] At the end the camera pulls back in a moment of self-reference to include an image of the banks of powerful lights set up to film the sequence.[19] Yet what is most striking about *Anjos da noite* is the way in which it is essentially a queer film, not just in its references to homosexuals and transvestites and the depiction of homoerotic desire, but in the way in which identities, sexual and otherwise, are unstable and situational.[20] One of the two best sex scenes in the film (the other is passionately interracial) involves the character of the has-been film star Marta Brum, played brilliantly by Marília Pêra, having sex with a gay escort, as she diverts his affections from his sometime male partner.[21]

Except for the film's ending, which takes place early in the morning of the next day, *Anjos da noite* is a braided series of images of the nightscape of the city. Moving in and out of various plot threads, the film literally pans the city repeatedly as approximately a dozen important characters move in and out of private spaces such as residences, cabarets, back rooms, and the street, in a movement through the city demanded by their pursuit of pleasure and livelihoods built on the sins of the night. The only significant extended take on the city at night is the aforementioned dance sequence and its build-up, as the actress and the taxi-boy negotiate the encounter of their bodies.[22] The film's action takes place on the all-important Avenida Paulista, the city's, and the continent's, financial centre. The dance sequence was filmed in the patio beneath the Museu de Arte de São Paulo (São Paulo Art Museum), located on the Paulista, as well as in the side streets off the Paulista and the chic and fast-paced environs of the Jardins area located just south of the Paulista.

If there is a unifying motif in the film, aside from the gay escort who interacts with all of the other characters, underscoring Barros's interest in capturing the prominence of gay/queer culture in the city, it is a young sociologist who is ostensibly engaged in a research project in which some of the characters are involved. Sociologist and escort come together at the end of the film, meeting on a park bench in the early sunlight. After agreeing that it is all very hard but worth it – life in the big city, one assumes – they separate after having shared only their first names. The escort predicts that they will find each other again because the city is "so small...." As the film closes, we see the sociologist walking along the Avenida Paulista, caught in the hustle and bustle of the city as it awakens to its sober daytime face.

Barros's ending is "happy" only in the sense that it underscores the necessary continuity of life and the way in which the individual will, in the end, likely find some way to survive. There is no socially or politic-ally anchored message in *Anjos da noite* because the director's primary interest lies in constructing a panorama of lives in the city at night. The various forms of self-reflexivity in the film, aside from providing some transient moments of humour, stand in juxtaposition to the controlled and distancing cinematographic approach of the Cinema Novo paradigm where viewers are encouraged to understand that what they are viewing is life in the process of being lived and that they are witnessing it through the privileged eye of the camera.[23] This identification of film with reality was reinforced by the documentary nature of many sequences and the frequent use of nonprofessional actors. Barros could well have filmed São Paulo at night in the same vein, taking his viewer into usually closed or less accessible realms of the denizens of the night and dwelling on the morbid and the scabrous, all with the aim of denouncing the essentially perverse nature of the nighttime face of a city whose much touted day-time face is that of the aggressive enterprise of modernity.

Barros's lack of interest in denouncing the nocturnal culture that takes place in the same spaces as the enterprise of the city's waking hours constitutes an eschewal of the moralistic tone of so much previous Brazilian filmmaking about social conditions. To be sure, the representation of many of the events of the night, such as sexual exploitation and police brutality, cannot be said to be represented in a naive or jejune fashion. Barros's point, rather, seems to be an adaptation to São Paulo of one of the famous apothegms of Nelson Rodrigues, who antedated him in describing a full range of the social life of Rio de Janeiro: "A vida como ela é": life as it is.[24] In the process, Barros has given us one of the most intriguing and playful films ever made in Brazil about São Paulo.

CONCLUDING REMARKS

The history of São Paulo in Brazilian film begins with Adalberto Kemeny's and Rudolf Rex Lustig's 1929 *São Paulo, sinfonia da metrópole* [*São Paulo, Symphony of a Metropolis*], modelled after Walter Ruttman's legendary *Berlin: Die Sinfonie der Großstadt* ([*Berlin: The Symphony of a Large Town*], 1927). The Brazilian film is much more than a propaganda paean to the icons of the commercial, financial, and industrial progress that had become the order of the day in the 1920s in São Paulo. Along with dynamic and positive images of the city are others that allude to the underbelly of marginalization, including the prison population. Kemeny and Lustig established the basis for scrutinizing the city visually and in correlating the unique material phenomena associated with it with lived human experience. Such a correlation is immediately apparent in the first film dealt with here, Luís Sérgio Person's *São Paulo, S.A.*, although by 1965 it was possible to refer to the alienated mechanization of individual life imposed by the city's structures of modernity.

Amácio Mazzaropi's comedy *O puritano da Rua Augusta*, also from 1965, takes place along one of the major commercial and residential thoroughfares of the period and turns on the inevitable social conflicts provoked by migration into the city from the countryside, instigated by the demands of industrialization and the inevitable commitments to new forms of social life brought by modernity. If alienation and social conflict are integral parts of modernity, corruption and cynical human relations are portrayed in Beto Brant's 2002 film *O invasor* as unquestionable correlatives of life in the fast lane as it is modelled by the city's privileged upper classes. Finally, Wilson Barros's *Anjos da noite*, made during the 1980s return to institutional democracy, departs from the rhetoric of the city as a destructive monster, to assume a more benevolent, yet nonetheless unflinchingly honest, discourse on the human topology of the city by night. The night is crucially present in *O invasor*, but in *Anjos da noite* it becomes fully invested as something like the alternative universe of São Paulo by day as the business centre of Latin America. Let me repeat: these four films, while not a representative sample of films on São Paulo, much less an exhaustive list, provide a window for understanding how, from the 1960s to the present, that megalopolis has functioned as a laboratory for Brazilian urban life.

WORKS CITED

Abreu, Nuno César. 2000. Mazzaropi, Amácio. In *Enciclopedia do cinema brasileiro*, org. Fernão Ramos and Luiz Felipe Miranda, 366–67. São Paulo: Editora SENAC São Paulo.

Araujo, Inácio. 1998. *Noite vazia*; Empty Night. In *Cinema brasileiro: The Films from Brazil*. Ed. Amir Labaki. 48–50. São Paulo: Publifolha.

Autran, Arthur. 2000. Wilson Barros. In *Enciclopédia de cinema brasileiro*, org. Fernão Ramos and Luiz Felipe Miranda. 49–50. São Paulo: Editora SENAC São Paulo.

Barnard, Timothy, and Peter Rist, eds. 1996. *South American Cinema: A Critical Filmography 1915–1994*. New York: Garland.

Barros, Wilson. 1987. *Anjos da noite* [script]. Porto Alegre, R.S.: Tchê!

Bernardet, Jean-Claude. 1995. Trajectory of an Oscillation. In *Brazilian Cinema*. Ed. Randal Johnson and Robert Stam, 281–89. Expanded ed. New York: Columbia Uniersity Press.

Bueno, Eva Paulino. 1999. *O artista do povo; Mazzaropi e Jeca Tatu no cinema do Brasil*. Maringá, Paraná: Eduem, Editora da Universidade Estadual de Maringá.

Caldeira, Teresa P.R. 2000. *City of Walls; Crime, Segregation, and Citizenship in São Paulo*. Berkeley: University of California Press.

Catani, Afrânio Mendes. 1997. Person, Luís Sérgio. In *Enciclopédia do cinema brasileiro*, org. Fernão Ramos and Luiz Felipe Miranda. 425–27. São Paulo: Editora Senac.

Cinema Novo and Beyond. 1998. New York: Museum of Modern Art.

Dennison, Stephanie, and Lisa Shaw. 2004. *Popular Cinema in Brazil, 1930–2001*. Manchester: Manchester University Press.

Foster, David William. 1999. *Gender and Society in Contemporary Brazilian Cinema*. Austin: University of Texas Press.

———. 2005. Downtown in São Paulo with Hildegard Rosenthal's Camera. *Luso-Brazilian Review* 42, no. 1: 118–35.

Johnson, Randal. 1984. *Cinema Novo x 5: Masters of Contemporary Brazilian Film*. Austin: University of Texas Press.

Johnson, Randal, and Robert Stam. 1995. *Brazilian Cinema*. 2nd ed. New York: Columbia University Press.

Moreno, Antônio. 2001. *A personagem homossexual no cinema brasileiro*. Rio de Janeiro: Ministerio da Cultura, FUNARTE; EdUFF, Editora da Universidade Federal Fluminense.

Nagib, Lúcia. 2004. Is This Really Brazil? The Dystopian City of *The Trespasser*. *New Cinemas: Journal of Contemporary Film* 2, no. 1: 17–28.

Peixoto, Nelson Brissac. 1998. *Anjos da noite*: Night Angels. In *Cinema brasileiro: The Films from Brazil*. Ed. Amir Labaki, 163–67. São Paulo: Publifolha.

Perlongher, Néstor Osvaldo. 1987. *O negócio do michê: prostituição viril em São Paulo*. São Paulo: Editora Brasiliense.

Reichenbach, Carlos. 1998. *São Paulo, S.A.*: São Paulo, S.A. In *Cinema brasileiro: The Films from Brazil*. Ed. Amir Labaki, 51–3. São Paulo: Publifolha.

Rodrigues, Nelson. 1992. *A vida como ela é--: o homem fiel e outros contos*. Sel. Ruy Castro. São Paulo: Companhia de Letras.

Travero, Antonio. 2007. Migrations of Cinema: Italian Neorealism and Brazilian Cinema. In *Italian Neorealism and Global Cinema*. Ed. Laura E. Ruberto and Kristi M. Wilson, 165–86. Detroit: Wayne State University Press.

Trelles Plazaola, Luis. 1989. *South American Cinema: Dictionary of Film Makers*. Río Piedras, P.R.: Editorial de la Universidad de Puerto Rico.

FILMS

Anjos da noite. [*Angels of the Night*]. Directed by Wilson Barros. Manchete Video, 1987.

Berlin: die Sinfonie der Großstadt [*Berlin: The Symphony of a Large Town*]. Directed by Walter Ruttmann. Fox Film Corporation, 1927.

Cidade de Deus [*City of God*]. Directed by Fernando Meirelles and Kátia Lund. Buena Vista International, 2002.

Invasor, o. Directed by Beto Brant. Artkino Pictures, 2002.

Ônibus 174 [*Bus 174*]. Directed by José Padilha and Felipe Lacerda. DVD. Hart Sharp Video, 2002.

Puritano da Rua Augusta, o. Directed by Amácio Mazzaropi. Reserva Especial, 1965.

São Paulo, S.A. Directed by Luis Sérgio Person. Videofilmes, 1965.

São Paulo, sinfonia da metrópole [*São Paulo, a Metropolitan Symphony*]. Directed by Adalberto Kemeny and Rudolf Rex Lustig. Columbia Pictures, 1929.

Tropa de elite [*Elite Squad*]. Directed by José Padilha. Universal Pictures do Brasil, 2007.

NOTES

1   By no means does this selection intend to be taken as a representative sample. Rather, I would insist that these are four particularly outstanding texts that might be complemented by a few more, but that should not be understood to constitute a random sampling, with each film representing some sort of major aspect of the city. I do not know what a series of dominant themes for the city might be, and thus no attempt is made to attach these films to such a series.

2   Some sources write out the acronym S.A., which means Sociedade Anónima, the Brazilian equivalent of Inc. In the context of the film, the subtitle becomes ironic, since it encompasses both the business meaning, as well as the literal meaning of "anonymous society," which is one of the ways in which Person's film portrays modern São Paulo. Unfortunately, Travero omits the film from his discussion of the influence of Italian neorealism in Brazil.

3   Reichenbach's short commentary on the film refers to the "progresso perverso e desordenado que assolou a metrópole de 1957 a 1961" ["perverse and disorderly progress that was a scourge to the metropolis from 1957 to 1961"].

4   The transition from European (especially German) economic dependence to American dependence as a consequence of Brazil's alliance with the United States is the basis of Chico Buarque de Holanda's 1978 play, *A ópera do malandro*, made into a film of the same name by Ruy Guerra in 1986. See the analysis by Foster (1999, 37–45).

5   The reference is to Sloan Wilson's 1955 novel, usually considered the paradigmatic representation of the American "company man."

6   There is a certain nostalgia for the Germanic in the film that must remain unexplored here. Yet both the Volkswagen and the Karmann-Ghia were being made in Brazil, as the sticker on the back window of the latter clearly announces, and Carlos mocks his employer for driving a "monstrous" imported American car.

7   For example, Trelles Plazaola does not include him in his registry of South American filmmakers, while none of his thirty-plus films makes its way into *South American Cinema*. On the other hand, Nuno César Abreu provides a superb encyclopedia entry on Mazzaropi's career. Mazzaropi is also discussed by Dennison and Shaw (149–55) and *ad passim*.

8   As Dennison and Shaw point out, the highbrow Cinema Novo is tied to Rio de Janeiro (141), whereas Mazzaropi is solidly a product of the state and the city of São Paulo.

9   Hildegard Rosenthal (1913–90), a Swiss-born German photographer, produced some three thousand images of São Paulo in the ten-year period from her arrival in Brazil in the late 1930s through the 1940s. One of her best known images is that of the *camarão*, the shrimp-coloured tram that carried passengers in and out of the financial and commercial center of São Paulo. See Foster (2005, 118).

10 There is a very clear consciousness in the film of the deleterious influence of

American values and their corruption of the traditional Brazilian way of life that Punduroso represents. He at one point demands the suppression of linguistic tokens in English in favour of "speaking Portuguese." At the same time, there is a clear juxtaposition in the film between the father's backlands pronunciation of Portuguese (a characteristic that Mazzaropi exploited over and over again in his films, such that his Jeca Tatu was a veritable case study of non-urban or pre-urban speech) and that of his city-dwelling children, who manifest all of the linguistic hipness of the day.

11   Dennison and Shaw relate Mazzaropi's persona as an actor to the tradition of the circus clown in Brazilian culture (15).

12   See Caldeira's effect metaphor of "a city of walls."

13   In one of the few critical interpretations of the film, Lúcia Nagib argues that Brant's film is primarily valuable for the ethical stance it takes against the privileges of a ruling economic class at the expense of extensive surrounding poverty. She is particularly interested in the aesthetics of the film, in its visual contrasts and how they are presented by the camera and enhanced by the important role of music in the film. Because she views the film in terms of the representation of modern Brazil as a whole, she is less interested in Brant's specific choice to locate his action within the hegemonic social dynamic of São Paulo, which is what I focus on here.

14   Whether or not this is true, the implication here is that the police will pursue crimes committed by social inferiors against social superiors, but will not pursue crimes carried out in the other direction, nor between social equals of whatever class unless there is a higher consideration, such as an upper-class victim who turns out to have more powerful allies than an upper-class perpetrator. This social dynamic is very much operant in a film like *Tropa de elite*, where multiple social players are involved (particularly a police unit that is socially superior to the regular police), affording a veritable *ars combinatoria* of the power relations involved.

15   The official English-language title of the film is *The Trespasser*.

16   *O invasor* is an anthology of São Paulo rap music, some of it by Paulo Miklos, who plays the part of Ansínio. In addition to Miklos's own music, tracks by Rica Amabis, Daniel Ganjaman, Sabotage, and Tejo are featured prominently. Dennison and Shaw make passing reference to the importance of music in *O invasor* as exemplary of the use of popular singers and musicians in contemporary Brazilian filmmaking (231).

17   Two major sources on the Cinema Novo are Johnson and *Cinema Novo and Beyond*.

18   Although Barros was an important figure in the Brazilian film industry, *Anjos da noite* is the only feature-length film he made. See the encyclopedia entry on his work by Arthur Autran, who notes that he was a key figure in the São Paulo incarnation of the Cinema Novo.

Peixoto (165–66) identifies the inspiration for the dance scene in Vincente Minelli's *The Band Wagon* (1953), where the Astaire-Charisse dance scene takes place in Central Park. Peixoto also speaks of other Hollywood reprises in the film and a certain noir dimension.

19 Despite the prizes it won and the critical acclaim it received, *Anjos da noite* is not mentioned in Johnson and Stam's *Brazilian Cinema*, perhaps because it breaks too radically from the sort of social-commitment filmmaking that prevails in their study.

20 The film is referenced ten times in Moreno's study of the "homosexual" character in Brazilian filmmaking, although it is never analyzed in any satisfactory way.

21 Marília Pêra tied with Betty Faria for the 1987 Gramado award for best actress. Faria's film, *Anjos de arrabalde [Angels from the Outskirts]*, directed by Carlos Reichenbach, also involved São Paulo, but in a dirty-realist fashion. Note that in *Anjos da noite*, the actress's name, Marta Brum, is an oblique reference to the significant Jewish community in São Paulo. This is one more indication of Barros's desire to accurately capture the social demographics of the city.

22 See Néstor Perlongher's famous study of the taxi-boys (*os michês*) of São Paulo and the gay urban culture they represent.

23 In addition to the delight of seeing the camera pull back to reveal the lights necessary to film the dance sequence, one particularly hilarious example is when, in the actress's boudoir, the escort reaches for her breast and she puts up her hand to block the gaze of the camera, as though on an actual set she were objecting to the way in which the director was constructing an unfavourable representation of her body. This gesture is particularly effective because it interrupts the mood of the scene of erotic foreplay to remind us that we are witnessing the staged action of a film. The fact that Pêra strategically overacts her role throughout the film can also be seen as a reminder that it is a film, not life, that we are viewing.

In terms of a Cinema Novo film on the night, one thinks of Walter Hugo Khouri's *Noite vazia* (1964), set in Rio de Janeiro, which includes the first lesbian scene in a Brazilian film, although hardly with the sense of queer *jouissance* found in Barros's *Anjos da noite*. Indeed, sex in *Noite vazia* is a metonym for the wasted and empty lives of the two couples who are the main characters of the film (see the discussion of the film by Araujo).

24 This was the general title given to the dozens of episodes of television series in the 1990s based on Rodrigues's famous chronicles about life in Rio (see Rodrigues).

BODIES SO CLOSE, AND YET SO FAR: SEEING JULIÁN HERNÁNDEZ'S *EL CIELO DIVIDIDO* THROUGH GILLES DELEUZE'S FILM THEORY

Gerard Dapena
Bard College

Although almost twenty-five years have passed since the publication in France of Gilles Deleuze's landmark two-volume study of the cinematographic image, *Cinema 1: The Movement-Image* and *Cinema 2: The Time-Image*, the impact of Deleuze's film theory has only recently become apparent in the field of Anglophone cinema studies. In 1997, David N. Rodowick wrote *Gilles Deleuze's Time Machine*, the first English-language study of Deleuze's film theory. *The Brain is the Screen*, a collection of essays edited by Gregory Flaxman, appeared in 2000, making a case for the currency of Deleuze's ideas. Since then, a proliferation of books on Deleuze's film theory testifies to the many possibilities that his ideas can bring to our understanding of the aesthetics of film and the nature of the cinematic experience. The current interest in Deleuze stems from a perception that psychoanalytic and post-structuralist film theories are no longer sufficient; for a growing number of film scholars, Deleuze stands as a viable alternative. Patricia Pisters, for instance, has stated that she wants to find out what other things one can see when one works with Deleuze instead of more traditional conceptions of the cinematographic apparatus (Pisters, 218). Along with Pisters, Steven Shaviro, Barbara M. Kennedy, Anna Powell, Laura U. Marks, David Martin-Jones, and Martine Beugnet make up a core group of writers who have brought Deleuze's original insights to bear upon the cinema of today.

Although Deleuze wrote very little about contemporary cinema, András Bálint Kovács argues that it is precisely in postmodern cinema and the new digital audiovisual culture that one may find the most fruitful developments and realizations of Deleuze's ideas: "What Deleuze underlines and conceptualizes vis-à-vis modernism are the very features that the digital culture of the 1990s has blown up and popularized to incredible proportions: namely, nonlinear, crystalline-structured narration, the coincidence of mutually exclusive worlds, and the constitutive role of the 'any-spaces-whatever'" (Kovács, 169). Martine Beugnet writes, and I agree with her, that some of the most exciting forms of filmmaking today – what she calls "the cinema of sensation" – are precisely those works which build on and develop the features Deleuze theorizes in his cinema books, combining narrative models with elements borrowed from modernist and experimental film in ways that undermine realism and representation, privileging instead an encounter with the materiality of film (Beugnet, 9).

None of the aforementioned authors, though, have much to say about contemporary Latin American cinema or whether the resurgent filmmaking scenes in countries like Mexico, Argentina, or Brazil might be producing movies that either embody Deleuzian ideals or could be read profitably through Deleuze's theories. Although Deleuze discusses the work of Glauber Rocha and the films from Luis Buñuel's Mexican period in *Cinema 2: The Time-Image*, overall Deleuzian thought has had only a moderate impact in the area of Latin American cinema studies.[1] I believe, however, that Deleuzian film theory can be a fruitful tool for the understanding of at least one recent Latin American film. In this article, I look at *El cielo dividido* [*Broken Sky*, 2006], the second feature by Mexican filmmaker Julián Hernández. By bringing *El cielo dividido* into a dialog with Deleuze's ideas, I intend to show what this film might have to say about new subjectivities and sexual identities as they are constituted in a world of time and sensation, of materiality and immanence. With its meandering, nonchronological narrative, its shuttling between the actual and the virtual, and its dilution of action into primarily optical and acoustic situations, *El cielo dividido* strikes me as a film that realizes to an unusual degree Deleuze's concept of an emergent cinema invested in the representation of time, affect, and sensation. By viewing *El cielo dividido* through the prism of Deleuze's film theory, I spotlight those aspects that make Hernández's film such a unique and revelatory experience: its rich and vibrant visual surface in a perpetual state of re-composition by the frequent use of racking focus, varying intensities of colour and light and intriguing counterpoint of image and sound; its depiction of human bodies as objects oscillating between motion and rest, in a constellation of shifting attitudes and postures, but also as entities gripped by and acting upon sexual desires; its concern with time and the experience of duration; and its meditation on the power of memory.

El cielo dividido follows Hernández's remarkable debut, the independent production *Mil nubes de paz cercan el cielo, amor, jamás acabarás de ser amor* [*A Thousand Clouds of Peace*, 2004]. Shot in black and white, the latter film recounts, in a style that is both lyrical and gritty, the story of Gerardo (Juan Carlos Ortuño), an adolescent boy searching for love in the wake of a failed relationship. One of the protagonists of Hernández's second feature is another adolescent named Gerardo (Miguel Ángel Hoppe); in *El cielo dividido*, he begins a love affair with a fellow student, Jonás (Fernando Arroyo). The young men meet on their urban college campus and immediately become lovers, but one night Jonás is approached and kissed by a young stranger on the dance floor of a discotheque; the stranger then disappears, leaving Jonás haunted by that kiss and the sudden conviction that in this ephemeral moment he has met his true soul mate. Gerardo becomes increasingly despondent over Jonás' detachment; at the same time, he is cruised by Sergio (Alejandro Rojo), a working-class youth. At first, Gerardo, obsessed with Jonás, takes little notice of Sergio's presence, but later yields to his advances during an escapade in a sex club. Little by little, Sergio's affection wins Gerardo over; after attempting for the last time to rekindle his dying romance with Jonás, Gerardo begins a relationship with Sergio. It is now Jonás' turn to suffer, as Gerardo's departure, which feels liberating at first, eventually fills him with an unremitting sense of loss.

This brief summary of *El cielo dividido*'s plot does not reveal the film's textual density, sensuous surface, and formal complexity, nor does it do justice to its philosophical undercurrents or convey its audacious treatment of gay desire.[2] One of the most explicit Spanish-language films to deal with this topic to date, both in terms of its depiction of physical intimacy between the male characters and its exploration of a wide range of feelings and emotions within a homosexual relationship, *El cielo dividido* approaches its subject matter without a trace of didacticism, moralizing, or guilt. However, the film can be a difficult experience for audiences unaccustomed to the narrative demands and temporal complexities of art cinema. Its running time of 140 minutes might feel even longer on account of the film's measured pace, minimal dialog, lack of intense motion, and restrained performances.[3]

Deleuze's cinema books describe a trajectory whereby, at a certain moment in history, films that privilege the representation of time over the depiction of action appear. In the preface to *Cinema 1: The Movement-Image*, Deleuze claims that he is not writing a history of the cinema, but rather a taxonomy whose goal is the classification of images and signs. Following in the footsteps of Charles Sanders Peirce's semiotic theory of signs, Deleuze comes up with his own terminology for a variety of visual and aural events that can be experienced in the course of a film projection; for instance, he speaks of *opsigns, sonsigns, tactisigns,* and *chronosigns* (Deleuze 1986, 18).[4] He also turns to the writings of Henri Bergson, in particular to Bergson's emphasis on perception, time, and memory. In *Matter and Memory*, Bergson asserts that any philosophical debate over the nature of the world must acknowledge that "we can only grasp things in the form of images"; therefore "we must state the problem in terms of images, and of images alone" (Bergson, 26). As their titles indicate, Deleuze's cinema books share with Bergson this concentration on images.

Deleuze devotes the first volume, *Cinema 1: The Movement-Image*, to a discussion of what he calls "the movement-image," the dominant mode in classical cinema and a concept whose invention he credits to Bergson. This category establishes "the absolute identity of image and movement" (Deleuze 1986, 2, 59). Under this paradigm, the representation of time is subordinated to and derives from movement. In the aftermath of World War II, however, Deleuze claims that the cinema underwent a series of important changes which gave rise to a new type of image: the time-image. Characters now find themselves in situations that preclude any possibility of action or reaction. Consequently, "the sensory-motor link is broken" and the characters are "no longer in a sensory-motor situation, but in a purely optical and aural situation" (Deleuze 1997, 51). This postwar cinema is a visionary one, as characters become seers rather than agents and "the viewer's problem becomes 'What is there to see in the image'? (and not now 'What are we going to see in the next image?')" (Deleuze 1989, 272). Editing patterns in these post-classical cinematic narratives also change, as shots become unlinked and autonomous. Motivation and causality are often weak and action can grind to a halt; the experience of time no longer derives from movement but is expressed in direct fashion, particularly through shots that foreground an experience of duration and depict states of boredom, acts of waiting, feelings of exhaustion in the midst of inaction (Deleuze 1997, 53). But Deleuze also remarks how time in these postwar films is interiorized rather than exteriorized; the time-image dramatizes movement into memory, into thought, into the brain.

Among the gamut of *chronosigns*, Deleuze recognizes the existence of two possible time-images: one grounded in the past (the virtual image), the other in the present (the actual image). For the time-image to exist, he states that the actual image and the virtual image must enter into a relation, constituting a double-sided image – a crystal image – built on their perpetual exchange and ultimate indiscernibility (Deleuze 1989, 98, 213–14, 273). Deleuze stresses the ambiguous nature of this crystal-image: "Instead of a linear development, we get a circuit in which the two images are constantly chasing one another round a point where real and imaginary become indistinguishable" (Deleuze 1996, 52).

For Angelo Restivo, the passage from the movement-image to the time-image signals the birth of modernist cinema. Restivo writes, "The demise of the action-image is what allowed the cinema finally to realize itself; liberated from the grip of narrative, the cinema was able ... to allow that which is seen to become charged with that which is unseen" (175). While Hernández has acknowledged the influence of modernist filmmakers like Marguerite Duras, Robert Bresson, Pier Paolo Pasolini, and Rainer W. Fassbinder, *El cielo dividido* is a work whose aesthetic concerns and narrative structure reflect and exemplify more contemporary audiovisual trends. The film observes at first a degree of linearity but then takes on an increasingly directionless flow, turning into the kind of open-ended, multi-directional and kaleidoscopic narrative that has become fashionable of late. However, unlike the films of another contemporary Mexican director, Alejandro González Iñárritu, which likewise experiment with fragmented narrative structures, *El cielo dividido* is much closer to the spirit of what Deleuze understands as the cinema of the time-image. For Rodowick, the latter is primarily an image of memory; in order to reproduce the way memory works, it entails dislocations of narrative time that establish nonlinear and nonchronological relations between past and present, resulting in contingent narratives of a multi-faceted and contradictory temporal dimension. In the cinema of the time-image, it is difficult to decide at any given moment between past and present, what might be a virtual image or memory and what might be an actual image (Rodowick, 88, 95). *El cielo dividido*'s concern with memory and the imbrication of different time registers differs from the scrambled nature of González Iñárritu's postmodern narratives, which intertwine actions and events in different spatial and temporal registers in order to expose their interconnectivity, but never aim for or achieve the level of indeterminacy of Deleuze's time-image nor are particularly preoccupied with conveying an experience of duration, of time lived and felt.

The representation of time takes on a subjective cast after the first hour of *El cielo dividido*, ushering in the domain of the crystal-image. On the one hand, memories of past events invade and supersede the present while, on the other, the narrative shifts between inner thought and exterior reality. In a couple of sequences, Jonás intrudes upon Sergio and Gerardo, but the spectator is left in a state of uncertainty about the nature of the scene (reality or fantasy?) or its location in narrative space or time. At later points in the film, the division between the imaginary and the real becomes even more unstable. Does Gerardo actually enter Jonás' bedroom, strip naked, and initiate sex or are we in the presence of a dream, a wish fulfillment, or a memory? And whose memory is it? In these sequences, rational time has yielded to the time of desire; as the latter imposes its own economy, the narrative loses itself in detours where the actual and the virtual can no longer be separated.

It is necessary to bear in mind, however, that Deleuze sees the time-image as an emergent potential for the cinema. Rodowick notes that even Deleuze was only able to offer a few examples of films purely governed by the time-image; instead, mixed or hybrid forms, where the movement-image and the time-image coexist and their boundaries remain fluid or indistinct, predominate (Rodowick, 89). *El cielo dividido* exemplifies this hybrid condition, with extended long takes displaying the highly kinetic camerawork that characterizes many contemporary films. However, instead of merely instilling in the viewer a sense of urgency and motion, the film's autonomous pans and tracking motions actually confront the viewer with their unfolding in time. Their significance lies less in the communication of meaning than in the way they infuse the traversal of space with the imprint of time.

In these sequences, bodies are highly mobile. In his second visit to the dance-club scene, for instance, Jonás is standing to the left of the screen; the camera tracks to the right for a stretch of time, parallel to the bar counter, and finally tilts downwards, coming to rest on Jonás, now sitting at a table on the right of the screen. The narrative's temporal freedom is equally startling. Temporal ellipses stand in tension with 360° camera movements that maintain the integrity and continuity of the spaces they travel through, making for complex and ambiguous representations of time. Thus, the camera will travel around a room in a circle or depart from one corner of the frame and travel past another adjacent space only to retrace its steps back to its point of origin; in the meantime, night has now turned to day or bodies in one spot and posture have shifted to another. Through its leisurely and self-conscious traversal of space, Hernández's camera achieves what Deleuze calls a "temporalization of the image"; its physical movements primarily register displacements in time (Deleuze 1989, 39).

Some of the film's most striking tracking shots occur in the disco-theque sequence. The camera circles Gerardo and Jonás as they dance in an embrace to a slow ballad. As the music speeds up to a techno beat, the camera follows Gerardo as he leaves Jonás on the dance floor and heads to the bar; climbing the steps to the upper level, he bypasses Sergio, who has been eyeing him from a distance. A number of swiveling camera movements, combined with readjustments of focal length, reposition Sergio and Gerardo, as the latter becomes aware of the former's intense gaze.

Fig. 1. Sergio (Alejandro Rojo, left) and Gerardo (Miguel Ángel Hoppe, middle). Courtesy of Jesús Torres Torres/Imcine/Mil nubes–Cine.

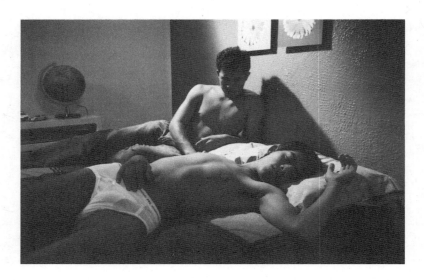

Fig. 2. Jonás (Fernando Arroyo, back) and Gerardo (Miguel Ángel Hoppe, front). Courtesy of Jesús Torres Torres/Imcine/Mil nubes–Cine.

The awkward exchange of glances, the simmering sexual tension, the unspoken feelings between the characters: all of these achieve prominence as a result of the manner in which the camera movements and the long takes emphasize the temporal nature of the actions depicted. Later on, as Gerardo stumbles into Sergio in a sex club, the camera circles and trails both men as they cruise each other, moving towards and away from the object of their respective desire in a tentative *pas de deux* that spins webs of erotic energy in time.

Other pans and tracking shots weave labyrinth-like spaces for this free reign of eros: in the library sequence, for instance, Jonás and Gerardo engage in a prolonged game of hide and seek among the book stacks, under the watchful eye of Sergio, perched on a ladder. Rodowick points out that in the cinema of the time-image, protagonists no longer act, but wander and observe (76). In the first half of the film, Sergio, who frequently gazes at Gerardo and Jonás wandering across the screen, takes on the role of passive seer. In the second half of the film, Jonás comes to occupy this position, as he spies on Gerardo and Sergio from afar.

Hernández also evokes the experience of duration by means of static long takes. Early in the film, as Gerardo and Jonás make love for the first time, a stationary camera shoots their different sexual positions from a removed distance; the lack of music, which allows occasional traffic sounds and other street noises to filter in, heightens the feeling of time unfolding. As Jonás's passion for Gerardo cools, the two boys spend long, uncomfortable stretches of time in silence, lying side by side in bed. Other scenes similarly drained of action – Jonás riding on a bus, Gerardo waiting at a bus stop for Jonás or on a overpass for Sergio, Jonás waiting in a club for the apparition of the stranger – generate boredom and anxiety from the characters' experience of the banality of time.

In *What is Philosophy?*, Deleuze and Félix Guattari assert that art is the language of sensation: "percepts, affects and blocks of sensation take the place of language" (Deleuze and Guattari, 176). Flaxman notes that for Deleuze "the image is not restricted to what we 'see'.... [r]ather the image is a collection of sensations." What Deleuze prizes about sensations, according to Flaxman, is that they "possess the capacity to derange the everyday, to short-circuit the mechanism of common sense, and thus to catalyze a different kind of thinking; indeed, sensations are encountered at a threshold we might call the 'thinkable'" (Flaxman, 12).

At first, Deleuze's references to a cinema of sensation might strike us as paradoxical, for the cinematic experience, after all, is predicated upon the spectator's contact with the immaterial play of fleeting light and shadows upon the flatness of a screen. Properly speaking, the bodies, objects, and sounds that our sensory organs perceive in a movie theatre are disembodied entities, lacking in substance and veracity. And yet, moviegoers often respond viscerally to moving images which Shaviro aptly describes as "at once intense and impalpable." Indeed, in his book, *The Cinematic Body*, Shaviro convincingly argues for the ways in which cinematic images and sounds can bring about "an intensification and disarticulation of bodily sensation" (Shaviro, 25–26, 51–52).[5]

Shaviro underscores that in *The Time-Image* Deleuze propounded a film theory built on the psychophysiology of the moving image, revelling in its powers of seduction and shock. Our visual contact with the bodies onscreen reminds us of our own bodily dimensions. Cinematic images arouse, sadden, frighten, disturb, and disgust us. We are immersed in affect and flooded with physical sensations that might be pleasurable or overwhelming. Deleuze speaks of *opsigns*, *sonsigns*, and *tactisigns*, each of which are capable of producing moments of intolerable beauty and shattering emotional intensity (1986, 18). In a discussion of Sergei Eisenstein's montage techniques and his aesthetic and conceptual reliance on shock, Deleuze most clearly articulates this connection between cinema and sensation, envisioning a state where, as spectators, "we can no longer say 'I see, hear,' but I FEEL, 'totally physiological sensation'" (Deleuze 1989, 58).

For Barbara Kennedy, Deleuze's main achievement lies precisely in the way his theories reclaim the need to examine the processes by which the materiality of the filmic image interacts with the materiality of the viewer, offering a model of subjectivity that recuperates the important role that sensation and affect play in our cinematic encounters (Kennedy, 16). As Shaviro and Kennedy have argued, what is significant about Deleuze is that he posits a shift away from signification – what a film might mean to a viewer – to sensation, materiality and affect – what a film does to the viewer. Deleuze's spectator, as Anna Powell points out, "does not exist as a separate entity, but is subsumed in the film event as part of it." Powell reminds us that "our eyes are embedded and embodied in flesh ... they feed our other senses." Vision, then, becomes grounded

Bodies So Close, and Yet So Far

in "the materiality of the agitated flesh"; it assaults our senses in a way that "thrusts us into the mysterious life of the body" (Powell, 258). In this scenario, audiovisual forms and human bodies share in a mutually dynamic experience of transformation: spectators become both movement and image, and the screen and the brain merge into what Deleuze calls an assemblage.

The aesthetics of sensation that Deleuze adumbrates gives right of place to the intense, even visceral responses that moviegoers have when stimulated by the material dimensions of the filmic projection. In this regard, *El cielo dividido* continuously positions its viewers as bodies impacted by waves of sound, colour, and light, by tracking shots that traverse the widescreen frame, or by the intensely carnal sight of bodies, often in tight close-ups that magnify faces in the throes of orgasm or sorrow. The viewer is drawn into the characters' psychological turmoil and invited to share not only their emotional journey but also their physical ecstasies. For instance, Hernández resorts to several 360° camera movements in order to register moments of convulsive emotions and shock. Early in the film, as Gerardo walks across campus, he comes to a stop the moment he eyes Jonás; the camera spins around him 360°, registering the impact of the encounter and, by extension, implicating the viewer in this vertiginous desire. As a visual device, it contributes little to our understanding of narrative space but is successful at linking time to sensation. A nearly identical camera movement, this time circling Jonás, occurs in the second half of the film, when he is stunned after spotting Gerardo and Sergio together in the street. More 360° camera movements are used in Jonás's flashbacks to the dance club; here the camera circles the two boys after the stranger kisses Jonás, conveying both the rapture and the shattering derangement of this sudden erotic revelation.

The virtuoso cinematography of Alejandro Cantú is another important feature of Hernández's cinema of sensation. Its complex colour palette and constantly shifting lighting scheme never cease to excite the spectator's eye, suddenly casting characters in shadow or light or silhouetting them by means of backlighting, at times challenging the viewer to make out shapes among the dimly lit corners. The film's lighting rhythms and modulations "temporalize" the image but also take on emotional and metaphorical qualities. In particular, there is a striking use of coloured spotlights and filters in order to shape and separate space, to dynamize

Fig. 3. Jonás (Fernando Arroyo) is kissed by the stranger. Courtesy of Jesús Torres Torres/Imcine/Mil nubes–Cine.

Fig. 4. Gerardo (Miguel Ángel Hoppe, left) and Sergio (Alejandro Rojo, right) kiss each other. Courtesy of Jesús Torres Torres/Imcine/ Mil nubes–Cine.

FIG. 5. GERARDO (MIGUEL ÁNGEL HOPPE) AND SERGIO (ALEJANDRO ROJO) EM-
BRACE. COURTESY OF JESÚS TORRES TORRES/IMCINE/MIL NUBES-CINE.

the frame, and to impart feeling and mood to the narrative. In the disco-
theque, bright, multi-coloured strobe lights circle around and over the
dancers, dissolving their bodies into fluid washes of colour. Jonás's various
flashbacks to the discotheque constitute immersions in coloured fields
throbbing with sexual energy. When Gerardo encounters Sergio in the
sex club, high-key neon lights create a stylized background for their mating ritual. Colour correspondences, too, echo throughout the film. In
early scenes, Gerardo sports a red jacket while Jonás wears a blue one, as
if anticipating in this contrast of warm and cool colours the emotional
dynamics to follow. Later on, as Gerardo and Jonás grow apart, their
embraces are photographed less and less in warm tones, as cold blue lights
progressively take over.

Even though *El cielo dividido* stands out for its limited use of dialog, it
is a film rich in acoustic sensations (*sonsigns*). Music replaces the spoken
word: the film features many scenes scored to pop songs and love bal-
lads or moments where characters lose themselves in music. Sprinkled
throughout the film, the songs are often utilized to comment on the

action or underline the characters' feelings, operating as important sources of affect. Furthermore, Hernández shows a penchant for extreme ranges of sound, from nearly imperceptible ambient noises (whispers, giggles, sighs) that force spectators to strain their sense of hearing to powerful waves of dance music that flood the screening room and immerse both characters and viewers in their propulsive electronic rhythms.

When Gerardo sneaks Jonás into his mother's apartment, their attempt to make it to the bedroom unnoticed hinges upon the silencing of every creaking footstep and rustle of clothes. The long take emphasizes both the traversal of space from the doorway to the bedroom, the time required to complete the action, and the effort to suppress sound. Their attempts to go unnoticed ultimately fail; Gerardo's mother wakes up and once again time and sound come together: we linger with her outside Gerardo's bedroom door as she strains to hear any sound that might clue her into the nature of what is taking place behind the closed door. At other times, subtle background sounds set up intriguing counterpoints with foregrounded sounds and the music track: in the sex club scene, for instance, muffled sighs and moans coming from the back room off-screen occasionally float over Renée Fleming's voice as she sings the aria *Invocation to the Moon* from Antonín Dvorak's opera *Rusalka*.

Hernández's fascination with a cinema of bodies inhabiting a universe of sensations is in evidence from the opening of *El cielo dividido*. The very first image is an overhead medium close-up of Gerardo lying shirtless on a bed, his torso and face bathed in a golden light that gives his dark skin the luster of burnished bronze. His eyes closed, he turns his head to the side and licks his right bicep. As a hand creeps up from the off-screen bottom part of the frame, making its way up his chest, Gerardo writhes with pleasure. In the shots that follow, a mouth kisses a neck and an ear and moves down to suck on a nipple. From the start, *El cielo dividido* confronts its viewers not only with the sight of flesh, but with a kind of haptic visuality triggered by images that invoke textures and appeal to the sense of touch. In the scene I just described, pleasure is demonstratively grounded in tactility and is something that is savored with a fierce concentration on the surface of the skin as well as inside the circuit of the brain. Throughout the rest of the film, haptic moments continue to command our eyes as well as our ears: hands caress faces, grab crotches, cup buttocks; mouths connect, tongues smack and explore the bodies'

Fig. 6. Gerardo (Miguel Ángel Hoppe) and Jonás (Fernando Arroyo) make love. Courtesy of Jesús Torres Torres/Imcine/Mil nubes–Cine.

Fig. 7. Sergio (Alejandro Rojo) and Gerardo (Miguel Ángel Hoppe) make love. Courtesy of Jesús Torres Torres/Imcine/Mil nubes–Cine.

crevices. Even the crystalline images – memories or reveries of bodies kissed and caressed – possess a haptic dimension. Other senses, too, such as taste and smell, are brought into play.

Beugnet remarks that many films affiliated with the "cinema of sensation" borrow visual strategies from what Linda Williams calls "body genres," namely gore and pornography, in order to foreground the material and the corporeal (Beugnet, 8–9). While the erotic imagery *in El cielo dividido* might recall the clichés of gay pornography, Hernández's highly aestheticized treatment of the lovemaking scenes differentiates them from standard pornographic representations. Moreover, I would argue that Hernández uses gay pornography's flair for spectacle and its intense corporeality to weaken the narrative flow and to underscore the material dimension of his images, exploiting porn's unsettling affective power so as to enhance the spectator's sensory and emotional response to his film.

In Hernández's film, bodies also function as bridges to the past and as triggers for the emergence of memory images. In *Matter and Memory*, Bergson describes how virtual images, as they slowly emerge out of the past's domain into the present, take on a material substance and provoke sensations which, in turn, give rise to sensory movements; their presence can be so intense that they control and shape psychic life to an extraordinary degree. In *El cielo dividido*, memories spring to life from the caress of a hand or the heat of a kiss; because of this physical source, they deliver an exceptionally physical and emotional punch absent from other types of crystal images. When halfway through the film Gerardo touches Jonás, he triggers in his lover an immediate flashback to the dance club. The coiling of Jonás's frame, the stiffness of his limbs, and the cooling of his desire lets Gerardo know that, as the memory image takes hold of his lover's mind and body, his present claim to Jonás's affection is increasingly tenuous; soon, he too will exist only as virtual memory image.

For Deleuze, our experience of cinematic time as something pleasurable or tedious – as a source of anxiety, boredom, elation, disaffection – is one path opening our bodies to thought. Corporeal sensations constitute another avenue. In this regard, Deleuze encourages us to think of a more central role for the body: "The body is no longer the obstacle that separates thought from itself, that which it has to overcome to reach thinking. It is on the contrary that which it plunges into or must plunge into, in

FIG. 8.   GERARDO (MIGUEL ÁNGEL HOPPE) AND JONÁS (FERNANDO ARROYO) MAKE
LOVE. COURTESY OF JESÚS TORRES TORRES/IMCINE/MIL NUBES-CINE.

order to reach the unthought, that is life … [the body] forces us to think what is concealed from thought, life." In Deleuze's words, then, it is through the body "that cinema forms its alliance with the spirit, with thought" (1989, 189). *El cielo dividido* charts a path from the body to the spirit, from the spasms of bodily pleasure to heights of happiness and depths of sorrow, from the ever-nagging edge of desire to the wistful oblivion of love, and from a sense of physical intimacy and wholeness to an unbearable emptiness. Film critic Armand White fittingly sums up the unsettling impact of the physical on the mind and soul of Hernández's characters: "As they 'learn about love through their bodies …' [t]he immensity of what they come to feel – physically, existentially – is overwhelming" (White, 2006).

Restivo asserts that Deleuze's importance lies in his repositioning of aesthetic debates back at the centre of film studies (Restivo, 189). According to Flaxman, Deleuze believes that "[a] work of art is a machine' constructed for the purpose of producing sensations … because sensations mobilize the differential forces that make thinking possible." Ultimately, starting from what Flaxman calls "a disorder of the senses," Deleuze's agenda seeks to elicit new modes of seeing and feeling and to provoke new types of sensations, all with the stated goal of instigating new patterns of thinking (Flaxman, 2–3, 12–13).

Pointing to an ethical and utopian strain in Deleuze's aesthetics, Rodowick maintains that the essence of the time-image is a thought that is "not yet"; it is an image that helps us "become other" by awaking us to "what yet remains unthought" (191, 200–201). Paola Marrati, for her part, states that the passage from the movement-image to the time-image reflected a rupture in the organic link between humans and the world. Deleuze, she argues, invests modern cinema with the power of restoring our belief in the possibility of creating new relations to and ways of being in this world. Through images that create what Marrati describes as "other livable configurations of thought," Deleuze's filmmakers of time potentially enable their viewers to perceive the world anew, to unveil alternative modes of existence (79, 85–89).

How might Hernández continue the utopian impulse of modernist cinema, compelling his audience to think differently and look at and feel the world as if for the first time? David William Foster describes how certain Latin American films dealing with the topic of homosexuality have created "alternative realms of erotic experience, protected spaces in a hostile world where homoeroticism ... can be pursued with relative impunity" (x). Within the last decade, Mexico's gay and lesbian community has experienced some important advances. An increasingly active gay and lesbian political movement has made impressive strides in the fight for anti-discrimination laws, gay marriage, and legal equality, the ingrained homophobia of much public and private discourses notwithstanding. In large urban centres, there is greater public visibility and acceptance of gays and lesbians and a flourishing network of bars, discotheques, and sex clubs. As the forces of globalization and capitalist practices of consumption proceed to permeate more sectors of Mexican society, many young Mexican homosexuals, like the protagonists of El cielo dividido, have eagerly embraced the fashions and popular culture of gay communities in Europe and the United States and adopted similar models of identity.

In El cielo dividido, Hernández imagines an almost gay-centred world from which the forces of intolerance have been banished and male bodies make love with abandon, free of shame or self-hatred. In this sense,

Hernández's cinema is a radical departure from mainstream Mexican cinema, which, as Sergio de la Mora describes in his book, *Cinemachismo*, has depicted homosexuality as a foil to male heterosexual identities in a manner that reaffirms an oppressive, patriarchal vision of masculinity (2–3, 18). In *El cielo dividido*, gay men take possession of college libraries and hallways, traverse streets hand in hand, and kiss with impunity in public spaces. Hernández's corporeal cinema of the time-image confronts its audience with the sights, sounds, and suggested textures of men having sex with other men, perhaps pinning its hope on the possibility that a cinema of sensation and duration might be able to expand and transform the mind through feeling; its utopian project, as Beugnet succinctly puts it, is "to reach a spectator's mind through the intelligence of the affective" (178). In imagining and imaging more affirmative modes of existence for gay men and in potentially making heterosexual viewers feel and think differently about the normalcy of homosexual desire, *El cielo dividido* opens new paths for Mexican and Latin American cinema in particular and pushes gay cinema into fresh directions. To paraphrase David Pendleton in his Deleuzian reading of queer cinema, I want to say that Hernández, too, presents homosexual desire as a creative force with the potential for thought and change. If *El cielo dividido* conforms to Pendleton's notion of a Deleuzian queer cinema, it might be because its purpose, too, is "[n]ot to show us what or how to think, but to ask us to question what images and identities and communities are" (Pendleton, 60).

El cielo dividido is one of the most visually arresting and thought-provoking films to come from Latin America in recent years. In tune with Deleuze's aesthetic proposals, *El cielo dividido* engages its spectators primarily in an experience in duration, materiality, and finally thought. In his foreword to *A Thousand Plateaus*, Brian Massumi states that the question of Deleuze and Guattari's philosophy of art is not whether it is true but rather "[w]hat new thoughts does it make possible to think? What emotions does it make possible to feel? What new sensations and perceptions does it open in the body?" (xv). *El cielo dividido* links corporeal sensation and affect to thought. In the final moments of the film, we see Gerardo and Jonás enter a hotel room and make love. At this point in the narrative, they are no longer together and, as a voice-off narrator informs us, have not spoken for some time. In this time-image, we cannot tell with any certainty where or when this event is taking place. The narrator tells us that, after a long period of silence, Jonás phones Gerardo to let him know that he deeply misses him and longs to hear his voice, that Gerardo's image involuntarily haunts his memory day after day. Gerardo, the narrator says, cries when he hears those words and is flooded by memories of a forgotten love, yet also horrified by that very forgetfulness; as the lyrics of an accompanying song indicate, the naked bodies embracing in the screen are "tan cerca, tan lejos" ["so close, so far"]. Silence and sound, bodies touching yet receding, tears and memories imprint this time-image with both carnality and affect, sensation and thought.

As it unreels assemblages of *chronosigns*, *opsigns*, *sonsigns*, and *tactisigns*, *El cielo dividido* implicates viewers in a wide gamut of sensations, emotions, and mental states, at the same time as it delivers a philosophical rumination on the tenuous and ever-changing nature of love. Through its celebration of bodies enthralled by lust and souls exalted by love, of young men in the grip of pleasure and suffering, driven by desire and haunted by loss, and never immune to the passage of time, the closing scene of *El cielo dividido* seems to substantiate Deleuze and Guattari's vision of existence as immanence; of a world where desire is contingent and in a perpetual state of flux, where subjectivities are fixed here only to be unraveled there, and where sensations can be endlessly prolonged when our encounter with matter, as Deleuze and Guattari so beautifully articulate it, takes place in time: "so long as the material lasts, the sensation enjoys an eternity in those very moments" (Deleuze and Guattari, 166–67).

WORKS CITED

Bergson, Henri. 1991. *Matter and Memory*. Trans. Nancy Margaret Paul and W. Scott Palmer. New York: Zone Books.

Beugnet, Martine. 2007. *Cinema and Sensation: French Film and the Art of Transgression*. Edinburgh: Edinburgh University Press.

Deleuze, Gilles. 1986. *Cinema 1. The Movement-Image*. Trans. Hugh Tomlinson and Barbara Haberjam. Minneapolis: University of Minnesota Press.

———. 1989. *Cinema 2. The Time-Image*. Trans. Hugh Tomlinson and Robert Galeta. Minneapolis: University of Minnesota Press.

————. 1997. *Negotiations*. Trans. Martin Joughin. New York: Columbia University Press.

Deleuze, Gilles, and Félix Guattari. 1996. *What is Philosophy?* Ed. and trans. Janis Tomlinson. New York: Columbia University Press.

Flaxman, Gregory. 2000. Introduction to *The Brain is the Screen: Deleuze and the Philosophy of Film*. Ed. Gregory Flaxman, 1–57. Minneapolis: University of Minnesota Press.

Foster, David William. 2003. *Queer Issues in Contemporary Latin American Cinema*. Austin: University of Texas Press.

Gundermann, Christian. 2005. The Stark Gaze of the New Argentine Cinema. *Journal of Latin American Cultural Studies* 14, no. 3: 241–61.

Kennedy, Barbara M. 2003. *Deleuze and Cinema: The Aesthetics of Sensation*. Edinburgh: Edinburgh University Press.

Kovács, András Bálint. 2000. The Film History of Thought. Trans. Sándor Hervey. In *The Brain is the Screen: Deleuze and the Philosophy of Film*. Ed. Gregory Flaxman, 153–70. Minneapolis: University of Minnesota Press.

Marks, Laura U. 2000. *The Skin of the Film: Intercultural Cinema, Embodiment and the Senses*. Durham, NC: Duke University Press.

Marrati, Paola. 2008. *Gilles Deleuze: Cinema and Philosophy*. Baltimore: Johns Hopkins University Press.

Martin-Jones, David. 2003. *Deleuze, Cinema and National Identity: Narrative Time in National Contexts*. Edinburgh: Edinburgh University Press.

Martins, Laura. 2007. Bodies at Risk: On the State of Exception. In *Argentinean Cultural Production During the Neoliberal Years 1989–2001*. Ed. Hugo Hortiguera and Carolina Rocha, 205–16. Lewiston, NY: Edwin Mellen Press.

Massumi, Brian. 1987. Foreword to *A Thousand Plateaus*, by Gilles Deleuze and Félix Guattari. Trans. Brian Massumi, i–xvi. Minneapolis: University of Minnesota Press.

Mora, Sergio de la. 2006. *Cinemachismo. Masculinities and Sexuality in Mexican Film*. Austin: University of Texas Press.

Noh, David. 2007. Review of *El cielo dividido*, by Julián Hernández. *Film Journal International*. 1 March. http://www.mrqe.com (accessed October 20, 2008).

Pendleton, David. 2001. Out of the Ghetto: Queerness, Homosexual Desire and the Time-Image. *Strategies* 14, no. 1: 48–62.

Pisters, Patricia. 2003. *The Matrix of Visual Culture: Working with Deleuze in Film Theory*. Stanford: Stanford University Press.

Powell, Anna. 2005. *Deleuze and Horror Film*. Edinburgh: Edinburgh University Press.

Restivo, Angelo. 2000. Into the Breach. In *The Brain is the Screen: Deleuze and the Philosophy of Film*. Ed. Gregory Flaxman, 171–92. Minneapolis: University of Minnesota Press.

Rodowick, David N. 1997. *Gilles Deleuze's Time Machine*. Durham, NC: Duke University Press.

Shaviro, Steven. 1993. *The Cinematic Body*. Minneapolis: University of Minnesota Press.

White, Armand. 2006. Review of *El cielo dividido*, by Julián Hernández. *The New York Press*, 27 September. http://www.nypress.com/19/39/film/Armond-White2.cfm (accessed October 20, 2008).

Williams, Linda. 1991. Film Bodies: Gender, Genre, and Excess. *Film Quarterly* 44, no. 4: 2–13.

Young, Deborah. 2006. Review of *El cielo dividido*, by Julián Hernández. *Variety*, February 23. http://www.variety.com (accessed October 20, 2008).

FILMS

El cielo dividido [*Broken Sky*]. Directed by Julián Hernández. Strand Releasing Home Video, 2006.

La ciénaga. Directed by Lucrecia Martel. Transeuropa Video Entertainment, 2001.

Memorias del subdesarrollo [*Memories of Underdevelopment*]. Directed by Tomás Gutiérrez Alea. Tricontinental Film Center, 1968.

Mil nubes de paz cercan el cielo, amor, jamás acabarás de ser amor [*A Thousand Clouds of Peace*]. Directed by Julián Hernández. Strand Releasing Home Video, 2003.

NOTES

1 Lucrecia Martel's *La ciénaga* (The Swamp, 2001) has elicited two Deleuzian-inflected readings: one by Christian Gundermann and another by Laura Martins. Angelo Restivo delivered a paper ("Third Cinema and the Time-Image,") at the 2008 conference of the Society of Cinema and Media Studies in which he discussed Tomás Gutiérrez Alea's *Memorias del subdesarrollo* (*Memories of Underdevelopment*, 1968) in connection with Deleuzian film theory.

2 Hernández has said that he was inspired to write his screenplay by Aristophanes' myth in Plato's *Symposium*: split in ancient times by Zeus into two symmetrical parts, men are doomed to spend their entire lives searching for their missing half in hopes of reconstituting the sundered whole. Early in the film there is a classroom scene where a professor explicates Aristophanes' myth.

3 *El cielo dividido* is the kind of film that elicits contrary yet intense audience responses; a viewer might feel at one moment exhilarated and bored the next, aroused and then disoriented, charged with energy and languid to the extreme. Some reviewers, for instance, have made explicit their displeasure over the film's pace. In *Variety*, Deborah Young called the film "a tedious aesthetic exercise." David Noh said of *El cielo dividido*: "To describe writer-director Julian Hernández's film as slow would be to seriously understate the issue. This thing crawls over a torturous 140-minute running length, with teenage love given a dire gravitas which verges on the absurd."

4 Deleuze defines *chronosigns* as images in which time ceases to be subordinate to movement and appears for itself. *Opsigns, sonsigns,* and *tactisigns* are images that privilege the experience of the visual, the acoustic, or the tactile aspects of a given film.

5 "Sitting in the dark, watching the play of images across the screen, any detachment from raw phenomena, from the immediacy of sensation or from the speeds and delays of temporal duration, is radically impossible.... I am confronted and assaulted by a flux of sensations.... I am violently, viscerally affected by this image and this sound... affected by continuities and cuts, movements and stillnesses, gradations of color and brightness" (Shaviro, 32, 255).

MYTH AND THE MONSTER OF INTERSEX: NARRATIVE STRATEGIES OF OTHERNESS IN LUCÍA PUENZO'S *XXY*

Charlotte E. Gleghorn[1]
Royal Holloway, University of London

The postdictatorship cultural climate in Argentina, as in many other Southern Cone countries, has been marked by an increased attention to the peripheral, forgotten characters of national history and their often unheard and unseen identities. This "attraction to society's marginal or abandoned figures, those who cast a dilemma about the representation of otherness'" (Masiello, 4) is reflected in recent filmic production and epitomized in features such as *Pizza, birra, faso* [*Pizza, Beer and Cigarettes*] (Adrián Caetano and Bruno Stagnaro, 1998), *Mundo grúa* [*Crane World*] (Pablo Trapero, 1999), and *La ciénaga* [*The Swamp*] (Lucrecia Martel, 2001), all associated with the so-called *nuevo cine argentino* [New Argentine Cinema].[2] Indeed, if one thing could be said to unite a number of films under the label of New Argentine Cinema, it is, according to Gabriela Copertari, "that they all stage narratives of disintegration" (279).

The diversity of experience, themes of social concern and the absence of a *grand récit* dominate these recent films, highlighting the fracturing of a unified concept of history and contesting official versions of truth as they had formerly been presented.

Amongst the films produced over the last decade are countless meditations – in short films, documentaries and features – on the last dictatorship in Argentina (1976–83), of which *Los rubios* [*The Blondes*] (Albertina Carri, 2003) stands out for its avant-garde aesthetic and the polemic it caused. Notably, however, a number of films have also turned their eye to the theme of sexual diversity. Carri's third feature, *Géminis* [*Gemini*] (2005), considers an incestuous relationship in a bourgeois family; *Vagón fumador* [*Smoker's Only*] (Verónica Chen, 2001) and *Ronda nocturna* [*Night Watch*] (Edgardo Cozarinsky, 2005) both portray male prostitution on the streets of Buenos Aires; *Un año sin amor* [*A Year without Love*] (Anahí Berneri, 2004) brings AIDS and gay sadomasochism to the centre of its narrative; and *Tan de repente* [*Suddenly*] (Diego Lerman, 2002) reinvigorates the traditional road movie with a lesbian kidnapping. *XXY* (Lucía Puenzo, 2007), the film discussed in this article, brings yet another narrative of diversity to the screen, that of an intersex adolescent.

XXY

Cited in the Argentine newspaper *Página 12* as "una de las películas más inquietantes que el cine argentino haya dado en bastante tiempo" ["one of the most disturbing films Argentine cinema has offered in a good while"] (Bernades), *XXY* has garnered a number of international awards and at the time of writing holds pride of place in countless GBLT film festivals around the world. This coproduction between Argentina, France, and Spain, won the Critics' Week Grand Prize at the 2007 Cannes festival and the 2008 Goya Award for best Spanish language film.[3] Adapted from Sergio Bizzio's short story "Cinismo" ["Cynicism"], the film constitutes the director Lucía Puenzo's feature debut.[4]

XXY is the story of a fifteen-year-old girl, Alex (Inés Efron), an intersex adolescent struggling with her identity. Alex's parents, Suli (mother) and Kraken (father) – played by Valeria Bertuccelli and Ricardo Darín

FIG. 1. ALEX (INÉS EF-
RON) FLOATING
ON THE WATER.
FILM STILL FROM
XXY (COURTESY
HISTORIAS CINE-
MATOGRÁFICAS).

respectively — decided not to operate on her unexpected phallus when she
was born, despite the encouragement of the doctors to normalize her female genitalia, and left Buenos Aires for Uruguay in search of a life away
from the judgmental gaze of others. Now her mother invites a friend,
Erika (Carolina Pelleritti), and her surgeon husband, Ramiro (Germán
Palacios) from the Argentine capital to study Alex's case and evaluate the
option of surgery to 'correct' Alex's body. The guests' son, Álvaro (Martín Piroyansky), develops a relationship with Alex, ultimately bringing
the recognition of Alex's ambiguous body out into the open. The film
concludes with the surgeon and his family returning to Buenos Aires and

Alex asserting her desire to break free from the world of secrecy which enshrouds her body.

In spite of the fact that the film's website and director repeatedly describe Alex, the protagonist, as an intersex adolescent, and not as a hermaphrodite, the majority of film criticism on the feature uses the mythic term of the hermaphrodite to denote Alex's status.[5] This is problematic, not only for its denial of the more general and recent term, intersex, but also for locating the narrative in the realm of myth with which the hermaphrodite is commonly associated. This tension between myth and reality, otherness and normality, reflected in these critics' perspectives on the film, is also to be found at the centre of the film's narrative structure. In order to discuss the strategies by which Puenzo brings Alex's otherness to the fore, I will first briefly outline the history of the myth and scientific treatment of hermaphrodites, or intersex individuals, as they are now widely known.

INTERSEXUALITY

As Anne Fausto-Sterling states in her book, *Sexing the Body*, "Intersexuality is old news" (32). While the term has only emerged in recent years, the existence of mixed-sex people has been documented since Antiquity under the guise of the hermaphrodite.[6] In classical Greek mythology, Hermaphroditus was the son of Hermes and Aphrodite who seemingly fused with the body of a water nymph, Salmacis, forming a body half male, half female.[7] The rejection of the term 'hermaphrodite' by members of activist groups, such as the Intersex Society of North America, was largely brought about to correct the inadequacy of the hermaphrodite model to describe a wide range of alternative configurations of the body, on the one hand, and, on the other, as a move away from the intense mythical status of the term.[8] Indeed, a study of the hermaphrodite over time demonstrates its persistent association with the Greek myth, a body belonging to the realm of the fantastical: an other-worldly body. The changing attitudes to the figure of the hermaphrodite mirror the changes in European societies, which increasingly sought to categories the human body. As Foucault documents in his introduction to *Herculine*

Barbin, "It was a very long time before the postulate that a hermaphrodite must have a sex — a single, a true sex — was formulated. For centuries it was quite simply agreed that hermaphrodites had two" (1980, vii). While not entirely devoid of stigmatization, the hermaphrodite did have certain rights and could, up to a point, enjoy its status as a Third Sex. As Gilbert Herdt notes in the volume *Third Sex, Third Gender*:

> The Greeks and the early Romans seem to have shared in folk beliefs and practices that were more open in their epistemology of sexual nature and sexual culture. Their acceptance of sexual and gender variations emerged from fundamental sources: the variety of life forms and genders that Zeus could temporarily inhabit, at one time desiring a woman and later a boy; the significance of the god Hermaphroditus in Greek thought; the acceptance of the legendary Tiresias, who changed from male to female to male again in one lifetime, and whose soothsaying powers hark back to such pansexuality. All of these Greek forms showed a lively attention to anatomical differences and sexual options, but with much more fluidity permitted in states of being and ways of acting human. (13–14)

However, with the rise of scientific reason in the nineteenth century, biologists focused on further dissecting and categorizing the human body. The French zoologist Isidore Geoffroy Saint-Hilaire in the 1830s developed a science of unusual births, *teratology*, which began to work towards the subdivision of hermaphrodites into the categories of "true" and "pseudo" hermaphrodites.[9] Moreover, the fusion of the two sexes became increasingly questioned during the nineteenth century, as it was assumed that one of them, male or female, would prevail, even in a hybrid body. Gradually the hermaphrodite became explained away to the point of societal obsolescence. The denial of the juxtaposition of the two sexes thus reinforced the binary sex system which marked male and female at opposing poles on a scale and obliterated their hybrid from the middle. Scientific advancement began to treat these "unusual" bodies not as freak phenomena but as disfigurements that could be "fixed" with the tools of science.

While today a growing number of accounts of intersex experience are coming to the fore in autobiographical narrations of embodiment and gender "normalization," it seems that little has changed since the nineteenth century with regard to the medical treatment of intersex individuals.[10] Indeed, as Alice Dreger makes patently clear in her excellent account of hermaphroditism and its treatment over time, there exists a disjuncture between what she terms the contemporary "postmodernistic" life histories from the perspective of intersex individuals themselves and the "extremely modernistic" medical-technological approaches to these biological anomalies (181). These approaches are based on the underlying assumption that, unless a child is brought up firmly in accordance with the societal gender norms of his/her given culture, s/he will be confused and severely unstable.[11] In line with this belief, doctors generally seek to take action promptly after birth to ensure an effective adjustment.

At birth, intersex children are declared a social emergency. Typically the parents are given twenty-four hours to make a decision about whether to operate on the baby's body and are rarely allowed the opportunity to talk to other parents of intersex children to understand their options. However, today activist groups such as the aforementioned Intersex Society of North America demand that "normalization" surgery should be decided with the patient at a later stage, giving the person the opportunity to choose and live with his/her chosen bodily configuration.[12]

XXY questions the surgical and hormonal methods used to control intersex bodies and as such overlaps with concerns of activist groups who seek to protect the corporeal autonomy of these children until they are of an age to make a decision for themselves. The film both highlights the scientific and illegitimate "fixing" of intersex individuals and allows the protagonist Alex agency in decisions over what should happen with her "deviant" body. This article considers both the film's important attempt to inscribe the body of the intersex person in the visual realm and the concomitant reiteration of this same body as other-worldly through the use of the marine myth.

BORDERLANDS

Alex's body is contested in multiple ways, and its corporeality suggests a borderland that is neither male, nor female, neither heterosexual, nor homosexual. Indeed, the figure of the intersex adolescent recognizes the limitations of sexual dimorphism, acknowledging that there are other combinations of gender and sexuality which are, in fact, humanly possible. Alex's corporeality, then, is "caught up in cultural 'border wars' – wars over the borders separating males and females, men and women, boys and girls, borders separating the acceptable heterosexual and the disfavored homosexual, borders separating those with authority from those without" (Dreger, 198). This frontier is evoked not only through Alex's hybrid body but also through her environment.

The borderland in *XXY* is inscribed from the outset in the location of the narrative. Set near Piriápolis in Uruguay, the family lead a reclusive life away from the big city and are deeply involved with marine and beach life. The beach, as a physical border which separates land and sea, becomes the landscape which epitomizes Alex's in-between state, as we learn in the film that she was in fact conceived on the sand. Alex's parents' decision to return to the place where she was conceived, and thus escape the judgment of people in the city of Buenos Aires, indicates a return to the very origin of Alex located in this desolate beach landscape. Far from depicting a hot, sunny beach with scantily dressed holiday-makers, however, the beach where Alex's family live is wild, windy, and grey. Furthermore, Alex's tomboyish appearance emphasizes the refusal of the film to eroticize the beach location, as in place of the usual swimming costume or bikini, Alex appears in a hooded top and knee-length shorts. Thus, the remote coastal setting of the film highlights Alex's reclusion and stakes out her diversity in terms of dress code and modes of leisure. Far from becoming the liberating space which her parents had desired, Alex's existence in this small-town locality is overshadowed by the secret she maintains hidden under her clothes. This secret is guarded throughout much of the film, and the spectator gradually realizes the nature of Alex's body from hints which are given in the dialogue. Yet it is the cinematography which most forcefully underlines the other-wordly status of Alex, alluding to the myth of the sea monster and depicting Alex's marginality from the opening of the film.

SEA MONSTERS

While the myth of Hermaphroditus is not specifically referenced in the film, I suggest that another myth, that of the sea monster Kraken – announced by way of Alex's father's name – structures its narrative. The film's proximity to the sea gives rise to the marine monster motif that perforates the film's symbolism.[13] The myth of the sea monster is invoked from the opening sequence when we see the protagonist Alex running breathlessly through a wood with a machete, intercut with the film credits depicting underwater scenes of pulsating squid-like creatures and subaquatic noises. This scene begins with a close-up of Alex's feet as she walks through the woods barefoot. As a largely gender indeterminate part of the body, the shot of the feet highlights the theme of Alex's bodily ambiguity from the onset. We then become aware that a girl, who turns out to be Alex's friend later in the film, is chasing her through the woods. But while this chasing game would purport to suggest innocent child's play, there seems to be a more malign spirit which encodes the spectator's first encounter with Alex. The sound of breathlessness emphasizes a sense of urgency and panic and this is interlaced with the underwater sounds of the credits. The cuts between the scene in the woods and the credits become shorter, giving the impression that someone else, or something else, is chasing Alex, and the sequence stops abruptly with a thud as Alex brings the knife down to the ground as if she has been dragged to the depths of the sea.[14] Furthermore, immediately following the credit sequence we see the guests from Argentina arriving at the family home with Alex framed as a beast of the underworld as she hides below the house and gazes on the new arrivals through the floorboards. Here a shot-reverse-shot sequence of point-of-view shots from Alex's and Álvaro's perspectives introduces the meeting between the two adolescents that will prove pivotal to the development of the characters throughout the film. This sequence of gazes also points to the economy of vision that is integral to the unveiling of Alex's secret in the narrative, and to which I will turn later. The opening, then, serves to alert the spectator to the spectral presence of the underwater monster.

SPECIES

Alex's connection with the underwater world occurs time and again in the film, from the clownfish which she keeps in a tank in her bedroom, to the refuge she seeks in the water. The fish she keeps in the house are not just an indication of her and her family's love for the marine world, but they also bear a symbolic weight in that the clownfish is also a protandrous hermaphroditic species, mutating from male to female with maturity. Indeed, the decision to include these fish in the *mise-en-scène* as a sign of Alex's gender indeterminacy points to the overt use of symbolism to accentuate aspects of her character.[15] On a formal level, then, Alex's clownfish suggest that she is interested in permeable and mutating identities akin to her own.

There is a further connection to the sea, however, in the character of her father, a marine biologist, who bears the name of Kraken. This naming strategy at once alerts the spectator to the myth of the marine monster in the film and to the special relationship that Alex holds with her father through their connection with the sea. In the film, Alex frequently assists Kraken with his work, not only pointing to her interest in the marine world but also providing narrative situations to make frequent suggestions of the similarities between the impulse to categories animals and human beings. On a number of occasions, the dialogue refers to humans as species, deepening the connections between the biological imperative to catalogue living organisms and humans alike. One such example occurs early on in the film, when Alex witnesses her father's naming of a stray turtle as *hembra*, female, as he carries out his work in his "consultation room." Building on this initial parallel established between animals and Alex, her exposed position in the community is emphasized in another scene when an argument between Kraken and Alex's friend Vando's (Luciano Nóbile) father also invokes the notion of species in reference to Alex's otherness. Here Vando's father goads Kraken by saying, "hay demasiadas especies en extinción por acá" ["there are too many species in extinction around here"], making reference to Alex's vulnerable status in the community.

The references to species in light of Alex's condition are not, however, limited to other characters but are also reflected in Alex's own comments, illustrating Alex's acute awareness of her alien position in society. In one scene Álvaro is playing with "un bichito raro" ["a strange bug"] on the beach when Alex confronts him with "¿qué sabés *vos* de las especies de mi casa?" ["what do *you* know about the species of my home?"], once again inferring that her world is a world-apart, another universe. The parallels established between the categorization of species in the animal world and in the world of humans once again emphasize the borderland that Alex inhabits – she belongs to both marine and human, male and female realms.

FUSION WITH THE SEA

Additional to the explicit references to Alex's otherness in the dialogue in the film, the cinematography (executed by Natasha Braier) frequently highlights and visualizes Alex's fusion with the marine world. In one scene we see Alex lying half-naked on her bed next to a huge window that gives directly onto the water, and the sound of the sea invades her private, and intimate, space. The structure of the shot visually emphasizes the absence of a barrier between her and the water; they literally become one.

The character of Alex, then, is to be found at the intersection of myth and reality through her straddling of human and animal realms. Her sexual otherness is underlined by way of the pet lizard she allows to roam her body. Indeed, the lizard, a colourful green reptile, is an extremely powerful evocation of otherness, a beast that often provokes fear, not fondness, in humans. Alex, by contrast, is at home with the lizard on her body and lets it crawl over her skin freely. This scene is erotically charged as the camera lingers on the skin-on-skin contact of the reptile with Alex, and the camera cuts to Alex's extremities as the lizard explores her body, highlighting the marrying of the image of a scaly beast with Alex's perceived dangerous sexuality. The camera here rests on the lizard as it slithers across Alex's skin, lending the scene more than a hint of sexual overtones.

Later on in the film, Alex's mother makes a point of returning, with the surgeon Ramiro and his wife, to the spot where Alex was conceived,

Fig. 2. Alex (Inés Efron) lying naked on her bed. Photo by Sebastián Puenzo (courtesy Historias Cinematográficas).

where she recounts the sexual encounter that resulted in Alex's birth. Given that the relationship between the three friends at this moment is fraught with tension as a result of the surgeon's fascination with Alex's body, it seems strange and certainly significant that Alex's mother should want to emphasize the exact location of her daughter's conception to the intruders in her family home. This serves to underline the fact that Alex's very existence is intimately linked to the coastal setting and the marine world on a number of levels.

Alex's other-worldly origins are further highlighted in a conversation that takes place between Kraken and the surgeon Ramiro. Here Kraken describes Alex's birth and remembers that she was *azul*, blue, when she was born. While Kraken, in the first instance, is actually referring to the fact that she could not breath for forty seconds, her apparent blueness could also be interpreted as referencing Alex's alien and Other status.[16] Kraken continues by saying: "Era perfecta. Desde el primer momento en que *la* vi, perfecta" ["*She* was perfect. From the very first moment I saw *her*, perfect"], evidencing his acceptance of her body in spite of its perceived irregularity. Moreover, Kraken's account of Alex as perfect at birth emphasizes his desire to classify her as a girl and the special father-daughter relationship that they hold.[17] Yet this description also challenges society's judgment that Alex should not be perfect, but a monstrous body that needs to be rectified.

THE MONSTRUOUS FEMININE

The blueness that characterizes Alex's birth reoccurs throughout the film since her skin has an iridescent quality, emphasized by the grey and blue hues that mark the desolate landscape of the Uruguayan coast. Her skin, clothes, and eye colour all complement the blue tones of the sea, under-lining her familiarity with the marine world. On one occasion, we see her seeking refuge in the sea following her sexual encounter with Álvaro, floating on the water's surface, as if at home there. Here the light is over-exposed on her body, giving her skin a bright quality, and the tag around her neck, actually a tag used to trace turtles as they migrate, alludes to a monitored, alien identity. In this way the tag is representative of her be-longing to the animal realm but also references a structure of control and monitoring.[18] The tag, or identity number, is doubly encoded, emphasiz-ing how Alex seamlessly bridges the human and aquatic kingdoms as she does the male/female divide. This duality, or hybridity, renders her body akin to the monstrous figures of the past.

The reference to the Kraken monster through the repeated marine motif and Alex's father's name is a signal that her intersex identity ap-pears monstrous to members of society. Indeed, her physical hybridity radically questions the very fundaments of the normative, heterosexual, and dualistic society in which many of us live.[19] As Foucault reminds us in *Abnormal*:

Fig. 3. Álvaro (Martín Piroyansky) and Alex (Inés Efron) exchanging gazes in the mirror. Photo by Sebastián Puenzo (courtesy Historias Cinematográficas).

The monster is essentially a mixture [...] of two realms, the animal and the human: the man with the head of an ox, the man with a bird's feet – monsters. It is the blending, the mixture of two species: the pig with a sheep's head is a monster. It is the mixture of two individuals: the person who has two heads and one body or two bodies and one head is a monster. It is the mixture of two sexes: the person who is both male and female is a monster. It is a mixture of life and death: the fetus born with a morphology that means it will not be able to live but that nonetheless survives for some minutes or days is a monster. Finally, it is a mixture of forms: the person who has neither arms nor legs, like a snake, is a monster (2003, 63).

The corporeal ambiguity and hybridity that surrounds Alex's existence is at the centre of her repression as she has persistently been taught that it is wrong to publicly acknowledge her "in-between state." Raised to be ashamed of her diversity, Alex is intensely aware of the labelling — evidenced through her wearing of the turtle identification tag — of her body as monstrous and the fascination that it provokes. At one point she even refers to herself as a monster in a discussion with Álvaro following their intimate sex scene: "Andá, decíles a todos que soy un monstruo" ["Go on, tell them all I'm a monster"]. In this way, the fascination with Alex's body as a phenomenon bears a striking resemblance to the fascination with the deformities of monsters.

In an essay on the cultural representation of monsters from Antiquity until Descartes, the Portuguese philosopher José Gil writes, "Os homens precisam de monstros para se tornarem humanos" ["Men need monsters to become humans"] (80). In other words, as a limit body, the figure of the monster represents a symbolic transgression of the norm and provides the marker by which all "normal" human beings should be understood. Unlike the monsters of which José Gil writes, however, our monster, Alex, does not flaunt her physical difference in public as a show of excess. Rather the act of seeing, looking at her body, in the film is codified as a violent and voyeuristic act, thus challenging the spectator to rethink the primacy of the visual in constructing notions of sex and gender identity. This is most clearly demonstrated in the lynching scene.

In this scene — which is extremely harsh and violent — Alex is attacked by a group of boys who want to know what lies beneath her clothes. Here we see the protagonist held down on a secluded beach and violated with the gaze of the boys, who pull her pants down to see if she really has a penis or not. While there is in fact no penetration — all the boys keep their shorts on — the scene is encoded as a gang rape whereby we see Alex completely stripped of the clothes that rendered the source of her difference invisible. Although Alex's diversity in the film is not only at the genital level, the suggestion is that vision, the very act of seeing and acknowledging the hybrid body physically, renders Alex powerless. Moreover, the boys who reveal her secret get a sexual kick out of seeing her mixed-sex genitalia, pointing to the power of the gaze in sexual interactions.

VOYEURISM AND VIOLENCE

Laura Mulvey's seminal essay "Visual Pleasure and Narrative Cinema" (1975) is instructive here in its analysis of voyeurism and scopophilia as integral to the architecture of cinema. According to Mulvey, "The place of the look defines cinema, the possibility of varying it and exposing it. This is what makes cinema quite different in its voyeuristic potential from say, strip-tease, theatre, shows and so on. Going far beyond highlighting a woman's to-be-looked-at-ness, cinema builds the way she is to be looked at into the spectacle itself" (46). Moreover, the gendered implications of Mulvey's seminal article point to the possibility of interpreting the monstruous in the context of *XXY* as a specifically feminine construct. Indeed, as Rosi Braidotti has emphatically demonstrated,

> The monstrous as the negative pole, the pole of pejoration, is structurally analogous to the feminine as that which is other-than the established norm [...] Within this dualistic system, monsters are, just like bodily female subjects, a figure of devalued difference; as such, it provides the fuel for the production of normative discourse (80).

She continues:

> Woman as a sign of difference is monstrous. If we define the monster as a bodily entity that is anomalous and deviant vis-à-vis the norm, then we can argue that the female body shares with the monster the privilege of bringing out a unique blend of *fascination and horror*. This logic of attraction and repulsion is extremely significant. (81)

Thus, both Mulvey's and Braidotti's analysis of the power of the gaze and its fascination with the Other, the woman, highlights the film's strategic mobilization of the motif of the monster through the body of an intersex girl in order to interrogate the structure of voyeurism in cinema and suggest the violence of the look in its objectifying form. The decision to use a female actress to portray the intersex character is fundamental here in the association of Alex with the female sex. While Alex presents a border body in her representation of an intersex adolescent, it is evident that the parents have brought her up as a girl from birth and that society expects her body to comply with this categorization. The actress Inés Efron provides a polished performance of the complexities of Alex's embodiment and identity, and her casting also reiterates the character's notional definition as a girl. This, in turn, emphasizes the connection I make between the logic of the monster and the economy of the gaze in cinema.

The implication that the spectator is bound up in the structure of voyeurism, which delineates the characters in their power relations in the film, highlights the role that the gaze, and the revealing or obscuring of Alex's body, plays in the film. Throughout *XXY* the spectator is almost "teased" by the idea that s/he will see the "offending" anatomy. While there are at least four key moments when Alex's genitals are revealed to other characters in the film (the sex scene; the shower scene with her friend; the lynching scene; and the goodbye scene between Alex and Álvaro), the spectator, in fact, never witnesses the physical secret. This withholding device also provides much of the tension in the film in that there is always an expectation that at some point the "truth" will be revealed, although the spectator does not know when or how.[20] *XXY* builds on the possibilities of voyeurism in cinema to emphasize the violent nature of the gaze, culminating in the violence of Alex's lynching and subsequent derobing, while ultimately refusing the spectator a role in that structure of power.

According to Gil, "ao exibir a sua deformidade, a sua anormalidade – que normalmente se esconde – o monstro oferece ao olhar mais do que qualquer outra coisa jamais vista. O monstro chega mesmo a viver dessa aberração que exibe por todo o lado a fim de que a vejam" ["by exhibiting its deformity, its abnormality – which is normally hidden – the monster offers more to the eye than any other thing ever seen. The monster even manages to live off that very same aberration that it exhibits everywhere, for everyone to see"] (78). Herein lies the fundamental difference between the monsters of myth and the reality that is depicted in the film. Gil suggests that monsters actively expose their deformities, defying humans to see and acknowledge their difference. Alex, on the other hand, does not flaunt the visual signs of her otherness. Indeed, as has been observed by a number of critics who consider the concept of the monster, the etymological origin of the word is closely related to the verb *mostrare*, the act of showing something publicly.[21] Alex is thus rendered monstrous through the act of revealing her perceived deformity. In this sense, the lynching scene serves to demarcate the realm of monster from the real experience of an intersex adolescent.

HAUNTING HOMOSEXUALITY

Over the course of *XXY*, however, it becomes clear that there is a second otherness that haunts the film. The surgeon's son, Álvaro, is a withdrawn teenager, struggling with his identity and his relationship with his father. Following the sexual encounter between Álvaro and Alex, where Álvaro realizes that he enjoyed being penetrated by Alex, the theme of dangerous homosexuality also invades the narrative. As Fausto-Sterling argues: "The debates over intersexuality are inextricable from those over homosexuality; we cannot consider the challenges one poses to our gender system without considering the parallel challenge posed by the other" (112). Historically hermaphrodites were forced to choose a sex at adulthood and then stick by it for life in order to conform to the heterosexual matrix. Those individuals who chose to be considered male and then pursued relationships with men were considered homosexual and constituted a threat to the established social order. The imperative to denote a category for the human body at birth, either male or female, corresponds to society's anxieties surrounding homosexuality, perceived as a threat to the normative heterosexual matrix. Thus, the character of Álvaro supplies the narrative flipside of intersex identity. Álvaro's father, the surgeon, is concerned that his son may be gay, and Alex is unsure whether she likes men, women, or both. Alex's parents, on recognizing that their daughter used her phallus (which according to her diagnosis is, in fact, a long clitoris) to penetrate another male, express concern for her development, once again highlighting the interconnectedness of genital ambiguity to concerns of homosexual propensity. These anxieties over sexuality haunt the film and evidence that it is much more than Alex's genital sex at stake in society's perception of her intersexuality. The possibility that she could, on a physical level, pursue sexual relations with both sexes constitutes a grave threat to society. This threat is illustrated in the repressive presence of the surgeon.

DISCIPLINE AND PUNISH

XXY presents the malevolent forces that repress Alex as masculine institutions, here embodied in the character of the surgeon, Ramiro. Ramiro is constructed as a harsh and unsympathetic father who is distressed at the idea that his son may be gay. When Álvaro, upset after the lynching of Alex, confronts his father in a fireside heart-to-heart, Ramiro admits to being disappointed in him. In turn, Ramiro is relieved by the fact that Álvaro appears to have fallen for a girl, albeit an intersexual, as he informs his son "Tenía miedo de que fueras puto" ["I was scared that you were queer"]. This anxiety over his son's sexuality is evidenced earlier in the film when Ramiro obliges Álvaro to drink some wine over a family meal, suggesting that his son should put something strong into his veins. These examples of Ramiro's dissatisfaction in his own son, and reluctance to accept a non-hetero sexuality, however, do more than just illustrate his own narrow-mindedness. They explicitly reference this surgeon's fascination with abnormalities and his desire to correct bodies (and monsters). Ramiro's attempt to mould Álvaro into a *real* man by forcing him to drink alcohol finds a parallel in his desire to mould Alex's body in accordance with normative sex-gender expectations.

Ramiro's profession is perceived as sinister from his very arrival in the family house as Kraken takes visible offence at his being invited in the first place. His fascination with Alex's 'case' is written in the surgeon's leading questions but also in his very sexualized gaze on his potential patient. In a kitchen scene, Alex is observed by Ramiro in a point-of-view shot to which she responds with a question: "¿Te gusta abrir cuerpos?" ["Do you like to open bodies?"] Alex's astute remark and awareness of his gaze and profession is also referenced in a conversation between Alex and Álvaro in Kraken's workplace, when she asks her new friend "¿Fuiste alguna vez ... al quirófano a ver como rebana cuerpos?" ["Have you ever been ... to the operating theatre to see how he cuts up bodies?"], to which Álvaro replies "No rebana cuerpos, los arregla" ["He doesn't cut up bodies, he fixes them"]. The use of the verb *rebanar*, literally to cut or to slice off a member/limb, and noun *quirófano* [operating theatre], harks back to the practice of violent repression during the Argentine Dirty War when the repressors used overtly medical vocabulary to refer to a range of torture practices.[22] The allusion made between the victim of torture and the patient at the end of the scalpel is relevant here insomuch as it demonizes the institution of medicine for its corrective tendencies and failure to consult the patients first. Many victims of intersex normalization surgery are damaged in their potential to fully function in the genital area, making it difficult to urinate and enjoy sex. The striking resonances between the attempt to cut away the cancer of society in the "operating theatres" in the dictatorship era – in the case of the Junta's rhetoric the cancers were *los subversivos* [the subversives] – and the efforts to cut away the offending piece of anatomy in the intersex body point to the overtly repressive and dehumanizing treatment of individuals that continues in contemporary society.

RESISTANCE AND HOPE

For all the repressive and controlling techniques used on Alex's body, the protagonist and her family actually present relatively positive approaches to intersex life. Alex's condition, congenital adrenal hyperplasia (CAH), is essentially a hormonal and enzyme irregularity, which in severe cases may cause genital ambiguity.[23] The virilization of CAH children, which normally occurs in adolescence, is usually controlled by hormone therapy, but in the film we see Alex refuse to take her medicine and throw the pills away. This is clearly expressed in the scene that takes place between Alex and her mother, when the former throws away her pills unequivocally stating "Quiero que todo siga igual" ["I want everything to stay the same"]. Moreover, Alex confronts the silence that enshrouds her body towards the end of the film when Kraken refers to the possibility of reporting the lynching incident: "Si querés, la hacemos, pero es tu decisión" ["If you want, we can go ahead with it but it's your decision"]. He then goes on to lament "se va a enterar todo el mundo" ["Everyone is going to find out"], to which Alex defiantly retorts "que se enteren" ["Let them"].

Ultimately Alex is not entirely sure of what she expects and hopes of the future, but for the time being, she wants to relieve herself of the burden of the secret and be able to acknowledge her ambiguous body publicly. Thus, her recognition of her body, and refusal of surgery and hormone therapy, constitute a rejection of the institution of medicine to "correct" these unruly bodies.

By rejecting these disciplining forces, Alex's body essentially questions the rigid gender and sex categories to which we have become so accustomed. Her body represents a more flexible interpretation of the tensions between sex, gender, and sexuality and as such defies control. Moreover, she is doubly unruly in the sense that she wishes neither to define her body as a stable entity nor to behave according to heterosexual gender norms – she penetrates Álvaro in the sex scene. This fluidity is precisely what threatens to disrupt notions of sexual diversity.

XXY negotiates the cultural malaise that the intersex body provokes through the trope of the monster, thus underlining Alex's otherness in a society that seeks to monitor discrete categories of sex and gender. Alex's decision that everything should stay the same defies the secrecy that has characterized her childhood and proposes that she might lead a full life with whichever embodied identity she chooses. Alex's body suggests that it is possible to envision an approximation of scientific knowledge and social constructionism and write the body's physical corporeality back into questions of gender. Alex's body, then, is a limit body. Presented as Other-worldly through its association with the marine myth, Alex becomes Other-worldly in an alternative sense. Alex's body belongs to a "postgender" world beyond the dualistic confines of the nature/nurture divide.[24]

The tensions inherent in the film's use of the gaze and encoding of Alex as Other by way of pre-existing tropes of difference as expressed in the figure of the monster (Hermaphroditus, Kraken and woman) echo Dreger's comments on the contemporary friction between modernistic and postmodernistic approaches to intersexuality. By shedding light on what Dreger defines as the modernistic treatment of intersex individuals, the film actively contributes to the development of "marginal" narratives associated with postmodern and postdictatorship cultural production in Argentina and recycles the motif of the monster in order to make social comment on the abuses committed against these invisible bodies.[25] Moreover, *XXY*'s underlying critique of the voyeuristic gaze of difference may be seen as representative of a number of Argentine films which, in a self-reflexive fashion, make reference to the camera as weapon. *Buenos Aires viceversa* (Alejandro Agresti, 1996) signals the camera as an "instrument of a voyeurism that is ethically not so distinguishable from the act of violence itself" (Page, 393). More recently, Albertina Carri wonders in *Los rubios* (2003), "¿en qué se parece una cámara a una picana?" ["How is a camera like an electric prod?"]. The critic David Oubiña, in an article considering the "omnipresence of politics" in recent Argentine films (Oubiña 2004), also highlights both the overlapping of social concerns with cinematic form and, significantly, reiterates the famous Benjaminian analogy between the surgeon and the cameraman from the seminal essay "The Work of Art in the Age of Mechanical Production" (Benjamin 1936). *XXY*'s narrative visualizes this same analogy, pointing to the similarities between the violence of the surgeon's gaze on the intersex body and the curious gaze elicited through the framework of voyeurism in cinema. However, by way of its self-reflexive reassessment of the gaze of difference in cinema, *XXY* suggests that in recognizing difference, the post- of postgender is not only possible but is already a reality for many, dislocating the myth from reality once and for all.

WORKS CITED

Amado, Ana. 2003. Cine argentino: cuando todo es márgen. *El ojo que piensa*, no. 0 (August), http://www.elojoquepiensa.udg.mx/espanol/numero00/very-ana/06_cineargentino.html (accessed July 20, 2008).

Avelar, Idelber. 1999. *The Untimely Present: Postdictatorial Latin American Fiction and the Task of Mourning.* Durham, NC: Duke University Press.

Benjamin, Walter. 1936. The Work of Art in the Age of Mechanical Production. http://www.marxists.org/reference/subject/philosophy/works/ge/benjamin.htm (accessed August 16, 2008).

Bernades, Horacio. 2007. El saludable arte de plantear preguntas. *Página 12*, June 14, http://www.pagina12.com.ar/diario/suplementos/espectaculos/5-6638-2007-06-14.html (accessed May 12, 2008).

Braidotti, Rosi. 1994. *Nomadic Subjects: Embodiment and Sexual Difference in Contemporary Feminist Theory.* New York: Columbia University Press.

Butler, Judith. 1990. *Gender Trouble: Feminism and the Subversion of Identity*. New York: Routledge.

———. 1993. *Bodies that Matter: On the Discursive Limits of "Sex"*. London: Routledge.

Copertari, Gabriela. 2005. *Nine Queens*: A Dark Day of Simulation and Justice. *Journal of Latin American Cultural Studies* 14, no. 3: 279–93.

Dreger, Alice. 1998. *Hermaphrodites and the Medical Invention of Sex*. Cambridge, MA: Harvard University Press.

Falicov, Tamara. 2007. *The Cinematic Tango: Contemporary Argentine Film*. London: Wallflower Press.

Fausto-Sterling, Anne. 2000. *Sexing the Body: Gender Politics and the Construction of Sexuality*. New York: Basic Books.

Feitlowitz, Marguerite. 1998. *A Lexicon of Terror: Argentina and the Legacies of Torture*. Oxford: Oxford University Press.

Foucault, Michel. 1972. Les insensés. Chap. 5 in *Histoire de la folie à l'âge classique suivi de mon corps, ce papier, ce feu et la folie, l'absence d'œuvre*. Paris: Gallimard.

———. 1980. Introduction to *Herculine Barbin: Being the Recently Discovered Memoirs of a Nineteenth-Century French Hermaphrodite*, trans. Richard McDougall, vii–xii. New York: Pantheon Books.

———. 2003. Lecture, January 22, 1975. In *Abnormal: Lectures at the Collège de France 1974–1975*, trans. Graham Burchell, 55–79. London: Verso.

Gil, José. 2006. *Monstros*. Lisbon: Relógio D'Água Editores.

Gundermann, Christian. 2005. The Stark Gaze of the New Argentine Cinema: Restoring Strangeness to the Object in the Perverse Age of Commodity Fetishism. *Journal of Latin American Cultural Studies* 14, no. 3: 241–61.

Herdt, Gilbert. 1994. *Third Sex, Third Gender: Beyond Sexual Dimorphism in Culture and History*. New York: Zone Books.

Hester, John. 2004. Intersexes and the End of Gender: Corporeal Ethics and Postgender Bodies. *Journal of Gender Studies* 13, no. 3: 215–25.

Kessler, Suzanne. 1998. *Lessons from the Intersexed*. New Brunswick, NJ: Rutgers University Press.

Masiello, Francine. 2001. *The Art of Transition: Latin American Culture and Neoliberal Crisis*. Durham, NC: Duke University Press.

Mulvey, Laura. 2000. Visual Pleasure and Narrative Cinema. In *Feminism and Film*. Ed. E. Ann Kaplan, 34–47. Oxford: Oxford University Press. [Originally published *Screen* 16, no. 3 (1975).]

Oubiña, David. 2004. Between Break Up and Tradition: Recent Argentinean Cinema. *Senses of Cinema* no. 31 (April–June), http://www.sensesofcinema.com/contents/04/31/recent_argentinean_cinema.html (accessed August 12, 2008).

Page, Joanna. 2001. Postmodernism, History and Social Critique in Post-Dictatorship Argentine Cinema: A Reading of Eliseo Subiela's *El lado oscuro del corazón*. *Modern Language Review* 96, no. 2: 385–96.

FILMS

Un año sin amor [*A Year without Love*]. Directed by Anahí Berneri. Distribution Company, 2004.

Buenos Aires viceversa. Directed by Alejandro Agresti. Argentina Video Home, 1996.

The Crying Game. Directed by Neil Jordan. Miramax Films, 1992.

La fe del volcán [*Faith of the Volcano*]. Directed by Ana Poliak. Cinemagroup, 2001.

Géminis [*Gemini*]. Directed by Albertina Carri. Distribution Company, 2004.

Mundo grúa [*Crane World*]. Directed by Pablo Trapero. Facets Multimedia Distribution, 1999.

The Pirates of the Caribbean: Dead Man's Chest. Directed by Gore Verbinsky. Buena Vista International, 2006.

Pizza, birra, faso [*Pizza, Beer and Cigarettes*]. Directed by Adrián Caetano and Bruno Stagnaro. Filmfreak Distributie, 1998.

Ronda nocturna [*Night Watch*]. Directed by Edgardo Cozarinsky. Cine Ojo, 2005.

Los rubios [*The Blondes*]. Directed by Albertina Carri. Women Make Movies, 2003.

Tan de repente [*Suddenly*]. Directed by Diego Lermán. Alfa Films, 2002.

Vagón fumador [*Smoker's Only*]. Directed by Verónica Chen. Strand Releasing, 2001.

XXY. Directed by Lucía Puenzo. Distribution Company, 2007.

NOTES

1 I would like to express my sincere thanks to the director Lucia Puenzo for her insightful comments and suggestions on an earlier version of this essay.

2 The concept of New Argentine Cinema has been widely discussed and disputed in both journalism and the academic sphere. While the mid-1990s certainly presented a revival in film production in the country, heralded by the emergence of Martín Rejtman's film *Rapado* (1992), the aesthetic and themes deployed by directors are extremely varied and could not easily conform to the tenets of a filmic movement *per se*. Amongst others, Amado (2003) and Gundermann (2005) both acknowledge that the term is as much a marketing strategy as an aesthetic category and although an interest in the marginal characters of Argentina surfaces in many recent films, they are not all produced in the same manner. I would have to concur with the aforementioned critics in that the New Argentine Cinema generally describes an umbrella movement for extremely diverse production qualities and techniques. For an account of the tensions between state assisted film development and production during the 1990s, see Falicov.

3 It is interesting to note that while *XXY* was praised by Argentine and international critics alike, and selected to represent the country in the 2008 Academy Awards, the film was not finally shortlisted in the Best Foreign Film competition.

4 Additional to his role as writer of a number of films, Sergio Bizzio directed *Animalada* (2001). Lucía Puenzo, also a writer, is the daughter of the renowned director Luís Puenzo, responsible for *La historia oficial* [*The Official Story*] (1985), winner of Best Foreign Film Oscar at the 1986 Academy Awards.

5 For just a few examples of the description of Alex as a hermaphrodite, see the reviews and synopses at: http://www.imdb.com; http://www.variety.com; http://www.siff.net (the Seattle International Film Festival website). The website of the film is available at: http://www.xxylapelicula.puenzo.com.

6 The term "intersexuality" was purportedly coined by the biomedical researcher Richard Goldschmidt in 1917.

7 The myth of the origin of Hermaphroditus is documented in Book IV of Ovid's *Metamorphoses*. It is repeatedly discussed in scholarly works dedicated to the theme of hermaphroditism and intersexuality. See Dreger, 31.

8 Dreger writes of the difference between the two terms: "'Intersexed' literally means that an individual is *between* the sexes – that s/he slips between and blends maleness and femaleness. By contrast the term, 'hermaphroditic' implies that a person has *both* male and female attributes, that s/he is not a third sex or a blended sex, but instead that s/he is a sort of double sex, that is, in possession of a body which juxtaposes essentially 'male' and essentially 'female' parts" (31).

9 See Herdt and Fausto-Sterling for detailed discussions of the development of scientific approaches to intersexuality.

10 See Dreger, 173–80, for an introduction to first-person experience of being intersex.

11 See Kessler, 14–16 and her account of John Money's research, which has led to these assumptions.

12 The Intersex Society of North America was established by the prominent intersex woman Cheryl Chase. In the UK, the AIS (Androgen Insensitivity Syndrome) Support Network, created in 1988, coordinates help for varied conditions leading to intersexuality. See the group's website: http://www.aissg.org, for further information.

13 The Kraken myth derives from Norse mythology, closely related to the word *krake*, which means an unhealthy or twisted animal, but is in fact now thought to be the true account of a giant squid which terrorized sailors in Scandinavian waters centuries ago. The Kraken monster has also been used in literature and film, most famously in Alfred Tennyson's poem, 'The Kraken,' published in 1830. John Wyndham also wrote the novel *The Kraken Wakes* (1953) and more recently the Kraken appeared as the sea monster in the second part of *Pirates of the Caribbean, Dead Man's Chest* (Gore Verbinsky, 2006).

14 Given the subject of the film, it would also be possible to interpret a Freudian gesture here in that Alex attempts to 'cut away' that element of her genitalia that might be displeasing to her – her phallus.

15 This prevalent use of symbolic short cuts to communicate Alex's hybridity is one aspect of the film that has elicited criticism. See Bernades.

16 Kraken states: "Alex nació azul, tardó 40 segundos en respirar" [Alex was blue at birth, she took 40 seconds to start breathing].

17 Kraken's recounting of his designating Alex as a girl at birth is reminiscent of Judith Butler's analysis of the performative function of the phrase "It's a girl!" in *Gender Trouble* (1990). Butler returns to this notion of the effect of this performative iteration at the birth scene in *Bodies that Matter* (1993) when she writes, "To the extent that the naming of the 'girl' is transitive, that is, initiates the process by which a certain 'girling' is compelled, the term or, rather, its symbolic power, governs the formation of a corporeally enacted femininity that never fully approximates the norm" (232). As Kraken reminds us later in the film when he states "no va a ser mujer toda la vida" [she will never be a woman], Alex's corporeality is persistently discordant with what is normally expected of her.

18 This method of controlling and tracking individual identities bears a striking comparison with the identification number given to the character of Ana in another Argentine film, *La fe del volcán* [Faith of the Volcano] (Ana Poliak, 2001), and the numbers prisoners are given in concentration camps and detention centres. This method of monitoring and dehumanizing identities, then, is a recurrent motif of many films and may be attributed to the surveillance society which neoliberalism endorses.

19 It is worth noting that a number of anthropological and historical studies have also considered non-Western practices of conceiving of gender roles, sexuality, and intersexuality. See Gilbert Herdt, "Mistaken Sex: Culture, Biology and the Third Sex in New Guinea," in *Third Sex, Third Gender*, 419–46, and Will Roscoe, "How to Become a Berdache: Toward a Unified Analysis of Gender Diversity," in *Third*

Sex, Third Gender, 329–72, for two in-depth studies of these indigenous approaches to gender.

20 This same narrative strategy was exploited in the British film *The Crying Game* (Neil Jordan, 1992), which toyed with Dil's bodily secret throughout. *XXY* differs from *The Crying Game*, however, in that the genitalia are never actually revealed to the camera's lens.

21 See Braidotti, 91; Foucault (1972), 162.

22 See Feitlowitz, for a thorough examination of the impact of the vocabulary used during the last dictatorship.

23 It is worth noting that the XXY condition of the title of the film is, in matter of fact, different than the condition that characterizes Alex. XXY (47) is a condition called Klinefelter's syndrome when several X chromosomes mix with one Y chromosome, potentially causing genital ambiguity. This leads me to believe that the title was used as a signifier to communicate the mixed-sex thematic of the narrative. Not surprisingly, however, the disjuncture between the title of film and Alex's actual condition has led some groups to criticize the film for ill-portraying the complexities of the various conditions. The Italian organization UNITASK (Italian Association for Klinefelter's syndrome) is one of the organizations that criticized Puenzo's film for misrepresentation. See http://www.centrotecnomed.it/articolopetizione.htm (accessed August 18, 2008). Also see Dreger, 35–40, for a breakdown of the specifics of different intersex conditions.

24 See Hester, for an analysis of the impact of the intersexual on the development of postgender thought.

25 Much debate has taken place regarding the specificities of the postmodern beyond the global North, particularly in terms of the judgment that a postmodern aesthetic precludes any possibility of social critique and evacuates any sense of the historical from cultural representation (Page 2001). Given postmodernity's intense association with the politics of late capitalism as a global phenomenon, it is important to note that the dictatorship in Argentina in many ways ushered in the subsequent and extremely severe 'opening up' and privitization of the economy that took place under President Menem's administration (1989–99). In this light, the postdictatorship years become, by extension, the embodiment of the postmodern logic *par excellence*. Indeed, for many critics, namely Idelber Avelar, the postdictatorship period is coterminous with postmodernity (Avelar, 79).

WATCHING RAPE IN MEXICAN CINEMA

Isabel Arredondo
State University of New York

In *From Reverence to Rape* (1974), one of the first works to examine rape in film, Molly Haskell describes how rape has been equated with romance. Since then, much more has been written about rape in the cinema. Sarah Projansky in particular has worked with the topic, first in her dissertation *Working on Feminism*; *Watching Rape* (1995), and later in the article "The Elusive/Ubiquitous Representation of Rape" (2001) and the book *Watching Rape: Film and Television in Postfeminist Culture* (2001). Inspired by Projansky's work, I have set out to examine representations of rape in Mexican film. As Projansky does, I restrict my analysis to films in which rape is represented as violation. Unlike Projansky's work, which builds a complete history of representations of rape in the history of U.S. film, my project is limited to analyzing key moments in the representation of rape in Mexican cinema. While Projansky is interested in demonstrating the pervasive and unacknowledged recurrence of rape in U.S. film and television, this article uses a historicized feminist perspective to focus on films by three renowned women filmmakers: Matilde Landeta, Marisa Sistach, and María Novaro.

In the pages that follow I compare two films from the classical period with three contemporary films in terms of how these reflect shifting societal notions about rape. The representation of rape in Matilde Landeta's *La negra Angustias* [*Black Angustias*, 1949] is compared to that in Fernando de Fuentes' *Doña Bárbara* (1943), an internationally acclaimed film from the same period. These films connect rape to a then-prevalent discourse on the nation and national identity; more recently, however, filmmakers Marisa Sistach and María Novaro represent rape less as a trope of a changing national ideology than as a key issue within a shifting set of feminist concerns. In *Conozco a las tres* [*I Know All Three Women*, 1983], Sistach explores the traumatic consequences of bringing rape into the public realm of the judiciary system, despite the solidarity (assumed in early feminism and in the film) between the victim and her friends. In *Perfume de violetas: nadie te oye* [*Violet Perfume, No One Is Listening*, 2000], Sistach reacts to a post-feminist environment by warning about the consequences of leaving feminist activism behind. María Novaro's *Sin dejar huella* [*Without a Trace*, 2000] follows up on Sistach's warning by pointing to the proportions rape has taken in the city of Juárez at the beginning of the twenty-first century.

TWO EARLY REPRESENTATIONS OF RAPE

Both Fernando de Fuentes' *Doña Bárbara* and Matilde Landeta's *La negra Angustias* present rape as an originary trauma in the lives of their principal characters. Both films also use rape as a trope reflecting changes in and anxieties about masculinity in 1940s Mexico and as the origin of "mannish" behaviour in women. However, de Fuentes' film represents this behaviour as monstrous and ultimately domesticates the "mannish" woman, while Landeta, herself considered a "mannish" woman in the film industry, celebrates the "masculine" woman as a revolutionary hero who helps rewrite gender constructions within the narrative of the nation.

Doña Bárbara, a Mexican adaptation of the well-known Venezuelan novel of the same name written by Rómulo Gallegos in 1929, uses an implied rape scene as a trope of societal anxieties about masculinity

FIG. 1. DOÑA BÁRBARA (MARÍA FELIX): DOMESTICATION OF THE "MANNISH WOMAN." CORTESY OF CINEMATECA DE LA UNAM.

performed by women. Gallegos's regionalist novel and de Fuentes' film, in which Gallegos collaborated, both represent Venezuela as a divided country in which civilization is located in the cities, while barbarism reigns in the countryside. Both the novel and the film take place in the Apure region of Venezuela, where barbarism is depicted as pervasive. Barbarism, whose traits include a will to power, cruel individualism, vengefulness, and expansionist motives, is associated with machismo but is represented here in the figure of Doña Bárbara. Fuentes' film gives rape a prominent role, orchestrating the entire narrative around the protagonist's violation. The murder of her lover and her subsequent rape transform the naïve Bárbara into "Miss Barbarous," the "man-eater."[1] While she does not literally eat men, she does make and impose her law and appropriates nearby territories; figuratively, she "eats men" by exerting power over them and assuming their masculine prerogatives.

Landeta's *La negra Angustias*, also an adaptation of a novel of the same name, written by Mexican novelist Francisco Rojas Gónzalez in 1944, also posits the trauma of rape as formative of the protagonist's "masculine" character, although in this case the rape is displaced onto an animal substitute. Rejecting the association of sex with violence that she observes in the animal world, Angustias becomes independent, brave, and willing to use violence to carry out justice – traits normally associated with masculinity. *La negra Angustias* begins in 1903 and develops during the Mexican Revolution. Angustias (María Elena Marqués), the daughter of pre-revolutionary hero Antón Farreras (Eduardo Arozamena), joins the Revolution and ascends to the rank of colonel because of her leadership qualities and fearless determination to defend revolutionary values.

In both *Doña Bárbara* and *La negra Angustias*, rape is understood as a life-altering trauma; both narratives, moreover, establish a cause-effect relationship between rape or rape-like experiences and "abnormal" behaviour. Raped women, both films argue, deviate from traits associated with "femininity" (humility, submission, gentleness) and show "masculine" attributes (bluntness, violence, resistance). In *Doña Bárbara*, rape triggers Bárbara's transformation into the respected and powerful Doña Bárbara (María Felix). As if she were a man, "barbarous" Doña Bárbara enjoys controlling the men around her and submitting them to her law. In *La negra Angustias*, the most obvious consequence of Angustias' having watched the billy goat "rape" her yellow pet goat is her rejection of marriage. This cause-effect relationship is established by positioning the rape scene at the beginning of the film, and by the return to this initial scene of trauma in the main body of the film.

The rape scenes in both films function as "primal scenes," which I analyze with help from Tanya Horeck's controversial and influential study of rape *Public Rape: Representing Violation in Fiction and Film* (2004). Horeck questions the emphasis feminists have placed on distinguishing between reality and fantasy. Horeck argues that the trauma of rape, like the trauma of the Freudian primal scene, haunts the psyche and is returned to obsessively in fantasy. In Freud, the primal scene is the original moment in which the child witnesses the fearful spectacle of her/his parents having sex. Unable to overcome the horror of what she/he has seen, the child returns to this scene, which becomes primal in the sense that it becomes the origin of the child's separation from the parents and development as an independent individual. Because of the traumatic effect of rape, the repetition of inescapable horror that constitutes trauma, Horeck posits that rape scenes have a foundational value similar to Freud's "primal scenes" (4–6).

In *La negra Angustias* and *Doña Bárbara*, rape functions as a "primal scene" that organizes the narrative. The experience of rape shapes the protagonists' perceptions and motivations by its recurrent return. Both films situate the rape sequence at the beginning of the narrative. *Doña Bárbara* begins with a short scene of Santos Luzardo's return to El Llano. As Luzardo (Julián Soler) travels in a boat, the boat master tells him the story of the infamous Doña Bárbara. A dissolve announces a flashback in which Bárbara, still an adolescent, travels up the Orinoco River in a boat filled with sailors. On the soundtrack, the voice of the boat master explains that Bárbara had fallen in love with a fellow passenger, whom one of the sailors then shoots in front of her. As the sailors argue over who is going to rape her first, the music on the soundtrack announces danger. The rape itself is implied; shots of the mob of sailors are followed by a dissolve and then by an image of Bárbara walking on the deck alone. The dissolve, a referential mark for an omission, also serves to suggest that Bárbara has only a nebulous idea of the criminal assault that has happened to her. Her invisible wound of rape explains, in Horeck's sense, the origins of all that will then happen in the present of the narrative.

La negra Angustias, also features a rape-like "primal scene" at the beginning of the film. In this scene, "La negra" Angustias, a young shepherdess whose dark features suggest her African descent, watches in horror as a huge billy goat mounts her favourite female yellow goat. After the mating, the female goat gets pregnant and dies. Traumatized by the loss of her pet, Angustias concludes that mating is a vicious attack on females; for her, animal mating is analogous to rape.[2] The film goes on to show adolescent Angustias angrily throwing stones at billy goats to prevent them from mounting female goats, exclaiming: "I hate those billy goats; they are mean." The substitute rape of the goat becomes a "primal scene" that triggers Angustias's rejection of accepted female roles.

In *Doña Bárbara* and *La negra Angustias*, rape is a foundational experience; this idea is expressed in the films through the narrative's obsessive return to it. Towards the end of de Fuentes' film, Doña Bárbara, heart-broken because Luzardo is in love not with her but with her daughter Marisela (María Elena Marqués), follows Luzardo with the intention of shooting him. When she sees him embracing her daughter, however, she has a flashback to the scene of the loss of her lover, which in the film is a visual marker of not only the loss of a lover but also of her rape. The shot of Luzardo's embracing Marisela is superimposed onto a similarly positioned shot of Bárbara and her lover. This superimposition suggests that Bárbara's experience in the boat frames her apprehension of the world; her understanding of love is distorted by her own traumatic experience. The recurrence of the past in *La negra Angustias* is created by parallel framing. The young Angustias has a suitor, El Coyote, a young male who wears a big hat, black clothes, and pointy shoes. El Coyote's father formally asks Antón Ferrara, Angustias' father, to give Angustias in marriage to El Coyote. Angustias does not want to marry him, and Ferrara decides to respect his daughter's wishes. Despite Ferrara's refusal, El Coyote is so persistent that Ferrara threatens him by brandishing a stick, an act reminiscent of the earlier scene in which Angustias threw stones at the billy goat. Through parallel framing, this scene induces the viewer's return to *La negra Angustia*'s primal scene and replicates her horror at the association between sex and female death. Later, when Ferrara dies, billy-goat-like, El Coyote attacks again. This time, however, Angustias avoids the yellow goat's ending; she stabs and kills El Coyote after he assaults her.

Despite comparable organization of the films' narratives through a return to a primal scene and similar associations between rape and masculine behaviour, *Doña Bárbara* and *La negra Angustias* are strikingly different in terms of the value they assign to a "masculine" woman's behaviours. In *Doña Bárbara*, the protagonist's qualities of strength, perseverance, clarity, and ability to govern are seen as negative traits that she acquired as a consequence of her rape. Thus, the film's main goal is to show the "reformation" of Doña Bárbara. Santos Luzardo, her neighbour, "enlightens" Doña Bárbara, making her realize that, in spite of her tragic victimization, she is harming herself by taking vengeance. At the end of the film, Luzardo's "teachings" pay off, as she accepts that revenge is taking her in the wrong moral direction, and repents. Doña Bárbara's transformation is manifested in the scene that superimposes the embrace between Luzardo and Marisela over that between Bárbara and her lover. When the flashback is about to show the sailor's shooting Bárbara's lover, the film narrative moves back to the present; rather than shooting Luzardo as she had planned, Doña Bárbara drops her gun and leaves. The film proposes that the cycle of return to the trauma scene has ended, as Doña Bárbara has realized that if she kills Luzardo, Marisela will likely become another *devora-hombres*. To propose this parallelism, however, the film has to forget its own explanation of Bárbara's trauma, which clearly includes rape as well as the murder of her lover. De Fuentes' film thus remains complicitous with the notion that women's "masculinity" is a perverse condition to be devalued and discouraged.

Unlike de Fuentes, whose film shows Doña Bárbara's "masculinity" as abnormal and rejoices at the character's withdrawal from violence, Landeta positively values Angustias' "masculine" traits and does not believe that her behaviour needs correction. This view is not shared by the female characters in *La negra Angustias*, who, armed with sticks, drive Angustias out of town for having refused to marry. Landeta explains that their expulsion of Angustias from the community was "La protesta ancestral contra la mujer que no sigue los rituales acostumbrados" ["Ancestral protest against the woman who does not follow the established rituals"] and that "Parecía muy inmoral que una muchacha, hija de familia, no se quisiera casar a la hora de que pedían su mano" ["It was considered immoral that a young woman, from a good family, rejected marriage when a man proposed"] (Arredondo, 201). In fact, the film presents La Negra as an able leader who plays a significant role in the Mexican Revolution. When she orders her troops to cut off the testicles of El Picado, a man who has been sexually aggressive towards her, the film presents this action, not as a sign of barbarism, but as an act of social justice, and thus a contribution to a better, more revolutionary society. *Doña Bárbara* seeks to reinforce the patriarchal power structure, while *La negra Angustias* attempts to legitimize the power of women. If we read *La negra Angustias* as a defiant voice against the mainstream values put forward by *Doña Bárbara*, then we can conclude that, in spite of the films' similarities, *La negra Angustias* undermines the masculine legitimacy that *Doña Bárbara* tries to maintain.[3]

Matilde Landeta, the director of *La negra Angustias*, was herself an embodiment of the threat to masculinity that characters like Angustias and Doña Bárbara represent. Landeta's many biographies, most importantly

FIG. 2. ANGUSTIAS (MARÍA ELENA MARQUÉS): CELEBRATION OF THE "MANNISH WOMAN." COURTESY OF CINEMATECA DE LA UNAM.

Matilde Landeta, hija de la Revolución [*Matilde Landeta, Daughter of the Revolution*, 2002, by Landeta, Burton-Carvajal et al.] and Patricia Díaz's film *My Filmmaking, My Life: Matilde Landeta* (1990), talk about two revolutions: the Mexican Revolution and the revolution that Landeta launched within the Mexican film industry in the 1940s. In protest against the male-dominated film industry, Landeta once arrived on the set wearing pants and a false moustache, and she also fought with the union of assistant directors to be able to join their ranks. These audacious actions, along with the three films that she directed in the 1940s, established Landeta as a film pioneer. *Doña Bárbara* uses rape as a trope to warn against women like Landeta who step outside the regimen of traditional women's roles, but *La negra Angustias* celebrates the courage and heroism of a "mannish" woman.

FEMINIST REPRESENTATIONS OF RAPE FROM THE 1970S TO THE 2000s

While *Doña Bárbara* and *La negra Augustias* use rape scenes to explore tensions about gender roles and portray rape as a primal scene and as a cause of the "masculine" behaviours and attitudes of women characters, more recent films represent rape as a reality with which victims, and feminists, must cope. This section examines three stages of Mexican filmmakers' responses to issues regarding rape: first, the film collective Cine-Mujer in the 1970s; second, Marisa Sistach's *Conozco a las tres* (1983) in the 1980s; and third, Sistach's *Perfume de violetas: nadie te oye* (2000) and Novaro's *Sin dejar huella* (2000). These films present rape and its aftermath in ways that both mirror and intervene in prevailing feminist views of rape during the three time periods.

The feminist film collective Cine-Mujer was founded in the mid-1970s, lasted for a decade, and was composed of eleven active members. I agree with Angeles Necoechea, a member of Cine-Mujer, and with scholars Márgara Millán and Elissa Rashkin, who claim that Cine-Mujer, by raising awareness about women's issues in Mexico, made significant contributions both to history and to filmmaking.[4] The collective aimed at opening up a discussion about women's issues by showing their films in cultural centres, universities, and other public spaces. Cine-Mujer's concerns included discrimination against women in the workplace, women's unequal access to resources and political power, and public discourse about women's bodies, especially in regard to rape and sexual liberation. Through Cine-Mujer, university students and other members independently produced and distributed non-commercial short and medium-length films in 16 mm. One member of Cine-Mujer, Rosa Martha Fernández, made a film about rape, *Rompiendo el silencio* [*Breaking the Silence*, 1979]. As I have been unable to locate Fernández's film, my comment is restricted to the film's title. *Breaking the Silence* presumably refers to the need to bring the unspeakable issue of rape into the public discussion.

Marisa Sistach, a film student at the Centro de Capacitación Cinematográfica [Film Training Centre], directed *Conozco a las tres* in early 1983, during the period when the members of Cine-Mujer were disbanding the collective and moving on to other projects. Using a feminist perspective and a realistic style close to that of documentaries, Sistach's medium-length fictional narrative builds on and reconsiders the collective's goal of opening a public discussion of rape. Rather than simply "breaking the silence," *Conozco a las tres* brings to the forefront the hardships raped women have to endure when making rape public, and thus complicates contemporary feminist discourse about bringing rape cases to justice.

The protagonists of *Conozco a las tres* – Ana (Irene Martínez), María (Laura Ruiz), and Julia (Chela Cervantes) – are three close friends who live outside the traditional family structure and who support each other. One day, María is raped in the street while she is running errands. The rapists drag her from the street to a nearby abandoned lot, where María struggles, in vain, to free herself from the attackers who outnumber and overpower her. Although the rape itself is elided, the shots showing María's wrestling depict sexual violence in a way that is disturbing for the audience.[5] Sistach thus recreates the horror of rape without making rape a public spectacle.

The aftermath of the rape in *Conozco a las tres* takes place at María's home, where the three friends and a boyfriend of one of them gather together. Ana and Julia try to console María by showing solidarity, while the boyfriend, a journalist, vehemently condemns rape in a letter intended to be published in a newspaper. To the friends' surprise, María reacts violently to this plan, showing that the grief of rape is not cured simply by the acknowledgment of victimization, and that publicizing the rape in a newspaper may contribute to further trauma.

In *Conozco a las tres*, bringing rape to the judicial system is a mechanism through which rape is acknowledged as a crime, but also a way in which the violated woman is further traumatized. María reports her rape, but she chooses to attend the hearing by herself because speaking publicly about her pain increases her hurt and embarrassment. The representatives of the justice system who receive her report do not take her seriously, further humiliating her. Thus, although she wins her case, her hearing is not presented as a complete "victory" of women over the silence imposed on them in cases of rape, but rather as a partial one that is painful. Elissa Rashkin, who sees the trial as a second rape, remarks that "the conditions that women face are depicted as bleak and almost hopeless, softened only by female solidarity and the ability to laugh in order to survive" (94). While María recognizes her social responsibility to report her rape, entering the judicial system delays her emotional recovery.

Cine-Mujer's goals and Sistach's reconsideration of these goals, while both feminist, show an evolution of thought regarding the cinematic representation of rape, a shift noticed by the Mexican press. In a 1984 review, Andrés de Luna states that *Conozco a las tres*'s aesthetic concerns and approach to the theme of rape are uncharacteristic of feminist cinema. Rather than showing characters engaging in social protest, de Luna explains, rape is seen from the perspective of the everyday lives of the three friends. Rashkin also posits a difference between *Conozco a las tres* and Cine-Mujer, arguing that Sistach moves from the collective approach characteristic of Cine-Mujer to a more subjective one, which Rashkin describes as an "overtly personal engagement" (94).

Seventeen years after making *Conozco a las tres*, Sistach, now an established feature film director, again brings the issue of rape to the forefront in *Perfume de violetas: nadie te oye* (2000). This time, Sistach's view of rape challenges contemporary post-feminist complacency and emphasizes the need for continued activism around the crime of rape. The post-feminist context in which Sistach's film is immersed has been described by Projansky in *Watching Rape*. After examining film and television representations of rape from the 1980s on, Projansky warns that the assimilation of feminist ideas into the mainstream media can not be taken as a sign that feminist activism in relation to rape is no longer necessary. Furthermore, she interprets 1980s representations of rape as a sign of post-feminist depoliticization, and not as a sign that issues surrounding rape have been resolved, much less that rape has disappeared. Overall, Projansky sees the lack of feminist support as a problem and calls for the re-establishment of feminist commitment.

The second part of *Perfume de violetas*' compound title, *nadie te oye* [*No One Is Listening*] alludes to the post-feminist disappearance of women's solidarity and mutual support around rape. *Perfume de violetas: nadie te oye* depicts an absence of solidarity between women: unlike the three friends in *Conozco a las tres*, women today cannot rely on one another for support in times of crisis. In the film, institutions and mothers who have not listened create a precarious situation for two high school girls, Yessica (Ximena Ayala) and Miriam (Nancy Gutierrez). *Perfume de violetas: nadie te oye* presents women of various ages, classes, and family structures, who deny or blame the victim for her rape, thus remaining complicitous with patriarchal ideologies despite the supposed triumph of feminism's counter-ideologies. Miriam is from a family in which, in spite of the father's absence, middle class values prevail, while Yessica's conflict-ridden family is working class, a family that struggles to make ends meet. While Miriam's single mother (Arcelia Ramírez) overprotects her, Yessica's working class mother (María Rojo) emotionally abandons her daughter, withholding both affection and trust. Yessica's mother also introduces Yessica to her abusive partner and his son. The son, Jorge (Luis Fernando Peña), orchestrates Yessica's rape.

In Sistach's film, Yessica's violation is once again implied rather than explicitly visualized. Sistach transmits the violence of the rape by showing Yessica's shock and disorientation as her abduction takes place and after the rape happens. The rape sequence begins with a medium shot of Yessica walking in a narrow street towards the camera. Miriam walks at some distance behind her. As Yessica walks, Jorge and his friends drive a minibus up behind her. The men inside the minibus grab her and roughly pull her inside. As she helplessly watches her friend's abduction, Miriam heartrendingly calls Yessica's name. A series of shots cross-cutting Miriam's report of the abduction to her mother and Yessica's rape follow. These shots contrast Miriam's mother's skepticism to the reality of the crime. Miriam's mother is presented as a woman lacking a feminist consciousness, an unsupportive self-absorbed woman. Holding a mirror in one hand and a lipstick pencil in the other, she says: "You are saying that they took her, but it could be the opposite, that she provoked them." She then accuses Yessica of being a whore. To counter Miriam's mother's point of view, the camera intersects intense shots that attest to Yessica's rape, such as a close-up of Jorge's legs as he walks impatiently around a fire pit in an abandoned lot and waits for the rapist to "finish." Directly behind him sits the minibus in which Yessica is being raped. This shot is followed by a medium shot and then a long shot of the minibus and lot. The camera then cuts to shots in which Miriam's mother, despite her denial of Yessica's violation, becomes afraid of leaving Miriam alone (thus admitting the possibility that Miriam did witness an abduction) and takes her daughter with her to work.

The shot of Miriam's mother taking Miriam to work is paired with a series of shots showing Yessica's disorientation in the aftermath of her rape. These begin with a close-up of linens in colourful floral patterns hanging on lines to dry; the shot is taken from a very low angle and accompanied by a rhythmic but dismal electronic beat that resembles a heartbeat. Then Yessica appears, and the camera follows her as she staggers in circles tangling herself in the colourful sheets. This long take is so narrowly framed that, at times, the camera misses Yessica's body, creating a claustrophobic sense of physical and emotional unbalance. This scene can be considered a "primal scene" in the sense that it represents the trauma of rape. However, rather than having the narrative return to the scene of rape as in the two classical films, the return is written in the movement of Yessica's traumatized body. Yessica's body goes around in circles trying to find its way. As the camera moves back to a long shot, the audience realizes that Yessica is in Miriam's backyard, trying to contact her friend. Miriam, however, is not there, having been taken to her mother's workplace. The movement of the camera, with low angles from odd perspectives, and the dismal beat induce a loss of balance in the body of the spectator. Sistach, however, is careful to show empathy towards Yessica's situation rather than distance from rape-trauma; the sheets hanging on the line around which Yessica staggers are clean and colourful, offering Yessica partial comfort and love.

Yessica's abandonment culminates when even her closest friend deserts her. After the rape, Yessica and Miriam meet in the school's bathroom to talk. Yessica anticipates her friend's love and comfort. To her surprise, Miriam, much influenced by her mother's view of Yessica, turns against her friend, repeating some of the same arguments her mother used in previous scenes. Miriam's sudden and unexpected betrayal throws Yessica "off balance" again, and her desperation peaks. The audience gets the sense that Miriam's support might have helped Yessica overcome her trauma; Miriam's turning against her makes Yessica feel lost and abandoned. Unable to put her despair into words, Yessica pushes Miriam, who accidentally knocks her head on the toilet and dies.

The final scenes of *Perfume de violetas: nadie te oye* warn about the possible consequences women might suffer should they fail to support each other. After the deadly bathroom accident, Yessica steals the key from Miriam's dead body; she then goes into Miriam's house and hides under the blankets in Miriam's bed. When Miriam's mother arrives home, she first reacts anxiously because she finds the door open and Miriam's keys in the lock; however, anxiety turns into comfort when she sees a body-shaped bump under Miriam's blankets. Next, a low-angle shot shows Miriam's mother in the background and Yessica's smiling face partially covered by the blankets in the foreground. The shot informs the spectator, but not Miriam's mother, that the bump in the bed is not her daughter. At the end of the film, the phone rings. One suspects that the caller has news that Miriam is dead. While one could argue that in her post-traumatic state Yessica is searching for motherly love by taking Miriam's place in bed, the final scene's ominous tone implies that Yessica is getting her revenge on two unsupportive women who have failed to learn feminist lessons about supporting rape victims, despite the supposed feminist conquest of mainstream ideology.

One of the most obvious differences between *Conozco a las tres* and *Perfume de violetas: nadie te oye* is the relationship between female characters. While in the former film María's friends are unanimously supportive, in the latter film Yessica's closest friend turns against her, and so does Miriam's mother, who converts her rape into provocation, and Yessica into a whore. Yessica's own mother admonishes her for returning home late the day she was raped and refuses to trust Yessica's explanations for any of her behaviour. Thus, with the exception of the school nurses who tell Yessica that she does not have to tolerate such violence, women in the film perpetuate myths that blame victims for their rapes. Sistach's view of women can be related to shifts within feminism; the solidarity of *Conozco a las tres* relates to the 1970s feminism, which presumes women's solidarity as a backdrop, while the lack of support in *Perfume de violetas: nadie te oye* points to a post-feminist era in which solidarity has collapsed. In its rendering of women's continuing complicity with patriarchy, *Perfume de violetas: nadie te oye* challenges the current situation and implicitly calls for social activism. A similar call for solidarity is hinted at in María Novaro's film *Sin dejar huella* [*Without a Trace*, 2000] in a brief segment alluding to the infamous series of ongoing rapes and murders of women in northern Mexico.

RAPE IN JUÁREZ AS A CAUTIONARY TALE

In *Sin dejar huella*, Novaro's fourth feature-length film, there is an important reference to a factual series of rapes in a specific location: the city of Juárez, directly across the border from El Paso, Texas. Prominent in the media yet notoriously unsolved, the ongoing rapes and murders of women in Juárez call for, first, an examination of the politics of representation of the mutilated bodies of young female workers, and second, an explanation of the reasons behind this seeming epidemic of sexual violence at the turn of the twentieth century and into the twenty-first century. *Sin dejar huella* answers this call in two powerful sequences; the first proposes respect for the desecrated bodies, and the second implicates the police in the violence. *Sin dejar huella* may thus be seen in connection with the post-feminist situation outlined in *Perfume de violetas: nadie te oye*. Novaro's film is a true cautionary tale that asks for solidarity and activism around the rapes and murders that are still taking place in Juárez.

Most Mexicans know that many female *maquiladora* workers have been raped, killed, and dismembered in the northernmost city of Juárez.[6] The crimes have been part of the news since they began in the early 1990s. As the wave of violence continued, the terms "femicide" and "feminicide" were created to refer to this specific phenomenon. Several documentaries have addressed the femicides of Juárez, including Ursula Biemenn's *Performing the Border* (1999), Saul Landau and Sonia Angulo's *Maquila: A Tale of Two Mexicos* (2000), and Lourdes Portillo's *Señorita extraviada* [*Missing Young Woman*, 2001]. The femicides have also inspired fictional films such as Hector Molina's *Espejo Retrovisor* [*Rearview Mirror*, 2002], Enrique Murillo's *Las muertas de Juárez* [*The Dead Women of Juárez*, 2002], Kevin James Dobson's *The Virgin of Juárez* (2006), and Gregory Nava's *Bordertown* (2006). Writers have also looked to understand and document the possible reasons behind the Juárez femicides.[7]

Although not exclusively about this subject, *Sin dejar huella* is another film that engages in a discussion about Juárez's femicides. Novaro's road movie begins in Juárez, where Aurelia (Tiaré Scanda), a *maquiladora* worker and mother of two, lives. Aurelia explains that she is leaving town because, at the *maquiladora* where she works, her employers do not allow her to take time off for breast-feeding her newborn. The film also hints that a second, unstated reason also motivates her to leave Juárez. As Aurelia and her oldest child, Juanito, are eating a pizza dinner on the couch of the living room, the local news is on TV. The presence of the news broadcast briefly takes the viewer outside the fictional narrative of the film. Unexpectedly, the viewer sees a medium shot of Juanito's eyes opening wide. The soundtrack coming from the television explains the horror in his eyes as the news broadcaster announces that "The lifeless body of a twenty-year-old *maquiladora* worker has been found in a garbage dump in one of Ciudad de Juárez's poor neighbourhoods; the body shows clear signs of sexual violence." The newscaster then provides background information that clarifies that the murder is not an isolated crime when he says: "This is the eighteenth case this year, and altogether the sex crimes in Ciudad Juárez add up to a total of 250." In contrast to the films examined above, this is the first time that rape is approached as a real-life external event and that sexual violence is related to a specific time and place, Juárez at the turn of the twentieth century.

Sin dejar huella intervenes in the discourse surrounding the representation of rape in the Juárez context, creating a feminist response to the onslaught of sensationalized accounts. In *Juárez: The Laboratory of Our Future* (1998), for example, journalist Charles Bowden writes about and photographs the dead bodies of young women in a crude and romanticized way, turning the dead bodies into fetishes.[8] Unlike Bowden's book, where mutilated and burned bodies occupy the centre of the photographs, in *Sin dejar huella* the body of the young murdered worker only leaves traces of its violent end. The scene in which Juanito is looking at the news continues with a shot in which Aurelia, who has been doing household tasks around the room, hears the broadcaster and anxiously asks her son: "What are you watching?" The camera moves to a long shot of Aurelia and Juanito, and then to a brief reverse-shot showing the television image of the place where the body was found. The victim's corpse has been removed, and the only indication of violence in the image is a thin trickle of blood. Here Novaro's strategy is similar to that defended by other feminist intellectuals; in "Towards a Planetary Civil Society," Rosa Linda Fregoso brings up the question: "How does one represents the dead in a respectful manner, in a way that does not further sacrilize their bodies, but honors the memory of their former existence?" (26). Fregoso sees in Portillo's *Señorita Extraviada* an example of respect because "Not a single dead body appears in the film" (26). The same thing can be said about *Sin dejar huella*, a film in which the raped body is respected in its absence.

Novaro's film alludes a second time to the chaotic and lawless Mexican border. This second sequence needs to be seen in the context of the debate surrounding the causes of the femicides. In "Towards a Planetary Civil Society," Fregoso critiques the ways in which the murders of Juárez have been explained. The accounts Fregoso refers to argue that femicides are a response to a change in normative sexuality brought by the global capitalism of the *maquiladoras*.[9] To counter these accounts, Fregoso proposes to look at the way Mexican law and local government treat domestic violence.[10] In line with Fregoso, *Señorita extraviada* includes a scene depicting Ramón Galindo, mayor of Juárez. Galindo appears in the news to explain that the women killed are women who do not conform to normative sexuality. Galindo recommends that Juárez's citizens stay at home at night to avoid the same thing happening to them. In Portillo's film, these televised remarks by the mayor show the extent to which the local government is complicit with the killings by presenting the victims as prostitutes rather than workers, and in that way justifying and blaming them for their deaths.

Sin dejar huella similarly calls attention to the government's, specifically the police's, involvement in the violence. The film refers to a widespread suspicion of police inaction during a conversation that takes place at a police station between a detainee, Spanish art dealer Marilú (Aitana Sánchez-Gijón), and the chief of police, Mendizabal (Jesús Ochoa). After Mendizabal blatantly sexually harasses her, Marilú asks him: "Why don't you solve the murders of Juárez and leave me alone?" Marilú directly challenges the police chief's priorities by asking why he is bothering her, an art dealer trafficking in falsified Mayan art, instead of trying to solve a more urgent matter, the femicides. At the same time, the scene also hints at the police's direct participation in the femicides by presenting the police chief as a sexual offender. This scene can be read in relation to extratextual information such as the testimony given by a rape survivor in *Señorita extraviada*, who explains that the police participated in the raping. *Sin dejar huella* points in the same direction, suggesting the direct implication of the police by making Mendizabal a sexual predator.

Unlike *Doña Bárbara* and *La negra Angustias*, narrative development in *Sin dejar huella* is not based on the main character's experience of rape and consequent personal transformation; in fact, hearing about or seeing the traces of rape does not transform Aurelia. What Novaro's film does is localize femicide, closely associating it with Juárez. The "primal scene" in *Sin dejar huella* appears on television. Although only one report of femicide appears in Novaro's film, the spectator is reminded that there have been 250 reports up to that moment. These implied instances haunt Aurelia, who reacts by calling her sister and arranging her departure to Cancún, a city as distant as possible from Juárez. The film does not compulsively return to the Juárez rape/murder, but Aurelia's fear does not disappear. In fact, in a complicated twist of events, the main narrative hinges on the attempts by Aurelia and Marilú to escape from police chief Mendizabal. Novaro's film is a true cautionary tale that warns that systematic sexual violence against women persists and is growing. When read together with Sistach's call for continued activism in a post-feminist era, *Sin dejar huella* suggests that much solidarity and activism are still needed in Juárez.

CONCLUDING REMARKS

Since rape has been and continues to be a central issue for feminism, my goal has been to examine some representations of rape in Mexican cinema, paying special attention to the emergence of a discourse on rape from a feminist perspective. My analysis of these representations suggests several conclusions. Firstly, representations of rape are historical; that is, they depend on the ways that rape is generally understood during a given period. My examination of two classical narratives, *La negra Angustias* and *Doña Bárbara*, demonstrates the use of rape as a narrative trope that can be contextualized as a 1940s approach. Two elements of this approach are the idea that rape is a traumatic "primal scene" to which the protagonists return and the notion that rape makes female characters into mannish women.

The historical nature of representations of rape can also be seen in the feminist films examined. My comparison of three feminist representations of rape produced in a three-decade span shows a historical shift in feminist concerns. Feminist discussion of rape evolves from stressing the need to go public in *Rompiendo el silencio* in the 1970s to considerations of the personal toll paid by women who go public in *Conozco a las tres* in the 1980s. In the 2000s, *Perfume de violetas: nadie te oye* responds to a post-feminist backlash against feminist activism. The historical shift referred to is especially clear in the case of Sistach, who presents supportive women characters in her films of the 1980s and unsupportive women in the post-feminist 2000s. Sistach's strategies to represent rape also evolve; in *Conozco a las tres*, María's wrestling with the rapist creates fear and anxiety in the spectators. By contrast, *Perfume de violetas: nadie te oye* focuses on the victim's post-traumatic disorientation.

Representations of rape are also contingent upon the political and cultural agendas of specific interest groups. The relationship to specific agendas is first illustrated by the contrast between women's interests and traditional patriarchal values. While de Fuentes reinforces mainstream values geared to undermine women's acquisition of social power, Landeta gives social power to her heroine. With the advent of the feminist movement, films made by women reflect yet another agenda. The feminist films examined here address rape, not as a trope, but as a sociological and psychological reality. This reality is the backdrop of *Rompiendo el silencio*, *Conozco a las tres*, and *Perfume de violetas: nadie te oye* and is especially important in *Sin dejar huella*, where rapes can be counted, where 250 women have been killed. The emergence of a feminist awareness has contributed to directly addressing the crime of rape in Mexican cinema.

WORKS CITED

Arredondo, Isabel. 2002. 'Tenía bríos y, aún vieja, los sigo teniendo': Reflexiones y entrevista a Matilde Landeta. *Mexican Studies/Estudios Mexicanos* 18, no. 1: 189–204.

Bowden, Charles. 1998. *Juárez: The Laboratory of Our Future*. New York: Aperture.

Brinkema, Eugenie. 2005. Rape and the Rectum: Bersani, Deleuze, Noe. *Camera Obscura* 58: 32–57.

Burton-Carvajal, Julianne. 1993. Regarding Rape: Fictions of Origin and Film Spectatorship. In *Mediating Two Worlds: Cinematic Encounters in the Americas*.

Ed. John King, Ana M. López, and Manuel Alvarado, 258–68. London: British Film Institute.

Crosthwaite, Luis Humberto, John William Byrd, and Bobby Byrd, eds. 2003. *Puro Border: Dispatches, Snapshots and Graffiti*. El Paso: Cinco Puntos Press.

Fregoso, Rosa Linda. 2003. *Mexicana Encounters: The Making of Social Identities on the Borderlands*. Berkeley: University of California Press.

Haskell, Molly. 1974. *From Reverence to Rape: The Treatment of Women in the Movies*. New York: Holt, Rinehart and Winston.

Hershfield, Joanne. 1996. *Mexican Cinema/Mexican Woman, 1940–1950*. Tucson: University of Arizona Press.

Hesford, Wendy S. 1999. Reading Rape Stories: Material Rhetoric and the Trauma of Representation. *College English* 62, no. 2: 192–221.

Horeck, Tanya. 2004. *Public Rape: Representing Violation in Fiction and Film*. London: Routledge.

Landeta, Matilde, Julianne Burton-Carvajal, Mauricio Montiel Figueiras, and Gustavo García. 2002. *Matilde Landeta, hija de la revolución*. Mexico: Arte e imagen. CONACULTA, Dirección de Publicaciones.

López, Ana M. 1991. Tears and Desire: Women and Melodrama in the "Old" Mexican Cinema. *Iris: A Journal of Theory on Image and Sound* 13: 29–51.

Luna, Andrés de. 1984. Las rasgaduras de lo inmediato. *Unomásuno*, March 31, Saturday supplement.

Millán, Márgara. 1999. *Derivas de un cine femenino*. Mexico City: Programa Universitario de Estudios de Género.

Projansky, Sarah. 1995. Working on Feminism: Film and Television Rape Narratives and Postfeminist Culture. PhD diss., University of Iowa.

———. 2001. *Watching Rape: Film and Television in Postfeminist Culture*. New York: New York University Press.

———. 2001. The Elusive/Ubiquitous Representation of Rape: A Historical Survey of Rape in U.S. Film, 1903–1972. *Cinema Journal* 41, no. 1: 63–90.

Quinones, Sam. 2001. *True Tales from Another Mexico: The Lynch Mob, the Popsicle Kings, Chalino, and the Bronx*. Albuquerque: University of New Mexico Press.

Rashkin, Elissa. 2001. *Women Filmmakers in Mexico: The Country of Which We Dream*. Austin: University of Texas Press.

Sommer, Doris. 1991. *Foundational Fictions: The National Romances of Latin America*. Berkeley: University of California Press.

FILMS

Bordertown. Directed by Gregory Nava. Capitol Film, 2006.

Conozco a las tres. Directed by Marisa Sistach. Zafra, 1983.

Doña Bárbara. Directed by Fernando de Fuentes. Clasa Films Mundiales, 1943.

Espejo retrovisor. Directed by Hector Molina. World Film Magic Distribution, 2002.

Las muertas de Juárez. Directed by Enrique Murillo. Laguna Productions, 2002.

La negra Angustias. Directed by Matilde Landeta. Técnicos y Actores Cinematográficos Mexicanos Asociados (TACMA). 1949.

Maquila: A Tale of Two Mexicos.. Directed by Saul Landau and Sonia Angulo. Cinema Guild, 2000.

My Filmmaking, My Life: Matilde Landeta. Directed by Patricia Díaz. Women Make Movies, 1990.

Perfume de violetas: nadie te oye. Directed by Marisa Sistach. TLA Releasing, 2000.

Rompiendo el silencio. Directed by Rosa Martha Fernández. Universidad Nacional Autónoma de México, 1979.

Señorita extraviada. Directed by Lourdes Portillo. Women Make Movies, 2001.

Sin dejar huella. Directed by María Novaro. Alta Films, 2000.

The Virgin of Juárez. Directed by Kevin James Dobson. First Look International, 2006.

VIDEOS

Performing the Border. Directed by Ursula Biemann. Women Make Movies, 1999.

NOTES

1 Doña Bárbara literally means "Miss Barbarous," and she is referred to as the "*devora-hombres*" or man-eater, a role performed by María Félix in other films as well.

2 According to Landeta, Angustias "había tenido el trauma de ver a la cabra hacer el amor" [was traumatizad by seeing the goat make love] (Arredondo, 201).

3 In "Regarding Rape: Fictions of Origin and Film Spectatorship," Julianne Burton-Carvajal expands on Doris Sommer's notion of foundational fictions in order to frame rape in Latin American film. Sommer suggests that each historical period creates narratives of national origin related to national historical processes. For instance, nineteenth-century novelists propose national unity through narratives in which heterosexual romance dominates. Burton-Carvajal creates the term "anti-foundational fiction" to refer to narratives in which national origins are established by chaos rather than order (260). For Burton-Carvajal, the fictions of Latin American Boom writers in which romance fails are examples of anti-foundational fictions. Burton-Carvajal suggests that rape is a trope that prevails in times in which "an era or a social sector perceives itself subject to threat" (261). During unstable periods, she explains, national discourse "recurs defensively to figures of violation to express its own desperate urge to reassert the legitimacy of its own claim to command." *Doña Bárbara* and *La negra Angustias* are anti-foundational fictions according to Burton-Carvajal's definition. If that is the case, what is the desperate urge that is at the heart of these narratives? What legitimacy needs to be reasserted? "In Tears and Desire: Women and Melodrama in the 'Old' Mexican Cinema," Ana María López uses Carlos Monsiváis studies in melodrama to establish the relationship between melodrama and the building of the Mexican nation in the post-revolutionary period. Following Monsiváis's argument about melodrama's socializing function, López writes that melodramas exposed the contradictions and desires within Mexican society at least in three ways: "The clash between old (feudal, Porfirian) values and modern (industrialized, urban) life, the crisis of male identity that emerges as a result of this clash, and the instability of the female identity that at once guarantees and threatens the passage from the old to the new" (511). López thus proposes that gender issues are at the core of the conflicts depicted in classical melodramas. Joanne Hershfield's detailed study of *Doña Bárbara* in *The Representation of Woman in Mexican Cinema 1943–50* (1993) also proposes that gender issues are at the heart of the conflict presented in de Fuentes' film. López and Hershfield's studies help answer to the question posed earlier of what legitimacy is at stake. *La negra Angustias* and *Doña Bárbara* engage shifts in gender roles and expectations in 1940s society, in which masculinity is threatened.

4 Jorge Ayala Blanco argued that Mexican feminist cinema, best represented by Cine-Mujer, was insignificant, among other things due to its failed representational strategies (Rashkin, 70). Angeles Necoechea responded

to Ayala Blanco's criticism in "Una experiencia de trabajo" [A Work Experience]. Márgara Millán and Elissa Rashkin dedicate sections of *Derivas de un cine femenino* (Millán, 111–23) and *Women Filmmakers in Mexico* (Rashkin, 68–74) to Cine-Mujer.

5   In "Reading Rape Stories," Wendy Hesford discusses the difficult question of whether or not rape should be represented on the screen, and if it has to be represented, how artists may avoid making rape into a sensational and entertaining spectacle.

6   *Maquiladora* is the name given to the U.S.-owned factories that are located on the Mexican side of the border; they became prominent after the North American Free Trade Agreement eased regulations for U.S. companies doing business in Mexico. The U.S. companies benefited from the agreement by paying low wages to Mexican workers, a majority of whom were women, many of them in their teens or twenties. The sex crimes in Juárez began in 1994, a little after the implementation of the Free Trade Agreement and the creation of most of the *maquiladoras*. Some propose that the sex crimes are the product of the *maquiladoras*, not in the sense that *maquiladoras* organize these crimes, but in the sense that they create a new social structure in which community is fragile and powerful social actors, such as drug dealers and police, can act with impunity.

7   The literature on femicides includes Charles Bowden's *Juárez: The Laboratory of Our Future* (1998), Sam Quinones' "The Dead Women of Juárez," in *True Tales of Another Mexico* (Quinones, 137–52), and *Puro Border* (2003), edited by Luis Humberto Crosthwaite,

John William Byrd, and Bobby Byrd, which includes a section entitled "May Our Daughters Come Home/Nuestras hijas de regreso a casa" (139–80). Rosa Linda Fregoso also wrote about femicides in "Towards a Planetary Civil Society" included in *Mexicana Encounters* (2003).

8   Bowden also writes a fantasy narrative for Adriana, one of the victims, in which he imagines life with Adriana and her two children in a terrestrial paradise (in Fregoso, 15).

9   Through her analysis of Saul Landau and Sonia Angulo's *Maquila: A Tale of Two Mexicos* (2000) and Ursula Biemann's *Performing the Border* (1999), Fregoso argues that the femicides have been seen through the prism of global capitalism in a meta-narrative that argues that the non-normative sexuality of the victims explains the crimes. The overall idea is that *maquiladora* culture altered prevailing gender power relations (*machismo*) and normative sexuality. The young women working in the *maquiladoras* have more mobility with the money they earn and, as a result, more sexual freedom. Portillo points out that this sexual freedom is presented as a disruption of the social fabric and as a facilitator of non-normative sexuality. This newly gained freedom produces hatred that finds expression in femicides. Fregoso argues that this narrative, although well-intentioned, is complicit with patriarchy because it sees women as objects in need of regulation and surveillance. Fregoso also remarks that this explanation blurs the difference between *maquila* workers and prostitutes, proposing that *maquila* workers are sex workers.

10 Fregoso proposes to look at the women raped and killed as abject subjects, as social rejects. She finds proof of this abjection in Mexico's judiciary system, in which sexual violence is treated as part of domestic violence, and set under the jurisdiction of the family, rather than a wider social realm. Fregoso also argues that Mexican law has rejected the creation of new regulations that could help solve the problem of sexual violence.

A SHAMANIC TRANSMODERNITY: JUAN MORA CATLETT'S *ERÉNDIRA IKIKUNARI*

Keith John Richards
Universidad Mayor de San Andrés, La Paz, Bolivia

The current political environment in Latin America, with its varied shifts towards self-determination and emancipation, requires a coherent theoretical and aesthetic framework in order to have lasting impact. It is a case, not only of emergence from present-day U.S. hegemony, but also of liberation from the legacy of European colonization. There is a growing awareness of the historical circumstances involved in the formation of Latin America and its current economic and social problems, even in those countries where popular political representation has not been achieved. Consumerism, evangelism, and a continued sense of Latin American inferiority to the 'developed' world are still deep-rooted presences, despite the new sense of political independence that is emerging in the early twenty-first century. In this context the term "postcolonial" seems problematic, not to say wishful thinking. Jorge Klor de Alva's rejection of the notion in a Latin American context is still persuasive in this region where the effects of globalization have replaced those of Iberian colonialism as the invasive force.

Nevertheless, the concept of decolonization is steadily gaining currency, despite the continued sense of unfinished business in terms of a satisfactory response to the upheaval created by a half-millennium of colonialism and its legacies. Conceptual alternatives to the notion of a "postcolonial" reality include the "coloniality" proposed by Aníbal Quijano as a means of avoiding the kind of problems outlined by Klor de Alva. According to Quijano, the global pattern of capitalist power: "is founded on the imposition of a racial/ethnic classification of the world's population as a cornerstone in said pattern of power and operates in each one of its levels, ambits and dimensions, both material and subjective, of daily social existence and at societal level. It originates and is globalized from America." (Quijano, 342). While Klor alerts one to the questionable application of concepts more valid in other parts of the world, Quijano's work identifies a global condition that has emerged from the Latin American situation.

However, in order to frame this discussion of Juan Mora Catlett's aesthetically innovative and discursively litigious 2006 film, *Eréndira Ikikunari* (*Indomitable Eréndira*), which follows on from his equally audacious *Retorno a Aztlán* (*Return to Aztlán*, 1991), I will consider aspects of Enrique Dussel's notion of transmodernity, a term conceptually related to a discussion of colonialism. Dussel has long been identified with a project of Latin American liberation philosophy, largely concerned with opposing what he sees as a Eurocentric version of modernity advanced by Friedrich Hegel and continued by Jürgen Habermas. Dussel speaks of the unwillingness or inability of European thinkers to assimilate and rectify the epistemological imbalance left over from the era of conquest and colonialism. Europe was shifted into the centre of world history and cartography, and, as Dussel puts it: "Modernity elaborated a myth of its own goodness, rationalized its violence as civilizing, and finally declared itself innocent of the assassination of the Other" (1992b, 50). This process, which implied the very conceptualization of Europe and accompanied the area's emergence from obscurity into domination, required ideological justification and rationalization (Dussel 2000). Dussel's *The Invention of the Americas. Eclipse of "the Other" and the Myth of Modernity* (1995b) supports his notion of modernity as a product of European domination with ample references to pre-Columbian civilizations (Guaraní, Aztec, Inca) as part of an indigenous world which, he argues, was "already humanized in its totality when Columbus arrived" (81). In this sense, Dussel's own project is "a project of political, economic, erotic, ecological, pedagogical, and religious liberation." As he puts in his own words, it proposes: "an *incorporative* solidarity between center/periphery, man/woman, different races, different ethnic groups, different classes, civilization/nature, Western culture/Third World cultures" (Dussel 1995a, 76). Dussel's eclectic methodology and his radical revision of the relationship between Latin America and the 'First World' offer a theory that is appealing and particularly relevant to the analysis of *Eréndira Ikikunari*. Dussel's interest in salvaging ancient non-European culture systems, his utopian focus on a genuinely multicultural future, non-Eurocentric perspective and emphasis on North–South dialogue is in keeping with the discourse and aesthetic focus of Juan Mora Catlett's cinema.

A brief synopsis of *Eréndira Ikikunari* should begin by mentioning the opening credits (of which more will be said below). They are crucial since they establish the film's tone and two of its sources – the codex commissioned by Don Pedro Cuynierángari, the Governor of Michoacán, in the sixteenth century as a report to the Viceroy, and a computer-generated reconstruction of a mural at Ixmiquilpan depicting the conquest from an indigenous perspective. By means of these and other sources, Mora Catlett sets out to create what he calls a "pre-Columbian cinematographic codex." The narrative itself opens at the court of Tangaxoan, lord of the Purépecha, an ethnic group based mainly in the Mexican state of Michoacán. Tangaxoan (Rubén Bautista) asks about the marriage to Eréndira (Xochiquetzal Rodríguez) of a young nobleman, Nanuma (Justo Alberto Rodríguez). The following scene introduces Eréndira, establishing her nonconformist attitude as she expresses dissent regarding the planned marriage to Nanuma, a man she finds loathsome. Eréndira rejects not only this choice of husband but the traditional role of women in general, a position in complete contrast to her aunt's acquiescence. From the opening sequences, we also learn of Eréndira's allegiances and admirers: Nanuma's brother, T'shue (Luis Esteban Huacuz Dimas), is secretly enamoured of the young woman, Eréndira identifies with the goddess Xarátanga, and her uncle Timas (Roberto Isidro Rangel) harbours a certain sympathy with her rebellious nature.

Fig. 1. Court of Tangaxoan (Rubén Bautista and uncredited actors). Photo by Toni Kuhn. (courtesy of Juan Mora Catlett).

An apocalyptic prophecy made by an old woman at court reveals that the ancestral gods are about to be vanquished by foreign deities who will behead Tangaxoan. Timas learns of the presence of the Spaniards and is prepared to fight. But Tangaxoan, fearful and dominated by omens, resolves to commit suicide before the prophecy can be fulfilled. Later, convinced that the foreigners do not come to harm them, he and his lieutenant Cuynierángari (Edgar Alejandre Pérez) decide to collaborate. A battle takes place in which the forces of Tangaxoan and Cuynierángari join the Spaniards to fight those of Timas, who allows Eréndira to fight. During the battle, Eréndira takes a white horse belonging to a fallen Spaniard. Nanuma is furious with Eréndira's rejection and her general disobedience: he eventually sides with the Spaniards, betrays Timas, and arouses the enmity of his own brother. The ambiguous outcome hints at Eréndira's survival as a constant challenge to the defeatism and self-betrayal represented by Tangaxoan. The affective element presents

Fig. 2. Eréndira (Xochiquetzal Rodríguez) with aunt (Adelaida Huerta): Eréndira's defiance is notable from her first appearance onward. Photo by Toni Kuhn (courtesy of Juan Mora Catlett).

another ambiguity because Eréndira displays far greater affinity with the horse than with any of the male characters. She resists the machismo and fatalism of her own culture as much as the threat of foreign invasion. It is a defiant position that reflects the aesthetic of a director who is as rigorous and uncompromising as he is eclectic. Mora Catlett insists upon the use of Purépecha, a language with little over 120,000 speakers, for its authenticity and sonorous qualities. He elects to tell this story, set in the sixteenth century, through the conjoined use of archaic and highly modern elements.

Some intriguing parallels are suggested, then, in considering Mora Catlett's work in the light of Dussel's theories. In addition, Mora Catlett's *Eréndira Ikikunari* does something akin to what the extraordinary Chilean filmmaker Raúl Ruiz proposes in his writings. In offering the notion of a "shamanic cinema" (Ruiz 1995, 73–90) Ruiz draws comparisons between the American continent and cinema itself – both of which, he argues, developed "in two directions: as industry and utopia." Both, too, were discovered on several occasions. Ruiz opposes the "predatory" industrial approach with the craft, a dichotomy he likens to witchcraft and science. Perhaps surprisingly, it is the film industry, with its tendency to capture souls, which is represented by the shamanic. Cinematic history could be explained as a periodic confrontation between industry and craft, were it not for a third force – that of the entrance of artists and intellectuals into filmmaking. Ruiz's notion of shamanic cinema is based on his rejection of conventional narrative in film as he yearns for "a cinema capable of accounting [...] for the varieties of experience in the sensible world" (Ruiz 1995, 90). A crucial element in this vision is the role and nature of memory. Ruiz argues that we all associate apparently disparate scraps of memory "so that incidents which did not actually happen in succession are juxtaposed." The human mind carries numerous films within it (1995, 79). However, whereas orthodox film practice reduces this apparently random association to orderly, immediately comprehensible patterns, the shamanic alternative permits new possibilities that we had not previously conceived or else had forgotten or consigned to our subconscious. If this can apply to the individual subject, why should it not also pertain to the collective? My contention here is that Mora Catlett's *Eréndira Ikikunari* does something akin to Ruiz's cinematic shamanism using elements that conjoin past, present, and pure imagination in order to re-establish a buried, suppressed cultural reality.

It is in this kind of environment of openness to previously little-explored subjectivities that Latin American cinema is finding ways of continuing the legacy of radical movements from the 1960s and 1970s. The undeniable achievements of the New Latin American Cinema of the 1960s and 1970s are a palpable legacy and by no means consigned to a bygone era, as is demonstrated by such powerful work as Fernando Solanas's *La dignidad de los nadies* [*The Dignity of the Nobodies*, 2005] or Patricio Guzmán's *Salvador Allende* (2004). In more recent times, Eliseo Subiela is only one of several Latin American filmmakers who have spoken of the movement's shortcomings in reaching a popular audience, since it produced: "un cine que tenía muy buenas intenciones pero que tenía una mala relación con el público" ["a very well-intentioned cinema but one which had a poor relationship with the public"] (Orell García 2006, 179). The concern with expressing social and political concerns in more poetic or accessible ways is visible in recent tendencies in Latin American film, perhaps most notably the movement towards an examination of individual and collective realities within their own context and without excluding the possibility of local responses to these conditions. Another is the variety of perspectives and subject-matter now being investigated, a development that accompanies a greater freedom in forging new forms of expression. Recognition of Latin America's cultural diversity is another tendency, a willingness to explore marginal subjectivities from within. This is a departure from previous inclinations to simply examine subjects as exotic case studies or as illustrations of a priori ideological assumptions. Even for the well-intentioned urban filmmaker in Latin America, the region's indigenous cultures have been the most remote and elusive of subjects, the most susceptible to erroneous perceptions and interpretation. Their treatment involves an approach to narrative techniques and forms of perception that have yet to be fully explored and satisfactorily executed in film. Ruiz, who is not addressing this problem specifically, nevertheless laments the expressive impoverishment of cinema generally. In speaking in terms of the shamanic in film, he proposes "nothing other than a cinema capable of inventing a new grammar each time it goes from one world to the next" (1995, 90).

A number of factors have given rise to an increase in representation of indigenous peoples in various Latin American national cinemas. That some of these factors are technical and economic is beyond doubt: one can cite far easier and cheaper access to audiovisual equipment through videotape followed by the digital revolution. This is accompanied by a readiness to fund organizations that foment audiovisual self-representation among indigenous communities. In Bolivia, there is the La Paz-based CEFREC (Centro de Formación y Realización Indígena, or Cinematography Education and Production Center). Mexican organizations include the Centre for Indigenous Video (Centro de Video Indígena, or CVI), which operates in Oaxaca, and Guatemala has its Centro Cultural y de Recursos Audiovisuales (Cultural and Audiovisual Resource Centre) or LUCIERNAGA, to name but a few. There is also continued activity on the part of non-indigenous Latin American filmmakers whose interest in native cultures is allied to a keen political awareness. Perhaps the best example of this is Jorge Sanjinés' *La nación clandestina* (*The Clandestine Nation*, 1988) in which the plight of an Aymara individual exemplifies

dilemmas of acculturation and economic need. The protagonist, Sebastián, is perceived as having betrayed his community not only through
his migration to La Paz but also in his collusion with the military. His
self-imposed martyrdom is also an act of cultural restoration since he
elects to perform the sacrificial *danzanti*, a ritual dance to death originally
conceived as an offering to ensure good harvests. In Sanjinés' film, this
serves to fuse and crystallize political and cultural concerns in a way that
is affecting and satisfying in its visual style and narration. However, its
mode of perception is still external to indigenous reality and its use of
the dance is removed from its ritual function in order to address a social
and political imbalance rather than a cosmological one; thus the cultural
is subsumed by the ideological. Nonetheless, this film can be seen as
the foremost example of a tendency that Sanjinés and the group refined
through films such as *Ukamau* (*And So It Is*, 1966) and *Yawar Mallku*
(*Blood of the Condor*, 1969).

If *The Clandestine Nation* has few equals in Latin American film, as
regards lucidity in conveying visions simultaneously within and outside
indigenous cultural positions, it is surprising that more has not been
achieved in this particular direction in Mexico, which has the largest
indigenous population in the Americas. The critic Jorge Ayala Blanco
was moved to comment in 1979:

> Si consideramos que cerca del 10% de la población mexicana
> pertenece a diversas razas indígenas, y que más de la mitad son
> mestizos, no podrá menos que asombrarnos lo parcamente que
> el cine mexicano ha tratado el tema de los indígenas.

> [If we consider that almost 10% of the Mexican population be-
> longs to diverse indigenous races, and that more than half are
> *mestizos*, it is nothing less than astonishing to see how scantly
> Mexican cinema has treated the subject of indigenous people.]
> (193)

Ayala Blanco is probably the fiercest critic of what he sees as a catalogue
of hypocrisies and misrepresentations of the native in Mexican film.
He is not alone. According to Charles Ramírez Berg, the Indian is a
"structured absence" in Mexican cinema (138). Ramírez Berg talks, not

only about the shortage of images, the native's marginalization from the screen, but also about how the notion of national essence, or *mexicanidad*, is constructed from the mainstream Mexican cinema's interaction with an "other" with which it coexists territorially but whose independent existence it is at pains not to recognize. Also it is undeniable that the indigenous in Mexican cinema has been confined to a representative cage restricting any radical cultural vision that defies Eurocentric orthodoxies.

Pre-Columbian Indian cultures have been constructed out of oblivion and silence, since not even well-intentioned filmmakers such as Mora Catlett and Nicolás Echeverría have access to materials for its creation. Such filmmakers must make use of anthropological observations. As well as his celebrated 1990 feature *Cabeza de Vaca*, Echeverría has made several ethnographic documentaries. There are also sources of doubtful accuracy like the fanciful engravings of the sixteenth-century Liège-based illustrator Theodor de Bry, who, significantly, never travelled to the Americas. However, it is not possible either to speak of a systematic demonization of the Mexican Indian like that seen in the North American Western. The native, indeed, has never been used as internal enemy for the demagogic purposes of the white or *mestizo* elite in Mexico, which has opted for a deceptive discourse of inclusion. Nevertheless, in spite of a rhetoric that, until recently, has denied it, the Indian has been seen as an obstacle to the notion of progress conceived in the national project. The famous postulation of a *"raza cósmica"* [*Cosmic Race*, 1925] by José Vasconcelos in 1925 does not incorporate the native as an active ingredient. This discourse acted as a smoke screen concealing a governmental policy that rendered autochthonous cultures malleable to a western vision of industrialization, capitalism, and individualism. Ramírez Berg sees in several Mexican films the traces of an internal colonialism that perceives whiteness as a "phenotypical ideal." The social status of the *mestizo*, according to him, improves due to its relative proximity to the required pale skin (137).

In his list of 'mythologies' of Mexican cinema, Carlos Monsiváis approaches the subject of indigenous marginalization somewhat obliquely (18–19). He places the trivialization of pre-Columbian history in his second category, "atmospheres," which includes "Xochimilco y el istmo de Tehuántepec: los paraísos perdidos" ["Xochimilco and the Isthmus of Tehuantepec: lost paradises"] as well as Broadway-style pseudo-folkloric dances, which he styles "gótico mexicano" ["Mexican gothic"], including "la secularización del Más Allá que utiliza aparecidos del virreintato, momias aztecas, hombres lobos, sacerdotes del culto a Huitzilopochtli, mujeres vampiro" ["a secularization of the Beyond that employs phantoms from the viceroyalty, Aztec mummies, wolf-men, high priests to the cult of Huitzilopochtli, vampire women."] The burlesque tone used by Monsiváis should not, however, distract from a reality in which, according to Juan Mora Catlett: "lo indígena es visto como retraso y obstáculo al desarrollo de los proyectos de la clase en el poder en México, donde mucha de su riqueza proviene del robo y de la explotación inhumana del indígena, desde la época de la colonia" ["the indigenous is seen as backward, as an obstacle to the development of the projects of those in power in Mexico, much of whose wealth has come from robbery and inhuman exploitation of indigenous people since colonial times."][1]

Accordingly, Monsiváis offers as his sixth mythology the "cultural nationalism" that he describes as fertile terrain for involuntary humour without ceasing to be a constant stimulant for societies isolated by poverty and the search for psychological compensations (27). Jorge Prior, the producer of *Return to Aztlán*, has recognized the power of myth in the national project, declaring "a mí se me hace envidiable lo que hicieron los japoneses por muchos años de aprovechar sus leyendas y su pasado de una manera impresionante y creo que el cine mexicano no lo hizo." ["I find enviable what the Japanese did for many years in making the most of their legends and their past in such an impressive manner and I think it's something Mexican cinema didn't do."] Prior fails to mention that such use of legend in Japan excludes that country's aboriginal Ainu population. Its adoption in Mexico would involve an assimilation of indigenous heritage in a way hitherto unknown. The adoption and re-signification of autochthonous legend in Mexico is precisely what Prior and Mora Catlett have achieved in both *Return to Aztlán* and *Eréndira Ikikunari*.

Up to now the Mexican nation has simply required the genetic, linguistic, cultural, and economic absorption of indigenous peoples. This passivity demanded of the Native has rarely been questioned in cinema, where the indigenous presence has often been latent and abstruse, serving to bolster the national imaginary rather than evoke a living entity. Such representation has characterized the work of Emilio "El Indio" Fernández, whose very nickname is a telling affectation (Fernández was a *mestizo*, son of a Spanish immigrant father and Kickapoo Indian mother). Andrea Noble's meticulous investigation of Fernández's *María Candelaria* (1943) is noteworthy here, particularly in the light of Serge Gruzinski's examination of the conflictive relationship between Christian and indigenous iconography (Noble, 81–84). According to Noble, Fernández's protagonist María Candelaria (Dolores del Río), rendered overtly representative of the Mexican nation, is "essentially hybrid" (81), subject to rival claims to her 'ownership' by indigenous and white men, and to contrasting associations which link her to "the imagistic dialogue between pre-Columbian past and Post-Columbian present" (82). Recent film practice in this area has sought a break with such paternalism and the convoluted semiotics that supported it.

The critic José Felipe Coria sees *Return to Aztlán* as the first Mexican film narrated from an indigenous viewpoint, using an indigenous aesthetic, as well as being acted and conceived in Náhuatl (34). For Coria, *Return to Aztlán* provides a rare link between the cinema of Fernández and the present. However, this putative heritage is something that Juan Mora Catlett rejects out of hand:

> En ningún momento tomé referencias de la representación del indígena en el cine mexicano que siempre parten de la visión condescendiente de la clase media, en mi opinión, mis películas están, en ese sentido, totalmente divorciadas de esa tradición, por eso creo que Jorge Ayala Blanco usó las palabras "insólita representación" al referirse a mi trabajo.

> [At no point did I take references from representations of the indigenous in Mexican cinema which, in my opinion, always depart from the condescending vision of the middle class. My films are, in that sense, totally divorced from that tradition. I think that's why Jorge Ayala Blanco used the words "unusual representation" to refer to my work.]

Implicit in Mora Catlett's approach to the indigenous presence in cinema is nothing less than an overhaul of the relationship between film and anthropology, not to mention the political and aesthetic ramifications of a genuine incorporation of the native into national life. It evokes the words of Jean Rouch when the legendary ethnographic filmmaker spoke of the minimal difference between film and ethnography. Rouch compares the activities of recording, editing, and distribution shared by the two professions (68). The distinction between them is also blurred by the celebrated Argentine cineaste Jorge Prelorán, who constantly refuses to be described as an ethnographer or anthropologist despite his non-fictional portrayal of marginalized or solitary individuals from the rural poor.

The character Eréndira has seen numerous manifestations; her story has been re-told in order to support the national project as well as ethnic and gender interests. As Ana Cristina Ramírez points out, she invites comparison with female figures, such as the Malinche-Guadalupe dichotomy, that are foundational in Mexican nationhood (Ramírez Barreto 2005). Ramírez shows how Eréndira has served as a contrast to the reviled Malinche by the writer and politician Eduardo Ruiz, who based his characterization of her (1971) partly on his own experience as a soldier resisting the French intervention in the 1860s. This emphasis on Eréndira as part of a heroic foundation for the Mexican nation also lends iconographical support to the Lázaro Cárdenas government, who named institutions after her. It is significant that the name is applied to girl children, despite its pagan origins, whenever there is a sense of political emergency or surge of nationalism (Ramírez Barreto 3). Mora Catlett's film spreads itself across a wide range of source material but excludes such commonplace manifestations. It does, though, tend far more towards the mural depiction by Juan O'Gorman (1941–42) of a young bare-breasted native woman with long hair, mounted on a white horse, controlling the steed with her legs to keep her hands free. This contrasts with an almost contemporaneous mural by Roberto Cueva del Río (1943) of a timid and puritanically clad Eréndira riding side-saddle, with none of the defiant eroticism of O'Gorman's version (Ramírez Barreto, 4).

Mora Catlett's protagonist is a curious and enlightening blend of the mythical and the everyday. She also bears characteristics of European mythical types, most notably nymphs, who, according to the Mexican essayist Roger Bartra, were "bellos seres femeninos que habitaban los bosques, los ríos y los campos, eran consideradas muchas veces bajo un signo noble y positivo, aunque en ocasiones podían ser terribles y nefastas." ["beautiful feminine creatures that inhabited woods, rivers and fields, were often considered under a noble and positive sign, although on occasion they could be terrible and destructive"] (17). Mora Catlett's eclectic

A Shamanic Transmodernity

Fig. 3. Eréndira (Xochiquetzal Rodríguez) on Horseback: the film-makers opt for the image of a warrior heroine. Photo by Toni Kuhn (courtesy of Juan Mora Catlett).

re-creation of indigenous or pre-Columbian worlds does not entail a culturally purist or exclusive approach, as can be seen in his inclusion of some western musical instruments in *Retun to Aztlán*. The prevailing aesthetic mood in *Eréndira* is one of dialogue between indigenous and European influences.

This use of material selected by Mora Catlett, at once distanced and familiar, makes use of both pre-Columbian and colonial imagery and does not baulk at employing non-indigenous sources, much in the same vein as the idea of transmodernity proposed by Dussel. Nevertheless, Mora Catlett has derived his plastic style for this film almost entirely from pre-Columbian and colonial codices and murals. The best example of the latter appears in the former convent of the Archangel Saint Michael of Ixmiquilpan in the state of Hidalgo, whose semi-human figures mark the film's opening credits. Mora Catlett explained to me that:

los caballos son representados como centauros monstruosos
con pies, cabezas y brazos humanos. Estas imágenes aparecen
en el comienzo de la película (donde tuve que crear digital-
mente una versión del templo, debido al deterioro del real, y
para poner los murales donde yo quisiera y hacerlos aparecer
como fantasmas, creando así la atmósfera introductoria mítica
y no realista) y en el sueño de Eréndira.

[the horses are represented as monstrous centaurs with human
feet, heads and arms. These images appear at the start of the
film (where I had to create, digitally, a version of the temple,
due to the deterioration of the real one, and to place the murals
where I wanted and make them appear as phantoms, thus creating the introductory mythical, not realist, atmosphere) and
in Eréndira's dream.]

Unlike Nicolás Echeverría, whose *Cabeza de Vaca* (1991) recreates indigenous artefacts such as houses, clothes, and body decoration, among
others, according to his own and his collaborators' imagination as well as
that of Theodor de Bry, Mora Catlett has elected to portray pre-Columbian cultures, namely Aztec and Purépecha, whose remains are to some
degree extant. Thus he has been able to exploit visual and testimonial
sources like those provided in the codex *Relación de Michoacán*. Akin to
Raúl Ruiz's rejection of conventional narrative in film and in an attempt
at accounting for the varieties of experience in the sensible world that
characterize shamanic cinema, the story of Eréndira seems to occupy
the interstices between chronicle and legend. Her nineteenth-century
manifestation was as an antidote to La Malinche, reviled and made a
scapegoat as the archetypal collaborator, while the Innocent Eréndira
prostituted by her heartless grandmother in the Gabriel García Márquez
story would appear to have more in common with a tale of unbridled
sexual appetite associated with Xarátanga.[2] Eréndira has always been
portrayed as heroine, adapted from pre-Columbian times to serve colonial, republican and now twenty-first-century concerns, as discussed by
Ana Cristina Ramírez Barreto. The difference is that here the interests
in question are largely those of the Purépecha themselves: Mora Catlett

assures us that all the aspects of his film have been discussed and approved in sessions with members of the community among whom it was filmed. This includes the construction of the script, the visual characterization of the community's ancestors, elements like costume and sound, as well as makeup. Julián Pizá, whose admirable efforts created the film's makeup, confirmed to me that the film's intention was to create a metaphorical interpretation of what life may have been like among the pre-Columbian Purépecha (personal communication, April 10, 2008).

Mora Catlett's approach is to some extent anthropological or even "ethnobiographical," if we adopt Jorge Prelorán's definition of a film that focuses on the life story of an individual through which the viewer can become familiar, not only with the personal story, but also with the cultural context. This technique of familiarizing the audience with an un-known culture through the everyday reality of an individual is designed for application to non-fiction and the present day. Eréndira, however exceptional she appears to us as a character, does present a number of problems which she faces both within her own culture and as external threats to that culture.

The reconstruction of pre-Columbian worlds represented by Mora Catlett, Echeverría and others is an approach that has had its imitators, some less interested than others in the faithful preservation of native cul-tural memory. Mel Gibson's "action" movie *Apocalypto* (2006) is a brazen distortion of those aspects of Mayan civilization most vulnerable to sen-sationalist representations: human sacrifice, the erosion of cultural values, the absence of Christianity. Gibson, moreover, has been accused by Mora Catlett himself of plagiarizing the visual style of *Return to Aztlán*.[3]

Neither does Mora Catlett concur with the metaphorical treatment of concrete historical guilt as explored in Octavio Paz's *The Labyrinth of Solitude*. Rather his vision resembles that of Elena Garro in her short story *La culpa es de los tlaxcaltecas* [*It's the Fault of the Tlaxcaltecas*, 1964] with its emphasis on creative re-examination (a reverse reading of history) and of a past simultaneous with the present. Mora Catlett acknowledges his condition as white middle-class: his is not a cinema that tries to recount 'from within' but which gets as close as possible to a salvage operation contributing to the restoration of cultural memory and identity. In this sense, he echoes Ruiz's cinematic shamanism for which memory is a crucial element. Mora Catlett's first feature-length film, *Return to Aztlán*,

FIG. 4. NANUMA (JUSTO ALBERTO RODRÍGUEZ) AND TANGAXOAN (RUBÉN BAU-
TISTA) SHARE THE SCREEN WITH TWO-DIMENSIONAL IMAGES FROM THE
CODICES. PHOTO BY TONI KUHN (COURTESY OF JUAN MORA CATLETT).

was filmed completely in Náhuatl, using images derived from the codices, with reproductions enveloped in flames, as in *Eréndira Ikikunari*, to
introduce each episode in the narrative. In contrast, in *Eréndira Ikikunari*,
the director is not content with simply endorsing the content in this way.
He rather allows the drawings to remain on screen after passing on to the
filmed narration. An example is the establishing shot of Lake Pátzcuaro
that precedes the journey by canoe of the cacique Tangaxoan, who intends to avoid humiliation from the Spaniards by drowning himself. The
editing provides phases of artificiality where gradually the colonial drawing yields to the live action. Elsewhere in the film, the inclusion of a
drawn scene, with parts of the codices amplified and simply 'cut out', is
even more obvious; it acts as a declaration of the simultaneity of history
with its consequences. After the battle in which Eréndira's beloved uncle
Timas dies, we see corpses piled up in their two-dimensional, mono-
chrome version, sharing the screen with the actors.

FIG. 5. Eréndira (Xochiquetzal Rodríguez) walking among dead figures from the codices. Photo by Toni Kuhn (courtesy of Juan
Mora Catlett).

Stylization also finds its way into the film through the schematic
nature of masks, used to represent both Spaniards and deities. These
are wooden masks from the dance of the Cúrpitis, which represents the
Spaniards as strange nonhuman beings. This implies that the supposed
'face-to-face' encounter between Indians and Europeans is anything but:
the outsiders are accorded a divine status that proves baseless. This approach initially alienates the viewer, who is obliged to share indigenous
perception of the strangers. Then, when the spectator has almost become
accustomed to this representation, she/he is submitted to an abrupt return to 'normality' as Eréndira perceives the sudden disappearance of a
Spaniard's mask, revealing the intruder for the first time as mortal instead
of divine. This is reminiscent of Dussel's call for a truthful reconstruction
of history as "modernity's other face" (1995a, 74). As the film's website
reminds us, the only figure that is never unmasked is the horse in a reference to the metal armour left by Eréndira when she unsaddles the animal.

FIG. 6. THE SPANIARDS' (UNCREDITED ACTORS) STRANGENESS AND SUPPOSED DIVINITY IS INITIALLY CONVEYED BY THE USE OF MASKS. PHOTO BY TONI KUHN (COURTESY OF JUAN MORA CATLETT).

The Purépecha deities in turn assume an active role. The goddess Xa-rátanga is repeatedly invoked by those who oppose the invaders – above all at the moment of Eréndira's confirmation as leader. Curi-Cáhueri is represented by a stone figure, transferred clandestinely from its place by the anxious natives so as to maintain its active and protective power. Also prominent is a wooden sculpture of Santiago apostle (according to Mora Catlett a piece of contemporary craftwork, bought in a common store). Tied to the back of the friar, it saves his life when it receives an arrow intended for the monk, who flees.

The desire to create an updated and non-stereotyped native aesthetic leads Mora Catlett to make use of sources of all kinds, including visual and auditory. At times this results in an incongruity that distances the spectator from any sense of comfort. It is a species of Brechtian *Verfrem-dungseffekt*, but if it breaks the illusion of the diegesis, it is largely through unexpected familiarity between the elements, particularly the modern music with the pre-Columbian codices. Perhaps the principal challenge to the viewer is the soundtrack: among its surprises is the use of a relatively little-spoken language. Purépecha, spoken in Hidalgo, Querétaro, Michoacán, and the state of Mexico, has benefited from official efforts to increase its use and turn it into a literary language. It is another example of the uncompromising approach taken by Mora Catlett, who had experts create a sixteenth-century form of Náhuatl for his first film, *Return to Aztlán*. Obviously such use of language contributes to the authenticity of both films, but it also conditions the experience of seeing them for the enormous majority of non-speakers. In the case of Eréndira, any difficulty in reading subtitles is attenuated by the clarity of the image, the repetition of certain settings like Tangaxoan's court or the council of Timas, the corral where the horse is kept, among others. The use of Purépecha also involves the use of local non-professional actors, joined by a handful of white Mexicans who play the invading Spaniards. Within the context of the film, the sudden and unexpected intrusion of the Spanish language has an alienating effect. In a scene in which the collaborator Cuynierángari tries to calm the foreigners, from one moment to the next the indigenous subject becomes object. The Spaniards retain the right to speak and despise the native language as 'Indian nonsense'. The third language heard is Latin, recited by the friar who accompanies the soldiers. It is heard particularly in the battle scenes or in other dangerous situations, lending symbolic and absurd qualities to a language, which only serves to communicate with an Almighty that the Indians do not recognize and that the rest of the Spaniards do not respect.

The inclusion of negative aspects about the natives, who at no point are idealized, helps to complicate the film and its reception as machismo, cannibalism, unrestrained violence, and factionalism are openly portrayed. As Robert Stam and Louise Spence wisely point out: "A cinema dominated by positive images, characterised by a bending-over-backwards-not-to-be-racist attitude, might ultimately betray a lack of confidence in the group portrayed, which usually has no illusions concerning its own perfection" (241). Accordingly, the old woman who correctly prophecies the arrival of the Spaniards, who is evidently in touch with ancestral deities, is repulsively shown being fed with the fresh blood of a captured youth.

The use of echo and dubbing also distances the spectator, making even immediate perception strange and unsettling. Mora Catlett has made use of what he calls "the speciality" of the Dolby system 5.1 and THX for "positioning the sounds in the spectator's internal spaces" when dealing with subjective elements like the voice of the narrator, or Eréndira's sobbing at the death of her uncle. Alternatively, there is a more conventional use of sound, where it perceptibly emanates from diegetic sources shown on the screen. Thirdly, there are the sounds that seem to emerge from all sides, such as "las voces de los dioses verdaderos en el volcán, o de los dioses falsos entre las pirámides, para enfatizar su sobrenaturalidad real o aparente" ["the voices of the true Gods in the volcano, or of the false Gods amongst the pyramids, to emphasize their supernatural qualities, real or apparent"]. The dialogues are reproduced in dubbed form, with the use of echo as at times the same line is spoken by two voices almost simultaneously. It is reminiscent of popular techno music, and it serves to emphasize the artificiality of the whole, reminding the public of the fact they are watching an approximation of the events. Mora Catlett explains:

> siendo una narración no realista, en este caso usé recursos técnicos para enfatizar la musicalidad o artificialidad del sonido, de hecho le pedí al músico que la construyéramos como una ópera, y algunas de las imágenes (el volcán o la corte de Tangaxoan) están trazadas operáticamente. De hecho hay mucho de operático en la puesta en escena. Ese es uno de los elementos occidentales que introduzco en la forma narrativa de esta película, ya que trata del encuentro del mundo precolombino con occidente.

> [as this is a non-realistic narration, in this case I used technical resources to emphasize the musicality or artificiality of the sound; in fact, I asked the composer to construct it like an opera, and some of the images (the volcano, or the court of Tangaxoan) are sketched out operatically. Indeed, there is a lot that's operatic in the mise-en-scène. That is one of the occidental elements I introduce into the narrative form of this film, since it deals with the encounter of the pre-Columbian world with the Occidental.]

The music consists of sounds and rhythms "recycled" using elements of the soundtrack such as dialogues and incidental sound. Unlike *Return to Aztlán*, *Eréndira Ikikunari* has a soundtrack that refers openly to its non-realist narration: here the incidental sounds have been "recycled" as music, whereas in *Return to Aztlán* musical instruments were used to create the sounds of beasts and other elements: "para sustituir ruidos incidentales (por ejemplo el vuelo de las flechas) o reforzar sonidos ambientales (el fuego del sacrificio humano) también se incluyeron en la música par-lamentos o segmentos de palabras usados de forma rítmica." ["In order to substitute incidental sounds (for example the flight of arrows) or reinforce ambient sounds (the fire of human sacrifice) speech was also included in the music, or scraps of words used in rhythmic form."]

The composer, Andrés Sánchez, is a young man with more interest in electronic rock music than in ethnohistory. As the director says in a shamanic tone: "Es una unión de los más arcaico con lo más moderno, porque lo mítico es atemporal y profundamente humano." ["It's a union of the most archaic with the most modern, because what is mythical is atemporal and profoundly human."] The effect on the spectator is, again, one of fertile alienation: an urban music, modern and occidental, suc-cessfully complements an oral, rural, pre-Columbian narration, with an indigenous perspective.

The conjunction of cinematographic and musical terms is particu-larly fecund for Mora Catlett, who sees a complementary interaction be-tween the two. Cinema and music, he argues, are temporal arts in that "para su creación y percepción necesitan desarrollarse *durante* el tiempo" ["for their creation and perception they need to be developed *through* time"] (author's emphasis). Using language that is fully musical, the dir-ector distinguishes between external editing, which handles the relation between shots and scenes to control the unity of the film, and internal editing, which does likewise with the elements within each shot. Thus, the shot contains three sets of elements: rhythmical, harmonic, and mel-odic. The rhythmical element gives the sensation of repetition, move-ment, visual temporality, and impact. The harmonic element provides the expressive value and establishes the basis of the spectator's interest. At the same time, the conscious interest, the "declared meaning" of the shot, in Mora Catlett's words, lies in the melodic motifs. These three sets of elements comprising the shot are put together and organized according to optical and acoustic perceptual principles, while the relations between juxtaposed shots depend on cuts that create new spaces and times that do not exist within any of the individual scenes but rather in the space-time "continuum" of the film as a whole. Control of all these elements and the relations between them are seen by Mora Catlett as orchestration.

Seeing *Eréndira Ikikunari* in this light, as a continuum, suggests that the aesthetic proposed by its creator in no way excludes foreign, ostensibly inimical, cultural elements. Here we see no spurious attempts at faithful recreation of a history now beyond the reach of any register, oral or written, but rather an effort to catch the essence and the spirit of times and events. If the rhythmical dimension of this film renders anecdotal violence and discord, the harmonic conveys the constant preoccupation aroused in the spectator by the fate of the Purépechas and the protagonist. The melodic line, drawing up the manifest development of history, is necessarily unfinished. The orchestration of these elements leads Mora Catlett to quote Siegfried Kracauer to the effect that editing is not only a question of narrative but also a means by which the objects shown must manifest "a very suggestive uncertainty" (Kracauer, 171). This very uncertainty is what convinces us of the validity of a film that evokes Raúl Ruiz's desire for "a cinema capable of accounting, above all, for the varieties of experience in the sensible world" (Ruiz 1995, 90) at the same time as it echoes Enrique Dussel's call "to put on methodically the skin of the Indian, the African slave, the humiliated *mestizo*, the impoverished peasant, the exploited worker, and the marginalized person packed among the wretched millions inhabiting contemporary Latin American cities" (1995b, 74). Mora Catlett and his Purépecha collaborators have created a pre-Columbian world that leaves the viewer wondering as to its authenticity, but it is no less convincing for that, in its readiness to use cinematic sorcery and incongruity to suggest ways of understanding historical and cultural circumstances beyond any question of faithful recreation and address them to both present and future.

WORKS CITED

Ayala Blanco, Jorge. 1979. *La aventura del cine mexicano.* Mexico City: Era Ediciones.

Bartra, Roger. 1992. *El salvaje en el espejo.* Mexico City: UNAM.

Coria, José Felipe. 2007. *Iluminaciones del inestable cine mexicano.* Mexico City: Paidós Crom.

Dussel, Enrique. 1995a. *The Invention of the Americas. Eclipse of "the Other" and the Myth of Modernity.* Trans. Michel D. Barber. New York: Continuum.

———. 1995b. Eurocentrism and Modernity. In *The Postmodernism Debate in Latin America.* Ed. John Beverley, José Oviedo, and Michael Aronna, 64–76. Durham, NC: Duke University Press.

———. 2000. The Semantic Slippage of the Concept of Europe. *Nepantla, Views from South* 1, no. 3: 465–78.

Gruzinski, Serge. 2001. *Images at War: Mexico From Columbus to Blade Runner (1492–2019).* Durham, NC: Duke University Press.

Guarini, Carmen. 2005. Cine antropológico: algunas reflexiones metodológicas. In *Cine, antropología y colonialismo.* Ed. Adolfo Colombres, 161–67. Buenos Aires: Ediciones del Sol.

Klor de Alva, Jorge. 1995. The Postcolonization of the (Latin) American Experience: A Reconsideration of 'Colonialism,' 'Postcolonialism,' and 'Mestizaje.' In *After Colonialism: Imperial Histories and Postcolonial Displacements.* Ed. Gyan Prakash, 241–75. Princeton, NJ: Princeton University Press.

Kracauer, Siegfried. 1971. *Theory of Film.* Oxford: Oxford University Press.

Monsiváis, Carlos. 1993. Las mitologías del cine mexicano. *Objeto Visual* 1: 13–28.

Noble, Andrea. 2005. *Mexican National Cinema.* Abingdon: Routledge.

Novarro, José. 1998. El sonido prehispánico en el cine: entrevista con Antonio Zepeda. *Estudios cinematográficos* 4, no. 17: 37–39.

Orell García, Marcia. 2006. *Las fuentes del Nuevo Cine Latinoamericano.* Valparaíso: Pontificia Universidad de Valparaíso.

Pacheco Colín, Ricardo. 2007. Cineasta mexicano acusa a Mel Gibson de plagio por Apocalypto; robó ideas de Regreso a Aztlán, afirma Juan Mora Catlett. *La crónica de hoy,* January 9.

Prelorán, Jorge. 2006. *El cine etnobiográfico.* Buenos Aires: Ediciones Universidad del Cine.

Quijano, Aníbal. 2000. Colonialidad del Poder y Clasificación Social. *Journal of World Systems Research* 6, no. 2: 342–86.

Ramírez Barreto, Ana Cristina. 2005. Eréndira a caballo. Acoplamiento de cuerpos e historias en un relato de conquista y resistencia. E-misférica 2.2; http://hemi.nyu.edu/journal/2_2/ramirez.html (accessed August 20, 2008).

Ramírez Berg, Charles. 1992. *Cinema of Solitude: A Critical Study of Mexican Film, 1967–1983.* Austin: University of Texas Press.

Rouch, Jean. 2005. ¿El cine del futuro? In *Cine, antropología y colonialismo.* Ed. Adolfo Colombres, 63–72. Buenos Aires: Ediciones del Sol.

Ruiz, Eduardo. 1971. *Michoacán: paisajes, tradiciones y leyendas.* Mexico City: Balsal Editores.

Ruiz, Raúl. 1995. Poetics of Cinema. Trad. Brian Holmes. Paris: Editions dis Voir.

Stam, Robert, and Louise Spence. 1999. Colonialism, Racism and Representation. In *Film Theory and Criticism: Introductory Readings.* Ed. Leo Braudy and Marshall Cohen, 235–50. Oxford: Oxford University Press.

FILMS

Apocalyto. Directed by Mel Gibson. Buena Vista Pictures, 2006.

Cabeza de Vaca. Directed by Nicolás Echeverría. Concorde Pictures, 1991.

La dignidad de los nadies [*The Dignity of the Nobodies*]. Directed by Fernando Solanas. Distribution Company, 2005.

Eréndira Ikikunari [*Indomitable Eréndira*]. Directed by Juan Mora Catlett. David Distribución, 2006.

María Candelaria. Directed by Emilio Fernández. Clasa Films Mundiales, 1943.

La nación clandestina [*The Clandestine Nation*]. Directed by Jorge Sanjinés. Grupo Ukamau, 1988.

Retorno a Aztlán [*Return to Aztlán*]. Directed by Juan Mora Catlett. Cooperativa José Revueltas, Dirección de Actividades Cinematográficas de la UNAM, Fondo de Fomento a la Calidad Cinematográfica, Instituto Mexicano de Cinematografía (IMCINE), Producciones Volcán S. A. de C. V., 1991.

Salvador Allende. Directed by Patricio Guzmán. First Run/Icarus Films, 2004.

Ukamau [*And So it Is*]. Directed by Jorge Sanjinés. Sanjinés, 1966.

Yawar Mallku [*Blood of the Condor*]. Directed by Jorge Sanjinés. Tricontinental Film Center, 1969.

NOTES

1   All quotes from Juan Roberto Mora Catlett are, unless stated otherwise, taken from an interview I conducted with the director in August 2007.

2   For a short description of de Xarátanga, see Relación de Michoacán in http:// www.colmich.edu.mx/ (accessed August 20, 2008).

3   See Ricardo Pacheco Colín's report in *La Crónica de hoy.*

WE ARE EQUAL: WOMEN AND VIDEO IN ZAPATISTA CHIAPAS

Elissa J. Rashkin[1]
Universidad Veracruzana

As the 1980s drew to a close, Mexican filmmaker Paul Leduc predicted the demise of traditional "dinosaur" cinema and the advent of small-scale "lizard" and "salamander" cinema (59). Two decades later, much as Leduc predicted, new technologies have made possible the emergence of a vibrant independent video sector affiliated with social movements such as campaigns for political reform and the struggle for indigenous rights. Challenging the exclusionary policies and limitations of mainstream media, under-represented social sectors, such as women, urban youth, indigenous Mexicans, gays and lesbians, have made their presences felt both on screen and behind the camera. Organizations such as Canal 6 de Julio [Channel July 6], Telemanita [Tele-sister], Voces contra el Silencio [Voices against Silence], local chapters of Indymedia, and many others form a mosaic that reflects the diversity of Mexican civil society.[2]

The state of Chiapas occupies a particularly interesting place in the development of this independent video sector. There, on January 1, 1994, the Ejército Zapatista de Liberación Nacional [Zapatista Army of National Liberation, EZLN] emerged after ten years of clandestine organizing and declared war on the federal government, shaking Mexican society to its core. After just a few days of fighting and many months of unproductive negotiation with the government as well as constant dialogue with civil society, the Zapatistas gradually moved toward becoming a peaceful civilian movement, a shift that culminated with the proclamation of local autonomous governing structures, or Juntas de Buen Gobierno [Good Government Councils], in 2003. In their *Sixth Declaration of the Lacandon Jungle* of June 2005, the Zapatistas announced a "national program of struggle" through which they would seek to strengthen alliances with and among marginalized groups around the country and at the United States border.

Launched during the 2006 electoral season, the Other Campaign, as they called their organizing drive, was also a critique "from below" of the presidential candidates and of electoral politics in general. This critique was extremely controversial, since many Mexicans, in particular many of the urban intellectuals who had constituted an important support base for the EZLN since 1994, backed the campaign of Partido de la Revolución Democrática [Party of the Democratic Revolution, PRD] candidate Andrés Manuel López Obrador. Given the close race and the intensity of propaganda launched against López Obrador's candidacy, the Zapatista position was seen as counterproductive, and EZLN spokesperson Subcomandante Marcos, the leader of the Other Campaign, was accused of betraying the movement's ideals in egotistical pursuit of a media spotlight now turned in other directions.

"El subcomandante Marcos rebasó los límites que tiene todo representante de un movimiento colectivo," wrote José Gil Olmos in the magazine *Proceso*, "No era sólo el líder, sino la encarnación misma del movimiento zapatista. Su voz era la única válida y su opinión la única" ["Subcomandante Marcos exceeded the limits that any representative of a collective movement has. He was not only the leader but the very incarnation of the Zapatista movement. His voice was the only valid one and his opinion the only one"] (Olmos 2006). Marcos and the Zapatistas were blamed for right-wing candidate Felipe Calderón's narrow victory, and, as the media were quick to point out, sympathy for their struggle declined.[3]

Not all intellectuals abandoned the Zapatista cause, however; on the website Znet, the Oaxaca-based writer Gustavo Esteva posted an eloquent defence of the Other Campaign in which he concluded that, given the bankruptcy and failure of the current political system, the Zapatistas' proposal to organize from below was, though fraught with obstacles, nevertheless "the only option against indescribable disaster" (Esteva 2006). The Mexico City newspaper *La Jornada*, long sympathetic to the PRD, covered the Other Campaign extensively and continues to run articles by pro-Zapatista journalists like Gloria Muñoz Ramírez and Herman Bellinghausen. In any case, the EZLN's effort to develop and sustain national networks of solidarity has gone forward since the elections, even as the Zapatista communities in Chiapas have struggled to survive and protect their achievements in the face of multiple threats and obstacles.[4]

The importance of electronic and audiovisual media to the Zapatista movement was widely noted from the beginning, including by representatives of the Mexican state. In April 1995, José Angel Gurría, Mexico's secretary of foreign relations, famously declared before a gathering of international businessmen that the conflict in Chiapas was a "guerra de tintas, de palabra escrita, una guerra en el Internet" ["war of ink, of the written word, a war of the Internet"] (Montes). This description blatantly downplayed the level of violence experienced by the Chiapan people, first during the armed conflict and later as a result of military occupation and paramilitary aggression; yet as a catchphrase, it served to highlight the important role of information and in particular the Internet as a tool used by activists to challenge what they considered to be the distortions and omissions of the mainstream news media (Cleaver). As Oliver Froehling points out, Internet access in Chiapas is scarce (291); nevertheless, thanks to an extensive communications network, letters from the EZLN leadership, news from remote communities, and discussions of Zapatista theory and practices went (and still go) out to the Internet on a daily basis, making it possible for observers in any net-wired location to follow the movement's trajectory in astonishing detail.

Along with the meteoric rise of the Internet, the EZLN uprising also coincided with a significant increase in the availability of both consumer and professional-quality video. Many of the thousands of visitors who have poured into Chiapas during the past fourteen years in more or less efficient acts of solidarity have brought their cameras with them; among these have been trained film and videomakers ranging from the famous (Oliver Stone and Edward James Olmos) to the anonymous (unidentified members of activist collectives), and many in-between. Thanks to their efforts, the region, which in the past was likely to appear in film as an exotic locale, home of lush jungles and colourfully "authentic" natives, is now indelibly associated with the Zapatistas and their struggle for social change (Saavedra Luna, 381).[5] While the exact number of films and videos that have been made about the Zapatista rebellion is unknown, it is quite likely the best-documented revolution in history.[6]

Many of these videos have focused on women, for good reason: the women's revolution-within-a-revolution has been one of the most striking and significant aspects of *zapatismo*. Even before the uprising began, EZLN organizers worked to combat sexism within communities that had long tended to treat women as male property and condone domestic violence as part of the status quo. Their effort was codified in a document called the Revolutionary Women's Law, which was developed through discussions among women in the communities where the Zapatistas were active, and was passed in March 1993. The law was then published as part of the Zapatistas' statement of principles on December 31 of that year. Opening with an explicit commitment to welcome women into the EZLN struggle "regardless of their race, creed, color or political affiliation," the law upholds a far-reaching vision of women's rights, including the right to participate in military and community affairs on an equal basis with men; the right to work and receive a just salary; the right to choose whom to marry and the number of children to bear and raise; the right to health care and education; and the right to live free from violence, sexual abuse, and discrimination (EZLN 1994).

The Women's Law represented a radical intervention, not only in the worldwide struggle for women's rights, but also in the battle to define, preserve, and reconstruct indigenous cultural identities. As Márgara Millán notes:

> La Ley Revolucionaria de Mujeres es el primer espacio normativo del despertar de una subjetividad específica, la de las mujeres indígenas, en un proceso de rearticulación comunitaria. Muestra un ejercicio de afirmación de la identidad

indígena (la permanencia) al tiempo que pone a prueba rad-
icalmente la democracia comunitaria (el cambio). Afirma la
identidad indígena porque reclama mejores condiciones para
su reproducción económica, social y cultural, y pone a prueba
la capacidad democrática comunitaria al exigir cambiar las
costumbres según nuevos consensos que tomen en cuenta la
voz de las mujeres, que extiendan el reconocimiento de su
trabajo (doméstico) en la esfera pública, de la gestión y toma
de decisiones comunitarias. (Millán)

[The Revolutionary Women's Law is the first normative space
of the awakening of a specific subjectivity, that of indigenous women, within a process of community rearticulation. It
serves as an exercise in the affirmation of indigenous identity
(permanence) at the same time as it radically puts community
democracy to the test (change). It affirms indigenous identity
because it demands better conditions for its economic, social
and cultural reproduction, and it puts the capacity for community democracy to the test when it demands that customs
change according to a new consensus that takes women's voices
into account and that extends recognition of their (domestic)
work into the public sphere and the community decision-
making process.]

The Law is a powerful expression of Zapatista women's desire to change
their culture from within, not by trading it for another model but by
building on its strengths while discarding its dysfunctional aspects, balancing respect for tradition with the need for change.

This has been a difficult struggle and one that is by no means over.
In an essay on rural women's activism through 2000, Lynn Stephen notes
that implementation of the Women's Law has been uneven and that in
many communities women receive little encouragement in the battle
for recognition of their rights (255–56). At an international gathering
held in Chiapas in December 2007, male attendees were assigned chores
such as cooking and babysitting and were prohibited from taking part in
the meeting in an effort to open the floor to women; this arrangement
precipitated a wealth of striking testimony from and discussion among

women participants (Pérez Vázquez and Kendall; Gutiérrez). Yet at the same time, its novelty, signalled by the proclamation that "el 1 de enero del 08 vuelve a lo normal" ["on January 1, 2008, everything goes back to normal"], revealed the continuing lopsidedness of gender roles within the movement.[7]

Nevertheless, as Guiomar Rovira and others documented early on, the strong presence of women leaders and soldiers in the EZLN set an example that, together with the Women's Law, empowered women to assert control over their own bodies and lives (Rovira).[8] One of these leaders was Comandante Ramona, a Tzotzil Maya woman from San Andrés Sacamch'en and a member of the Zapatistas' governing council, the Comité Clandestino Revolucionario Indígena [Clandestine Revolutionary Indigenous Committee], until her death in 2006. In February 1995, a tense moment in which negotiations between the EZLN and the government of Ernesto Zedillo had broken down, the Zapatistas were being hunted by federal forces, and their usual spokesperson, Subcomandante Marcos, had retreated into silence, Ramona appeared in a videotaped message to the nation. The exact date and location of production were unknown; yet the tape reached the national and international press, which reported its message worldwide the day after its distribution in Mexico City on February 19.

The video consists of a single medium shot, in which Ramona is shown seated at a table with a newspaper in front of her and a white banner reading "EZLN" in the background. No one else appears, although noises in the background indicate the presence of the anonymous videographer. Looking at the camera, Ramona announces her location as "un lugar en la Selva Lacandona" ["someplace in the Lacandon Jungle"] and proceeds to address the people of Mexico, whom she specifies by group: women, youth, and men, and finally "todos los habitantes de nuestro país" ["all the inhabitants of our country"]. She describes the many problems experienced by women in her community and cites her own chronic illness as an example of the poor nutrition and health conditions from which a majority of Chiapan villagers suffer. She then calls on all women and men to organize to create a more just society.

At the time this video was released, the federal government was trying to undercut support for the Zapatista insurgency at all costs. In a speech televised on February 9, President Zedillo "unmasked" a photo of

Marcos, removing a superimposed ski mask to "expose" the leftist philosophy professor Rafael Sebastián Guillén Vicente underneath. Issuing arrest warrants for Guillén and four other alleged leaders, the president announced triumphantly that these were "neither popular, nor indigenous, nor from Chiapas" (Serrill). Zedillo's strategy not only deliberately ignored the EZLN's substantial support base in Chiapas but also insulted indigenous people by portraying them as easily manipulated and incapable of organizing on their own behalf. Ramona counters the government's accusations by explaining, from a self-aware indigenous woman's perspective, the social conditions behind the rebellion.

"On the tape," observes Ellen Calmus, "there is a sort of intimate catch in her voice, as if she were speaking with great restrained emotion" (6). Indeed, Ramona's quiet yet firm speech seems to implicitly repudiate the centuries of silence to which indigenous women have been consigned. The video is simple, yet also powerful: a stark contrast to so many Mexican *telenovelas* and other programs in which indigenous characters appear, if at all, as abject caricatures. In *Comunicado del Ejército Zapatista de Liberación Nacional en voz de la Comandante Ramona* [*Communiqué of the EZLN in the Voice of Commander Ramona*], the Zapatista leader occupies the privileged and colonized space of the television screen, if only for a few minutes, with strength and dignity that challenges the audience and shatters stereotypes (Rashkin, 234).

Besides this telecommuniqué, many other videos portraying the Zapatista women appeared during the 1990s. Some were made by women, mostly from Mexico City; in 1995, for instance, the Las Brujas collective released the video *El EZLN y las mujeres, las siempre olvidadas* [*The EZLN and Women, the Ones Always Forgotten*], while Guadalupe Miranda and María Inés Roqué's student film *Las compañeras tienen grado* [*Zapatista Women*] brought the testimony of female Zapatista combatants to film audiences in Buenos Aires, New York, Salzburg, Santiago de Chile, and other cities in Europe and the Americas. Carmen Ortiz, a Mexico City videomaker with the Colectivo Perfil Urbano, also directed several videos about the Zapatistas in the 1990s. In a 2000 interview with the video organization Telemanita, Ortiz spoke of her background as a housewife and mother who came into videomaking after separating from her husband, not long before the Zapatista uprising. She and her new partner, José Luis Contreras, became involved in the situation in Chiapas and were among the first to portray the Zapatistas on video. According to Ortiz, their 1994 video *Los más pequeños* sold 11,000 copies, a figure that indicates the thirst for information about Chiapas that prevailed during those years.

What is also interesting, however, is the effect that these projects had on Ortiz herself. Her assertion that "the Zapatistas saved us too.... I don't know what would have happened if the Zapatistas didn't exist" suggests that the relationship between the EZLN and Mexican civil society was more than one of simple solidarity. For Ortiz, as for many Mexicans, the Zapatistas represented the rebirth of a hope for revolutionary social change that was long thought to be dead and buried; her participation was not simply the documentation of someone else's struggle, but a form of personal commitment and transformation.

Perhaps the most visceral images of women's participation in the Zapatista struggle were filmed by Carlos Martínez Suárez, a veteran documentary maker and video activist based in San Cristóbal. His 1996 video *Oventic: Construyendo dignidad* [*Oventic: Building Dignity*] opens with shots of men working collectively to build what will become the "Aguascalientes" or regional cultural centre of Oventic, in the municipality of San Andrés Sakamch'en. The men's work is interrupted by the appearance of a helicopter flying low overhead in an obvious act of surveillance. The implications of this sinister portent are borne out a short time later, when army tanks are shown entering the road to the village. In silence, the women, men and children of Oventic join hands in a human chain along the road to await the invasion. Their backs are turned in avoidance of the soldiers' cameras, which are captured by Martínez Suárez's lens in a subtle reminder of the political investments inherent in documentary representation. Close-ups of women's faces register simultaneous nervousness and resolve.

As the tanks move in, the silence is broken by a few voices shouting at the soldiers to leave. Then, the incursion of the vehicles is momentarily halted by a barrier of women bearing handwritten placards denouncing the soldiers' actions. Variations of this scene are repeated on tape over several days, with women playing a central role in the protests. In the background, tree-covered mountains with peaks shrouded in mist are a dramatic presence whose beauty contrasts with the tension on the ground. On day three, a group of villagers runs to confront the soldiers whose armoured vehicles are now parked along the road. The men wear boots; the women, sandals or bare feet, despite the cold and muddy ground. With increasing vehemence, the men shout at the soldiers. The women stand to one side, but suddenly they too erupt in protest, as if no longer able to contain their fury.

The confrontation continues; the soldiers refuse to respond, but their facial expressions suggest discomfort. With their bodies shielded by tanks and guns and swathed in dark protective clothing and headgear that contrasts with the women's colourful shawls and bare limbs, the soldiers seem to embody the stony indifference of the government they serve, and the political, social, and economic structures of a nation that refuses to acknowledge its most disadvantaged and oppressed inhabitants. When the soldiers finally withdraw to the site where they are building their camp, the villagers chase after them. The tanks have been repelled for the moment, but the conflict is far from over.[9]

In addition to these documentaries produced by EZLN supporters, there have also been videos made by the Zapatistas themselves through organizations such as the Chiapas Media Project/Promedios de Comunicación Comunitaria. CMP/Promedios is a binational partnership based in Mexico and the United States that emerged a decade ago during a particular phase in the Zapatista movement's evolution. By the late 1990s, after the failure of negotiations was followed by outright as well as covert persecution, the Zapatistas had given up hope of resolving their differences with the government and had begun instead to create their own administrative structures. Enlisting the financial help of international solidarity groups, they built hospitals, clinics, and schools, developed systems for communal land use and ownership, and complemented traditional agricultural production with a variety of economic development strategies, principally worker and consumer cooperatives. They also sought to increase their access to communications technologies. CMP/Promedios was founded in 1998 to provide these autonomous communities with the means to produce and distribute their own media. As of late 2009, twenty-eight video productions were in distribution; about 250 students from at least fifty communities had been trained in basic camera usage, and the most advanced of these were now teaching the introductory courses in their native languages. In addition to the digital media centre in San Cristóbal, regional media centres had been built in

Fig. 1. Videomaker, Ejido Morelia, Chiapas. Photo by Francisco Vásquez. Courtesy Chiapas Media Project/Promedios de Comunicación Comunitaria, 1999.

four Zapatista communities (Oventic, Morelia, Roberto Barrios, and La Garrucha) with video production and post-production equipment, audio production equipment, and satellite internet access.[10]

Like other international no11n-governmental organizations (NGOs), CMP/Promedios receives the bulk of its funding and support from abroad, while its projects are developed and carried out by local communities in Chiapas and other parts of southern Mexico. In spite of the potential for inequality that such an arrangement implies, the project would seem to exemplify the kind of positive alliance that Miguel Pickard of the Centro de Investigaciones Económicas y Políticas de Acción Comunitaria [Centre for Political and Economic Research for Community Action] discusses, in which partners from North and South collaborate on a non-hierarchical basis to achieve common goals (Pickard). Such an alliance differs radically from the paternalistic approach often seen in government-initiated indigenous media programs, described by Tzeltal videomaker Mariano Estrada at the Encuentro Internacional de Imágenes, Memorias e Identidades Amerindias [International Gathering of Amerindian Images, Memories and Identities] held in San Cristóbal in 2006:

> El hoy desaparecido Instituto Nacional Indigenista ... dotó a varias comunidades del país (entre las cuales nos contamos) del equipo de producción audiovisual para registrar los momentos más bellos o alegres de la comunidad, como sus fiestas, pues, como se sabe, al gobierno le interesa más ver a los indígenas en fotografías o esculturas para museo que verlos de carne y hueso ... los ve como atractivo turístico y no como pueblos vivos y sinceros. (Molina)

> The now-disappeared National Indigenist Institute ... gave various communities in the country (ours among them) audiovisual production equipment to record the community's most attractive and joyful moments, like its festivals, since, as is well known, the government is more interested in seeing indigenous people in photographs or sculptures than in seeing them as flesh and blood ... they see them as a tourist attraction and not as peoples who are alive and sincere.

Members of these communities, Estrada continues, rejected the aims of the government and began instead to document their struggles, asserting themselves as *"sujetos de la historia y no objetos de estudio"* ["subjects of history, not objects of study"] (Molina). Video became a means of reporting events as well as reflecting on issues in ways that could lead to dialogue. Indeed, the videos made by Zapatista community groups are often used to share organizing strategies and knowledge between communities (Halkin, 56–57); they are also, as Alfonso Gumucio Dagrón reports, an effective way of documenting and in some cases even preventing abuse at the hands of military and paramilitary forces (Gumuncio Dagrón, 47).

Several of the Zapatista videos distributed by CMP/Promedios focus specifically on women. *We Are Equal: Zapatista Women Speak* [*La vida de la mujer en resistencia*], made in 2004 by men and women of the EZLN stronghold Resistencia hacia un Nuevo Amanecer [Resistance towards a New Dawn] in the Tzeltal municipality of Francisco Villa, addresses the changing social role of Mayan women as experienced by members of a Zapatista community.[12] As we have seen, the empowerment of women has long been a priority for the EZLN, whose Revolutionary Women's Law outlines a human rights agenda that gives women full equality with men. Yet more than a decade after its passage, this video shows that change has not come easily.

We Are Equal: Zapatista Women Speak portrays the struggle of socially and economically marginalized subjects whose existence has never been recognized. As some of Mexico's poorest inhabitants, they are an invisible part of a nation supposedly in the throes of modernization; moreover, as women, they are silenced by patriarchal attitudes that view women's words and actions as worthless. As the video begins, women speak about their grandparents' hard lives as peons on feudal plantations, then reflect that their own lives are not that much different, in spite of their liberty from peonage. Their descriptions of gruelling workdays that begin before dawn and end around midnight are borne out visually; the camera follows the women as they carry out their many daily chores, paying homage to the female labour that is too often taken for granted. Although men also work hard in the fields, they do not suffer the double or triple burden borne by the women. They wake to the hot breakfast that the women have been up for hours preparing; their clothes are washed, their children

Fig. 2. Videomaker, Ejido Morelia, Chiapas. Photo by Francisco
Vásquez. Courtesy Chiapas Media Project/Promedios de
Comunicación Comunitaria, 1999.

cared for, their homes clean. On Sundays they rest. The women's chores,
on the other hand, never end.

Compounding this unequal division of labour is the misogynistic
attitude prevalent in the communities. Interviewees talk about the total
control men exercised over women prior to 1994; women were not allowed to leave their homes, and if they did they were automatically accused of wrongdoing. Domestic violence was endemic.[13] The women,
illiterate and isolated, were, as one interviewee explains, "ignorant of our
rights" and had little choice but to accept their lot. Although these conditions did not change overnight, the coming of the Zapatistas represented
a turning point in the women's lives, especially in terms of their political
participation and presence outside the home. As the women began to
organize in support of the insurgency, the men realized that their wives
and daughters might have something positive to contribute and began to

permit their participation. As the women became aware of their rights and empowered by their collective effort, they realized they no longer needed to ask permission.

That the achievement of equality is a complex process is made clear in several ways in *We Are Equal: Zapatista Women Speak*. In one sequence, while we watch women go through the various steps of preparing tortillas, a male voice on the soundtrack sings in Spanish about the need for men to respect women's rights. Later, we hear a broadcast on the same subject from the EZLN radio station. The broadcast, in which alternating male and female voices cite the Revolutionary Women's Law and emphasize the need for women's full social participation, is also spoken in Spanish. The women, on the other hand, speak in Tzeltal, for while men in Chiapas often learn Spanish in the course of their interactions with the world outside their villages, most women do not. The contrast between the two languages serves to highlight a certain distance between the ideals of the revolution and the reality on the ground.

The EZLN use of Spanish as a lingua franca to address males in linguistically diverse communities, however, does not override the fact that the women's Tzeltal testimony is, in fact, recorded by the video itself and transmitted to audiences far beyond the local context. In the video's closing credits, we find acknowledgments of a Service Employees International Union local and of supporters in San Francisco, California. In this respect, *We Are Equal: Zapatista Women Speak* operates on multiple levels as an example of what Néstor García Canclini, in his essay "Will There Be Latin American Cinema in the Year 2000?," refers to as "multicontextuality." "National and local identities," he writes, "can persist if we resituate them in a context that is multicontextual. Identity, made more dynamic through this process, will not be only a ritualized narration, the monotonous repetition of outmoded principles. Identity, as a narrative we constantly reconstruct with others, is also a coproduction" (García Canclini, 257). The multiple contexts registered in and by the video attest to this notion of identity as a work perpetually in progress.

The process of construction and reconstruction of identity is expressed symbolically in the face coverings worn by the video's interviewees. While the women filmed during their daily activities mostly have their faces uncovered, those who address the camera use the bandanas or knit ski masks that identify them as Zapatistas. Gary Gossen, an anthropologist who has sought to articulate ancient Mayan beliefs and traditions with contemporary practices, has speculated that the Zapatista use of masks, beyond its protective and propagandistic functions, is linked to the Mayan understanding of identity as something that is not only internal to the individual but also made up of multiple external relationships. The EZLN's masks, writes Gossen,

> may suppress individual identities, but they do not disguise them, for [among the Zapatistas] all participants are known to one another. Contextually, in suppressing individual identities, the wearing of the half-masks is expressing group identity – an identity that ... is a relationship among a set of individual identities, identities that are influenced by something beyond themselves. (Gossen, 280n4)

It is precisely this group identity, founded on the symbolic suppression of individual identities, that enables the women shown in *We Are Equal: Zapatista Women Speak* to challenge their previous condition of invisibility.

The women in the video never talk specifically about being Zapatistas. Their status as such can be inferred from the title and production context, since they are identified from the outset as residents of an EZLN *caracol* or regional centre, but it is also made clear by their masks, which signify the leap that the women have taken from abjection to empowerment, from passivity to participation, and from silence to self-assertion. The statement *We Are Equal: Zapatista Women Speak* thus refers not only to women's equality with men, but to the equality claimed by women who choose to hide their identities behind masks. In symbolically suppressing their individuality, they are able to identify themselves with a transcendent ideal beyond the scope of their particular lives. At the same time, the video's emphasis on the ordinary, down-to-earth aspects of their existence prevents the ideal from overtaking the real. Indeed, the last part of the video shows the women working together in a collective kitchen rather than in isolation, sharing joyfully with their community. The song played over the final credits, with the refrain "porque esto ya comenzó, y nadie lo va a parar" ["because this has already begun, and nobody is going to stop it"], underscores the sense of pride and dignity that the women have acquired in their struggle.

The emergence of women-run cooperatives is an indicator of the changing role of women in Zapatista Chiapas. The video *Xulum'chon* (2002), also distributed by CMP/Promedios, was made in the Tzotzil-speaking municipality of San Juan de la Libertad to document and promote the weavers' collective of that name. Yet it is neither an "infomercial" nor an ethnographic documentary, at least as these genres are normally practised. The video opens with close-up shots showing different stages of weaving and embroidering, followed by the telling of the first half of a local legend whose meaning will not become clear until the end of the film. From there, an abrupt transition takes us into the daily labours of the women's collective. There is no unifying narration; instead, through interviews and images, the video recounts the cooperative's history from its founding in 1999 and provides a matter-of-fact portrayal of rural women's labour similar to that in *We Are Equal: Zapatista Women Speak*. A particularly striking shot shows a woman awkwardly trying to weave while her baby nurses at her breast; neither the nursing nor the weaving is romanticized, and instead we get an image that encapsulates the difficulty of balancing women's multiple roles – an image with which any working mother can surely identify.

The beauty and skill of the weaver's craft is expressed visually in sequences that show the production process as well as the finished textiles, some of which follow traditional patterns while others, such as an embroidered insignia of the Mut Vitz coffee cooperative, respond to more recent developments in the community. In their verbal testimony, the women discuss their work not as an art form, but rather as an activity that they rely on to make ends meet. This income source is especially crucial due to the insufficiency of the community's coffee crop and the instability of the local agricultural economy in general. Yet it too is precarious; the women say that the sale of their work in the city of San Cristóbal often does not even cover costs, and that what little money they earn usually goes into maintaining the cooperative rather than feeding their needy families. Foreign buyers such as Denver-based coffee importer Kerry Appel, who appears briefly onscreen, provide essential economic support and at the same time reinforce the community's ties to an international network of solidarity. The emphasis is thus not on women carrying out an ancient tradition but rather on women attempting to carve out a place in the modern global economy. Difficult as their situation may be, the video portrays them not as victims but rather as active subjects in a process of social transformation.

CMP/Promedios is not the only organization involved in indigenous video production in Chiapas. Sna Jtz'ibajom [House of the Writer], a Maya literary workshop in San Cristóbal, has worked in video, as has the Comité de Defensa de la Libertad Indígena Xi'nich [Committee in Defence of Indigenous Freedom "Ant"]. Another key player is the Proyecto de Videoastas Indígenas de la Frontera Sur [Indigenous Video-makers of the Southern Border Project, PVIFS], sponsored by the Centro de Investigaciones y Estudios Superiores en Antropología Social [Centre for Research and Higher Education in Social Anthropology, CIESAS]. Founded in 2000, PVIFS's stated mission is "to encourage a collaborative and decolonized anthropology" in which intercultural dialogue between academics and community members takes the place of traditional ethnographic observation; as with CMP/Promedios, the project funds and trains indigenous participants to become "'multipliers' or 'popular video-makers' able to promote a new cultural politics" (Leyva and Köhler). Videos produced by the project include several by or about women, among these the collectively directed *Se abren las flores de las regiones. Las mujeres en la realidad de Chiapas* (*The Flowers of Our Regions Are Opening: Women in the Reality of Chiapas*, 2002) and Pedro Agripino Icó Bautista's *Saberes de las parteras indígenas en Los Altos de Chiapas* (*Knowledge of Indigenous Midwives in the Chiapas Highlands*, 2004). These and other videos are collaborations between PVIFS and local NGOs, a productive model that has encouraged diversity in the project's themes and approaches.

The videos discussed in these pages, made largely by women and men with scarce resources and no access to commercial media networks, raise many questions. First, the obvious challenge is how these projects will be sustained in the long term. As I mentioned, CMP/Promedios and similar projects rely on funding from abroad, whether from sales, donations, or grants from foundations and other institutions. Their work, like that of the Xulum'chon weavers, has non-monetary value to their communities, who use the videos as a catalyst for dialogue and reflection and to preserve the communities' history and collective memory. Yet also like the weaving and coffee cooperatives of Zapatista Chiapas, the video projects depend financially on a kind of alternative export economy based on principles of fair trade and solidarity, and this economy is precarious.

Indeed, the very sectors in the United States that had been most sympathetic to the Zapatistas during the 1990s found themselves under siege during the Bush administration, struggling over issues such as the Iraq war, civil liberties restrictions, anti-immigrant legislation, and mounting racism and discrimination at the local level. The economic crisis of the late 2000s exacerbated the problem, and, in spite of the Obama administration's softer attitude toward progressive activism, there is no guarantee that Zapatista media projects will continue to attract donors.

Given the limitations of international solidarity, can it be considered a sufficient means of support in the long run? Or rather, if and when this support runs out, will community media producers be left stranded, with their equipment wearing out beyond repair or becoming obsolete and their videos deteriorating on shelves in an uncontrolled storage environment? If it is relatively simple to distribute video equipment and train people to use it in an efficient manner, it is much more difficult to create an alternative media infrastructure that will meet the needs of historically marginalized communities, especially in a rural setting. The Zapatistas have tried to do just that, in collaboration with their international allies and supporters. Yet as they well understand, this work cannot be done from outside but must ultimately become the responsibility of the communities themselves. Meanwhile, these communities struggle to meet their basic needs in an environment characterized by ongoing conflict and harassment. Thus, while local and national networks of support may sustain the project to some degree, it is obvious that a truly level mass media playing field requires profound social change.

Access to information, education, and resources were among the Zapatista's original demands in 1994. Now, nearly seventeen years later, the Zapatistas have moved from being a military movement fighting against the government to being an alternative civilian government operating autonomously within the borders of the Mexican nation and working to bring about an all-encompassing social transformation, including in the area of communications. If, down the road, this model succeeds, it will be exciting to see what new kinds of structures for media production and distribution develop.

In the meantime, it is interesting to reflect on the relation videos like *Xulum'chon* and *We Are Equal: Zapatista Women Speak* bear to the broader history of Mexican cinema in its commercial and state-supported forms.

As I noted at the beginning of this chapter, the independent video sector that has emerged in Mexico in recent years, which encompasses not only producers but also training centres, festivals and distribution networks, has created an alternative to a national film industry whose view of indigenous Mexico has long been based on formulas and stereotypes. Within this sector, the influence of the Zapatista rebellion, both as subject matter and as ideological compass, has been crucial. What is certain is that, as Saavedra Luna suggests, Chiapas can no longer be considered a "set," providing exotic colour for images of the nation scripted from the perspective of the metropolitan centre (371). In Zapatista Chiapas, indigenous women and men have claimed their place as speaking subjects, declaring "never again a Mexico without us."

The very concept of "Mexico" contained in this slogan, however, implies a revision and a challenge. What we see today are strategies of media production and distribution that are, in effect, simultaneously local and international, bypassing to a large extent the traditional category of the nation as the entity defining both media-making practices and cultural identity. Community-based videomakers represent micro-communities and groups whose identification is less with the nation as such than with other categories, such as Maya, *indígena*, Zapatista, or simply "from below." Moreover, using tools such as the Internet, speaking tours, and Zapatista-led or inspired international *encuentros* [gatherings], these smaller entities network with each other and with other similar groups and communities in other countries, expanding horizontally – multicontextually – rather than seeking to rise to prominence on a national level.

Is this what Paul Leduc meant when he proclaimed the end of big-budget dinosaur cinema and the advent of lizard and salamander cinema? Perhaps, in this case, the image is more apt than even Leduc realized, for as we learn in the last minutes of the weavers' video, the name 'Xulum'chon' refers in the Tzotzil Maya language to a kind of lizard. And like the women weavers who adopted the lizard's name for their cooperative, perhaps independent grassroots video producers can find inspiration in the story told in the video, of the small but clever animal that faces up to the threat of imminent destruction, damns the floodwaters, and saves the community from oblivion.

WORKS CITED

Aumenta la militarización en Chiapas, afirman. 2007. *La Jornada*, 18 November. http://www.jornada.unam.mx/2007/11/18/index.php?section=politica&art icle=011n2pol (accessed July 10, 2008).

Belausteguigoitia, Marisa. 2007. Rajadas y alzadas: De Malinches a comand-antes; Escenarios de construcción del sujeto femenino indígena. In *Miradas feministas sobre las mexicanas del siglo XX*. Ed. Marta Lamas, 191–236. Mexico City: Fondo de Cultura Económica.

Calmus, Ellen. n.d. We Are All Ramona: Artists, Revolutionaries, and Zapa-tistas with Petticoat. *ZoneZero*. http://www.zonezero.com/magazine/essays/distant/fcalmus2.html (accessed July 10, 2008).

Centro de Documentación sobre Zapatismo. 2005. Libros, Revistas, Videos y Música. http://www.nodo50.org/cedoz/libros/indi_librosvid.htm (accessed August 8, 2008).

Cleaver, Harry. 1995. The Zapatistas and the Electronic Fabric of Struggle. Chiapas95. http://www.eco.utexas.edu/faculty/Cleaver/zaps.html#17. Also in *Zapatista! Reinventing Revolution in Mexico*. Ed. John Holloway and Eloína Peláez, 81–103. London: Pluto Press, 1998.

Ejército Zapatista de Liberación Nacional (EZLN). 1994. Women's Revolution-ary Law. In *Zapatistas! Documents of the New Mexican Revolution*. Brooklyn: Autonomedia. http://lanic.utexas.edu/project/Zapatistas/chapter01.html (accessed August 8, 2008).

———. *Sixth Declaration of the Lacandon Jungle*. 2005. Enlace Zapatista. http://enlacezapatista.ezln.org.mx/especiales/2/ (accessed August 8, 2008).

Esteva, Gustavo. 2006. The 'Other Campaign' and the Left: Reclaiming an Al-ternative. Trans. Holly Yasui. *ZNet*. 17 December. http://www.zmag.org/znet/viewArticle/2514 (accessed August 8, 2008).

Filmoteca de la UNAM. 2003. Filmografía Mexicana. http://www.filmoteca.unam.mx/Bases/bases.htm (accessed August 8, 2008).

Froehling, Oliver. 1997. The Cyberspace 'War of Ink and Internet' in Chiapas, Mexico. *Geographical Review* 87: 291–307.

García Canclini, Néstor. 1997. Will There Be Latin American Cinema in the Year 2000? Visual Culture in a Postnational Era. In *Framing Latin American Cinema: Contemporary Critical Perspectives*. Ed. Ann Marie Stock, 246–58. Minneapolis: University of Minnesota Press. Originally published as "¿Habrá cine latinoamericano en el año 2000? La cultura visual en la época del postnacionalismo." *Nueva Época* 21 February 1993, *La Jornada*: 27–33.

Gossen, Gary H. 1999. *Telling Maya Tales: Tzotzil Identities in Modern Mexico*. London: Routledge.

Gumuncio Dagrón, Alfonso. 2001. *Making Waves: Stories of Participatory Communication for Social Change*. New York: Rockefeller Foundation. http://www.comminit.com/strategicthinking/pdsmakingwaves/sld-1893.html.

Gutiérrez, Eugenia. 2008. La Comandanta Ramona y las zapatistas (Una reseña del Encuentro de Mujeres). *Rebelión* 28 January. http://www.rebelion.org/noticia.php?id=62494&titular=la-comandanta-ramona-y-las-zapatistas- (accessed August 12, 2008).

Halkin, Alexandra. 2008. Outside the Indigenous Lens: Zapatistas and Autonomous Video-making. In *Global Indigenous Media: Cultures, Poetics, and Politics*. Ed. Pamela Wilson and Michelle Stewart, 54–77. Durham, NC: Duke.

Henríquez, Elio. 2007. Denuncian nueva embestida contra bases del EZLN. *La Jornada*, 21 November. http://www.jornada.unam.mx/2007/11/21/index.php?section=politica&article=023n2pol (accessed August 8, 2008).

Hernández Castillo, Rosalva Aída, ed. 1998. *La otra palabra: Mujeres y violencia en Chiapas, antes y después de Acteal*. San Cristóbal: CIESAS.

Leduc, Paul. 1989. Dinosaurs and Lizards. Address to the 1987 Festival of New Latin American Cinema in Havana. In *Latin American Visions*. Ed. Patricia Aufderheide, 57–59. Philadelphia: Neighborhood Film/Video Project of International House.

Leyva, Xochitl, and Axel Köhler. 2004. Introducción/Introduction. Proyecto Videoastas Indígenas de la Frontera Sur. http://sureste.ciesas.edu.mx/Proyectos/PVIFS/pagina_principal.html (accessed August 10, 2008).

Millán, Márgara. 1996. Las zapatistas del fin del milenio. Hacia políticas de autorepresentación de las mujeres indígenas. *Chiapas* 3. http://www.ezln.org/revistachiapas/No3/ch3.html (accessed August 20, 2008).

Molina, Javier. 2006. El video indígena comunica hechos reales sin maquillarlos: Estrada. *La Jornada*, 31 October. http://www.jornada.unam.mx/2006/10/31/index.php?section=espectaculos&article=a08n1esp (accessed August 20, 2008).

Montes, Rodolfo. 1995. Chiapas es guerra de tinta y Internet. *Reforma*, 26 April. Chiapas95 Archives, http://www.eco.utexas.edu/~archive/chiapas95/1995.04/msg00340.html (accessed August 28, 2008).

Muñoz Ramírez, Gloria. 2007. Alarma ofensiva en Chiapas. *La Jornada*, 29 September. http://www.jornada.unam.mx/2007/09/29/index.php?section=opinion&article=014o1pol (accessed August 28, 2008).

Olmos, José Gil. 2006. López Obrador y Marcos. *Proceso* online edition. 28 September. http://www.proceso.com.mx/ (accessed August 28, 2008).

Pérez Vázquez, Hilda, and Tamil Kendall. 2007. "Relatoria de la plenaria de las mujeres del Caracol de la Garrucha: como se vive las ninas y madres Zapatistas." Centro de Medios Independientes/Indymedia Chiapas. 29 December. http://chiapas.indymedia.org/display.php3?article_id=153295&keyword=Relatoria+de+la+plenaria+de+las+mujeres+&phrase= (accessed September 2, 2008).

Pickard, Miguel. 2006. Una reflexión sobre relaciones entre agencias financiadoras del Norte y organizaciones de la sociedad civil del Sur. Centro de Investigaciones Económicas y Políticas de Acción Comunitaria. *Boletín Chiapas al Día* 528 (8 December). http://www.ciepac.org/boletines/chiapasaldia.php?id=528 (accessed September 2, 2008).

Primero Noticias. 2006. Interview with Subcomandante Marcos by Carlos Moret de Mola. Televisa Channel 2, Mexico City. 9 May. Transcript: http://enlacezapatista.ezln.org.mx/la-otra-campana/327/ (accessed June 15, 2008).

Promedios. 2008. Chiapas. http://www.promediosmexico.org (accessed June 2, 2008).

Rashkin, Elissa. 2001. *Women Filmmakers in Mexico: The Country of Which We Dream*. Austin: University of Texas Press.

Rovira, Guiomar. 1997. *Mujeres de maíz*. Mexico City: Era.

Saavedra Luna, Isis. 2000. El cine en Chiapas durante la década de los noventa a partir de la visión de la prensa de la ciudad de México. In *Microhistorias del cine en México*. Ed. Eduardo de la Vega Alfaro, 367–81. Guadalajara: Universidad de Guadalajara.

Serrill, Michael S. 1995. Unmasking Marcos. *Time*, 20 February. http://www.time.com/time/magazine/article/0,9171,982550,00.html (accessed June 2, 2008).

Speed, Shannon, Rosalva Aída Hernández Castillo, and Lynn Stephen, eds. 2006. *Dissident Women: Gender and Cultural Politics in Chiapas*. Austin: University of Texas Press.

Stephen, Lynn. 2006. Rural Women's Grassroots Activism, 1980–2000: Reframing the Nation from Below. In *Sex in Revolution: Gender, Politics, and Power in Modern Mexico*. Ed. Jocelyn Olcott, Mary Kay Vaughn, and Gabriela Cano, 241–60. Durham, NC: Duke University Press.

Telemanita. 2000. Interview with Carmen Ortiz, Mexican Video Maker and Zapatista. *Boletín Video-Red Mujer* 13 (April–May), English edition. http://www.laneta.apc.org/telemanita/index.html (accessed September 2, 2008).

VIDEOS

Las compañeras tienen grado. Directed by Guadalupe Miranda and María Inés Roqué. Centro de Capacitación Cinematográfica, 1995.

*Comunicado del Ejército Zapatista de Liberación Nacional en voz de la Comandante Ra-
mona.* Ejército Zapatista de Liberación Nacional, 1995.

El EZLN y las mujeres, las siempre olvidadas. Colectivo La Brujas, 1995.

Los más pequeños: Un retrato del Ejército Zapatista de Liberación Nacional. Directed by
Carmen Ortiz y José Luis Contreras. Colectivo Perfil Urbano, 1994.

Oventic: Construyendo dignidad. Directed by Carlos Martínez Suárez. Video Trópi-
co Sur, 1995.

Saberes de las parteras indígenas en Los Altos de Chiapas. Directed by Pedro Agripino
Icó Bautista. Organización de Médicos Indígenas del Estado de Chiapas and
Proyecto Videoastas Indígenas de la Frontera Sur, 2004.

Se abren las flores de las regiones. Las mujeres en la realidad de Chiapas. Directed by
Rogelio Vázquez Bolom, Sara Duque Sosa, Catalina Casillas Moreno and
Maria López Sánchez. Comité de Derechos Humanos Fray Pedro Lorenzo
de la Nada; Enlace, Comunicación y Capacitación; and Proyecto Videoastas
Indígenas de la Frontera Sur, 2002.

We Are Equal: Zapatista Women Speak. Caracol Resistencia hacia un Nuevo
Amanecer. Distributed by Promedios, 2004.

Xulum'chon: Weavers in Resistance from the Highlands. Directed by José Luis.
Xulum'chon Cooperative. Distributed by Promedios, 2002.

NOTES

1   I would like to thank Alexandra Halkin of CMP/Promedios, Nayibe Bermúdez Barrios, and the anonymous reviewers for their helpful comments on earlier versions of this chapter.

2   Canal 6 de Julio, named for the date of the fraudulent 1988 presidential elections, produces and distributes videos that critique Mexican politics, state-sponsored violence and repression. Telemanita, whose name is a neologism combining "tele" with an informal diminutive of "sister" that can also mean a "helping hand," provides training and support to women videomakers from many social sectors, and especially promotes sexual diversity, reproductive rights, and environmental sustainability. Voces contra el Silencio is an advocacy organization that promotes independent documentary video. Indymedia is a decentralized international network of alternative media producers.

3   Marcos appeared on the Televisa network's *Primero Noticias* [News First] program on May 9, 2006, in a predictably sensationalist interview in which, among other topics, host Carlos Loret de Mola highlighted the apparent unpopularity of the Other Campaign in comparison to earlier EZLN initiatives. Marcos responded that in opposing López Obrador, the Zapatistas had made a calculated sacrifice that they saw as necessary to maintain their integrity and move their agenda forward. The role of the mass media in shaping public opinion about social movements, actors, and issues was not addressed.

4   In late 2007, *La Jornada* published numerous reports about rising levels of militarization, violence, and insecurity in the region. See, for instance, "Aumenta la militarización en Chiapas," Muñoz Ramírez and Henríquez.

5   A survey of Chiapas-made films in the database of the National University's Filmoteca [Film Archive] suggests that much interest in the region has been anthropological, with emphasis on native myths and legends and not on present-day social conditions. The disproportionate attention given to the isolated Lacandon people, rather than other ethnic groups who have long interacted with *mestizo* society, suggests a fetishistic preoccupation with authenticity and the exotic on the part of many filmmakers. At the same time, Chiapas has often served as a generic jungle locale for Hollywood action films such as *Predator* (1987) and *Immortal Combat* (1994).

6   The Centro de Documentación sobre Zapatismo [Center for Documentation of *Zapatismo*] website lists 111 videos made between 1994 and 2003, and notes that its list is incomplete. Also see Saavedra Luna for an overview of film and video activity during the 1990s.

7   The phrase "On January 1 ..." was posted on the signs that announced the rules for the meeting.

8   Other accounts of women and *zapatismo* include Hernández Castillo; Speed, Hernández Castillo, and Stephen; and Belausteguigoitia.

9   My descriptions are based on an un-
     finished version that circulated among
     activist groups at the beginning of
     1996. The tape that was released later
     that year concludes with a new year's
     celebration taking place in the newly
     built cultural centre.

10   Organizational data comes from the
     CMP/Promedios website and from
     founder Alexandra Halkin, personal
     communication, August 29, 2009. For
     a detailed and illuminating account of
     CMP/Promedios' history see Halkin
     (2008).

11   Part of *We are Equal* was produced dur-
     ing a women's video workshop con-
     ducted by a Zapatista videomaker from
     La Garrucha (Halkin, personal com-
     munication, August 29, 2009).

12   Though not mentioned in the video,
     Rovira shows sexual abuse to be a com-
     mon problem, one exacerbated by the
     heavy use of alcohol among men.

13   Halkin also points out that video
     production has been "one of the only
     projects in the communities that is
     truly integrated" in terms of men and
     women working together, a situation
     she says "has created some interesting
     interactions and learning experiences"
     (personal communication, August 29,
     2009).

SEXPLOITATION, SPACE, AND LESBIAN REPRESENTATION IN ARMANDO BO'S *FUEGO*

Nayibe Bermúdez Barrios
University of Calgary

While recently more and more literature addressing lesbian issues in Latin America has appeared in sociology and literary criticism, in the area of film this is a rather new territory. This essay, therefore, seeks to explore such "territory" by establishing a much-needed connection between representation, sexploitation, and spatio-temporal relations. My analysis of the Argentine film *Fuego* (*Fire*, Armando Bo, 1968), will show the correlation between the cultural and the socio-economic by linking sexploitation to the social and mental spatio-temporal structures that help in the construction of the lesbian subject's representation and identity.[1]

The idea of lesbian identity has been highly contentious because the term "lesbian," as criticism has shown, is very hard to define (Farwell, 10, 16; Zita, 110–11). This is particularly so in the Latin American contexts, where sociologists emphasize the difficulty in locating not only 'lesbian,' but also 'gay' experience, as these identities are considered a "recent, urban and middle-class affair" (Bleys, 9; Thayer, 395).[2] Equally important is the fact that not all of these identities have been generally included in existing homosexual networks (Bleys, 9; Brown, 123). Also, while some critics have explained lesbian invisibility as being due to fear (Kaminsky, 51; Thayer, 396), and several readers and critics of lesbian discourse have assumed it to belong to a presumably personal and private realm (Martínez, 5), others argue that a broadly defined political space, both internal and external, as well as economic-structural factors, contribute to creating possibilities and/or foreclosing options for how lesbians and their movements conceive of their own identities (Thayer, 389; Brown, 126).[3] The difficulty in locating lesbianism informs other spheres as well. Lourdes Arguelles and B. Ruby Rich report that in pre-revolutionary Cuba, one of the common practices for "Cuban heterosexual men, was the procurement of a lesbian prostitute's favors for a night" (687). As implied by their analysis of the commodification of homosexual desire, these prostitutes were coveted because of their lesbianism. At the same time, in daily life these '*tortilleras*' were either ignored or ridiculed (Arguelles and Rich, 686, '*tortilleras*' in the original). Although it is true, as Stephen Brown states, that lesbian and gay organizations now exist in every country in Latin America, some of them dating back to the mid-1980s, judging by the myriad of mostly negative terms used to designate or to denigrate the lesbian subject, scorn, among other feelings, continues to permeate this region (119).[4] Stephen Murray counts eighteen terms in Spanish-speaking America that refer to the "lesbian," many of which metonymically refer to sexual behaviour while others point to appearance, as if to stress the dichotomy between 'feminine' and 'masculine' and to confirm a heterosexist optic (190). Beyond simply showing that "lesbian" is a contested sign, the previous outline also speaks of a spatialization that is created by and through factors such as identity politics, social class, the academic canon, marketing, and the commodification of desire, among others. This spatialization both produces and limits the performance of lesbianism.

Here "lesbian" refers to the representation of women who have erotic and sexual interest in each other, as seen in Armando Bo's *Fuego*.[5] The film portrays, Laura, a nymphomaniac, who in an effort to quench the sexual fire that consumes her, spends her time and energy having sex mostly in open natural settings, such as forests and mountain tops. As generally observed, some of these soft-core sex situations underlying a moralistic ending cause laughter in contemporary audiences. However, they are catastrophic for the protagonist as her condition is medically diagnosed as a sexual neurosis. Finding herself out of options to perform correctly within the limits of a society that privileges marriage, heterosexuality, and monogamy, Laura commits suicide. The terms of Laura's entrapment are enhanced through the film's focus on a lesbian subordinate, Andrea, with whom the protagonist has an intense relationship. This erotic liaison also produces a sense of cultural and economic verisimilitude as it serves to underlie sex, social class, and gender dynamics as constitutive key elements in the contest for the commodification of desire. This means that the lesbian both provides a pretext to showcase leading actor Isabel Sarli, especially her breasts, and the means, as Andrea Weiss has noted for another context, to soothe male sexual anxieties about female autonomy or independence from men (4). The lesbian, then, occupies a threefold space. In view of the situations in which she gets entangled, she becomes a tool for selling the film; due to her erotic and sexual interest in the protagonist, she is a threat to sexual "normalcy"; and through her role of working woman, she represents a menace to gender relations.

As implied above, representation and genre necessarily pertain to the socio-spatial discourses that shape the bodily contours of the subject. Following Henry Lefebvre's ideas about "bodily lived experience," subjects experience spatio-temporal relations through a non-hierarchical triad (31–33, 38–40). The first sphere entails the physical parcellization of space, including the spatial practices which embrace production and reproduction, and the particular locations and spatial sets characteristic of each social formation. The next one, known as representations of space, includes the images, symbols, and codes of conceptualized or conceived space that serve to impose an order to the relations between subjects. These two areas come together to generate or undermine a successful performance of subjecthood in the third sphere, known as representational space, or space as directly lived. Due to its inception in the body, it has been widely shown that directly lived space is both gendered and sexualized.[6] As I will demonstrate through my analysis of *Fuego*, space can also be aestheticized and commodified in response to market concerns, global demands, and genre aesthetic conventions. Extending beyond a strict Marxist sense focused on the study of social class, Lefebvre's theory of space can serve as a cartography encompassing film genre in its triple existence as aesthetic practice, industrial mechanism, and arena of cultural-critical discursivity, as formulated by Christine Gledhill (221–23).[7] Since these three aspects involve a spatial organization and productions of relations within and with "out" the film industry, including those fostered by production, distribution, exhibition, and reception, it is appropriate to study genre as a socio-spatial phenomenon. In particular, I will see how sexploitation in *Fuego* puts in place its representation of the lesbian and how it becomes implicated in the production, reproduction, and reformulation of spatial practices.

There has been at least one early attempt at situating Bo's filmography within the framework of genre. In the 1990s, Sergio Wolf probed into this matter, albeit only in the restricted sense of the thematic, coupled with a derivative although also innovative aesthetic connection to the literary source of the *folletín* [serials]. Moving from the identification of melodramatic themes of what he deemed "folletín salvaje" ["wild serials"] to Bo's "contraseña autoral" ["author signature"], Wolf was trying to restore value to an otherwise mostly reviled filmography (80, 87). However, even if stressing the optic of auteurism, what is missing in this particular analysis is a move beyond the aesthetic, and especially a literary origin, to a consideration of the industrial mechanisms and cultural-critical discursivity concerns that also make up genre, that have an effect on film as an industry, and which were of importance for Armando Bo and Isabel Sarli.[8] More recently Bo's films have been celebrated within the phenomenon of exploitation, more precisely as sexploitation, for their penchant for sex and nudity (Curubeto 1996, 142; Ruétalo, 80). According to Eric Schaefer (1999), the term "exploitation film" is derived from the practice of exploitation, advertising or promotional techniques that went over and above typical posters, trailers, and newspaper ads. During the 1960s and 1970s, the term was modified to indicate the subject that was being exploited, such as "sexploitation" and "blaxploitation" movies (4).[9] Sexploitation, as such, emerged in the form of pictures known as "nudie cuties," which included nudity and sexually suggestive scenes, and were low-budget and lurid (Schaefer 2007, 19–20). Since sexploitation generally refers to low-budget fast-made film vehicles, often intended for the United States and European markets, as Greene puts it, I find this categorization of Bo's films more encompassing as, beyond mere thematic or aesthetic concerns, sexploitation also refers to industrial mechanisms such as production values and market strategies, as well as to various levels of reception (1). Due to inaccessibility of data, I will leave the analysis of reception responses for future research and I will concentrate in this essay on the interconnection between culturally rooted aesthetic and thematic decisions as well as on industrial mechanisms.

In the 1960s and 1970s, Argentina saw an avalanche of what are now called sexploitation movies in the works of the duo formed by filmmaker Armando Bo and star/sexual symbol Isabel Sarli. Several of the sexploitation works by Sarli and Bo featured protagonists who sometimes had sex with other women, as seen in *Fuego* (*Fire* 1968), *Intimidades de una cualquiera* (*Intimacies of a Prostitute*, 1972), *Insaciable* (*The Insatiable Widow*, 1976), and *Una mariposa en la noche* (*A Butterfly in the Night*, 1977). In view of space limitations, this paper will only address lesbian representation and space in the film *Fuego*. The initial investment of $15,000 dollars that was used to shoot this movie ties production values to minimal investment, as Bo emphasized on several occasions this important aspect of his relationship to film as an industry (Bo quoted in Fontán, 62, and in Martín, 34; Fernández and Nagy, 63). As a matter of fact, when asked why he starred in all of his movies, Bo emphasized the need to economize money as he jokingly said that his performance was low-cost (Martín, 102). For these economic reasons, *Fuego* was filmed in fourteen days on locations including Sarli's residence in Buenos Aires, the south of Argentina, and New York (Bo quoted in Martín 1981, 34).

Anecdotes apart, the film brings to the fore the intrinsic connection between cultural and socio-economic boundaries, not only by introducing the theme of lesbianism, which was considered taboo in the 1960s in Argentina, but also by consolidating Isabel Sarli's status as a film star.[10] Armando Bo's thematic interest in portraying sex, including lesbian scenes, was according to him, attuned to developments in the global marketplace, in a period where sex symbols such as Gina Lollobrigida, Silvana Mangano, and Sofia Loren had provided their national cinematography the opportunity to break into the international film market (Bo quoted in Martín, 101, and in Fontán, 60). Bo was also apparently responding to internal socio-spatial constraints that through strong censorship film policies put explicit sex off limits for Argentine screens. Industrial and economic concerns, then, played a role in Bo and Sarli's attempt at profiting from a transnational market.[11] What was needed was an Argentine sex symbol, which up to that moment had not existed in a national media space dominated for quite a while by the *status quo* image and persona of actors such as Libertad Lamarque and Nini Marshall.[12] Sarli and Bo saw an opportunity to enter the transnational market by supplying an identified demand for hot topics and sizzling divas. Even if the actor's working-class background may have limited the types of roles that she got to play in her movies, as Victoria Ruétalo asserts (81–82), Sarli's participation in low-budget sexploitation films is also linked to their potential, in the 1960s and 1970s, as an untapped source of fame and revenue. As a matter of fact, sexploitation not only guaranteed a long and active twenty-seven-film business collaboration between Sarli and Bo during almost three decades; the exploitation genre also helped the duo's partnership transcend national boundaries through co-production deals with producers from Uruguay, Brazil, Paraguay, Venezuela, and Mexico, among others (Curubeto 1996, 334). As a result of the reproduction of socio-spatial imaginaries about the female body as an erotic and transnationally marketable product, Bo and Sarli were able to move their films beyond national borders and on to the screens of New York, Miami, Brazil, Europe, and Japan. It is precisely this transnational dimension, together with the innovative thematic concerns of Bo's and Sarli's films, that spurred my curiosity, not only about *Fuego*, but also about the question of genre.

Further than stressing the point about the questioning and possibly about the modification of a national media space not attuned to global paradigms, the focus on Sarli's body also turns us to the question of industrial mechanisms other than those contemplated by production. Sarli was undoubtedly a significant asset for the duo's sexploitation project, her commodified star-studded status having already been recognized by several critics (Curubeto 1996, 333; Fontán, 61; Kuhn, 38–38; Romano, 21; Ruétalo, 80–81). Distribution of Bo and Sarli's vehicles was based on Sarli's sex appeal, as indicated both by the filmmaker and the actor (Bo quoted in Fontán, 60; Sarli quoted in Calleja). As early as 1964, Columbia Pictures started distributing their films in the United States. Consequently, the advertising machinery featuring large photos of Sarli was set in motion. For example in New York, a promotional ad for *Fuego* displayed a shirt-clad Sarli in a semi-lotus position with open arms connected to six close-ups of the actor's face hanging over her head and body (Martín, 35).[13] While this position creates the image of a flame to reference the movie, it also achieves the goal of tying the idea of sexual fire to Sarli's body. This is done by using the shirt to emphasize the actor's breast and thighs and by having her arms shoot out what appear to be six close-ups of pleasure. For instance, in one of the close-ups, Sarli looks directly at the viewer while in the others she assumes a more subdued position by averting and closing her eyes. Simultaneously, the close-ups create a sense of movement by varying the positioning of the actor's face. This is accompanied by fiery descriptions of the reactions she is supposed to provoke, including squeezing "sexual frisson" and turning "men into raging beasts." According to the ad, all of these attributes help Sarli out-stage such stars of the moment as Rachel Welch and Brigitte Bardot. Such eroticized use of the female body for advertising the genre of exploitation does not come as a surprise. However, in the ad, Sarli's money-making significance, while being associated with her body and pleasure, was also used to inscribe her within the same rhetoric used by Bo, only this time with an emphasis on American and non-Italian stars-products of the period. The ad, then, intensifies Sarli's transnational dimension as it has her rubbing shoulders with such a select company of divas. Such a move situates advertising discourses within a global market and spatial imaginings that illustrate the idea of "bodily lived experience" in connection with aesthetic practices of production and reproduction and to images and codes for situating the female as producer and the male as consumer of pleasure. These forms of heterosexual disciplining mark the body in ways that link the economic to the cultural, not only through the production and reproduction of representations of space, but also by their way of direct male address.

The rhetoric and images used in the ad might also explain the conditions imposed by the Columbia Pictures contract, which, according to Sarli, required Bo's filmic direction and her starring role (quoted in Calleja). Here one is bound to remember that no other Argentine director, except for Emilio Vieyra, was creating this type of film which, if judging by the ad, was catering to a male public, as seen in the quotes above. If Sarli did not actually turn men into raging beasts, at least her role in *Fuego* seems to have turned them into avid spectators, as in terms of reception the film is counted, together with *Fiebre* (*Fever* 1979), among the couple's most successful. For its United States release in October 1969, *Fuego* was screened for fourteen weeks in eighty-three theatres in New

York (Bo quoted in Martín, 34). According to Diego Curubeto, in the United States only *Fuego* grossed one million dollars and it was also premiered in Australia, Canada, Italy, Japan, and almost everywhere in Latin America (2001, 86). Although not only cut, but banned in Argentina, this film was also successful during its 1971 release in that country (Romano, 101, 111). It becomes clear that industrial mechanisms, as seen through the production and distribution factors underlined, mark the deep relationship between the film market and the machinery set in motion to tap into sexploitation, including the emergence of Isabel Sarli and the treatment of soft-core sex. All of these elements weigh in when assessing the spatio-temporal interactions in which the film is engaged.

The cost-effective conjunction of sexploitation, Sarli, and Bo also calls for an analysis of lesbian representation within *Fuego*. The type of sexual and taboo roles called for by sexploitation as a non-mainstream sector of the industry, while creating Sarli's persona and on-screen image, also helped Sarli and Bo to actively shape the genre, as within sexploitation circles in Argentina their films, as well as Vieyra's, went a step further than most local sexploitation movies in their depiction of sex (Curubeto 1996, 142). Sarli not only did the first full-frontal nude scene in Argentine cinema, she also interpreted controversial roles, including, among others, lesbians, as I have already noted, and prostitutes.[14] She even played a woman affected by zoophilia in *Fiebre*. This sort of articulation, capable of generating specific and distinctively different generic formulae in particular historical conjunctures, as Gledhill identifies in her description of genre (229), is what further explains a connection between Sarli, lesbianism, global consumption, and the commodification of desire. Turning mainly to the filmic text, I will now study the physical parcellization of space and some of the images, symbols, and codes for the representation of the lesbian that were common during Sarli and Bo's given historical conjuncture and which find their way into *Fuego*.

Besides having shock value used to entice the public, as is characteristic of sexploitation, lesbianism enters the film as a tool to display Sarli's body. As I have already mentioned, in *Fuego* Sarli plays a fiery nymphomaniac. Although Laura, the protagonist, has sexual intercourse with several men, including lower-class workers, she also has a more stable relationship with Andrea, her housekeeper and assistant. In fact, more screen time is devoted to this erotic relationship than to any other, including the one Laura has with her fiancé, Carlos. Moreover, more body parts are seen by the spectators when Laura is engaged in sexual intercourse with Andrea, interpreted by Alba Mujica, also a staple in Bo's movies. In two scenes at a lake, for example, the assistant is seen caressing and kissing Laura's legs, her crotch, breast and upper thighs as the protagonist stands nude and passive on the beach, except when she responds by touching her own breasts. By contrast, when Laura is with at least six men with whom she has sex in the film, her body parts are not singled out, although she is sometimes seen nude. Laura's complete exposure when she is with Andrea is also accentuated by the fact that the latter is always dressed. This detail also establishes a contrast between the two women as Laura's disrobed and excessive beauty, clearly tied to exotizing ideas about South America, its geography and its women, underlines Andrea's severity and her less feminine identification. Andrea is also very active as she initiates sex and seems unable to resist Laura's voluptuous body. However, the love-making scenes between the two, by means of multiple close-ups of Laura's breasts, her thighs, and face, focus the viewers' attention on Laura's sexual attributes. This of course is in line with Sarli and Bo's sexploitation project, but it also highlights the place of woman-to-woman sex in the exploitation genre as the pleasure that Laura receives from Andrea becomes a mechanism, as Weiss has said for another context (1992), to appeal to male voyeurism about lesbians. In this sort of imaginings, not only is one of the two women passive, the other one also has a less feminine identification both in looks and in behaviour. Before addressing the issue of the iconographic inscription of the lesbian, I will describe physical spacialization in more detail in order to further contextualize lesbian representation.

Besides serving as an excuse to expose Sarli's abundant breast from various lens' distances, Laura and Andrea's love-making highlights the protagonist's connection with nature. As a way of emphasizing a natural environment, even the film's credits are superposed on trees, the mountains, and various views of what looks like the tributary of a river. The film starts with one of the lake scenes mentioned above, as Laura is seen bathing under the desiring eye of Andrea, who with an open mouth observes her lustfully. As Laura exits the water onto the beach, a long shot with a slow zoom-in shows the assistant kneeling down as she starts caressing and kissing Laura's legs and crotch. At that moment Laura discovers Carlos, who as an uninvited guest, is watching the two women from a distance. The three-way exchange of glances, with Andrea's gaze on Laura, Laura's on Carlos, and Carlos's on the two of them, introduces the three main characters of the film and at the same time posits Andrea's lesbian gaze in opposition to Carlos's heterosexual one as the two characters vie for Laura's favours. In this scene, physical spatialization allows for a connection between a seemingly wild and untouched environment and the unravelling of hidden desires and instincts in a stereotypical move that connects geographical background to sexual excess in an exoticized Latin American landscape represented by San Martín de los Andes. Since this film was intended for the United States and other international audiences, citations of the north-south narrative trope, in which the South is presented in a way that will be easily recognizable and consumable by the North, are to be expected.[15]

More importantly, in the segment described above, it is through Carlos's gaze that extradiegetic spectators see the lesbian scene. In this sense, if it is true, as Bo said, that his filmmaking is responding to global demands for sex, then one has to consider again the male audience posited both by Carlos and the advertisement mentioned above. In addition to being an excuse to displaying Sarli's body, lesbianism in this film provides a shock component that is mediated, at least at two levels, through Carlos's intradiegetic gaze and the film's intended extradiegetic male audience. Again, this is also to be expected as until the 1970s, according to Weiss, the few lesbian images offered by the cinema were for heterosexual male viewers to appeal to male voyeurism about lesbians (4). Spatio-physical representation and the object of desire in *Fuego*, then, set up spectatorial expectations and procure visual recognition by stressing competing lesbian and heterosexual yearning in reaction to strategies for the commodification and heterosexualization of desire and in response to male fantasies about the lesbian.

No wonder the film also includes a scene which in the Something Weird Video Inc. DVD is subtitled as "Lucha del gato" ["Cat fight"]. In this scene, typical of the heated eroticism of trash cinema, especially because it takes place after Laura has taken a shower, Andrea physically attacks her mistress. On learning about Laura's decision to marry Carlos, Andrea throws Laura on the floor and hits her as Laura remains almost inert but sexually provocative. After a while Andrea starts crying and

Laura resolutely utters: "He has something you don't." Even if the film will go on to show Laura's entrapment within institutions that fail her, such as marriage and the medical establishment, this scene functions to soothe society's anxieties by turning to the legality of matrimony and heterosexuality. The heterosexual male gaze proves essential to the idea of lesbian (in)visibility as the inclusion of lesbianism, both as a strategy for audience enticement and its exclusion as an option for Laura, are seemingly negotiated through Laura's cultural reference to a revered place for the penis. However, in the same scene summarized above, Laura keeps telling Andrea that their relationship can go on. That comment, and the fact that at the end of the film nymphomaniac Laura has to die, destabilizes a heterosexual matrix that proves unable to contain the lesbian. As a matter of fact, although Andrea is eventually expunged from the film due to Carlos's resolve, the woman's final words promising eternal love to Laura express a commitment that can probably only be controlled by Laura's death.

Lesbian (in)visibility is further promoted in the film through universalizing iconographic signs. In the particular segment of the lake described above, and in contrast to the protagonist, Andrea sports short hair and a black loose dress that makes for a flat-chested look. In addition, the white lace framing the collar of her dress together with her flat shoes recall the stereotypical maid's uniform. Also, her unglamorized appearance is highlighted by strategic close-ups showing her older face, especially as it contorts in a grimace when she sees Carlos for the first time. In this sense, the film renders the lesbian visible for an audience of spectators familiar with universalizing signs for lesbianism, such as Andrea's subordinate role as Laura's servant and assistant, her attire, her age, and her overall aggressiveness.[16] As a matter of fact, the back cover of the DVD of the film describes Andrea as a "lizard-like lesbian housekeeper." However, beyond that, and in contrast to her plain dress, Andrea's face is covered with heavy makeup around the eyes as well as on the lips, in order to accentuate her gaze and her desire, as she watches Laura in open-mouthed rapture. In this case, in accordance with exploitation aesthetic conventions, the focus on desire and the initiation of sex between the two women is what gives the lesbian away, even if Andrea's body is never seen nude. This representation marks a difference, for example, with Hollywood film noir and lesbian vampire films from the 1930s on in cinemas of the United

States, Great Britain, France, West Germany, Belgium, Spain, and Italy, in which lesbianism is often not directly tied to sexuality or eroticism but is commonly associated with the supernatural, as well as with blood and violence.[17] It also differentiates itself from Argentine prison movies, which, starting in the 1950s, as Natalia Taccetta and Fernado Peña note, due to its association with crime, perversion, and sadism, privilege the jail as a double space for the sordid possibility of lesbianism and its appropriate disciplining (116).[18] Thinking in terms of aesthetic conventions and spatio-temporal relations, previous global and local iconographies are both displaced and reutilized. It is also clear that the sex thematic supported by Bo addresses the taboo of lesbianism by highlighting the corporeal side of desire between two women. This would situate *Fuego*, independently of whether Bo and Sarli were aware of social movements, within a global space of identification of lesbianism and the body, much in the vein that was being discussed in the 1960s and 1970s in the United States. If as Brown states, gay publications in Argentina from the 1970s on show a close identification with the lives, struggles, and cultural activities of lesbians and gay men around the world, especially in the United States and Europe (125), then it might be possible to position *Fuego* within such a paradigm of lesbian identity as a contemporary context for Bo. This does not mean that the film furthers the feminist and/or lesbian causes. As I have shown, its ambiguous politics renders the lesbian invisible through iconographic and cultural citations that reinforce the place of the lesbian within heterosexually regulated representations of space. Rather, this film might be an example of what Leon Hunt calls "permissive populism," or the popular appropriation and commodification of elitist 'liberationist' sexual discourses (2). At the same time, through the direct erotization of Andrea's desire, the film also gets implicated in the global political discussion and recognition of forms of embodied sexuality other than the heterosexual.

In *Fuego*, changes in spatio-temporal relations affect not only sexuality but extend also to the realm of work. In the film, Laura's relationship with Andrea is encoded within a tyrannical form of employer/employee relationship, similar to the one Richard Dyer has identified for lesbians in Hollywood film noir (63). While Laura asks Andrea to be on call just in case she needs her sexually, Andrea is a possessive and violent lover who spies on her mistress. Even though it is her working-woman status that allows Andrea to be close to Laura, it is also this same marker that proves contentious for its obvious relationship to lesbianism as a negative identity trait. This is introduced early in the film, during the first private conversation between Carlos and Laura, when the man comments: "I'm a bit curious. That woman that helped you at the beach; unnatural, strange, somehow I got a bad impression." To which Laura responds: "Andrea? She works for me at home, my housekeeper and assistant. I couldn't do without her, she's devoted." Through her response, the protagonist tries to hide Andrea's erotic role, even when acknowledging the interdependence between the two. In fact, Laura does not have any close connection with any other female, although women in her upper social class milieu discuss her and express their hesitation as to whether they should admire or envy her. At a party, early in the film, and as a not too subtly concealed tool of character presentation two women look at her through a framed door. As they admiringly stare at Laura, they take turns at saying that the protagonist "has nerves and money," and that "she uses all of her men like toys." The two women's more traditional societal position is established through their appreciative gaze and the framing device that separates them from Laura and posits them as observers and commentators. Even if belonging to Laura's social class, the two women are not Laura's friends and can only admire or envy her from a distance. Only men are allowed to have close contact with Laura. However, since she is still not sexually satisfied, Andrea provides the relief needed. It is noticeable that, in many scenes, and in contrast to the scene with the two women, even when presented through a mirror, Laura is framed together with Andrea. This proximity highlights Andrea's working status as a means that allows easy access for the lesbian to her object of desire.

Andrea's untamable independent working status, in its connection with her identity as a lesbian, accounts for her final displacement from the film. In fact, her encounters with Laura are explained, not only through the protagonist's sexual neurosis, but also as a result of Andrea's predatory nature, which is freely released at work. When he finally convinces Laura to get rid of her assistant, Carlos clearly states so by saying to Andrea: "You abused a woman that was sick in her mind when you wanted to satisfy your unnatural instincts." Since this idea is not used to chastise any of the men Laura has sex with, including the electrician found by Carlos with Laura in the couple's own bed, it looks like it is only natural for men to respond to male drives when confronted with a woman's power of seduction. Also, since most of the men with whom Laura has sex are identified with work, either because they talk about it or are seen working, then it appears that work is also a natural given for them as a marker of identity, and not necessarily a pretext to have access to Laura in order to wreak havoc in the family. As a result, the idea about Andrea's "unnatural" and "strange" ways, beyond simply voicing concerns about a 'perverted' sexual instinct, also articulates male sexual anxieties about the autonomy and pleasures that work can provide for a female.

Although the narrative articulations of Bo and Sarli's sexploitation project created a space for the lesbian, this representation was highly regulated. Among such regulations were iconographic and cultural citations, including cinematic codes overseeing the ways people "saw" lesbians, conservative global ideologies concerning proper gender identities, and, in particular, market concerns related to the titillation of a presumably heterosexual audience. This conjunction speaks of a dynamic social space where genre functions as a socio-economic and culturally conditioned aesthetic framework for the representation and consumption of images. The dynamism of space as a triad is further proven through perceptions about changes in the consumers of Bo and Sarli's films. While Rodolfo Kuhn, in a move that stresses social class, speaks of a transition from an uncultured public to an intellectual one that revered these films as "camp" (11), Sarli also points gender demographics, including men at the beginning of her career, women in the 1960s, and a more intellectual and snobbish public in the 1970s (Romano, 121). Such changes, and the previous analysis, mean that both creators and consumers are actively implicated in spatial practices that help shape and transform the images, symbols, and codes that make up the mental spaces we inhabit. Referring back to Lefebvre, through their bodily lived experiences, subjects may attain some agency in order, as Sarli notes, to shift positions, including those concerning their relationship to a film product and the images it creates and recreates.

In relation to this, it should be stated that, not only their films, but also both Sarli and Bo, have, since the 1960s, recurrently caught the imagination of critics and the general public.[19] Sarli's stardom has already been documented and is further proven by the recent blogs, filmographies, and articles found online.[20] There are also a number of biographies

(Fernández and Nagy 1999; Romano 1995), monographs (Kuhn 1984; Martín 1981), articles (Ruétalo 2004; Wolf 1992), interviews (Fontán 1974), and casual references (Maciel 2002). Beyond these written signs of attention, Sarli's image was chosen in 2001 to feature in T shirts by Ona Saéz, a Buenos Aires designer brand (Satragno 156). Also, on November 24, 2007, as reported by Ángel de Brito, the actor was honoured at the Festival de Cine Iberoamericano de Huelva, in Spain, where Argentine film critic and filmmaker Diego Curubeto was also scheduled to screen his documentary *Carne sobre carne, Intimidades de Isabel Sarli* (2008). Besides appealing to Bo's and Sarli's followers through the citing of two of their movies in its title, this feature includes censored clips from the duo's work.[21] The 2007 Festival de Cine Iberoamericano de Huelva's screening of *Carne* (*Meat*, 1968) and *Fuego* (*Fire* 1968), now considered classics among the duo's films, attests to Bo's and Sarli's enduring trasnsnational allure, which de Brito connects to Sarli's persona as: "el gran mito erótico argentino" ["the great Argentine erotic myth"], and to a filmography that, due to its incorporation of nudity and sex, "ha[n] marcado un antes y un después en la cinematografía iberoamericana" ["changed Hispanic filmmaking"] (no pagination). Sarli also received a tribute at the XXIII Guadalajara International Film Festival, held in Mexico on March 7–14, 2008, where *La diosa virgen* [*The Virgin Goddess*, 1973] was screened.[22] Although all this attention might be proving Bo right when he said that Sarli's films would be seen a hundred years after their making, it specifically speaks of a set of spatial interactions where commodity products obtain a transnational status. Since commodities can be understood as the product and embodiment of social relations of production, a means of realizing an exchange value, and a resource allowing the objectification of social relations for consumers, among other things, transnational commodity culture, in the sense proposed by Crang, Dwyer, and Jackson, marks a space inhabited by a whole range of differently positioned actors (448). This interrelated dimension is what I have tried to explore by using the concepts of genre and space in their triadic formulation. Sexploitation mixes genre aesthetics with industrial mechanism in response to transnational spatial business practices in which very often the female body, as I have said with respect to female representation within and without the filmic text, responds to global stylizations that in seeking to produce shock value also manage to sell consumable and palatable images, in addition to images that are reclaimed by ever-changing publics, as Kuhn and Sarli note (Romano, 121). Particular ideas, production values, film vehicles, and representations get mobilized and contested by this lived social field, which also bridges the gap between the economic and the cultural.

WORKS CITED

Arcila Gonzalez, Antonio. 1969. *Las lesbianas.* Bogotá: Ediciones sexo y cultura.

Arguelles, Lourdes, and B. Ruby Rich. 1984. Homosexuality, Homophobia, and Revolution: Notes toward an Understanding of the Cuban Lesbian and Gay Male Experience, Part I. *Signs: Journal of Women in Culture and Society* 9, no. 4: 683–99.

Avritzer, Leonardo. 2005. Culture, Democracy, and the Formation of the Public Space in Brazil. In *Imagining Brazil.* Ed. Jessé Souza and Valter Sinder, 37–59. Lanham, MD: Lexington Books.

Baron, Joe. 2003. Lesbian Space, Lesbian Territory: San Francisco's North Beach District, 1933–1954. In *Wide-Open Town: A History of Queer San Francisco to 1965.* Ed. Nan Alamilla Boyd, 68–107. Berkeley: University of California Press.

Bergmann, Emilie L. 1998. Abjection and Ambiguity: Lesbian Desire in Bemberg's *Yo, la peor de todas.* In *Hispanisms and Homosexualities.* Ed. Sylvia Molloy and Robert McKee Irwin, 228–47. Durham, NC: Duke University Press.

Bermúdez Barrios, Nayibe. 2008. *Sujetos Transnacionales: La Negociación en Cine y Literatura.* Colección In Extenso. Ciudad Juárez: Universidad Autónoma de Ciudad Juárez.

Blanco Cano, Rosana. 2004. Dislocamientos sexuales, genéricos y nacionales en *Infinita* de Ethel Krause. *Ciberletras* 11. http://dialnet.unirioja.es/servlet/articulo?codigo=925932 (accessed April 20, 2008).

Bleys, Rudi C. 2000. *Images of Ambiente: Homotextuality and Latin American Art, 1810–Today.* New York: Continuum.

Borim, Dário, Jr. 1996. Intricacies of Brazilian Gayness: A Cross-Cultural and Cross-Temporal Approach. In *Bodies and Biases: Sexualities in Hispanic Cultures and Literatures.* Ed. David William Foster and Roberto Reis, 333–58. Minneapolis: University of Minnesota Press.

Breckenridge, Janis. 2003. Outside the Castle Walls: Beyond Lesbian Counter-plotting in Cristina Peri Rossi's *Desastres Íntimos*. In *Tortilleras: Hispanic and U.S. Latina Lesbian Expression*. Ed. Lourdes Torres and Inmaculada Pertusa, 118–26. Philadelphia: Temple University Press.

de Brito, Ángel. 2007. "La Coca Sarli, mito internacional." Infobae.com. http://www.infobae.com/contenidos/345581-100912-0-La-Coca-Sarli,-mito-internacional.

Brown, Stephen. 2002. Con discriminación y represión no hay democracia: The Lesbian and Gay Movement in Argentina. *Latin American Perspectives* 29, no.2: 119–38.

Calleja, Pedro. 2006. Entrevista con la coca Sarli: la historia de amor más grande jamás contada. http://pedrocalleja.blogia.com/2006/072703-entrevista-con-la-coca-sarli-la-historia-de-amor-mas-grande-jamas-contada.php (accessed April 20, 2008).

Cantú, Lionel. 2002. De Ambiente: Queer Tourism and the Shifting Boundaries of Mexican Male Sexualities. *GLQ* 8, nos. 1–2: 139–66.

Carrier, Joseph M. 1989. Gay Liberation and Coming Out in Mexico. In *Gay and Lesbian Youth*. Ed. G. Herdt, 225–52. New York: Haworth Press.

Chanan, Michael. 1998. Latin American Cinema in the 90s. Representational Space in Recent Latin American Cinema. *Estudios Interdisciplinarios de América Latina y el Caribe*. 9, no. 1 http://www.tau.ac.il/eial/IX_1/chanan.html#foot3 (accessed February 2, 2008).

Cooper, Sara E. 2004. Family in Levi Calderón's *Dos mujeres*: Post-Traumatic Stress or Lesbian Utopia? In *The Ties That Bind: Questioning Family Dynamics and Family Discourse in Hispanic Literature*. Ed. Sara E. Cooper, 171–83. Lanham, MD: University Press of America.

Cortina, Guadalupe. 2000. *Invenciones multitudinarias: escritores judíomexicanas contemporáneas*. Series: estudios de literatura latinoamericana. Ed. Tom Lathrop and Juan de la cuesta. Newark, DE: Hispanic Monographs.

Crang, Philip, Claire Dwyer, and Peter Jackson. 2003. Transnationalism and the Spaces of Commodity Culture. *Progress in Human Geography* 27, no. 4: 438–53.

Curubeto, Diego. 1993. *Babilonia gaucha: Hollywood en la Argentina, la Argentina en Hollywood*. Buenos Aires: Planeta.

———. 1996. *Cine bizarro: 100 años de películas de terror, sexo y violencia*. Buenos Aires: Editorial Sudamericana.

———. 2001. .Vampiros argentinos for export. *Kinetoscopio* 12: 84–6.

D'Lugo, Marvin. 2002. Transnational Film Authors and the State of Latin American Cinema. In *Film and Authorship*. Ed. Virginia Wexman, 112–30. New Brunswick, NJ: Rutgers University Press.

De La Mora, Sergio. 2006. Cinemachismo: Masculinities and Sexuality in Mexican Film. Austin: University of Texas Press.

Dyer, Richard. 1993. *The Matter of Images: Essays on Representation*. London: Routledge.

Falicov, Tamara. 2003. *B-Movies in the Pampas. Hemisphere: A Magazine of the Americas* 12: 25–28.

Farwell, Marylin R. 1996. *Heterosexual Plots and Lesbian Narratives*. New York: New York University Press.

Fernández, Rodrigo, and Denise Nagy. 1999. *La Gran aventura de Armando Bo: Biografía total*. Buenos Aries: Libros Perfil.

Fittipaldi, Luis Maria. n.d. Reina Isabel, el sexo ingenuo. RosarioCine.com. http://www.rosariocine.com.ar/?sitio=in14 (accessed April 20, 2008).

Fontán, Dionisia. 1974. "El pensamiento vivo de Armando Bo." *Siete Días Ilustrados*, 58–62.

Foster, David William. 2002. *Mexico City in Contemporary Mexican Cinema*. Austin: Uniersity of Texas Press.

Gledhill, Christine. 2000. Rethinking Genre. In *Reinventing Film Studies*. Ed. C. Gledhill and Linda Williams, 221–43. London: Arnold.

Gossy, Mary S. 1996. Not so Lonely: A Butch-Femme Reading of Cristina Peri-Rossi's *Solitario de amor*. In *Bodies and Biases: Sexualities in Hispanic Cultures and Literatures*. Ed. David William Foster and Roberto Reis, 238–45. Minneapolis: University of Minnesota Press.

Greene, Doyle. 2007. *The Mexican Cinema of Darkness: A Critical Study of Six Landmark Horror and Exploitation Films, 1969–1988*. Jefferson, NC: McFarland.

Hankin, Kelly. 2001. Lesbian Locations: The Production of Lesbian Bar Space in *The Killing of Sister George. Cinema Journal* 41 (1): 3–26.

Hetherington, Kevin. 1997. *The Badlands of Modernity Heterotopia and Social Ordering*. London: Routledge.

Hopkins, Lori. 2000. *La vida según Muriel* and the Marking of Feminine Space. Proceedings of the International Conference on Hispanic Literatures and Cinematographies: *Cine Lit 2000: Essays on Hispanic Film and Fiction*, Febrary 18–21. Ed. George Cabello Castellet, Jaume Martí-Olivella and Guy H. Good, 67–76. Corvallis, OR: Oregon State University.

Hueso Montón, A. Luis. 1983. *Los Géneros Cinematográficos: Materiales bibliográficos y filmográficos*. Burgos: Mensajero.

Hunt, Leon. 1998. *British Low Culture: From Safari Suits to Sexploitation*. London: Routledge.

Jussila, Heikki. 1999. *Marginality in Space – Past, Present and Future: Theoretical and Methodological Aspects of Cultural, Social and Economic Parameters of Marginal and Critical Regions*. Aldershot, UK: Ashgate.

————. 2001. *Globalization and Marginality in Geographical Space: Political, Economic and Social Issues of Development in The New Millennium*. Aldershot, UK: Ashgate.

Kaminsky, Amy. 1989. Lesbian Cartographies: Body, Text, and Geography. In *Cultural and Historical Grounding for Hispanic and Luso-Brazilian Feminist Literary Criticism*. Ed. Hernan Vidal, 223–56. Series Literature and Human Rights. Minneapolis: Institute for the Study of Ideologies and Literature.

Keith, Michael, and Steve Pile, eds. 1993. Introduction to Part 2: The Place of Politics, 24–32. *Place and the Politics of Identity*. London: Routledge.

Knights, Vanessa. 2003. Modernity, Modernization and Melodrama: The bolero in Mexico in the 1930s and 1940s. In *Contemporary Latin American Cultural Studies*. Ed. Stephen Hart and Richard Young, 127–39. London: Arnold; New York: Oxford University Press.

Kuhn, Rodolfo. 1984. *Armando Bo: El Cine, la Pornografía Ingenua y Otras Reflexiones*. Buenos Aires: Ediciones Corregidor.

Lefebvre, Henry. 1991. *The Production of Space*. Trad. Donald Nicholson-Smith. Oxford: Blackwell.

Leiner, Marvin. 1994. *Sexual Politics in Cuba: Machismo, Homosexuality, and Aids*. Boulder, CO: Westview Press.

López, Ana M. 1991. Celluloid Tears: Melodrama in the Classical Mexican Cinema. *Iris* 13: 29–52.

————. 1993. Tears and Desire: Women and Melodrama in the 'Old' Mexican Cinema. In *Mediating Two Worlds: Cinematic Encounters in the Americas*. Ed. John King, Ana López, and Manuel Alvarado, 147–63. London: British Film Institute.

Lumsden, Ian. 1996. Gay Life in Havana Today. In *Machos, Maricones and Gays: Cuba and Homosexuality*. 130–59. Philadelphia: Temple University Press.

Maciel, Alejandro. 2002. *El trueno entre las páginas. Diálogos entre Augusto Roa Bastos y Alejandro Maciel*. Asunción: Intercontinental Editora.

Magnusson, Warren. 1996. *The Search for Political Space: Globalization, Social Movements, and The Urban Political Experience*. Toronto: University of Toronto Press.

Martín, Jorge Abel. 1981. *Los films de Armando Bo con Isabel Sarli*. Buenos Aires: Ediciones Corregidor.

Martínez, Elena M. 1996. *Lesbian Voices from Latin America Breaking Ground*. New York: Garland.

Monsiváis, Carlos. 1994. Se sufre, pero se aprende: El melodrama y las reglas de la falta de límites. *Archivos de la Filmoteca: Revista de Estudios Históricos sobre la imagen* 16: 7–19.

Munt, Sally R. 1998. *Heroic Desire: Lesbian Identity and Cultural Space*. London: Cassel.

Murray, Stephen O. 1995. *Latin American Male Homosexualities*. Alberquerque: University of New Mexico Press.

Naficy, Hamid. 1996. Phobic Spaces and Liminal Panics: Independent Transnational Film Genre. In *Global/Local: Cultural Production and the Transnational Imaginary*. Ed. Rob Wilson and Wimal Dissanayake, 119–44. Durham, NC: Duke University Press.

Noble, Andrea. 2005. *Mexican National Cinema*. New York: Routledge.

Oroz, Silvia. 1992. *Melodrama: O cinema de Lágrimas da América Latina. Rio de Janerio*: Rio Fundo Editora.

Pécora, Paulo. 2008. Isabel Sarli vuelve al cine con 'Arroz con leche.' TELAM: Agencia de noticias de la República Argentina. http://www.telam.com.ar/vernota.php?tipo=N&idPub=91991&id=208448&dis=1&sec=12 (accessed February 2, 2008).

Quinziano, Pascual. 1992. La comedia: un género impuro. In *Cine argentino: La otra historia*, comp. Sergio Wolf, 129–46. Buenos Aires: Editorial Buena Letra.

Radcliffe, Sarah A. 1993. Women's Place/El lugar de mujeres: Latin America and the Politics of Gender Identity. In *Place and the Politics of Identity*. Ed. Michael Keith and Steve Pile, 102–16. London: Routledge.

Randall, Margaret. 1993. To Change our Own Reality and the World: A Conversation with Lesbians in Nicaragua. *Signs: Journal of Women in Culture and Society* 18, no. 4: 907–24.

Romano, Néstor. 1995. *Isabel Sarli al desnudo*. Montevideo: Ediciones de la Urraca S.A.

Ruétalo, Victoria. 2004. Temptations: Isabel Sarli Exposed. *Journal of Latin American Cultural Studies* 13, no. 1: 79–95.

Sapere, Pablo. n.d. http://www.pasadizo.com/portada1.jhtml?cod=77&desp=2& disp=5051&dos=0 (accessed January 20, 2008).

Satragno, Lidia. 2002. *Pinky Conversaciones*. Buenos Aires: Grulla.

Schaefer, Eric. 1999. *Bold! Daring! Shocking! True! A History of Exploitation Films, 1919–1959*. Durham, NC: Duke University Press.

———. 2007. Pandering to the "Goon-Trade": Framing the Sexploitation Audience through Advertising. In *Sleaze Artists: Cinema at the Margins of Taste, Style, and Politics*. Ed. Jeffrey Sconce, 19–46. Durham, NC: Duke University Press.

Schaefer-Rodriguez, Claudia. 1996. Monobodies, Antibodies, and the Body Politic: Sara Levi Calderón's *Dos mujeres*. In *Bodies and Biases: Sexualities in Hispanic Cultures and Literatures*. Hispanic Issues 13. Ed. David William Foster and Roberto Reis, 217–37. Minneapolis: Univesity of Minnesota Press.

Shaw, Deborah. 1996. Erotic or Political: Literary Representations of Mexican Lesbians. *Travesía, The Journal of Latin American Cultural Studies* 5, no. 1: 51–62.

Soliño, María Elena. 2001. From Perrault through Disney to Fina Torres: Cinderella Learns Spanish and Talk Back in *Celestial Clockwork*. *Letras Femeninas* 27, no. 2: 68–84.

Steimberg, Oscar. 1988. *La recepción del género: Una investigación sobre los juicios de calidad acerca de los medios*. Buenos Aires: Secretaría de publicaciones, Facultad de Ciencias sociales, Universidad Nacional de Lomas de Zamora.

Sternbach, Nancy, Marysa Navarro-Aranguren, Patricia Chuchryk, and Sonia Alvarez. 1992. Feminisms in Latin America: From Bogotá to San Bernardo. *Signs: Journal of Women in Culture and Society* 17, no. 2: 393–434.

Taccetta, Natalia, and Fernando Peña. 2008. El amor de las muchachas. In *Otras historias de amor: gays, lesbianas y travestis en el cine argentino*, comp. Adrian Melo, 115–33. Buenos Aires: Ediciones Lea.

Tajbakhsh, Kian. 2001. *The Promise of the City [Electronic Resource]: Space, Identity, and Politics in Contemporary Social Thought*. Berkeley: University of California Press.

Tassara, Mabel. 1992. El policial: la escritura y los estilos. In *Cine argentino: La otra historia*. Comp. Sergio Wolf, 147–67. Buenos Aires: Editorial Buena Letra.

Thayer, Millie. 1997. Identity, Revolution, and Democracy: Lesbian Movements in Central America. *Social Problems*, 44, no. 3: 386–407.

Tierney, Dolores M. 1999. Tacones plateados y melodrama mexicano: Salón México y Danzón. *Archivos de Filmoteca: revista de estudios históricos sobre la imagen.* 31: 212–27.

Tonkiss, Fran. 2005. *Space, The City and Social Theory: Social Relations and Urban Forms.* Cambridge and Malden: Polity.

Torres, Lourdes, and Inmaculada Pertusa, eds. 2003. *Tortilleras: Hispanic and U.S. Latina Lesbian Expression.* Philadelphia: Temple University Press.

Vianello, Mino. 2005. *Gender, Space and Power: A New Paradigm for the Social Sciences.* London: Free Association Books.

Villalobos, José P. 1994. La novela lésbica en México: *Amora* de Rosamaría de Roffiel y *Dos mujeres* de Sara Levi Calderón. *Los Discursos de la Cultura Hoy,* 103–7.

Weiss, Andrea. 1992. *Vampires and Violets: Lesbians in the Cinema.* London: Jonathan Cape.

Williams, Bruce. 2002. A Mirror of Desire: Looking Lesbian in María Luisa Bemberg's *I, the Worst of All.* Quarterly Review of Film and Video 19: 133–43.

White, Patricia. 1998. Female Spectator, Lesbian Spectre: *The Haunting.* In *Women in Film Noir.* Ed. Ann Kaplan, 130–50. London: British Film Institute.

Wolf, Sergio. 1992. "Armando Bo con Isabel Sarli: El folletín Salvaje." In *Cine argentino: La otra historia,* comp. Sergio Wolf, 77–90. Buenos Aires: Editorial Buena Letra.

Zita, Jacquelyn N. 1992. Male Lesbians and the Postmodernist Body. *Hypatia* 7, no. 4: 106–27.

FILMS

Almejas y mejillones [*Clams and Mussels*]. Directed by Marcos Carnevale. VHS. Argentina Video Home, 2000.

Alucarda, la hija de las tinieblas. Directed by Juan López Moctezuma. Neon Video, 1978.

Arroz con leche [*Rice and MIlk*]. Directed by Jorge Polaco. Produced by Oscar Marcos Azar and Sebastian Perillo. 2009.

Carne. Directed by Armando Bo. Cinematografica Landini, 1968.

Carne sobre carne, Intimidades de Isabel Sarli. Directed by Diego Curubeto, 2008.

La ciénaga. [*The Swamp*]. Directed by Lucrecia Martel. Cowboy Booking International, 2001.

La dama regresa. Directed by Jorge Polaco. Produced by Carlos Gorosito and Fernando Sokolowicz, 1996.

La diosa impura. Directed by Armando Bo. Películas Mexicanas, 1963.

La diosa virgen. Directed by Dirk de Villiers. Produced by Bevil Films and Armando Bo Productions, 1973.

Esperando al mesías [*Waiting for the Messiah*]. Directed by Daniel Burman. Argentina Video Home, 2000.

Éxtasis tropical. Directed by Armando Bo. Haven International Pictures, 1969.

El favor. Directed by Pablo Sofovich. Primer Plano Film Group, S.A., 2004.

Fiebre [*Fever*]. Directed by Armando Bo. Variety Films, 1970.

Fuego [*Fire*]. Directed by Armando Bo. Something Weird Video Inc., 1968.

Gringo in Mañanaland. Directed by Dee Dee Halleck. Dee Dee Halleck Productions, 1995.

Insaciable. Directed by Armando Bo. Armando Bo Productions, 1976.

Intimidades de una cualquiera. Directed by Armando Bo. S.I.F.A., 1972.

Lujuria tropical. Directed by Armando Bo. S.I.F.A., 1962.

La niña santa [*The Holy Girl*]. Directed by Lucrecia Martel. Transeuropa Video Entertainment, 2004.

Una mariposa en la noche. Directed by Armando Bo. Armando Bo Productions, 1977.

Relación prohibida. Directed by Ricardo Suñez. VHS. Barba Azul, 1987.

Setenta veces siete. Directed by Leopoldo Torre Nilsson. Something Weird Video Inc., 1962.

Video de familia. Directed by Humberto Padrón. Instituto Cubano del Arte e Industria Cinematográficos, 2001.

NOTES

1   Once considered a concern of social theorists and anthropologists, space has now become a subject of study for feminists, semioticians, phenomenologists, and scholars working in various fields. For the past twenty years, one line of analysis has been devoted to connecting space with resistance and transgression. From Lefebvre and Keith and Pile, to Magnusson and Jussila (1999; 2001), space has been linked with sites for exerting radical opposition and attaining political freedom. More recently, there has been a visible shift accompanied by another strain of thought, one which allows for alternate modes of social ordering by linking space to processes of "becoming" rather than to "being" (Naficy; Hetherington; Tajbakhsh). It should be noted that questions of economics, social class, modernity, modernization, and transnationalism are dealt with in these works in terms of what position is occupied by the heterosexual subject. This line of questioning has opened the door for research connecting space with gender configurations (Tonkiss; Vianello). However, with the exception of Munt and a few others (Hankin; Baron), lesbians have thus far been left out of these conceptualizations of space, as if to further imply the marginality of this subject.

In the Latin American context, scholars, such as Radcliffe, Schaefer-Rodriguez, Chanan, Cantú, Foster, Avritzer, and Noble, have focused on space, its meanings, and its implications in the lives of the subjects who inhabit it. Nevertheless, studying the relationship between, on the one hand, "public and private space" (Radcliffe; Avritzer; Noble) with, on the other, "zones of tolerance and danger" (Schaefer-Rodriguez), including notions of "queer tourism" (Cantú), the representation of the city, "real social space," and "queer issues" (Chanan; Foster), criticism has contributed to the establishment of a canon that has tended to ignore the specificity of the lesbian subject(s) in favour of general theories of democratization and a generalized queering of space. The problem with this last move is methodological as it, not only re-establishes the binary opposition between a gender/sex norm and its "deviant," but it also seems to dilute the lesbian subjects.

2   With respect to the gay experience, it has been noted that Latin American men are generally not classified into homosexual or heterosexual categories simply according to their supposed sexual behaviour. Rather, what is important is the dichotomy of 'active' and 'passive,' according to which the active partner would even confirm his masculinity, that is, his not being homosexual, while having male-to-male sex (Arguelles and Rich, 686; Carrier, 227–28; Borim, 339; Lumsden, 132–33; Bleys, 9). This seems to be changing among the young, in particular in Cuba, where the label of "*completo*," has been used to indicate reciprocal sex (Lumsden, 150), while in Mexico the term is "*internacionales*" (Carrier, 231; De La Mora, 188). For a summary of statements from gays and lesbians detailing how they experience their identity in 1990s Cuba, see Leiner (49–52). For a chapter on gay life in Havana in the 1990s, see Lumsden. In his short *Video de familia* (2001), filmmaker Humberto Padrón, portrays the pangs and pains of family life and homosexuality in

contemporary Cuba. For a testimony of lesbian experiences in Nicaragua in the 1990s, see Randall. Brown historizes identity politics within the Argentine lesbian and gay movements from the 1960s up to the beginning of the twenty-first century.

3   In the literary and academic worlds, the silencing of lesbians identified by critics has somehow been challenged in the last few years, with the development of lesbian theory and criticism and the emergence of literary works. Writers who have dealt with lesbian themes include, among others, Sabina Berman, Ethel Krauze, Sara Levi Calderón, Cristina Peri Rossi, Mercedes Roffé, Reina Roffé, and Rosamaría Roffiel. Critics include Amy Kaminsky, José P. Villalobos, Mary S. Gossy, Elena M. Martínez, Claudia Schaefer-Rodríguez, Deborah Shaw, Guadalupe Cortina, Janis Breckenridge, Lourdes Torres and Inmaculada Pertusa, Rosana Blanco Cano, and Sara Cooper, among others.

In Latin American cinema, the lesbian subject(s) continue to be scantily represented or studied, although one has to recognize that starting in the 1990s there are more film samples, the majority of which have been produced either in Argentina or in Mexico. At the same time, in Latin American Film Studies, up until now, only a few scholars, including Emily Bergmann, Lori Hopkins, María Elena Soliño and Bruce Williams , have talked about lesbianism, although sometimes only in passing.

4   Taking into account existing criticism on Latin American feminisms and lesbian movements, there are historical similarities in their genesis, as in some countries they were born at the same time as parallel or interdependent groups, and also with respect to their rapport with politics. See Sternbach et al. and Thayer. For an account calling for the legal penalization of lesbianism at the end of the sixties, see Arcila. In Argentina, Brown cites cases of disappearances of lesbians and gays both during the dictatorship of the 1970s and after the redemocratization of the 1980s, as well as continued and more recent police harassment (121, 123).

5   Other more recent Argentine films that portray or hint at lesbianism, and which form part of my larger project to study genre, space and lesbian representation, include *Almejas y mejillones* [*Clams and Mussels* 2000]; *El favor* (2004); *Esperando al Mesías* [*Waiting for the Messiah* 2002]; *La ciénaga* [*The Swamp* 2001]; *La niña santa* [*The Holy Girl* 2004]; *Relación prohibida* (1987); and *Tan de repente* [*Suddenly* 2002], among others. This project will also include the study of samples from Mexico, Venezuela, Cuba, Chile, and Peru.

6   See, for example, the work of Munt, Tonkiss, and Vianello, respectively.

7   This way of reformulating the idea of genre provides an answer to the impasse experienced by authors such as A. Luis Hueso Montón, who in his book *Los Géneros Cinematográficos* (1983) is unable to move beyond literary concerns in his attempt to tie film genres with Eurocentric national origins, thematic specificity, and aesthetic elements (*ad passim*). In the Argentine context, in a study made in the 1980s, Oscar Steimberg (1988) emphasizes a more dynamic approach to the issue, as he recognizes intra- and extramediatic factors, including production values,

marketing, and critical commentary. Besides placing genres in relation to one another, he also establishes connections to the historic moment, to reception issues, and to the resurgence of new genres. However, Steimberg's study is restricted to television. See his "Diez proposiciones comparativas" (1988, 19–43).

8   To my knowledge, a comprehensive examination of genre as a tripartite phenomenon has not been yet undertaken in Latin American Film Studies, least of all in association with a study of lesbian representation. In Latin American Film Studies, genre concerns have been addressed by several film scholars, including Ana López (1991), Silvia Oroz, Pascual Quinziano, Mabel Tassara, Carlos Monsiváis, Dolores M. Tierney, Vanessa Knights, and Andrea Noble, among others. Although most of this criticism refers to melodrama (López 1991; Oroz; Monsiváis; Tierney; Knights; Noble), other aesthetic practices, which do not exclude melodramatic turns, such as comedy (Quinziano) and police dramas (Tassara), have also been of interest. All in all in these articles, particular aesthetic, filmic, and/or thematic elements have been studied to describe specific historical and contextual periods and to explain the ties of genre to issues such as Hollywood conventions (Tassara, Curubeto 1996), national identity (López 1991; Monsiváis), affect and reception (López 1991; Oroz; Tassara, Monsiváis), modernity and modernization (López 1991; Knights).

9   Blaxploitation cinema deals with African-American representations and urban crime. Although Schaefer's study of exploitation (1999) is restricted to the period comprised between 1919 and 1959 in the United States, many of the characteristics he describes for exploitation movies can also be seen in Bo's films. These traits, almost all found in Bo's features, include: a forbidden topic, low production values, independent distribution, and small exhibition circles (1999, 4–6). On a narrative level, exploitation films also lack continuity (1999, 43). For a study of Bo's techniques, including continuity, chronology, and dubbing glitches, see the essay by Wolf, who classifies them as Bo's author signature (*ad passim*).

10   For a study of Sarli's stardom, see Ruétalo. According to Schaefer, lesbianism constituted a major theme in sexploitation films in the United States in the late 1960s (2007, 30).

11   For an analysis and a problematization of the continued film market exchanges between the United States and Argentina, see Curubeto (1993) and Falicov. Marvin D'Lugo speaks about cinematic movement beyond the borders of the local or "national" culture, but while mentioning Mexican *ranchera* comedies, Brazilian *chanchadas*, and auteurs such as Argentina's Leopoldo Torre Nilsson, he conspicuously leaves Bo's sexploitation films out of the equation (115).

12   Romano (21) and Ruétalo (81) also note this lack.

13   The cover of the Something Weird Video Inc. DVD quotes this ad without the six close-ups. However, it does materialize the idea of fire because Sarli's provocative body is surrounded by flames.

14   Sarli's full-frontal nude caused quite a stir among audiences of Bo's *El trueno entre las hojas* [*Thunder among the Leaves*, 1957].

15 For a compendium of images in Hollywood movies tying Latin America to the excessive and the exotic, see Dee Dee Halleck's documentary *Gringo in Mañanaland* (1995). In my book, *Sujetos Transnacionales: La Negociación en Cine y Literatura* (2008), the analysis of the novel and film *Ilona llega con la lluvia* [*Ilona Arrives with the Rain*] provides another example of the uses of the north-south narrative trope.

16 Richard Dyer (60–65) has identified these characteristics as part and parcel of lesbian characters in Hollywood film noir.

17 Patricia White (1998) has written about the recourse to the supernatural in her analysis of film noir in Hollywood cinema. For a review of cultural myths to which the lesbian vampire film subscribes, see Weiss's chapter on "The Vampire Lovers" (84–108). In his study of the Mexican film *Alucarda, la hija de las tinieblas*, in *The Mexican Cinema of Darkness*, Greene also finds an equation of lesbianism with madness and vampirism.

18 Natalia Taccetta and Fernando Peña present an overview of lesbian characterization in Argentine prison films. According to them, instead of becoming more complex from film to film, lesbian characters, on the contrary, embody caricature traits, including a lack of femininity often related to sadism, violence, and crime.

19 As the bibliography shows, Armando Bo has received critical attention in several books and articles. He died in 1981. In 1998 Sarli made appearances at the Teatro de Variedades in Buenos Aires and in 2006 she was featured in the TV program *Tiene la palabra*. I would like to thank David W. Foster for giving me access to this program.

20 See Pedro Calleja's blog, "Chicas en biquini buscando a Norman Bates," which, besides an interview with Sarli, also contains two other texts with comments about her films. Pablo Sapere in, an e-zine devoted mainly to horror and science fiction, also offers an entry on Sarli. I have to thank Antonio Lazaro-Reboll for his help in finding these sites. For a commented filmography online, see Fittipaldi.

21 Bo's collaboration with Sarli boasts such telling titles as *Lujuria tropical* (1962), *La diosa impura* (1963), *La tentación desnuda* (1966), *Éxtasis tropical* (1969) and *Fiebre* (*Fever* 1970), among others.

22 Although Sarli made most of her movies with Bo, she also performed in Leopoldo Torre Nilsson's *Setenta veces siete* (*The Female, Seventy Times Seven*, 1962) and worked with Dirk de Villiers in the Argentina/South Africa co-production *La diosa virgen* (1973), in which Armando Bo was her co-star. More recently, Sarli has collaborated with Jorge Polaco in *La dama regresa* (1996) and in *Arroz con leche* (2009), a comedy about old age. For comments on the latter film, see Pécora. I was unable to verify rumours concerning the dedication of an exhibition room to Isabel Sarli in the Museo del Cine Pablo Ducrós Hicken in Buenos Aires. The museum is closed to the public and is apparently undergoing renovations as part of the Proyecto Polo Sur Cultural. Apparently, the museum has not had a permanent site since 1998. I would like to thank Victoria Ruétalo and Serge Zaïtzeff for their time and help in finding this information.

AT THE TRANSNATIONAL CROSSROADS: COLOMBIAN CINEMA AND ITS SEARCH FOR A FILM INDUSTRY[1]

Juana Suárez
University of Kentucky

In 2005, the Oscar nomination of Catalina Sandino for best actress in a leading role seemed to have placed Colombian cinema in the global sphere. Sandino earned her nomination for her performance in *María llena eres de gracia* [*María Full of Grace*] (2004), a U.S./Colombian film by American director Joshua Marston, which was partially filmed in Ecuador due to security issues, given the political instability in Colombia.[2] As in the case of *Real Women Have Curves* (Patricia Cardoso, 2002), the film was post-produced and distributed by HBO. Both casting and plot signal the type of geopolitical movements that make ideas of nation and national boundaries problematic and set the stage for a dialogue on how Colombian films are gaining ground transnationally and globally.

Michael Chanan has warned of the need to tread carefully when discussing the position of cinema in the multinational era since "cinema has been transnational from the very start and global in reach and operation by the 1930's, before postmodernism" (41–42). In a certain sense, the emphasis on the transnational that is recurring now has always been present in Colombian filmmaking. As Rito Torres states in the introduction to *Largometrajes colombianos en cine y video 1915–2004,*

> Muchos ejemplos evidencian la presencia extranjera en el cine nacional durante toda su historia, por lo cual, aun cuando se tenga arte propio, es impreciso elaborar un listado categórico del cine colombiano ya que, desde sus orígenes, las fronteras entre lo propio y lo extraño, lo nacional y lo extranjero, son difusas. (2004, 17)

> [Many examples bear witness to the foreign presence in national filmmaking throughout its entire history, due to which, even when Colombia has its own art, drawing up a categorical list of Colombian film production is imprecise, since from its origins the boundaries between what has come from within and from without, between what is national and what is foreign, are vague.][3]

The filmography of the Colombian productions reviewed in that book provides an idea of the constant inclusion of foreign technicians, actors, directors, and co-screenwriters that over time has resulted in numerous international projects.[4]

In *Magical Reels*, John King mentioned that Colombian cinema was characterized by its "sporadic and uneven quality" and remained largely neglected, especially when compared to the scope of criticism devoted to the cinematic traditions of Cuba, Mexico, Argentina, and Brazil (207). This situation is now slowly changing. Currently, Colombian cinema is still seen as something of a novelty but is merely continuing the cinematographic tradition that began back in 1897 when the Italians Francesco and Vincenzo Di Domenico sought their fortune in the Americas and introduced filmmaking in Colombia, upon settling in Bogotá in 1910. Despite its long history, extensive in years but not in number of productions, Colombian cinema remains largely unknown and is often summarized through a couple of films or a list of directors rather than in a chronological fashion. As is the case in other countries where state control has intervened in the regulation of film policies, in Colombia, FOCINE (Compañía de Fomento Cinematográfico) was influential for years, the history of Colombian cinema may be examined through the continuities and gaps that derive from King's statement.[5] However, at the thematic level, various outbreaks of violence and the need to represent political events seem to have provided the impetus on several occasions to reactivate the cinematic tradition. Such an examination is not my goal here, yet these considerations are important in a discussion about the possibilities for Colombian cinema to go transnational since violence becomes a ubiquitous presence that defines its history.[6]

These pages focus on analyzing some of the crossroads at which Colombian cinema finds itself in its aim to enter the transnational arena. Inexorably, the directions taken by Latin American cinema in its current trends impose a number of anxieties that can hardly be ignored by Colombian filmmakers. The recent success of Latin American films and of Latin American directors in the transnational sphere has increased the interest in cinema in countries like Colombia and has renewed the interest that already existed where there was a more solid national film tradition, such as in Mexico, Brazil, and Argentina. Therefore, in the first part of this discussion, I will compare the case of present-day Colombia with some representative cases of success alluded to above. Of special interest here is a discussion of the effect that the work of Mexican directors Alejandro González Iñárritu, Alfonso Cuarón, and Guillermo del Toro has had in increasing the visibility of Latin American filmmaking. The mega-success at the box office of Brazilian movies such as *Cidade de Deus* [*City of God*] (Fernando Meirelles and Kátia Lund, 2002) and the growing attention towards what has come to be called New Argentine Cinema, which groups such directors as Adrián Caetano, Juan Pablo Trapero, and Lucrecia Martel, among others, will also be commented on.[7]

In the second part, I will scrutinize the current state of Colombian cinema in light of Law 814 on filmmaking (2003) (referred commonly as "La ley de cine"), whose general terms will be explained later. Since in both cases the background of the discussion is the location of Latin American cinema in the transnational flux, it is important to keep in mind that discussions on transnationalism are quite broad and complex. In the case of Latin American cinema, as with other minor cinemas, those discussions become more problematic, given the field's own fluctuating position within film studies. In terms of theory, it has been included in discussions on third cinema (Getino y Solanas), Eurocentrism and polycentrism (Shohat and Stam), and world cinema (Chapman; Dennison and Song Hwee Lim; Badley and Barton); there has even been a proposal to treat it as a genre in its own right (Poblete).

With no intention of being prescriptive, and rather than define "transnational," which is important but is not the objective of this discussion, I prefer to turn here to Françoise Lionnet and Shu-Mei Shih's considerations in "Thinking through the Minor, Transnationally" along with those of Philip Crang, Claire Dwyer and Peter Jackson in "Transnationalism and the Spaces of Commodity Culture." For both works, transnationalism and globalization share the same historical moment of late capitalism. Thus, it is important not to use the terms interchangeably. For Lionnet and Shih, transnationalism demands an analysis that is not filtered through utopian/dystopian readings from the liberal high ground of globalization or through the critical model of the local and the global, where the local is necessarily associated with a subaltern figure that resists the advance of global capital (2005, 5–7). In their observations, they stress that "[t]he transnational, on the contrary, can be conceived as a space of exchange and participation wherever processes of hybridization occur and where it is still possible for cultures to be produced and performed without necessary mediation by the center" (2005, 5). For their part, Crang, Dwyer and Jackson express their concerns "over geographical 'grounding' of transnational discourse" with regard to "scope, specificity and politics" (440). These authors conceive transnationalism "as a multidimensional space that is multiply inhabited and characterized by complex networks, circuits and flows" (441).

In these considerations, there is an invitation to regard the transnational both horizontally and transversally. As Lionnet and Shih observe,

> This cultural transversalism includes minor cultural articulations in productive relationships with the major (in all its possible shapes, forms and kinds), as well as minor-to-minor networks that circumvent the major altogether. This transversalism also produces new forms of identification that negotiate with national, ethnic, and cultural boundaries, thus allowing

At the Transnational Crossroads

for the emergence of the minor's inherent complexity and multiplicity. (8)

For this reason it becomes imperative not to think about Colombia's case in an isolated way or to focus exclusively on the current status of its cinema vis-à-vis Hollywood. The commercial visibility of recent Latin American cinema raises certain questions that allow us to consider briefly both its connections and disconnections to Colombian filmmaking. With regard to the connections, leaving aside monetary comparisons, the case of Cuarón and González Iñárritu, who have directed big Hollywood stars, is relatively similar to the steps taken by directors like Patricia Cardoso, mentioned above for her film *Real Women Have Curves*, in trying to open up a space in one of the most difficult and competitive film industries in the global circuit.[8] Rodrigo García's case is similar, although his films may have a greater thematic affiliation with independent filmmaking in the United States, recognizing that a large part of his work has been developed for HBO. For Julián Gorodisher, García's filmmaking achieves "a strange harmony between auteur films and Hollywood productions. The latter nourish the former with shining stars" (2).[9]

For her part, in an interview for *DGA Magazine*, Cardoso has defended her intention to keep her perspective on success and carefully scrutinize her offers to direct films. She states that she has rejected six proposals, adding, "I don't want to be the flavor of the month. I want to do good work. Of the projects that I have been offered, about 30% were Latino and 70% were not Latino projects, which is encouraging, because they see me as a filmmaker and not just a Latino filmmaker."[10] Her position differs from that of the three Mexican directors (González Iñárritu, Cuarón, and del Toro) whose incursion into Hollywood's global entertainment industry adheres to "a politics of recognition," similar to the one that theories of transnationalism, according to Lionnet and Shu-mei Shih, continue to exercise, since the predominating binary model presupposes "that minorities necessarily and continuously engage with and against majority cultures in a vertical relation of opposition and assimilation" (7). Unlike this paradigm, Lionnet and Shu-mei Shih recognize minority cultures as "part of our transnational moment, not a reified or segregated pocket of cultures and mores waiting to be selectively incorporated into what qualifies as global or transnational by the powers that be." (7–8) Conscious of her condition as a minority within the United States, Cardoso seems to be clear about her inherently transnational condition as a migratory subject and opts not to play up an exoticism implicit in her being a foreign woman filmmaker.

Colombian cinema also shares certain similarities with Brazilian cinema through its preoccupation with abundant representations founded on violence. For example, *Cidade de Deus* was highly polemical due to its insistence on reducing its treatment of Rio de Janeiro to the *favelas*, as was the "excess" of violence in other recent film portrayals of the city. Along the same lines, in objecting to the repeated presence of violence in contemporary Brazilian filmmaking, and as Randal Johnson comments, critics have coined the phrase "cosmetics of violence" – playing off Glauber Rocha's *Cinema Novo* manifesto on the "aesthetics of violence" (13).[11] Randal Johnson sums up the polemic about cinematic modes of representation, politics, and aesthetics by starting from the division of opinions among the directors themselves and the critics, as opposed to the viewers. Regarding the representation of violence and its excess, Johnson includes two dominant positions: those directors who are committed to an ideological purity, and those who see an unfavourable Manichaean division in the disassociation between culture and commerce. For the latter, the insistence on ideological purity, still practised in a form that is very close to *Cinema Novo* and by extension to New Latin American Cinema, is an obstacle to re-establishing the presence of Brazilian filmmaking in the globalized international realm and relegates it to a ghetto (2005, 11–38). Johnson suggests that *Cinema Novo* is and will continue being a point of reference but that filmmakers nowadays are not – and cannot be – limited to its considerable legacy (2006, 126). In general, the legacy of diverse manifestations of New Latin American Cinema can be thought of in similar terms, given that political contexts, modes of production, distribution, and consumption have changed. Of particular interest in Johnson's discussion is his review of the consensus among directors that the recent exploration of different genres, including romantic comedies, comedies of manners, *neo-cangaceiro*, literary adaptations, and children's films, has to do with "a film industry that has been long characterized by atomization rather than concentration;" he also points out "the attempts by filmmakers to explore diverse ways of reestablishing communication with the Brazilian public" (2005, 18).

Likewise, Argentine cinema is more interested in developing a vital and diverse industry than it is in political considerations (Falicov, 115–56; Konstantarakos, 135–36). For example, the success of such productions as *Nueve reinas* [*Nine Queens*] (2000) by the late Fabián Bielinsky generated a diverse spectrum of approaches to what the *corralito*, economic measures taken in Argentina at the end of 2001 to stop the exodus of currency, and its context of corruption have revealed about long-standing problems in Argentine society. This subject has inspired particular metaphors in *El bonaerense* (Juan Pablo Trapero, 2002) and *Un oso rojo* [*Red Bear*] (Adrián Caetano, 2002). There are also new approaches to subjects that have seemingly been addressed quite frequently in Argentine cinema; for example, the dismantling of the cherished myth of immigration as a component of Argentine identity that is depicted in *Bolivia* (Adrián Caetano, 2001) or the renovation of ways to approach the question of the disappeared. An example of the latter, *Los rubios* [*The Blonds*] (Albertina Carri, 2003) is a personal reflection on family memory and the impossibility of recording historical trauma.[12] Along these lines, both young and veteran Colombian directors are searching for other filmic languages. *Bluff*, a dark comedy (Felipe Martínez (2007), *Al final del espectro* [*At the End of the Spectra*], a horror film (Juan Felipe Orozco, 2006), and *Yo soy otro* [*Others*], an essay film (Óscar Campo, 2008) are examples of Colombian filmmaking's interest in reactivating less explored genres and/or venturing into film approaches less common in Colombia.

The examples from Argentine, Mexican, and Brazilian cinema serve to show that the dilemmas confronted by Colombian filmmaking are not unique. However, they also show that "Latin American Cinema" as a category has become increasingly complicated: it makes homogeneous a diverse geography that confronts similar challenges yet offers heterogeneous responses that are formulated as much around production as reception. For this reason, Juan Pablo Poblete postulates "the existence of a second degree genre, the genre Latin American film." In his view, "[t]hrough such a poetics, these [Latin American] directors, both with extensive publicity and commercial experience, respond in their own way to the debates over the artistic or industrial condition of film as manifested in the discussions over the opposition (national) auteur/(international) cultural apparatus" (223). Such recent, highly visible examples of Latin American filmmaking open new paths yet also raise expectations due to the type of production and the mechanisms filmmakers employ to insert themselves in the transnational industry.[13]

Perhaps it would be more appropriate to consider the phenomenon in terms of directors rather than national industries, since the transnational flux also offer directors the flexibility of filming in other geographic locations and directing in foreign countries. In the case of Brazil, Johnson relates the success in the marketplace by directors such as Fernando Meirelles and Walter Salles Jr. to their use of an "international film language" (2006, 127); obviously, such language has to do with the transnational order but, at the same time, it incorporates visual products as commodities. Not in vain has so-called world cinema, mentioned above as one of the categories where Latin American cinema is frequently placed, been put on a level with the awkward category of world music, whose popularity, like the commodification of ethnic food, has become problematic, as Dennison and Song Hwee Lim attest in their introduction to *Remapping World Cinema* (3–4).[14] The flow of commodity products can be understood either as a derogatory extension of homogenizing colonial powers or as a potential tool to increase interest in and exposure to other cultural forms. In the case of filmmaking, insertion into the transnational is also valued as having greater market capability for producers or distributors and a growing number of audiences interested in seeing and consuming these films. The success of this type of production finds an echo in the jubilant voices of critics, such as Deborah Shaw, who seem to see a certain epiphany in the commercial success of recent filmmaking: "A combination of factors is behind this change in fortunes for films from Latin America, but in broad terms, directors and producers are aware of the international market and have learned how to raise funds, *create more audience-friendly films,* and market their finished products" (1, emphasis added). Comments of this nature imply the idea that "going transnational," in regards to Latin American cinema, means that it needs to become more "understandable"; hence, more consumable by ever-wider and more global audiences.

In the case of Colombia, those two angles are connected: the economic profits that film may generate and its adaptability to other audiences are protected by Law 814 from 2003.[15] Up to now, this recent legislation constitutes the most ambitious project yet to ensure that Colombian cinema functions on a continual basis and solidifies itself as an industry since it attempts to guarantee appropriate channels for distribution and exhibition. In keeping with different commercial policies, this law intends to revitalize both the production and the number of Colombian films. Other goals contemplated by Law 814 include exploring new strategies to obtain national and international subsidies for cinematic production, drawing larger audiences, and decentralizing filmmaking. The law also pays attention to the considerations of region and diversity that characterize cultural discussions in Colombia; this is suggested in the rhetorical emphasis on a sense of "colombianidad" suggested in the way Law 814 is advertised (La Ley de Cine, 6).

Colombian productions have begun to be represented at festivals and in film series with greater frequency and through a larger number of films, reflecting a positive balance in regard to quantity. Directors may decide to adhere to the conditions of this law, or they may decide to continue making films outside it; nonetheless, the law emerges as a point of comparison for the success or failure of contemporary Colombian cinema. Naturally the concept of success is also quite complex, since one can speak of financial success, but a good result at the box office does not equate to excellence in production, or success in critical circles, which in any case often depends on subjective aesthetic judgments. If directors become beneficiaries of the law, the challenge for their films will be to demonstrate its success in order to guarantee continuity in the regulations. If they decide to operate outside the law – after all, the law is not the only way to subsidize filmmaking in Colombia, directors can find their own way to produce films – the results of other modes of production will be compared in the future to those generated by Law 814.

The law's formulation came about in response to the void left by the closure of FOCINE. Its explanatory pamphlet states:

> El Gobierno Nacional ideó unos incentivos de inversión y generó unos mecanismos que tienen como fin desarrollar integralmente el sector y promover toda la cadena de producción cinematográfica colombiana: desde los productores, distribuidores y exhibidores, hasta la preservación del patrimonio audiovisual, la formación y el desarrollo tecnológico, entre otros. ("La ley de cine" 5)

[The National Government devised some incentives for investment and created some mechanisms that have the goal of integrally developing the film sector and promoting the entire chain of Colombian cinematographic production: from producers, distributors, and exhibitors, to the preservation of our audiovisual heritage, its formation, and its technological development, among others.]

In addition to a review of FOCINE's missteps and accomplishments, planning of the law also paid attention to regulatory processes and film legislation in other Latin American countries. In its attempts to rectify formerly weak policies on distribution and exhibition, Law 814 had to recycle and rearrange FOCINE's positive aspects, along with the policies that preceded the latter's creation, including the Surcharge Law, and combine them with the survival strategies from the ten years between FOCINE's closure in 1993 and the promulgation of the Law on Filmmaking in 2003.[16] One such strategy is the Fondo Mixto de Promoción Cinematográfica (Mixed Fund for Cinematographic Promotion), an entity that tries to obtain public contributions; private sector contributions are regulated by the Ministry of Culture by means of investment certificates and are allocated to films on an individual basis. Too complex to be summarized in a few lines, the main attraction of the law is its tendency to favour private investment through securitization in the stock market and tax exemptions. With the possible securitization of cinematographic projects, "each director will be able to make his/her project available on the open market so that it can be acquired through the purchase of stocks by private investors" ["cada director podrá llevar su proyecto al mercado de valores para que pueda ser adquirido a manera de acciones por compradores privados."] ("La ley de cine" 13). The analogy offered in the explanatory pamphlet on the law is the real estate practice of selling apartments by floor. To date, this purchase of stocks is regulated but not working due to the still small size of the Colombian film industry.

The law appears at a time that is complex and full of contradictions for Colombian filmmaking. We can cite three aspects that characterize the current state of Colombian filmmaking and that have an impact on the solutions as a whole sought by Law 814. First, we have the growing professionalization of the field and the increase in the number of formative programs on filmmaking at universities and private and public schools. The formation of professionals in the audiovisual field is an expensive investment in any country. As such, just as in other professions, no one wants to pursue a career that may not be profitable. Unlike earlier directors who accomplished heroic feats of survival, whether in the FOCINE years or afterwards, few novice students want to continue with a career in film if it is not financially worthwhile. Recently graduated directors are more interested in combining a film career with a career in directing soap operas, in advertising, or in teaching, which in the past provided jobs for film directors, often by accident and as an option in order to stay afloat in the industry.[17]

Similarly, institutions such as the National University of Colombia, the Department of Social Communication at the Universidad del Valle, in the southwestern city of Cali, and bold efforts from the private sector such as the Black María School of Filmmaking and other schools at universities and institutes are producing a good crop of filmmakers. On the other hand, despite the proliferation of centres for training in cinematography and the growth in film studies programs at universities, the typical curriculum is oriented towards artistic and technical aspects and neglects the area of production and financial aspects. This hinders commercial autonomy: when professionals who understand how distribution circuits and international exhibitions operate in short supply, the most practical solution for filmmakers to achieve transnational exposure for their movies is to hand them over to the *majors* or leave that part of the business in the hands of a foreign co-producer.

In the same vein of having access to both theoretical and practical training, new directors are benefitting as well from an increase in international exchanges and workshops with transnational institutions such as Ibermedia and Fond Sud Cinéma; facilitating their participation is another mission of Law 814. There are also workshops for new creative talent at numerous film festivals in economically developed countries where directors and producers can gauge the future viability of their projects. In both cases, the calls for entries are publicized periodically in *Claqueta* and *Pantalla Colombia*, the two electronic bulletins put out by Mincultura and Proimágenes en movimiento, respectively. The possibilities for studying filmmaking abroad are greater now, which is not to say that they are more economical. Travel, mobility, migrancy, flow, and displacement – words associated with transnationalism – have contributed a small share since new generations of Colombians raised abroad are choosing filmmaking as a university course of study and can join academic programs that are recognized worldwide. For those studying filmmaking, Argentina and Cuba – in particular the Escuela Nacional de Experimentación y Realización Cinematográfica and the Escuela Internacional de Cine y Televisión de San Antonio de los Baños – are also two main destinations. There is already an extensive group of directors whose formation has straddled two countries, whether they were trained partially in Colombia and are filming abroad, or they were trained abroad and are alternating between international and national film projects: they include Juan Fisher, Patricia Cardoso, Diego García Moreno, Ricardo Gabrielli, Simón Brand, and Catalina Villar, among others.[18] If in keeping with Lionnet and Shu-mei Shih we consider that "minor cultures as we know them are always already mixed, hybrid and relational" (10), the transcultural experience of these directors contributes to destabilizing the aspirations to authenticity that Colombian audiences often demand of Colombian filmmaking.

Second, besides stipulating regulations and establishing budget items, a function that belongs rather to the work of the Consejo Nacional de Cine [National Council on Filmmaking], a Ministry of Culture office for public policy on the film industry with representatives from the Colombian filmmaking sectors, Law 814 has the implicit and difficult task of drawing Colombian audiences who after the FOCINE years became more resistant to consuming Colombian films. Distribution becomes a key element here: although we are discussing how Colombian filmmaking could insert itself in the transnational film industry, we cannot ignore that Latin American countries are not the largest consumers of their own cinema. García Canclini's overview of the decline in local audiences for national cinemas, the marked difference between cinema buffs and "video buffs," and various changes in habits of consumption of visual products all resonate here (2001, 109–22; 2007, 36–39). Although in recent years the number of Colombians who watch Colombian films has increased, that was not the case in the past.[19] There have been improvements in distribution, but we cannot ignore the thorny subject of piracy, which affects both the national and the foreign film industry and is also a transnational problem. With the expansion in the system of

Multiplex theatres in Latin America, the possibility of competing with the foreign film industry and the perennial presence of Hollywood are even more daunting. In the same way, production methods and film consumption are changing every day, but they continue being strongly marked by access to technology. In analyzing these challenges, Pedro Adrián Zuluaga warns that in situations like that of Colombia, whose film industry is not yet consolidated, it no longer suffices to consider distribution via DVDs alone: Internet downloading, "pay per view" access, and digital technologies must also be taken into account (68–71). Paradoxically, it should be noted that Colombia has an extensive tradition of alternate venues, film series in museums, and film clubs that persist in the face of huge monopolies. The profusion of video-bars that provide spaces for screenings, such as "In-vitro" in Bogotá, for example, and showcases such as "Pandora's Box" at the *sui generis* Santa Fe de Antioquia Film and Video Festival are crucial in light of the deficient infrastructure for film distribution.[20]

Third, together with increasing professionalization and the problem of drawing audiences to the theatre, the subject of violence continues dividing investors as well as viewers. The topic has been somewhat exhausted, and large sectors of the viewing public confess that they are tired of it and want to see other approaches to or stories about violence, or simply other subjects altogether.[21] For public groups who defend such positions, the uses and abuses of the subject of violence in Colombian filmmaking are deplorable, and for them it makes no sense to support an industry that – unlike that dealing with the exporting of goods – does not honour the name of Colombia; to the contrary, the image it offers works to the detriment of the idealized "tourist" vision of the country. This became extremely conspicuous in polemics that arose around *La virgen de los sicarios* [*The Virgin of the Assassins*] (Barbet Schroeder, 2000), a film based on the homonymous novel by controversial writer Fernando Vallejo. Even journalists such as Germán Santamaría called for banning the film for being – in his view – "a production against Colombia."[22] Santamaría's anxieties arise from a sense of patriotism that understands filmmaking as a means to export a consumable image of the nation. According to this view, filmmaking ought to continue clinging to the nationalist sentiments with which, at the beginnings of Latin American cinema, *actualités* propagated and helped construct nationalist discourses.

We should not overlook that the text of Law 814 implies the construction of a sense of national identity with its reminder that "filmmaking allows us to see ourselves and recognize ourselves as individuals and as groups with diverse ways of understanding all aspects of life, something that is especially important in a country like ours that has inexhaustible cultural diversity" ("La ley de cine," 5).[23] The precise term used in the text is *"colombianidad"* ("La ley de cine," 6). Beyond the reference to diversity, what this trait of belonging to the country would consist of is unclear; at the risk of getting off the point, we should caution that as in any prescriptive formulation about national identities, a standard definition may become essentialist and lead to problems of inclusion and exclusion.

Five years after the promulgation of Law 814, it is premature to declare its achievements, but it is possible to detect dominant trends that have survived the trauma of FOCINE and have given rise, at least temporarily, to a preoccupation with breaking into the transnational industry. In the long term, it is probable that as discussions on the national recede, "Colombian movies" and "Colombian filmmakers," not "Colombian cinema" *per se*, are likely to become significant pieces of the global puzzle. As Chanan argues, "given the nature of today's international film market, co-productions are the order of the day, in which Latin American filmmakers have often turned, willingly or unwillingly, to trading on the exotic" (46). González Iñárritu, Cuarón, and Del Toro are recognized precisely as Mexican filmmakers; however, their films have very blurry traces of their national affiliation. Their success has not been achieved without using the master's tools.

Clearly, up to this point no aesthetic judgment about the work of these Mexican directors has been offered because this discussion has focused on the mechanism of commercialization, an aspect without which their success and their entrance in the global industry could not have been achieved. Speaking of commercial formulas with regard to Colombia is a thorny subject because the obvious reference is to Gustavo Nieto Roa's filmmaking. This director's work intersected with the FOCINE era and left behind two lexical contributions to Colombia's filmmaking vocabulary: *nietoroísmo* and *benjumeísmo*. Each alludes to the plainly commercial style that Nieto Roa adopted, basing his film work on television series and casts, Carlos Benjumea being one of his favourite actors for histrionic roles, thereby accentuating the inability to acknowledge differences between film and television as means of communication. When Paulo Antonio Paranaguá referred to Colombian filmmaking as predominantly characterized by its "chapucería y chatura estética" ["slapdash work and low artistic level"] (1996, 372), he was probably referring to productions such as those by Nieto Roa. Nevertheless, it must be taken into account that Nieto Roa's *modus operandi* was quite self-sufficient and capable of carrying out a continuous production that did not depend exclusively on support from FOCINE. Ironically, he has been one of the Colombian directors with the highest box-office success and, for better or for worse, one of the most prolific and memorable.

Nowadays Dago García can be identified as the heir apparent to Nieto Roa. Soccer, life in the neighbourhood, family, popular music, and love are recurring themes of his. The financial success of his work mirrors Hollywood's pre- and post-production strategies: García has set about accustoming audiences to a film for the Christmas holiday, opening usually on December 25, just as "summer blockbusters" and "holiday releases" are timed in the U.S. market; likewise, the films come with a whole display of publicity on television entertainment shows and in entertainment magazines, usually owned by the same entities [for example, Caracol television co-produced *El carro* [*The Car*] (Luis Orjuela, 2003, written by Dago García) and *La pena maxima* [*Maximum Penalty*] (Jorge Ecehverri, 2001; also written by García)]. In other highly commercial cases such *Paraíso Travel* (Simón Brand, 2007), the soundtrack appears on the market at the same time as the film, and copies in the original format as well as on DVD are ready in time to take advantage of promotion and participation in film festivals and foreign distribution circuits. Dago García, in particular, is not interested in DVD sales, which in Colombia are minimal and besides are affected by piracy, nor in film festivals; nevertheless, some of his films circulate internationally through such channels as Amazon, Netflix, and Blockbusters.

Interviews with Nieto Roa and Dago García confirm that they are unapologetic directors who demonstrate clarity and absolute conviction about the type of commercial and entertainment films that they want to make; they are clearly cognizant of the possibilities for production in Colombia and, as such, they understand the reach and limitations of their productions. Moreover, García has no qualms about acknowledging the strong influence that his lengthy television career has had on his filmic language (García, 20–23; Nieto Roa, 16–19). Along with Dago García, directors such as Harold Trompetero and Rodrigo Triana have also demonstrated their success at exploiting the star system of soap operas, beauty pageants, and situation comedies with notably "light" productions such as *Como el gato y el ratón* [*Like Cat and Mouse*] (Rodrigo Triana, 2002)and *Dios los junta y ellos se separan* (Harold Trompetero, 2006).

By insisting on discussing such phenomena as Nieto Roa or Dago García, I hope to elicit a more in-depth examination, not of aesthetic issues, but of filmmaking's whole machinery and of what is harboured in its representations. Beyond critical judgments – it would be difficult to laud the artistic value of these films convincingly – *nietoroísmo, benjumeísmo,* and the Dago García and the Nieto Roa phenomena, as well as the long list of similar directors in Colombian cinema, merit a political reading of what they bring to the screen and why it is so popular, despite critical insistence on pointing out the caricature and deformation of society that this type of filmmaking offers. Mexican film criticism has done it with the *comedia ranchera,* and Cantinflas's movies, for example. Brazil has also done it with its *chanchada.*[24]

In both cases I am aware of the apparent futility of insisting on traces of the national when the concept of the nation is in jeopardy, but these films also reveal components of what nations are about. They address cultural *difference,* understood here in the sense that Arjun Appadurai employs the term as a "useful heuristic that can highlight points of similarity and contrast between all sorts of categories: classes, genders, roles, groups and nations" (12). Depictions of social groups in these films reveal *fragments of the nation* that are not inherently Mexican or Brazilian or Colombian; however, we can understand them as "cultural dimensions" inasmuch as they speak of "situated difference," which for Appadurai is "difference in relation to something local, embodied, and significant" (12). In their naiveté, their boastful showing-off, their political criticism that comes from below and not from great intellectuals, and in many other components of this commercial film industry, there are remnants of the nation, of how cultures are formed and deformed, and of how filmmaking shapes and distorts them.

Colombian filmmakers who have an explicit interest in addressing social problems confront the challenge of whether to modify scripts or insist on violence as a mechanism of resistance. As mentioned, the recurrence of this topic in Colombian filmmaking is frequently attacked, but the way it is represented by the commercial film industry needs to be examined. It is also worthwhile to explore whether Law 814 is opening up new directions in Colombian filmmaking, given the ubiquitous presence of the subject of violence. Until very recently, the majority of Colombian films known abroad belonged to the FOCINE period and the majority of them dealt with *La Violencia*, the bloody bipartisan conflict that divided the country politically from the late 1940s to the late 1960s. They include *Cóndores no entierran todos los días* [*Man of Principles*] (Francisco Norden, 1984), *Tiempo de morir* [*Time to Kill*] (Jorge Alí Triana, 1985), and *Técnicas de duelo* [*Details of a Duel*] (Sergio Cabrera, 1988). These were followed by productions that put elements on screen in order to explore the convergence of multiple forms of violence and their relationship to socio-economic, political, cultural, and regional factors, as well as, obviously, to the consequences of drug-trafficking. Specifically, two of the last productions from the FOCINE period anticipated these same explorations: *Rodrigo D. No futuro* [*Rodrigo D: No Future*] (Víctor Gaviria, 1990) and *La estrategia del caracol* [*The Snail's Strategy*] (Sergio Cabrera, 1993 – recipient of a FOCINE award but not produced by this institution), which are also two of the better-known Colombian films. Even in the search for new filmic languages and in the experimental filmmaking that has been done in Colombia, either *La Violencia* or multiple forms of violence are visible in the background. In this way, elements from the past and present can be recontextualized and transformed, but violence is a referent with which Colombia coexists and it forms part of what defines the country.

In that context, it is remarkable that no film has yet embarked on a serious or in-depth approach to guerrilla upheavals. In their use of humour, the two most popular films on guerrilla groups in Colombia, *Golpe de estadio* [*Time Out*] (Sergio Cabrera, 1998) and *Soñar no cuesta nada* [*A Ton of Luck*] (Rodrigo Triana, 2005), trivialized one of the most convoluted episodes in the country's history. In the latter case, we can question whether the current nature of the events portrayed on screen represents its passport to transnationalism. Based on a true story, this dark comedy recreates the story of a group of soldiers who come upon a cache of $16.5 million dollars. The money was hidden in the Caguán region and was undoubtedly part of the FARC's earnings, obtained from payments for kidnap victims and profits from drug-trafficking. This gift from God soon becomes the Devil's handiwork for the soldiers.

The reception of this film aids in understanding other connections with the audience, along with film as a commodity. It is an obvious example of theories on modes of consumption that emphasize the agency of consumers and the fact that audiences are not passive. García Canclini, for example, characterizes consumption "as more complex than the simple relation between manipulative media and docile audiences" (2001, 37) and elaborates on "the ensemble of practices of sociocultural processes in which the appropriation and use of products takes place" (2001, 38). Although the intense publicity apparatus of *Soñar no cuesta nada* did not leave out a single detail, as is evident on the movie's website, the film's huge box-office success, one of the highest of all time according to statistics on Proimágenes's website, undoubtedly has to do with the level of controversy generated among Colombians by the soldiers' trial.[25] Whether people had seen the film or not, having brought such a recent event to film made *Soñar no cuesta nada* a catalyst for discussions about the ethical implications of an event that, on various metaphorical levels, represents daily life in Colombia. The problem at the heart of the case of the hidden cache itself was ethical in nature, since it put the soldiers in a position of deciding whether to fulfill their moral and military duty or appropriate the money while knowing that the State would never pay them a comparable sum for their services. The greatest misstep in the film, as in many other Colombian productions where entertainment meets violence, lies in the absence of any psychological exploration of the event while keeping to a merely anecdotal level. Echoing Bentes' criticism of *Cidade de Deus*, the problem with the representation of violence here, as in other similar films, has to do with "transforming violence into a spectacle without offering the necessary contextualisation and without indicating the underlying causes of violence." (quoted in Johnson 2006, 126) Humour here prevents from any serious reflection on the intensity of the real life drama.

Another unresolved issue in this kind of commercial cinematic approach to Colombian events is the poor quality of the acting and the caricatures and stereotypes of the popular classes, a hackneyed practice that runs throughout a large part of Colombian filmmaking. In the framework of this study, my discussion does not focus on aesthetic or value judgments but on emphasizing that a democratic and healthy industry should open up spaces to make all types of movie genres and portray all types of subject matter. Notwithstanding, I must mention that Colombian films function more as a social and anthropological document. With very few exceptions, Colombian cinema offers slim possibilities for substantive analysis of films that allow for positive consideration of their mastery of visual elements. This aesthetic deficiency was addressed in "Las latas en el fondo del río: el cine colombiano visto desde la provincia," by Luis Alberto Álvarez and Víctor Gaviria. The dependence on television's common tropes that they criticized in Colombian filmmaking in 1982 does not seem to have been overcome in today's cinema. Such films as *Soñar no cuesta nada* are successful due to their adherence to formulas from television, but, by doing so, they become television made for the big screen. In a way, this corresponds to what García Canclini identifies as the rise of certain aesthetic and cultural features that are not exclusive to the United States; however, they indicate the economic control wielded by that country and condemn Latin America to continue being a suburb of North America (2001, 32). These films, as he states, find in United States cinema "an exemplary representative: the predominance of spectacular action over more reflective and intimate forms of narration; the fascination with a memoryless present; and the reduction of differences among societies to a standardized multiculturalism where conflicts, if admitted, are 'resolved' according to very Western and pragmatic modalities" (2001, 32). Moreover, representations of the periphery and the marginal in these productions perpetuate a series of stereotypes that already alienated audiences from productions during the FOCINE years.[26]

The instances and examples of Colombian cinema that best lend themselves to substantive reflection are precisely those that, by distancing themselves from the anecdotal and the easy path, have opted to vindicate the imagination as the driving force for the image in movement. I have in mind here films such as *La sombra del caminante* [*The Wanderer's Shadow*] (Ciro Guerra, 2004), as well as *Cóndores no entierran todos los días* and *Yo soy otro* (both mentioned above), in which the geographic and historical contexts of their narratives are not reduced to a decorative backdrop. Additionally, directors like Víctor Gaviria, through their subject matter and visual proposals, have consistently demonstrated their awareness that New Latin American Cinema's moment has passed, without assuming that its legacy must be completely discounted. Even Harold Trompetero whose trademarks have linked him with Dago García has made *Violeta de mil colores* [Violet of a Thousand Colors] (2005), a profoundly poetic film and a great visual product on a low budget. Filmed in New York, this production reveals Trompetero's multifaceted nature as a director and producer.

The challenges for Colombian filmmaking are not only financial, technical, and artistic; they also border on the imagination in their need to explore other narrative horizons, even in their representation of violence. Law 814 is not a complete panacea, but it is a good start, or, at least, it has been well received. Interviews with Colombian film producers published in the journal *Kinetoscopio* in 2007, confirm this. Most of the producers are quite convinced that Law 814 meshes well with their own way of doing business and they understand it as a protectionist measure. With the exception of Jorge Echeverri, a producer and director whose films are considered experimental, there seems to be a consensus to support entertainment cinema that produces a return on investment. Similarly, they all consider that, although this is a good time for Colombian filmmaking, the law needs a great deal of refining, and the true challenge for Colombian cinema continues to be its consolidation as an industry.[27] The greatest difference of opinion in this survey surfaces in their answers about the stories yet to be told. Comments by Alberto Amaya and Efraín Gamba synthesize an opinion that is heard frequently in Colombian film circles and forums: the deficit of stories arises from problems with scripts; stories exist, but they are not told well (2007, 14 and 25). Perhaps this explains the relative dependence on literature, especially on literature about narcotrafficking, that Colombian filmmaking is experiencing, along with the tendency to turn violence into spectacle to attract international co-productions.[28]

As we have explained, if Law 814 contemplates a discourse of cultural diversity, beyond tokenization, then Colombia's aspiring film industry can benefit from a new approach to the role of such diversity, transcending what Katharyne Mitchell labels as "the hype of hybridity" (quoted in Crang et al., 446). There various spaces of invention and re-invention can exist from which other courses of action can be articulated for a film industry that no longer wants merely to survive. Perhaps this ought to be the other position taken by Colombian filmmaking if it is finally to become a solid industry and part of the transnational order: venturing more into the realm of imagination and relying less on facile formulae as a passport into the transnational sphere.

WORKS CITED

Alvaray, Luisela. 2008. National, Regional, and Global: New Waves of Latin American Cinema. *Cinema Journal* 47, no. 3: 48–65.

Álvarez, Luis Alberto, and Víctor Gaviria. 1982. Las latas en el fondo del río: el cine colombiano visto desde la provincia. *Cine* 8: 1–36.

Amaya, Alberto. 2007. Nos falta tomar decisiones sobre el mercado para poder consolidarlo. *Kinetoscopio* 17.79: 13–15.

Appadurai, Arjun. 2000. *Modernity at Large. Cultural Dimensions of Globalization*. Minneapolis: University of Minnesota Press.

Badley, Linda, and R. Barton Palmer. 2006. Introduction to *Traditions in World Cinema*. Ed. Linda Badley, R. Barton Palmer and Steven Jay Schneider, 1–12. Edinburgh: Edinburgh University Press.

Chanan, Michael. 2006. Latin American Cinema: From Underdevelopment to Postmodernism. In *Remapping World Cinema. Identity, Culture and Politics in Film*. Ed. Stephanie Dennison and Song Hwee Lim, 38–51. London: Wallflower Press.

Chapman, James. 2003. *Cinemas of the World: Film and Society from 1895 to the Present*. London: Reaktion.

Crang, Philip, Claire Dwyer, and Peter Jackson. 2003. Transnationalism and the Spaces of Commodity Culture. *Progress in Human Geography* 27, no. 4: 438–53.

Dennison, Stephanie, and Song Hwee Lim. 2006. Situating World Cinema as a Theoretical Problem. In *Remapping World Cinema. Identity, Culture and Politics in Film*. Ed. Stephanie Dennison and Song Hwee Lim, 1–15. London: Wallflower Press.

Falicov, Támara. 2007. Young Filmmakers and the New Independent Argentine Cinema. Chap. 4 in *The Cinematic Tango: Contemporary Argentine Film*. London: Wallflower Press.

Gamba, Efraín. 2007. Hay que mirar el cine como una industria cultural. *Kinetoscopio* 17.79: 24–27.

García, Dago. 2007. La única forma de seguir haciendo cine es cuidando el negocio. *Kinetoscopio* 17.79: 20–23.

García Canclini, Néstor. 2001. *Consumers and Citizens: Globalization and Muticul-
tural Conflicts*. Trans. George Yúdice. Minneapolis: University of Minnesota
Press.

———. 2007. *Lectores, espectadores e internautas*. Barcelona: Gedisa.

Geffner, David. 2002 Patricia Cardoso's *Real Women Have Curves*. Interview.
DGA Magazine. http://www.dga.org/news/v26_6/indie_cardosowomen.
php3 (accessed April 27, 2007).

Getino, Osvaldo, Fernando Solanas, and Grupo Cine Liberacieon. 1988. Hacia
un tercer cine. Apuntes y experiencias para el desarrollo de un cine de liberación en el Tercer Mundo. In *Hojas de cine.Testimonios y documentos del Nuevo
Cine Latinoamericano. Volumen I. Centro y Sudamérica*, 29–62. Mexico: SEP,
UAM y Fundación Mexicana de Cineastas.

Gorodisher, Julián. 2008. Rodrigo García en *In Treatment*, cómo narrar sutil-
mente una sesión de psicoanálisis. *Página 12*. Cultura y Espectáculos. July 18.
http://www.página12.com.ar (accessed July 18, 2008).

Johnson, Randal. 2005. TV Globo, The MPA, and Contemporary Brazilian
Cinema. In *Latin American Cinema. Essays on Modernity, Gender and National
Identity*. Ed. Lisa Shaw and Stephanie Dennison, 11–38. Jefferson: McFarland
and Co.

———. 2006. Post-*Cinema Novo* Brazilian Cinema. In *Traditions in World Cinema*.
Ed. Linda Badley, R. Barton Palmer, and Jay Schneider, 117–29. Edinburgh:
Edinburgh University Press.

King, John. 1990. *Magical Reels: A History of Latin American Cinema*. London: Verso.

Kostantarakos, Myrto. 2006. New Argentine Cinema. In *Traditions in World
Cinema*. Ed. Linda Badley, R. Barton Palmer, and Jay Schneider, 130–40.
Edinburgh: Edinburgh University Press.

La ley de cine para todos. 2004. Bogotá: Ministerio de Cultura, Proimágenes en
Movimiento. *Largometrajes colombianos en cine y video, 1915–2004*. Bogotá:
Fundación Patrimonio Fílmico Colombiano.

Lionnet, Françoise, and Shu-mei Shih. 2005. Introduction to *Minor Transnationalism*. Ed. Françoise Lionnet and Shu-mei Shih, 1–23. Durham, NC: Duke
University Press.

Mora, Carl J. 1989. *Mexican Cinema: Reflections of a Society, 1896–1988*. Berkeley:
University of California Press.

Morales, Miguel Ángel. 1996. *Cantinflas: Amo de las carpas*. Mexico: Editorial
Clío.

Nieto Roa, Gustavo. 2007. O hacemos un cine que tenga respuesta del público o perdemos la última oportunidad. *Kinetoscopio* 17.79 (July–September): 16–19.

Ochoa, Ana María. 2003. *Músicas Locales en tiempos de globalización*. Bogotá: Editorial Norma.

Paranaguá, Paulo Antonio, ed. 1995. *Mexican Cinema*. Trans. Ana M. López. London: British Film Institute and IMCINE.

———. 1996. El Nuevo Cine Latinoamericano frente al desafío del mercado y la televisión (1970–1975). In *Historia General del Cine*, vol. 10. *Estados Unidos (1955–1975). América Latina*. Ed. Carlos Heredero and Casimiro Torreiro, 347–83. Madrid: Cátedra.

Poblete, Juan. 2004. New National Cinemas in a Transnational Age. *Discourse* 26, nos. 1/2: 214–34.

Shaw, Deborah. 2007. Introduction: Latin American Cinema Today. A Qualified Success Story. In *Contemporary Latin American Cinema: Breaking into the Global Market*. Ed. Deborah Shaw, 1–10. Lanham, MD: Rowman & Littlefield.

Shohat, Ella, and Robert Stam. 1994. *Unthinking Eurocentrism: Multiculturalism and the Media*. London: Routledge.

Stam, Robert, and Randal Johnson, eds. 1995. *Brazilian Cinema*. New York: Columbia University Press.

Stavans, Ilan. 1998. *The Riddle of Cantinflas: Essays on Hispanic Popular Culture*. Alburquerque: University of New Mexico Press.

Suárez, Juana. 2008. Cine y violencia en Colombia: claves para la construcción de un discurso fílmico. In *Versiones, subversiones y representaciones del cine colombiano*. Investigaciones recientes. Memorias de la XII Cátedra Anual de Historia Ernesto Restrepo Tirado. Bogotá: Ministerio de Cultura and Museo Nacional, 87–108.

Torres, Rito Alberto. 2004. 'Hemos de tener arte propio.' Noventa años de cine colombiano. In *Largometrajes colombianos en cine y video 1915–2004*. 17–20. Bogotá: Fundación Patrimonio Fílmico Colombiano.

Vieira, João Luiz. 1987. A Chanchada e o Cinema Carioca (1930–55). In *História do Cinema Brasileiro*. Ed. Fernão Ramos, 129–87. São Paulo: Art Editora.

Wolf, Sergio. 2002. La estética del Nuevo Cine Argentino: el mapa es el territorio. In *El nuevo cine argentino: Temas, autores y estilos de una renovación*. Ed. Horacio Bernades, Diego Lerer, and Sergio Wolf, 29–39. Buenos Aires: Ediciones Tatanka.

Zuluaga, Pedro Adrián. 2007. La exhibición y distribución del cine. ¿El tercer acto? *Kinetoscopio* 17.79: 68–71.

FILMS

Bluff. Directed by Felipe Martínez. Laberinto Producciones, 2007.

Bolivia. Directed by Adrián Caetano. Fundación Proa, 2001.

El bonaerense. Directed by Juan Pablo Trapero. Argentina Video Home, 2002.

El carro. Directed by Luis Orjuela. Cinema Tropical, 2003.

Cidade de Deus. Directed by Fernando Meirelles. Miramax Films, 2002.

Como el gato y el ratón. Directed by Rodrigo Triana. CMO Producciones, 2002.

Cóndores no entierran todos los días. Directed by Francisco Norden. Procinor, 1984.

La desazón suprema: retrato incesante de Fernando Vallejo. Directed by Luis Ospina, 2003.

Dios los junta y ellos se separan. Directed by Harold Trompetero, Orlando Jiménez, and Fabián Torres. Harold Trompetero Producers, 2006.

La estrategia del caracol. Directed by Sergio Cabrera, Argentina Video Home, 1993.

Al final del espectro. Directed by Felipe Orozco. Paloalto Films, 2006.

Golpe de estadio. Directed by Sergio Cabrera. Alta Films, 1998.

María llena eres de gracia. Directed by Joshua Marston. Tayrona Entertainment Group, 2004.

Nueve reinas. Directed by Fabián Bielinksky. Argentina Video Home, 2000.

Un oso rojo. Drected by Adrián Caetano. Transeuropa Video Entertainment, 2002.

Paraíso Travel. Directed by Simón Brand. Grand Illusions Entertainment, 2007.

La pena máxima. Directed by Jorge Echeverri. Canal Caracol, 2001.

Perder es cuestión de método. 2004. Directed by Sergio Cabrera. Films Sans Frontières, 2004.

Real Women Have Curves. DVD. Directed by Patricia Cardoso. Home Box Office Video, 2002.

Rodrigo D. No futuro. Directed by Víctor Gaviria. Facets Multimedia Distribution, 1990.

Rosario Tijeras. Directed by Emilio Maillé. First Look International, 2005.

Los rubios. Directed by Albertina Carri. Barry Women Make Movies, 2003.

Satanás. Directed by Andy Baiz. Little Film Company, 2007.

La sombra del caminante. Directed by Ciro Guerra. Ciudad Lunar Producciones, Tucán Producciones y Cinematográfica Ltda, 2004.

Soñar no cuesta nada. Directed by Rodrigo Triana. Venevisión Internacional, 2006.

Técnicas de duelo: Una cuestión de honor. 1988. Directed by Dir. Sergio Cabrera. FOCINE, 1988.

Tiempo de morir. Directed by Jorge Alí Triana. FOCINE and ICAIC, 1985.

Violeta de mil colores. Directed by Harold Trompetero. The Latino Group, 2005.

La virgen de los sicarios. Directed by Barbet Schroeder. Paramount Classics, 2000.

Yo soy otro. Directed by Óscar Campo. One Eyed Films, 2008.

NOTES

1   Translated by Laura Chesak, University of North Carolina, Greensboro

2   For an explanation of Marston's decision to film the sequences related to cut-flower production in Amaguaña (Ecuador), see an interview in *Filmmakermagazine* (http://www.filmmakermagazine.com/summer2002/features/25_faces21-25.php) (accessed July 18, 2008).

3   Unless a source is already available in English, all translations of quotes in Spanish are the work of the translator of the present article.

4   This reference book published by *Patrimonio Fílmico Nacional* (Colombian Film Heritage Foundation) synthesizes the technical information for every fictional feature-length film made in Colombia up to 2004. Subsequent updates have been published in downloadable versions on the foundation's website for succeeding years. Seehttp://www.patrimoniofilmico.org.co.

5   FOCINE stood for *Compañía de Fomento Cinematográfico* (Cinematographic Development Company). Before FOCINE, the *Ley de sobreprecio* (Surcharge Law) sought to favour the national industry, stimulating production of short subjects and protecting production as well as exhibition and distribution; it increased the price of admission to movie theatres and simultaneously required the inclusion of a national short film with every show. The excess of production and the poor quality of the shorts defeated the good intentions of that project but left two great difficulties to be resolved. On one hand, interest in using film for sociopolitical commentary grew, although it was im-

peded by the commercial impetus that undercut the aesthetic level of many productions. The heirs of the surcharge argued over mixing the commercial with the political, without managing to resolve the dilemma in a way that would positively affect the formation of a national cinema. On the other hand, the failure of the Surcharge Law made it clear that the country needed clearly defined state policies regarding the sponsorship, production, exhibition, and distribution of films. As a state-sponsored institution devoted to the patronage of filmmaking, FOCINE was born with the intent of making national cinema possible. It attempted to focus on the impetus toward and interest in filmmaking, hoping to rectify a few vague paragraphs in its constitution over the long term. The good intentions of FOCINE could not sustain the hope that its problems would straighten themselves out along the way. Unfortunately, behind a great number of productions, a series of bureaucratic pressures, differences of opinion about the films that should be produced, budgetary intrigues, and general crises became entangled and led inevitably to FOCINE's dissolution.

6   See Suárez.

7   Falicov refers to alternative labels such as "*las películas argentinas jóvenes de éxito* (Young Argentine Film Successes)" and "*el nuevo cine independiente argentino* (New Independent Argentine Cinema)" (115). See also Konstantarakos's "New Argentina Cinema" in *Traditions in World Cinema* and Sergio Wolf's "La estética del Nuevo Cine Argentino: el mapa es el territorio" in *El nuevo cine*

argentino: Temas, autores y estilos de una renovación.

8   Cuarón directed *Harry Potter and the Prisoner of Azkaban* (2004, the third film in the Harry Potter series). Before the success of his *Y tu mamá también* (2002), he had adapted Charles Dickens' novel *Great Expectations* (1998), starring Ethan Hawke and Gwyneth Paltrow. After his success with *Amores perros* (2000), González completed his trilogy with *21 Grams* (2003, starring Sean Penn, Naomi Watts, and Benicio del Toro) and *Babel* (2006, starring Brad Pitt, Gael García Bernal, and Cate Blanchett).

9   In the original, "una extraña armonía entre el cine de autor y la producción de Hollywood. La segunda nutre de nombres rutilantes al primero" (2). Seldom associated with Colombian cinematic circles, Rodrigo García is the son of writer Gabriel García Márquez; he was born in Bogotá and educated during his formative years in Mexico. His first film was *Things You Can Tell Just by Looking at Her* (2000, starring Glenn Close and Cameron Díaz). His film *Nine Lives* (2005, starring Holly Hunter, Glenn Close, and Jason Isaacs) was co-produced by González Iñárritu. García has also participated in directing episodes of such U.S. television series as *Six Feet Under* (2001) and *The Sopranos* (1999). He is the executive producer, director, and writer of HBO's *In Treatment* (2008).

10 Cardoso currently resides in Los Angeles. The term "Latino" in this context has to do with the predominant divisions in U.S. culture in which "Latino" refers to cultures of Latin American origin: in other words, to the generations that have resulted from the diverse geo-political and migratory movements that have characterized the reterritorialization of the idea of U.S. nationality.

11 Randal Johnson summarizes various critical positions in Brazil with regard to expressing a continuation of or a rift with *Cinema Novo* and in particular the legacy of Glauber Rocha.

12 Before 2000, we could also include *Hombre mirando al sureste* [*Man Facing Southeast*] (Dir. Eliseo Subiela, 1986), *Moebius* (Dir. Gustavo Mosquera, 1996) and *La sonámbula* [*Sleepwalker*] (Dir. Fernando Spinner, 1998), three examples of science fiction that, as Chanan reminds us, "function to create allegories of the disappeared, or the seeming amnesia which followed the dirty war" (47).

13 As Luisela Alvaray shows in her study of Argentine, Brazilian, and Mexican cinemas, national policies, regional agreements, and global marketing strategies now form the intricate waves in which [Latin American] films navigate (61).

14 For other useful discussions on the problematic category of world music in the case of Latin America, see Ana María Ochoa.

15 The complete text of Law 814 is available in PDF format on the Ministry of Culture's website (http://www.mincultura.gov.co in the section entitled "Legislación cultural") and on the website of *Proimágenes en Movimiento* (http://www.proimagenescolombia.com/legislacion). Quotes in this essay are taken from an explanatory pamphlet entitled "La ley de cine para todos" prepared by the Ministry of Culture for the presentation of the law. Special thanks to Pedro

Adrián Zuluaga for further explanations on the intricacies of the law.

16   See the description of the Surcharge Law in note 5.

17   Luis Alberto Restrepo, Jorge Alí Triana and the late Carlos Mayolo are among the directors who have combined their work in film with frequent incursions into television series and soap operas. Felipe Aljure and Raúl García, Jr. are among the directors who have alternated between working in film and in advertising. Many other men and women filmmakers have worked as instructors, whether in universities or centres for audiovisual studies. Specific information on each director is taken from profiles that appear on the website of *Proimágenes en Movimiento: Fondo Mixto de Promoción Cinematográfica*, a division of the Ministry of Culture that is in charge of matters related to cinema (http://www.proimagenescolombia. com).

18   With regard to Colombian directors trained abroad, the list is quite long. Information corresponding to the directors mentioned has been taken from the following websites: for Diego García Moreno and Patricia Cardoso, *Proimágenes en Movimiento* (http://www. proimagenescolombia.com, "Perfiles" section); for Juan Fisher, the program of the cultural festival *Colombiage 2007*, an independent initiative put together by Colombians residing in the United Kingdom (http://www.colombiage. com); for Ricardo Gabrielli, *Fundación Nuevo Cine Latinoamericano* (http:// www.cinelatinoamericano.org) and for Catalina Villar, *Programa de Documental en Creación* through the Universidad del Valle (http://documentaldecreación. com; all accessed July 18, 2008). Infor-

mation on Simón Brand is from his own website (http://www.simonbrand.net; accessed April 20, 2008).

19   This information is based on statistics kept by *Proimágenes en Movimiento* on its website and updated frequently. Its graphs demonstrate a significant increase in the number of viewers between 1994 (the date of Sergio Cabrera's *La estrategia del caracol* [*The Strategy of the Snail*]) and 2005/2006 with films like *Rosario Tijeras* and *Soñar no cuesta nada* [A *Ton of Luck*], respectively (http://www.proimagenescolombia. com) (accessed July 18, 2008).

20   According to its website, *Laboratorios Black Velvet* is "a company dedicated to audiovisual development and the promotion of Colombian filmmaking in diverse areas such as the circulation, promotion, and design of audiovisual products" ["una empresa dedicada al desarrollo audiovisual y a la promoción del cine colombiano en diversas areas como la divulgación, promoción y diseño de productos audiovisuales"]. With the motto, "The best of young Colombian filmmaking" ["Lo mejor del cine joven colombiano"], Black Velvet organizes frequent screenings at its "In-vitro" location in a bar of the same name. Complete information is available at http://www.blackvelvetlab. com.

According to the website of the Santa Fe de Antioquia Film and Video Festival, "Pandora's Box" is "a selective sample of recent Colombian audiovisual production (from the last two years). Over two days in consecutive five-hour sessions, within the framework of the Ninth Santa Fe de Antioquia Film and Video Festival, the latest in documentaries, fiction, experimental films, and video clips made in our country is shown" ["una muestra selectiva del audiovisual colombiano reciente (dos últimos años en la producción). Durante dos días en jornadas de cinco horas consecutivas, en el marco del IX Festival de Cine y Video de Santa Fe de Antioquia, se muestra lo nuevo del documental, la ficción, el video experimental y el video clip que se ha hecho en nuestro país"]. The Festival has been celebrated since 1999, usually during the first week in December. It has been a cultural initiative led by Víctor Gaviria, and its aspiration, once the festival is over, is that the selections will tour the country. The sample and the festival itself are not competitive. Complete information appears at http://www.festicineantioquia.com.

21 This weariness on the part of audiences towards stories about violence has been discussed explicitly in various public forums in which directors have been questioned about the lack of other stories. This occurred, for example, during a presentation by Víctor Gaviria at the *Pura Colombia* Film Festival, organized by Florida Atlantic University (Boca Ratón, March 19, 2005) and during Luis Alberto Restrepo's discussion after a screening of *La primera noche* (April 20, 2003). Director Andy Baiz also revealed his lack of agreement with a criticism that he frequently receives for not making "more tourist-friendly films" ("películas más turísticas") about Colombia during a panel entitled, "Para dónde va el cine colombiano" ["Where is Colombian Filmmaking Headed"] organized by the magazine *El Malpensante* (Bogotá, June 28, 2008).

22 This particular comment is recorded in Luis Ospina's documentary *La desazón suprema. Retrato incesante de Fernando Vallejo* [*The Supreme Uneasiness. Incessant Portrait of Fernando Vallejo*, 2003] on the life and work of Fernando Vallejo.

23 In the original, "el cine permite vernos y reconocernos como personas y como grupos con distintas maneras de entender todos los aspectos de la vida, algo especialmente importante en un país, que como el nuestro, tiene una diversidad cultural inagotable" ("La ley de cine," 5).

24 In each case, the bibliography is extensive. For *comedia ranchera*, see, for example, Paulo Antonio Paranaguá and Carl J. Mora; on Cantinflás, see Morales and Stavans. On the Brazilian *chanchada*, see Stam and Johnson and Vieira.

25 See http://www.cmoproducciones.com/sncn/index.htm (accessed March 29, 2007).

26 It should be added that, echoing the literary panorama, the history of Colombian filmmaking appears fragmented into regions: there is a more conspicuous production in Bogotá, Medellín, and Cali. Álvarez and Gaviria's article comments not only on issues related to television formulas but also on the misrepresentation of the margin resulting from Bogotá's hegemonic position in filmmaking.

27 The interviews followed a more or less standard format and primarily included questions on Law 814; other topics included film's relationship to the language and format of television, piracy, opinions about international co-productions, and the international recognition being accorded to Colombian

filmmaking. Besides Dago García and Nieto Roa (who are also producers), Clara María Ochoa, Alberto Amaya, Efraín Gamba, Rodrigo Guerrero and Matthias Ehrenberg were also interviewed.

28 One of the characteristics of contemporary Colombian cinema is the frequent adaptation of novels. Some of the recent literature that has been adapted to film include *Satanás* by Mario Mendoza (adapted by Andy Baiz, 2007); *Rosario Tijeras* by Jorge Franco Ramos (adapted by Mexican director Emilio Maillé, 2005); *Paraíso Travel* by Jorge Franco Ramos (adapted by Simón Brand, 2007); and *Perder es cuestión de método* [*The Art of Losing*] by Santiago Gamboa (adapted by Sergio Cabrera, 2005).

NOTES ON CONTRIBUTORS

PAOLA ARBOLEDA RÍOS is a journalist. She is currently pursuing a PhD in Latin American Literature at the Spanish and Portuguese Department of the University of Florida. She has a master's degree in Women's and Gender Studies from the University of British Columbia. She is the co-author of *La presencia de la mujer en el cine colombiano* (Ministerio Colombiano of Cultura, 2003). Her research interests include film, literary theory, and gender studies. She is particularly interested in the literary work and visual texts of queer women from Latin America and the Caribbean.

ISABEL ARREDONDO is an associate professor of Spanish at SUNY Plattsburgh, where she teaches Latin American film. She received her PhD in Hispanic Languages and Literatures from the University of California at Berkeley. She is the author of *"Palabra de Mujer": Historia oral de las directoras de cine mexicanas (1988–1994)*. Recently she has written about dress in Mexican cinema, including an article on dress in Adela Sequeyro's *La mujer de nadie*. She was the winner of a Fulbright grant to study the work of avant-garde Venezuelan filmmaker Diego Rísquez. For the last four years, she has been part of the research project, Women and the Silent Screen. She is also finishing a book on images of motherhood in Mexico's classical and contemporary films.

NAYIBE BERMÚDEZ BARRIOS is an associate professor in the Department of French, Italian, and Spanish at the University of Calgary, where she teaches Latin American film, literature, translation, and culture. She holds a master's degree from the University of Arkansas and a

PhD from the University of Kansas. She is the author of *Sujetos Trans-nacionales: La Negociación en Film y Literatura* (Universidad Autónoma de Ciudad Juárez, 2008). Other publications include articles on film and literature. Her current research project deals with lesbian representation, space, and genre in Latin American cinemas.

GERARD DAPENA is a visiting assistant professor of Film Studies at Bard College. He received his PhD in Art History at the Graduate Center, CUNY, with a dissertation on cinema in post-Civil War Spain. He also held a Mellon Postdoctoral Fellowship at Macalester College. His research interests include Spanish Fascist Cinema, Contemporary Spanish Cinema, Latin American Cinema, and Visual Arts in Spain and Latin America. He has written extensively on these topics.

DAVID W. FOSTER is Regents' Professor of Spanish, Humanities, and Women's Studies at Arizona State University. He completed both his master's degree and his PhD at the University of Washington. His research interests focus on urban culture in Latin America, with emphasis on issues of gender construction and sexual identity, as well as Jewish culture. He has written extensively on Argentine narrative and theatre, and he has held Fulbright teaching appointments in Argentina, Brazil, and Uruguay. He has also served as an Inter-American Development Bank Professor in Chile. His most recent publications include: *Urban Photography in Argentina* (McFarland, 2007); *Queer Issues in Contemporary Latin American* Cinema (University of Texas Press, 2004); *Mexico City and Contemporary Mexican Film-making* (University of Texas Press, 2002) and *Contemporary Brazilian Cinema* (University of Texas Press, 2000). Foster is also the translator of novels by Enrique Medina (*Las Tumbas/The Tombs* and *The Duke*), Aristeo Brito (*The Devil in Texas*), Miguel Méndez M. (*Pilgrims in Aztlán, The Dream of Santa María de las Piedras*, and *Between Literature and Bricks: An Autobiography in the Form of a Novel*), and Ana María Shúa (*Patient*).

CHARLOTTE E. GLEGHORN is a post-doctoral researcher at the Royal Holloway University in London, United Kingdom. She completed her master's degree in World Cinemas at the University of Leeds and received her PhD in Latin American Film Studies at the University of Liverpool. Her research interests include the themes of memory and trauma in comparative perspective, particularly in light of recent film production from Argentina and Brazil, as well as gender and the representation of urban space in contemporary Latin American cinema. She is currently working on indigeneity and performance in theatre and film in the contemporary world, with an emphasis on indigenous filmmaking in Latin America.

REBECCA L. LEE is an assistant professor of Latin American Literature and Culture at the University of Missouri, Kansas City. She completed her PhD at Cornell University. She teaches 19th and 20th century Latin American literature and film, as well as gender and cultural studies. Her primary research focuses on race, gender, and nation in Latin America. She has published articles on Latin American narrative and popular culture. She is currently working on a book project examining the virilisation of national identity within nationalist projects in Latin America.

ELIZABETH MONTES GARCÉS is an associate professor in the Department of French, Italian, and Spanish at the University of Calgary. She earned both her master's degree and her PhD at the University of Kansas. She is the author of *El cuestionamiento de los mecanismos de representación en la novelística de Fanny Buitrago* (Peter Lang, 1997). She also edited *Relocating Identities in Latin American Cultures* (Calgary: University of Calgary Press, 2007). She has published many articles dealing with Latin American women's writing.

MYRIAM OSORIO is an assistant professor of Spanish at Memorial University of Newfoundland. She received her PhD in Spanish from the University of Wisconsin-Madison and has taught in the United States and Canada. She specializes in contemporary Latin American literature, women writers, and feminist theory. She is the author of *Agencia femenina, agencia narrativa: Lectura feminista de la obra en prosa de Alba Lucía Ángel* (Peter Lang, 2010). She has published articles on Albalucía Ángel and Rosa Montero and a collectively written dictionary for the reading of Rigoberta Menchu's testimony. Her current research focuses on the visual and narrative representation of Cuban women in the cigar industry.

ELISSA J. RASHKIN is a researcher at the Universidad Veracruzana. She is the author of *The Stridentist Movement in Mexico: The Avant-Garde and Cultural Change in the 1920s* (Lexington, 2009) and *Women Film-makers in Mexico: The Country of Which We Dream* (University of Texas Press, 2001) as well as many articles on Mexican and international film, literature, and cultural history.

KEITH JOHN RICHARDS divides his time between teaching at the Universidad Mayor de San Andrés, in La Paz, Bolivia, and writing. He was awarded a PhD from King's College, University of London, for a thesis on the Bolivian writer Néstor Taboada Terán, which was published as *Lo Imaginario Mestizo* (Plural, 1999). His critical bilingual anthology *Narratives from Tropical Bolivia* was published by La Hoguera, Santa Cruz, in 2004. He has taught Latin American film, literature, and popular culture at universities in Britain, the United States, and Bolivia. He has published widely on all of these subjects and co-organized Latin American film symposia and festivals at the universities of Leeds and Richmond. He is currently preparing a book on Latin American cinema.

JUANA SUÁREZ is an assistant professor of Latin American Film and Visual Culture at the University of Kentucky. She received her PhD from the Arizona State University. Her area of specialty includes visual culture, gender Studies and US Latino and Latin American literature. She is the author of *Cinembargo Colombia: ensayos críticos sobre cine y cultura colombiana* (Universidad del Valle, 2009) and *Sitios de contienda: producción cultural colombiana y el discurso de la violencia* (Madrid: Iberoamericana Vervuert, 2010). Her articles on Colombian cinema have appeared in journals such as *Revista Iberoamericana*, *Chicana/Latina Studies*, and *Cuadernos de Investigación de la Cineteca de Caracas*.

INDEX

crystalline-structured narration, 126
Cuarón, Alfonso, 281, 283, 292, 304n8
Cuba, 252
Cueva del Río, Roberto, 210
La culpa es de los tlaxcaltecas (Garro), 213
cultural difference, 294
cultural diversity, 205, 298
cultural nationalism, 208
Curi-Cáhueri, 216
Curubeto, Diego, 258, 265

D

Dalma (fictional character), 7, 33–35, 37–38
Dapena, Gerard, 310
    "Bodies So Close, and Yet So Far," 10
Darín, Ricardo, 7, 28, 150
Darío (fictional character), 31–33, 39
Dayan, Daniel, 50
De Brito, Ángel, 265
De Domenico, Francesco, 280
De Fuentes, Fernando, 12, 176–77, 180
    reinforces mainstream values, 193
    women's masculinity is perverse, 181
De la Rua, Fernando, 29
De Lauretis, Teresa, 11
De Luna, Andrés, 185
De Man, Paul, 58
deaestheticization, 68–69
decolonization, 8, 10, 200
defamiliarization, 13, 48, 51, 56, 58, 67,
    75n4
Del Río, Dolores, 209
Del Toro, Guillermo, 281, 283, 292
Deleuze, Gilles, 10, 13, 129–31, 135, 140–
    42, 144
    Cinema 1: The Movement-Image, 125, 128
    Cinema 2: The time-Image, 125–26, 134
    film theory, 125–28
    What is Philosophy?, 133
democracy, 115, 118
denaturalizing the apparently natural order,
    50, 57, 64, 66, 68
Dennison, Stephanie, 282
    Remapping World Cinema, 286
desire, 57, 59, 65, 130
    commodification of, 252–53, 258
    fever related to, 67
DGA Magazine, 283

Díaz, Patricia, 182
digestive appropriation of cultures, 8, 13
digital culture (1990s), 126. *See also*
    electronic and audiovisual media
La dignidad de los nadies (2005), 204
Dios los junta y ellos se separan (2006), 294
La diosa virgen (1977), 265
Dirty War (1976–83), 49, 167
disease, 8. *See also* illness as metaphor of
    corruption
    parallel to corruption of state, 82, 84,
        86, 88
Dobson, Kevin James, 189
Doña Bárbara (1943), 12, 91, 176–78
    patriarchal power structure in, 180–82
    rape as foundational experience, 179
    rape as "primal scene," 179, 192
    rape makes women mannish, 192
Donizetti, Gaetano, 90
Dreger, Alice, 154, 168
Driscoll, Catherine, 64
drug trafficking, 110–11, 295–96, 298
Duchesne Winter, Juan, 5, 10
Duras, Marguerite, 129
Dussel, Enrique, 1–2, 4, 11–13, 203, 211,
    215, 220
    The Invention of the Americas, 200
    Latin America's relationship to the 'First
        World,' 201
DVDs, 291, 293
Dvorak, Antonín, 138
Dwyer, Claire, 2, 6, 265, 282
Dyer, Richard, 262

E

Ecehverr, Jorge, 293
Echeverría, Nicolás, 207, 212–13
Ecuador, 3, 279
Educuentro Internacional de Imágenes,
    Memorias e Identidades Amerindians
    (San Cristóbal, 2006), 235
Efron, Inés, 150, 164
Eisenstein, Sergei, 134
Ejercito Zapatista de Liberación. *See* EZLN;
    Zapatista movement
Él (1952), 91
electronic and audiovisual media. *See also*
    Internet
    importance to Zapatista movement, 227

national allegory paradigm, 50, 75n3, 294
    reinterpretation of, 49
    women directors' departure from, 48
"National Belonging in Juan José
        Campanella's *Luna de Avellaneda*"
        (Lee), 6
national elites, 30, 34, 37, 44n17. *See also*
        social class
national identity, 292
National Indigenist Institute, 235
National Institute of Cinematography and
        Audiovisual Arts (INCAA), 26
National University of Colombia, 289
nationalism, 2–3, 291
nation-state, 3, 26
    breakdown of, 7–8, 10
    questioning of, 5–6
'natural' subordination (woman to man,
        child to adult), 54
Nava, Gregory, 189
Necoechea, Angeles, 183
La negra Augustias (1949), 12, 91, 180
    celebration of masculine woman, 176,
        178, 181–82, 192
    rape as foundational experience, 179
    rape as "primal scene," 179, 192
neo-cangaceiro, 284
neocolonialism, 7
neo-liberal economic reforms, 2, 40
    crisis of state responsibility, 33
neoliberalism
    dissatisfaction with, 7
    social inequity, 38
neoliberalism as form of neo-colonialism,
        21n7
Netflix, 293
Network against Violence toward Women, 3
Network of Popular Educators, 3
Neuman, Shirley, 64
New Argentine Cinema, 25, 43n4, 49, 149,
        172n2, 281
    obsession with the gaze, 55
New Latin American Cinema, 49, 76n7,
        204, 284, 297
Nieto Roa, Gustavo, 292
La niña santa [The Holy Girl], 48
Nóbile, Luciano, 157
Noble, Andrea, 209

nonprofessional actors, 76n5
    in *Anjos de noite*, 116
    Eréndira Ikikunari, 217
    in *O invasor*, 113
Norden, Francisco, 295
'normalcy,' 11
normality, 58
normalization surgery. *See* intersex
        normalization surgery
Novaro, María, 12, 175–76, 183
nudie cuties, 254
Nueve reinas (2000), 285
nuevo cine argentine. See New Argentine
        Cinema
nymphomaniacs, 252, 258, 261

O

Obama administration, 242
Ochoa, Jesús, 191
O'Gorman, Juan, 210
Ojos que no ven (2003), 8–9, 79–95
    critical attention, 99n1
    gendered proscription of agency and
        power, 88
    rape shown on screen, 91
Olmos, Edward James, 228
Olmos, José Gil, 226
Ona Saéz, 265
Ônibus 174 (2000), 110
opsigns, 128, 134, 144
Orjuela, Luis, 293
Orozco, Juan Felipe, 15, 285
Ortiz, Carmen, 231–32
Ortuño, Juan Carlos, 127
Un oso rojo (2002), 285
Osorio, Myriam, 8, 311
Other Campaign, 226–27
The Other Francisco (1974), 91
Oubiña, David, 169
Oventic (1996), 232

P

Padilha, José, 110
Página 12, 150
Palacios, Germán, 151
"Pandora's Box," 291
Pantalla Colombia, 289

Promedios de Communicación Communitaria. *See* CMP / Promedios

prostitutes and prostitution, 91, 107, 186, 188, 191, 252, 258

Proyecto de Videoastas Indígenas de la Frontera Sur, 241

psychophysiology of the moving image, 134

Public Rape (Horeck), 178

Puenzo, Lucía, 11, 13, 150–69

Purépecha culture, 212

Purépecha deities, 216

Purépecha language, 203, 217

O puritano da Rua Augusta (1965), 9, 107–9, 117

  counterpoint between two value systems, 109

  music in, 109

  "rock around the clock" house party, 108

  snapshots of São Paulo in mid-1960s, 108–9

  urban lifestyle, 108

Q

queer cinema, 115, 143

queer *jouissance*, 123n23

Quijano, Aníbal, 2–4, 200

R

radical populism, 114

Ramírez, Arcelia, 186

Ramírez Barreto, Ana Cristina, 210, 212

Ramírez Berg, Charles, 206–7

Ramiro (fictional character), 151, 158–59, 166

  sexualized gaze, 166

Ramona, Comandante, 230–31

Rangel, Roberto Isidro, 201

Raoul, Valerie, 60

  "Women and Diaries," 59

Rapado (1991), 49

rape, 8, 12, 80–82, 88–90, 162, 186

  as cause of mannish behaviour in women, 176–78, 180–81, 192

  in city of Juárez, 176, 189–92

  connection to nation and national identity, 176

equated with romance, 175

feminist representations of (1970s to 2000s), 183–88

in judicial system, 184–85

lack of agency and justice, 88

life-altering trauma, 178

in Mexican cinema, 175–93

from the perspective of everyday lives, 185

as "primal scene," 178–79

raped bodies as metaphor for violence against society, 81

representation of corruption and injustice, 95

shifting societal notions about, 176

shown on screen, 91

social responsibility to report, 185

rape, women, and the nation connection, 90–92

Rashkin, Elissa J., 15, 183–84, 312

  "We Are Equal," 14

"raza cósmica," 207

Real Women Have Curves (2002), 279, 283

Red Bear. See Un Oso rojo (2002)

Rejtman, Martín, 49

Relación de Michoacán (codex), 212

religiosity and sexuality, 61

religious activism, 59

religious ecstasy

  fever related to, 67

religious hymns, 109

religious zealots, 109

Remapping World Cinema (Dennison), 286

representation, 10

  dominant system of, 11

  feminist representations of rape (1970s to 2000s), 183–88

  of indigenous peoples, 13–14, 205–7

  instability of, 15

  lesbian representation, 255, 258–59

representation of the dead, 190–91

representations of the female body. *See also* sexploitation films

  global stylizations, 14

Restivo, Angelo, 129, 141

Restrepo, Luis Alberto, 305n17

Return to Aztlán (1991), 200, 213, 217

  indigenous viewpoint, 208–9

  music, 211, 219

woman as monstrous, 163, 168
women, 2. *See also* indigenous women;
    maquiladora workers
  agency, 95
  autonomy, 253, 264
  blaming the victim for her rape, 186,
    188, 193
  complicity with patriarchy, 188
  defined as passionless sex, 66
  mannish, 176–78, 180–81, 192
  place in modern global economy, 240
  submissive, 92
  systemic sexual violence against, 192
  traditional role of, 201
  unaware and helpless victims, 90
  victimization and powerlessness, 92
Women, the Ones Always Forgotten (1995), 231
"Women and Diaries" (Raoul), 59
women-run cooperatives, 240. *See also*
    Zapatistas
women's autobiographies, 64–65
"The Work of Art in the Age of Mechanical
    Production" (Benjamin), 169
Working on Feminism (Projansky), 175
World Bank, 40
world cinema, 282, 286

X

Xarátanga, 212, 216
Ximenes, Mariana, 113
Xulum'chon (2002), 240, 242
Xulum'chon weavers, 241
XXY (2007), 11, 150–69. *See also* Alex
    (fictional character)
  beach in, 155
  borderland in, 155, 158
  erotically charged scenes, 158
  intersexuality (*See* intersex adolescent)
  lynching scene, 162, 164, 166–67
  questions rigid gender and sex categories,
    168

Y

Yawar Mallku (1969), 206
Yessica (fictional character), 185–88
Yo soy otro (2006), 285, 297

Z

Zapatista movement, 3, 226
  access to information, education, and
    resources, 242
  electronic and audiovisual media, 227
  influence on independent video sector,
    243
  pro-Zapatista journalists, 227
  turning point in women's lives, 237
  women leaders and soldiers, 230
Zapatistas, 243
  face coverings or masks, 238–39
  videos, 231–33, 236
  women-run cooperatives, 240
  women's involvement, 231–32, 236–37
  women's revolution-within-a-revolution,
    228
Zedillo, Ernesto, 230–31
Zeus, 153
Znet, 227
zoophilia, 258
Zuluaga, Pedro Adrián, 291
Zylberberg, Julieta, 61